A MOSAIC NOVEL

WILD CARDS III
JOKERS WILD

Editor GEORGE R.R. MARTIN was born September 20, 1948 in Bayonne, New Jersey. He began writing very young, selling monster stories to other neighborhood children for pennies, dramatic readings included. Later he became a comic book fan and collector in high school, and began to write fiction for comic fanzines (amateur fan magazines). Martin's first professional sale was made in 1970 at age 21: "The Hero," sold to *Galaxy*, published in the February, 1971 issue. Other sales followed.

Four-time winner of the Hugo Award, two-time winner of the Nebula Award, and six-time Locus Award winner, Martin is the author and editor of over two dozen novels and anthologies, and the writer of numerous short stories. His *New York Times* bestselling novel *A Storm of Swords*—the third volume in his epic fantasy series "A Song of Ice and Fire"—was published in 2000. Martin lives in Santa Fe, New Mexico.

"Martin has assembled an impressive array of writers. . . . Progressing through the decades, Wild Cards keeps its momentum to the end . . . I'm looking forward to the next episodes in this saga of mutant Americana."

—*Locus*

"Well written and suspenseful and a good read . . . The authors had a lot of fun rewriting recent American history."

—*Aboriginal Science Fiction*

"Commendable writing . . . a zany premise . . . narrated with rueful humor and intelligence."

—*Publishers Weekly*

WILD CARDS III
JOKERS WILD
A MOSAIC NOVEL

EDITED BY
GEORGE R.R. MARTIN

and written by:
Melinda M. Snodgrass ♦ Leanne C. Harper
Walton Simons ♣ Lewis Shiner ♥ John J. Miller
George R.R. Martin ♦ Edward Bryant

ILLUSTRATIONS BY TOM PALMER

ibooks
new york
www.ibooksinc.com

DISTRIBUTED BY SIMON & SCHUSTER, INC

An Original Publication of ibooks, inc.

An ibooks, inc. Book

Distributed by Simon & Schuster, Inc.
1230 Avenue of the Americas, New York, NY 10020

ibooks, inc.
24 West 25th Street
New York, NY 10010

The ibooks World Wide Web Site Address is:
http://www.ibooksinc.com

ISBN 0-7434-3489-7
First ibooks, inc. printing January 2002
10 9 8 7 6 5 4 3 2 1

Cover art by Brian Bolland
Cover design by J. Vita

Printed in the U.S.A.

This editorial hat trick is dedicated
to the editors who have helped me along the way

to Ben Bova, and Ted White, and Adele Leone,
to David G. Hartwell, and Ellen Datlow, and Ann Patty,
to Betsy Mitchell, and Jim Frenkel, and Ellen Couch,
to the memory of Larry Herndon and the Texas Trio,

and of course to Shawna and Lou,
who knew a winning hand when they saw one.

JOKERS WILD

PROLOGUE

There is Mardi Gras in New Orleans, *Carnival* in Rio, Fiestas and Festivals and Founders' Days by the hundreds. The Irish have St. Patrick's Day, the Italians Columbus Day, the nation its Fourth of July. History is full of mummers' parades and masques and orgies and religious pageants and patriotic extravaganzas.

Wild Card Day is a little of all of that, and more.

On September 15, 1946, in the cold afternoon sky over Manhattan, Jetboy died and the Takisian xenovirus—known colloquially as the wild card—was loosed upon the world.

It is unclear just when the observances began, but by the late sixties, those who had felt the touch of the wild card and had lived to talk of it, the jokers and aces of New York City, had taken the day as their own.

September 15 became Wild Card Day. A time for celebrations and lamentations, for grief and joy, for remembering the dead and cherishing the living. A day for fireworks and street fairs and parades, for masked balls and political rallies and memorial banquets, for drinking and making love and fighting in the alleys. With each passing year, the festivities became larger and more fevered. Taverns and restaurants and hospitals did record-setting business, the media began to notice, and finally, of course, the tourists arrived.

Once a year, without sanction or statute, Wild Card Day engulfed Jokertown and New York City, and the carnival of chaos ruled the streets.

September 15, 1986, was the fortieth anniversary.

CHAPTER 1

6:00 a.m.

It was as dark as it ever gets on Fifth Avenue, and as quiet.

Jennifer Maloy glanced at the streetlights and the steady stream of traffic, and pursed her lips in annoyance. She didn't like all the light and activity, but there wasn't much she could do about it. This was, after all, Fifth Avenue and 73rd Street in the city that never sleeps. It had been equally as busy the past few mornings she'd spent checking out the area and she had no reason to expect that conditions would ever get any better.

Hands thrust deep into the pockets of her trench coat, she strode past the five-story graystone apartment building and slipped into the alley behind it. Here was darkness and silence. She stepped into an area of the alley that was screened by a garbage dumpster and smiled.

No matter how many times she'd done this, she thought, it was still exciting. Her pulse speeded up and she breathed faster in anticipation as she put on a hoodlike mask that obscured her finely sculpted features and hid the mass of blond hair tied in a knot at the back of her head. She took off her trench coat, folded it neatly, and set it down next to the dumpster. Under the coat she wore only a brief black string bikini and running shoes. Her body was lean and gracefully muscular, with small breasts, slim hips, and long legs. She bent down, unlaced and removed her sneakers and put them next to the trench coat.

She ran a hand almost caressingly over the rear wall of the graystone apartment building, smiled, and then walked right through the wall.

It was the sound of a power saw biting into sodden hardwood. The whine of steel teeth made Jack's own teeth ache as the all-too-familiar boy struggled to hide deeper within the cypress tangle.

"He in dere somewhere!" It was his uncle Jacques. The folks around Atelier Parish called him Snake Jake. Behind his back.

The boy bit his lip to keep from crying out. He bit deeper, tasting blood, to keep from *changing.* Sometimes that worked. Sometimes–

Again the steel saw shrieked into wet cypress. The boy ducked down low; brown, brackish water slopped against his mouth, into his nose. He choked as the bayou washed over his face.

"Tol' you! Dat little gator-bait right dere. Get 'im." Other voices joined in.

The power saw blade whined one more time.

Jack Robicheaux flailed out in the darkness, one arm trapped in the sweaty sheet, the other reaching for the phone. He slammed the Tiffany lamp back against the wall, cursed as he somehow caught its petals-and-stems base and steadied it on the bed table, then felt the cool smoothness of the telephone. He picked up the receiver in the middle of the fourth ring.

Jack started to curse again. Who the hell had this number? There was Bagabond, but she was in another room here in his home. Before he could get his lips to the mouthpiece, he knew.

"Jack?" said the voice on the other end of the line. Long-distance static washed out the sound for a second. "Jack, this is Elouette. I'm callin' you from Louisiana."

He smiled in the darkness. "Figured you were." He snapped the lamp switch, but nothing happened. The filament must have broken when the lamp toppled.

"Never actually called this far before," said Elouette. "Robert always dialed." Robert was her husband.

"What time is it?" Jack said. He felt for his watch.

" 'Bout five in the morning," said his sister.

"What is it? Is it Ma?" He was waking up finally, pulling free from the fragments of the dream.

"No, Jack, Ma's fine. Nothin'll ever happen to her. She'll outlive us both."

"Then what?" He recognized the sharpness in his voice and tried to tone it down. It was just that Elouette's words were *so* slow, her thoughts so drawn-out.

The silence, punctuated by bursts of static, dilated on the line. Finally Elouette said, "It's my daughter."

"Cordelia? What about her? What's wrong?"

Another silence. "She's run off."

Jack felt an odd reaction. After all, *he'd* run away too, all those years before. Run away when he was a hell of a lot younger than Cordelia. What would she be now, fifteen?

Sixteen? "Tell me what happened," he said reassuringly.

Elouette did. Cordelia (she said) had given little warning. The girl had not come down for breakfast the morning before. Makeup, clothing, money, and an overnight bag were also gone. Her father had checked with Cordelia's friends. There weren't many. He called the parish sheriff. The patrols got the word. No one had seen her. The law's best guess was that Cordelia had hitched a ride out on the blacktop.

The sheriff had shaken his head sadly. "Gal looks like that," he'd said, "well, we got cause to worry." He'd done what he could, but it had all taken precious time. It had finally been Cordelia's father who'd come up with something. A girl with the same face ("Purtiest little thing I seen in a month," the ticket clerk had said) and long, luxuriant, black hair ("Black as a new-moon bayou sky," said a porter) had boarded a bus in Baton Rouge.

"It was Greyhound," Elouette said. "One-way fare to New York City. By the time we found out, the police said it wasn't none too practical to try and stop it in New Jersey." Her voice shook slightly, as though she wanted to cry.

"It'll be okay," said Jack. "When's she supposed to get here?"

"About seven," Elouette said. "Seven your time."

"*Merde.*" Jack swung his legs off the bed and sat up in the darkness.

"Can you get there, Jack? Can you find her?"

"Sure," he said. "But I gotta leave now for Port Authority, or I won't make it in time."

"Thanks be," Elouette said. "Call me after you've met her?"

"I will. Then we'll figure out what to do next. Now I go, okay?"

"Okay. I'll be right here. Maybe Robert will be back too." Trust filled her voice. "Thanks, Jack."

He put down the phone and stumbled across the room. He found the wall switch and finally was able to see in the windowless room. Yesterday's work clothes were strewn over the rough slab bench to one side. Jack pulled on the well-worn jeans and green cotton shirt. He grimaced at the fragrant work socks, but they were all he had. Today being his day off, he'd planned to spend it at a laundromat. He laced the steel-toed leather boots quickly, catching every other pair of eyelets.

When he opened the door leading into the rest of his home, Bagabond, the two huge cats, a passel of kittens, and a goggle-faced raccoon were all there in the doorway, silently staring at him. In the dimness of the lamp-lit living room beyond, Jack made out the gleam of Bagabond's dark brown hair and even darker eyes, her high, shadowed cheekbones, the lightness of her skin.

"Jesus, Mother Mary!" he said, stepping back. "Don' scare me like that." He took a deep breath and felt the tough, grainy hide on the back of his hands become soft again.

"Didn't mean to," said Bagabond. The black cat rubbed up against Jack's leg. His back nestled along the man's kneecap. His purr sounded like a contented coffee grinder. "Heard the phone. You okay?"

"I'll tell you on the way to the door." He gave Bagabond a précis as he stopped in the kitchen to decant the last of yesterday's coffee sludge into a foam cup he could carry with him.

Bagabond touched his wrist. "Want us to come along? Day like this, a few more eyes might be valuable at the bus station."

Jack shook his head. "Shouldn't be any problem. She's

sixteen and never been in any big city before. Just watched a lot of TV, her mama says. I'll be right there at the bus door to meet her."

"She know that?" said Bagabond.

Jack stooped to give the black a quick rub behind the ears. The calico meowed and moved over to take her turn. "Nope. Probably she was going to phone me once she got here. This'll just save time."

"Offer's still open."

"I'll have her back here for breakfast before you know it." Jack paused. "Maybe not. She'll want to talk, so maybe I'll take her to the Automat. She won't have seen anything like that back in Atelier." He straightened up and the cats yowled disappointedly. "Besides, you've got an appointment with Rosemary, right?"

Bagabond nodded dubiously. "Nine."

"Just don't worry. Maybe we can all have lunch. Depends on how much of a zoo downtown turns into. Maybe we can pick up take-out at a Korean deli and have a picnic on the Staten Island ferry." He leaned toward the woman and gave her a quick kiss on the forehead. Before she could even halfway raise her hands to grasp his arms and reciprocate, he was gone. Out the door. Out of her perception.

"Damn it," she said. The cats looked up at her, confused but sympathetic. The raccoon hugged her ankle.

Jennifer Maloy slipped through the lower two floors of the apartment building like a ghost, disturbing nothing and no one, neither seen nor heard. She knew that the building had gone condo some time ago and what she wanted was on the uppermost of the three floors that were owned by a rich businessman with the unfortunate name of Kien Phuc. He was Vietnamese. He owned a string of restaurants and dry-cleaning establishments. At least that's what they'd said on the segment of *New York Style* she'd seen on PBS two weeks ago. Jennifer really enjoyed that show, which took its viewers on tours of the artsy and stylish homes of the city's upper class. It presented her with endless possibilities and tons of useful information.

She floated through the third floor, where Kien's servants lived. She had no idea what was on the fourth floor, since it had been ignored by the television cameras, so she bypassed it and headed for Kien's living quarters on the top floor. He lived there alone in eight rooms of unrelieved luxury and opulence—decadence, almost. Jennifer had never realized there was that much money in laundromats and Chinese restaurants.

It was dark on the fifth floor, and quiet. She avoided the bedroom with the circular, mirror-ceilinged bed (a little tacky, she'd thought when she'd seen it on TV), and the fabulous hand-painted silk screens. She bypassed the Western-style sitting room with its two-thousand-year-old bronze Buddha gazing benignly from a place of honor next to a fabulous electronic entertainment center complete with a wide-screen television, VCR, and compact disc player with accompanying racks of video and audio tapes and discs. She wanted the study.

It was as dark there as it was on the rest of the floor, and she started when she saw a vague, shadowy figure looming beside the huge teakwood desk that dominated the room's back wall. Although impervious to physical attack while ghosting, she wasn't immune to surprise, and this figure hadn't been filmed by the *New York Style* cameras.

She quickly faded into a nearby wall, but the figure

didn't move or even show any sign that it had noticed her. She cautiously slipped into the study again, and was relieved and astonished to see that the thing was a large, nearly-six-foot-tall terra-cotta figure of an Oriental warrior. The workmanship of the piece was breathtaking. Facial features, clothing, weaponry, all were molded with exquisite delicacy of detail. It was as if a living man had been turned to clay, baked to a flawless finish in a kiln, and preserved down through the millennia, ending up in Kien's study. Her respect for Kien's wealth—and influence—went up another notch. The figure was undoubtedly authentic—Kien had made it clear during the television interview that he had no truck with imitations—and from what she knew, the 2200-year-old terra-cotta grave figures of the emperor Ying Zheng, first emperor of the Qin dynasty and unifier of China, were absolutely positively unavailable to private art collectors. Kien must have gone through considerable feats of legerdemain and bribery to obtain it.

It was a fantastically valuable piece, but, Jennifer knew, too large for her to remove and probably too unique for her to fence.

She felt a sudden wave of dizziness ripple through her insubstantial form, and quickly willed herself to solidity. She didn't like that feeling. It happened whenever she overextended herself, as a warning that she had stayed insubstantial for too long. She didn't know what would happen if she remained a wraith for too long. She never wanted to find out.

Now substantial, she looked around the room. It was lined with display cases containing Kien's collection of jades, the most beautiful, extensive, and valuable collection in the Western world. Kien had been profiled on *New York Style* because of them and they were what she had come for. Some of them, at least. She realized that she couldn't get them all even if she made a dozen trips back to the alley, because her ability to turn extraneous mass insubstantial was limited. She could only ghost a few jades at a time. But a few, really, were all she needed.

First, though, before starting on the jades, there was something else she had to do. The thick pile of the luxurious carpet feeling quite sensuous on the soles of her bare feet, she glided around the teakwood desk almost as quietly as if she were insubstantial, and stood before the Hokusai print hanging on the wall behind it.

Behind the print, so Kien had said, was a wall safe. He had mentioned it because, he had said, it was absolutely, one hundred percent, totally, and irrevocably, burglarproof. No thief knew enough about microcircuitry to circumvent its electronic lock and it was strong enough to withstand a physical assault short of a bomb big enough to bring down the whole building. No one, no how, at no time, could possibly break into it. Kien, who had looked very smug as he'd said all this, evidently was a man who liked to brag.

A mischievous smile on her face as she wondered what riches Kien had hidden in his high-tech safe, Jennifer ghosted her right arm and put her hand through the print and the steel door behind it.

He juggled her in his arms while he fished for his key, and finally unlocked the door.

"You idiot, put me down. Then you can open the door."

"Nope, going to carry you over."

"We haven't gotten married."

"Yet," he said, and grinned down into her face.

Her angle, from where she reclined in his arms, intensified the deformity of his neck, and made his head look like a baseball perched on a pedestal. Aside from that neck—a legacy of the wild card virus—he was a rather handsome man. Short-cropped brown hair, beginning to gray at the temples, merry brown eyes, strong chin—a nice face.

He negotiated the door, and set her on her feet. "My castle. Hope you like it."

It proclaimed the blue-collar origins of this man. Serviceable couch, recliner placed before the television, a stack of *Reader's Digests* on the coffee table, a large and poorly executed oil painting of a sailing ship clawing through improbably high seas. The sort of painting one found at starving-artist sales in Hilton hotels.

But it was scrupulously clean, and in a touch that seemed out of character in so large and powerful a man, a row of multicolored African violets lined the windowsills.

"Roulette, I haven't stayed out all night since my high school prom."

"I'll just bet you stayed out all night."

He blushed. "Hey, I was good Catholic boy."

"My momma always warned me about good Catholic boys."

He moved in, wrapped brawny arms about her waist. "I'm not quite so 'good' anymore."

"I hope that refers to your morals, and not to your performance, Stan."

"Roulette!"

"Prude," she teased.

He nuzzled her neck, and nibbled on her earlobe, and Roulette pondered yet again the random nature of wild card that it should have struck this very ordinary "sandhog," and made him more than human.

She reached up, and stroked her hands down the sides of his swollen throat. "Does it ever bother you?"

"Being the Howler? Hell, no. Makes me special, and I always wanted to be special. Used to drive my old man crazy. He always said water was good enough for our kind of people, meaning not to get above myself. He'd sure be surprised now. Hey." He reached out, caught a tear on the tip of one thick finger. "What are you crying about?"

"Nothing. I just . . . I found that sad."

"Well, come on. I'll show you how good my performance can be."

"Before breakfast?" she asked, trying to delay the inevitable.

"Sure, give us a better appetite."

She followed him resignedly into the bedroom.

Jennifer felt around inside of the safe and touched something that felt like a stack of coins nestled in a small pouch. She tried to ghost one of the coins and frowned when it remained solid.

Probably gold, she thought, Krugerrands or Canadian Maple Leafs.

It was difficult to ghost dense materials like metal, particularly gold, requiring a deeper level of concentration and a greater input of energy. She decided to leave the coins where they were for now, and continued to explore the safe.

Her hand caressed a flat rectangular object that ghosted a lot easier than the coin. She drew three small notebooks through the wall, and, unable to see details in the darkness, switched on the small tensor lamp that sat on the top of the teakwood desk. Two of the books, she could now see, had plain black covers. The third had a blue cloth cover with a bamboo pattern. She flipped open the top book in the stack.

Squares of brightly colored bits of paper were stuck in rows of pockets on the notebook's thick pages. Postage stamps. The ones in the top row seemed to be British, but they had words in another language and the date 1922 over-printed on them. She bent down closer to examine them, and froze as a tiny sound came from somewhere outside the cone of light illuminating part of the desktop.

She glanced up and saw nothing. Her eyes now accustomed to the light, she tilted the shade of the lamp outward, throwing illumination over the far reaches of the desk.

And she froze, her heart suddenly in her throat.

On the far corner of the desk was a five-gallon jar, about the size of a water cooler jug. Only this jar was glass, not plastic, and it wasn't connected to anything. It stood on a flat base on the edge of the desk, home to the thing that floated in it.

It was little more than a foot high, with green, glabrous, somewhat-warty skin. It floated with its head clear of the water, its web-fingered hands pressed against the glass, its human eyes staring at Jennifer out of a pinched face. They looked at one another for a long moment and then it opened its mouth and cried out in a high-pitched, wailing voice, "Kiennnnnn! Thiefffff! Thiefffff!"

New York Style had said nothing about Kien having a batrachian joker watchdog, Jennifer thought giddily as lights snapped on in other rooms. She heard sounds of commotion in other parts of the condo and the joker in the glass jar continued to scream for Kien in an ululating voice that seemed to bypass her ears and pierce directly into her brain.

Concentrate, she told herself, concentrate, or the daring sneak thief, the self-proclaimed Wraith, will be captured and exposed as Jennifer Maloy, reference librarian at the New York Public Library. She'd lose her job and go to jail for sure. And what would her mother think?

There was motion at the door and someone flicked on the study's overhead light. Jennifer saw a tall, slim, reptilian-looking joker. He hissed at her, his long, forked tongue lolling out an impossible length. He raised a pistol and fired. His aim was accurate, but the bullet ricocheted harmlessly off the wall. Jennifer was rapidly sinking through the floor, the three notebooks clutched tightly against her chest.

With Jack gone, Bagabond entered her morning ritual still wearing the tiger-striped robe he had given her. Sitting back in one of the red velvet overstuffed chairs, she closed her eyes and pinpointed the creatures who shared her life. The calico cat fed her young kittens as the black cat guarded them. The raccoon slept with his head against her ankles. He was tired from a night of prowling around Jack's Victorian lodgings. Bagabond hoped he had not disturbed anything important. She had set guards in the raccoon's head, warning him off Jack's belongings. Lately they had proven quite effective, but she never forgot the fight she had had with Jack when the raccoon had removed every one of his Pogo books from their shelf.

Reaching to stroke the raccoon, she expanded her consciousness out into the city. It was easy now, a waking ritual—although more and more, when she wasn't around Jack, Bagabond kept a nocturnal schedule. For years she had maintained their relationship as a casual one, showing up only when the weather was extremely bad or on days like this, when strangers found their way into places where they normally were too timid to venture. If Jack was home, she stayed. If he was gone, she moved on to another burrow. Lately, though, she had begun to seek his company more often, finding excuses to visit. Jack and Rosemary had both become very important to her, in ways she was not always able to define. It had taken years to trust them, but once she granted that trust, it was frighteningly easy to depend on them to be there for her. She shook her head angrily, unhappy to be distracted into thinking about things that were not under her control, and losing track of the creatures which were.

Waking and hurting with her creatures seemed more natural now. Her mind moved among the rats in the tunnels, the moles, rabbits, opossums, squirrels, pigeons and other birds. She took the night's death toll. There were always many who did not survive. She had learned that there could be no escape for the victims. Many died to feed the predatory animals; others were killed by men. Once she had tried to save them, to protect the prey from the predators. It had nearly driven her insane again. The natural cycle of life, death, and birth was stronger than she, and so Bagabond had begun to work within it. The animals died; there were more to take their places. Only human interference could upset the rhythm. She couldn't control humans yet. Briefly she touched the inhabitants of the zoo. Hate for the cages colored her impression. *Someday*, she promised the zoo prisoners again. *Someday . . .*

A warm paw on her cheek brought her back. The black cat, all forty pounds of him, lay across her chest. When her eyes opened, he licked her nose. She reached up and scratched him behind his ear.

There was a touch of gray on his muzzle now, but he

still moved like a younger cat most days. She sent him the warm feeling she thought of as love. He purred and sent her the image of the calico keeping the kittens away from Jack's Victorian furniture. If not closely watched, the kittens found the lion's-paw legs wonderful scratching posts.

Well, old friend, Jack turned me down again last night. What do you think is wrong? The subvocalized question received only a querying look from the cat at first, but then he sent the image of a hundred of Bagabond's creatures around her.

Yes, I know you're all there, but every once in a while I want another human. She created the image of the black and the calico together as mates. The black returned a vision of Bagabond and a human-sized cat. Bagabond nodded as she looked over at the kittens at play. *Not my type, unfortunately.*

She wondered why Jack refused to sleep with her. Her frustration and lack of understanding were beginning to turn to anger. It had only begun the last year. Each time she played with the kittens, she felt a lack in her own life.

The feeling angered her, but she couldn't deny it. Recently she had turned to Jack for confort, but for once he had turned her away. She resolved not to ask again.

Without the layers of dirt and ancient clothing that protected her in the world outside, she knew she was not unattractive. To spare her other friend Rosemary embarrassment, she had learned to dress on rare occasions in an acceptable fashion. It never felt right, though. Those were the times she was really in costume and she hated them. Perhaps she had become too involved with Jack and Rosemary. Perhaps it was time to go underground again.

The black followed the tone of her thoughts, even if he could not translate their abstract meanings. He added his approval of their severing the relationship with the humans by sending an image of some of their former lairs.

But not today. Today I have to go over to see Rosemary. Bagabond pulled herself up out of the chair and walked over to piles of old, dirty and shapeless clothing, which provided most of her wardrobe. The black cat and two kittens followed.

No, you're staying here. Jack may want to reach me. Besides, it is hard enough for me to get into her office without you along. She shifted her attention. *Blue coat or green army jacket?*

There were thirteen black candles in the room. When they burned, the wax turned the color of fresh blood and ran down the sides. Now the room was turning gray and their narrow circles of light were starting to fade.

"Do you know what time it is?"

Fortunato looked up. Veronica stood next to him in pink cotton panties and a ripped T-shirt, arms crossed over her breasts. "Almost dawn," he said.

"Are you coming to bed?" She turned her head sideways and waves of black hair fell across her face.

"Maybe later. Don't stand like that, it makes your stomach stick out."

"Yes, *o sensei.*" The sarcasm was muted, childish. A few seconds later he heard the bathroom door lock. If she wasn't Miranda's daughter, he thought, he would have put her back on the street weeks ago.

He stretched, stared for a few seconds at the murky clouds taking shape in the eastern sky. Then he went back to the Work in front of him.

He'd covered the five-pointed star on his floor with tatami, and on them he'd laid the Mirror of Hathor. It was about a foot long, with an image of the goddess where the handle met the solar disk. Her cow horns made her look a little like a medieval jester. It was made of brass, the front reflective for clairvoyance, the back abraded to rebound an enemy's attacks. He'd ordered it from an aging hippie in the East Village and had spent the last two days purifying it with rituals for all nine major deities.

For months he'd been increasingly unable to think of anything but his enemy, the one who called himself the Astronomer, who'd commanded a vast network of Egyptian Masons until Fortunato and the others had destroyed the nest he'd made at the Cloisters. The Astronomer had escaped, even if the evil thing he'd brought from space hadn't. The months of silence had only made Fortunato more and more afraid.

The Bornless Ritual, the Acrostics of Abramelin, the Spheres of the Qabalah, all of Western Magick had let him down. He had to use the Astronomer's own Magick against him. Had to find him, somehow, despite the blocks he'd set up that made him invisible to Fortunato.

The trick to Egyptian Magick—the real thing, not the Astronomer's warped and bloody version—was to go at it from their reverence for animals. Fortunato had spent his entire life in Manhattan, Harlem at first, then downtown once he could afford it. To him animals were poodles that left their shit on the sidewalk or listless, foul-smelling caricatures that slept their lives away at the zoo. He'd never liked or understood them.

It was an attitude he could no longer afford. He'd let Veronica bring her cat to the apartment, a vain, overweight gray tabby named Liz, in honor of the movie star. At the moment the cat was asleep on his crossed legs, her claws hooked into the silk of his robe. The cat's primitive value system was a doorway into the Egyptian universe.

He picked up the mirror. He just about had the mind-set. He watched his reflection: lean face, brown skin a little blotchy from lack of sleep, forehead swollen with *rasa*, the Tantric power of retained sperm. Slowly his features began to melt and run.

He heard a sound from the bathroom, a muffled sigh, and his concentration broke. And then, instead of the Astronomer, he was looking into the mirror and seeing Veronica. She sat on the toilet, her panties around her ankles. In her left hand was a pocket mirror, in her right a short piece of red-striped soda straw. Her head rolled loosely on her neck and she rubbed her cheek against her shoulder.

He put the Mirror of Hathor back on the mat. The junk didn't surprise him; it was just that she would do it here, right here in his apartment. He moved the protesting cat off his lap and went to the bathroom. He popped the lock with his mind and kicked the door open and Veronica's head jerked up guiltily. "Hey," she said.

"Pack your shit and get out," Fortunato said.

"Hey, 's jus' a li'l coke, man."

"For Christ's sake, how stupid do you think I am? Do you think I don't know smack when I see it? How long you been on this shit?"

She shrugged, dropped the mirror and straw into her open purse. She stood up, nearly tripped, then saw her feet tangled in her panties. She balanced herself on the towel rack while she pulled them up and snapped the purse closed. "Couple months," she said. "But I'm not *on* anything. I jus' do it sometimes. 'Scuse me."

Fortunato let her by. "What the hell's the matter with

you? Don't you care what you're doing to yourself?"

"Care? I'm a fucking hooker, why should I care?"

"You're not a hooker, goddammit, you're a geisha." He followed her into the bedroom. "You've got brains and class and—"

"Geisha my ass," she said, sitting heavily on the end of the bed. "I fuck men for money. That's the goddamn bottom line." She pushed her unresisting leg into her pantyhose, the big toenail laddering a run all the way down the right side. "You like to kid yourself with all this geisha shit, but real geishas don't fuck for money. You're a pimp and I'm a whore and that's all there is to it."

Before Fortunato could say anything somebody started hammering at the front door. Lines of tension and urgency radiated from the hallway, but nothing threatening. Nothing that couldn't wait.

"I don't put up with junkies," he said.

"You don't? Don't make me laugh. Half the girls in your stable take at least a snort now and then. Five or six are on the needle. Big time."

"Who? Is Caroline—"

"No, your precious Caroline is straight. Not that you'd know if she wasn't. You don't know *what* the fuck is going on."

"I don't believe you. I can't—"

There was a scraping sound in the front room and the door came open. A man named Brennan stood in the doorway, a strip of plastic in one hand. In the other was a slightly oversized leather attaché case. In it, Fortunato knew, was a disassembled hunting bow and a rack of broadhead arrows.

"Fortunato," he said. "Sorry, but I—" His eyes moved to

Veronica, who had peeled off her T-shirt and was holding her breasts in her hands.

"Hi," she said. "Wanna fuck me? All it takes is money." She teased her nipples with her thumbs and licked her lips. "How much you got? Two dollars? Buck and a half?" Tears ran out of her eyes and a line of mucus leaked out of one nostril.

"Shut up," Fortunato said. "Shut the fuck up."

"Why don't you slap me around?" she said. "That's what a pimp's supposed to do, isn't it?"

Fortunato looked back at Brennan. "Maybe you should come back later," he said.

"I don't know if it can wait," Brennan said. "It's the Astronomer."

CHAPTER 2

7:00 a.m.

By the time he got to the Port Authority Bus Terminal, Jack wished he had taken his electric track-maintenance car and sped uptown playing hopscotch with the trains. But what the hell, he'd thought as he'd ascended the stairs to the passenger levels of the City Hall station—this was a *holiday.* He didn't want to think about work. What he wanted to do more than anything else was to get all his clothes laundered, read a few chapters of the new Stephen King novel, *The Cannibals*, and maybe wander up to Central Park to have some cheap vended hot dogs with Bagabond and the cats.

But then the uptown 7th Avenue express had screeched into the station, and it had seemed like a good idea to step aboard. As the train sped uptown though Tribeca, the Village, and Chelsea, Jack noticed through the smeared panes that the stations seemed awfully busy for a holiday—at least this early.

When he got off at Times Square and walked the block

west in the tiled tunnels beneath 42nd, he overheard one transit cop disgustedly say to his partner, "Wait'll you take a gander topside. It looks like a cross between spring break at Lauderdale and the Bronx Zoo."

He came up for air at Eighth Avenue, ascending out of the strong morning scent of disinfectant barely masking the smell of vomit. The street population looked to Jack like any rush-hour weekday morning, except that the average age looked fairly youthful, and gray suits had been replaced by considerably more garish attire.

Jack stepped off the curb to avoid having to confront a swaggering trio of teenaged boys—normals by the look of them—who wore outrageous styrofoam headgear. The hats featured tentacles, drooping lips, segmented legs, horns, melting eyes, and other, more unappetizing appendages that jiggled and bobbed with the wearer's movements.

One of the boys put his thumbs to his cheekbones and wagged his fingers at passersby. "Ooga, booga," he cried. "We muties! We bad!" His pals laughed uproariously.

A block further, Jack passed one of the sidewalk sellers peddling the foam hats. "Hey!" the vendor called. "Hey, c'mere, c'mere. Y' don't got to *be* a joker to look like one. T'day's your chance to *act* like one. You interested?"

Jack shook his head wordlessly, scratched the back of his hand, and walked on.

"Hey!" yelled the man to another potential customer. "Be a joker for a day! Tomorrow you can go back to being yerself."

Jack shook his head. He wasn't sure now whether it would be better to go on being depressed, or just go back and rip out the hat vendor's throat. He looked at his watch. Five before seven. The bus would be in. The salesman's life was temporarily safe.

The Port Authority building was a darker gray, bulking large in the chill gray of the Manhattan morning. Then Jack noted that most of the human traffic seemed to be exiting rather than entering the building. It reminded him of an Avenue A apartment after the exterminators set off their chemical bombs—an exodus of cockroaches carpeting every exit.

He fought his way through one of the main doors, ignoring the hulking men importuning, "Hey, man, want a cab? Want an escort in to your bus?" Most of the storefronts along the interior promenade were locked and dark, but the snack bars were doing a land-office business.

Jack looked at his watch again. 7:02. Ordinarily he would have stopped and appreciated the huge "42nd St. Carousel" kinetic sculpture, a glass box enclosing a marvelous and musical Rube Goldberg contraption, but now there was no time. Less than no time.

He checked the arrival board. The bus he wanted was coming in at a gate three levels up. *Merde!* The escalators were broken. Most of the foot traffic was coming down. Jack made his way up the stationary metal flights. He felt like a salmon struggling upstream to spawn.

Only a minor current of the incoming tidal crest of humanity seemed to be the usual sorts of people who arrived in Manhattan by bus. Most seemed either to be tourists—Jack wondered whether *this* many people would actually be coming into the city for this particular holiday—or jokers themselves. Jack noted wryly that the normals were obliged by the constraints of the stairs and escalator steps to associate much more closely with jokers than they might otherwise have wished.

Then someone elbowed him painfully in the side, and the opportunity for musing was over. By the time he reached the third level and stepped outside the down-traveling crowd, Jack felt as if he'd used as much energy as he would normally burn climbing to the crown of the Statue of Liberty.

Somebody in the crush patted him on the rear. "Watch it, jerk," he said without rancor, not looking.

He found the section holding the gate he wanted. The area was packed. It looked as if at least half a dozen coaches had arrived and were unloading simultaneously. He waded into the aimless melee and aimed himself at the right gate number. He stopped to allow a dozen traditionally garbed nuns to move past him at right angles. A big joker with leathery skin and pronounced tusks protruding from beneath his upper lip tried to muscle through the nuns. "Hey, move it, penguins!" he yelled. Another joker, one with huge puppy-like brown eyes and what appeared to be stigmata wounds on his palms, voiced exception. The shouting match looked as if it might escalate into something more violent. Naturally an increasingly dense crowd of onlookers stopped to gawk.

Jack tried to bypass the mess. He stumbled into an apparent normal, who shoved back. "Sorry!"

The normal was well over six feet tall, and proportionately muscled. "Buzz off."

And then Jack saw her. It was Cordelia. He knew that as surely as he knew anything, though he hadn't seen her before in his life. Elouette had sent pictures the Christmas previous, but the photographs didn't do the young woman justice. Looking at Cordelia, Jack thought, was like looking at his sister when she'd been three decades younger. His niece was wearing jeans and a sweatshirt. The sweatshirt was a faded crimson with screaming yellow letters spelling out FERRIC JAGGER. Jack recognized the name even though he wasn't terribly interested in heavy metal groups. He could also make out some sort of pattern made up of lightning bolts, a sword, and what looked like a swastika.

Cordelia was about ten yards away, on the other side of a thick flow of disembarking passengers. She held a battered floral-print suitcase with one hand, a leather handbag with the other. A tall, slender, expensively dressed Hispanic man was trying to help her with the suitcase. Jack was instantly suspicious of any helpful stranger wearing a purple pinstripe suit, slouch hat, and a fur-trimmed coat. It looked like baby harpseal pelts.

"Hey!" Jack shouted. "Cordelia! Over here! It's me—Jack!"

She obviously didn't hear him. For Jack, it was like watching television, or perhaps the view seen through the wrong end of a telescope. He couldn't attract Cordelia's attention. With the noise of the terminal, the buses revving their engines, the massed roar of the crowd, his words wouldn't cross the intervening distance.

The man took her suitcase. Jack yelled helplessly. Cordelia smiled. Then the man took her elbow and steered her toward a near-side exit.

"No!" It was loud enough that even Cordelia turned her head. Then she looked puzzled briefly, before continuing toward the exit at the behest of her guide.

Jack uttered a curse and started to pull and shove people out of his way as he tried to cross the waiting area. Nuns, jokers, punkers, street bums, it didn't matter. At least not until he fetched up against the bulk of a joker who looked to have the general shape and about half the mass of a Volkswagen Beetle.

"Goin' somewhere?" said the joker.

"Yes," said Jack, trying to move past.

"I come all the way from Santa Fe for this. I always heard you people here was rude."

A fist the size of a two-slice toaster grabbed Jack's shirt lapels. Fetid breath made him think of a public restroom after rush hour.

"Sorry," said Jack. "Look, I've got to get my niece before a son-of-a-bitching pimp steals her out of here."

The joker looked down at him for a long moment. "I can dig it," he said. "Just like on TV, huh?" He let loose of Jack, and the latter scooted around him like rounding the flank of a mountain.

Cordelia was gone. The nattily attired man guiding her was gone. Jack got to the exit where the two had presumably left. He could see hundreds of people, mainly the backs of their heads, but no one who looked like his niece.

He hesitated only a second. There were eight million people in this city. He had no idea how many tourists and jokers from all parts of the world had flooded into Manhattan for Wild Card Day. More millions, probably. All he had to find was one sixteen-year-old from rural Louisiana.

It was all instinct for the moment. Without thinking further, Jack headed for the escalators. Maybe he'd catch up with them before the man and Cordelia got outside. But if not, then he'd just find Cordelia on the street.

He didn't want to think about what he'd tell his sister.

Spector hadn't slept. He picked up the amber bottle of pills on the bedside table and dropped them into the trash. He'd have to find something stronger.

The pain was always there, like the smell of stale smoke in a seedy bar. Spector sat up and breathed slowly. The early morning light made his apartment look even grayer than usual. He'd furnished the efficiency with cheap beat-up junk from pawnshops and secondhand stores.

The phone rang.

"Hello."

"Mr. Spector?" The voice had the refined edge of a Bostonian. Spector didn't recognize it.

"Yeah. Who are you?"

"My name is unimportant, at least for now."

"Right." They were going to play cagey with him, but most people did. "So why are you calling me? What do you want?"

"A mutual acquaintance named Gruber indicated that you have certain unique abilities. A client of mine might wish to employ you, initially on a freelance basis."

Spector scratched his neck. "I think I see what you're getting at here. If this is some kind of a setup, you're a dead man. If you're legit, it's going to cost you."

"Naturally. Perhaps you've heard of the Shadow Fist Society? It could be very profitable for you to work within that organization. However, they are cautious and would require a demonstration first. Would this morning be too soon?"

Word had it that the Shadow Fist Society was run by the city's anonymous new crime lord. They were leaning hard on the older gang bosses. Spector would feel right at home in the upcoming bloodbath. "I got nothing else to do. Who do you have in mind?"

"That's really of no importance to us." He paused. "Mr. Gruber seems to know quite a bit about you, and he's far from discreet."

"Fine by me."

"Be at Times Square at eleven-thirty this morning. If

we're satisfied that you meet our needs you'll be contacted there."

"What about money?" Spector heard a buzz at the other end.

"That will be negotiated later. If you'll excuse me, I have another matter to attend to. Good-bye, Mr. Spector."

Spector dropped the receiver into the cradle. He smiled. Gruber wasn't one of his favorite people. He never gave anyone a fair price for their goods. Killing a greedy fence would be something of a public service.

He walked naked to the bathroom and stared at the mirror. His stringy brown hair needed washing and his mustache was overgrowing his thin upper lip. Other than that he looked the same as the day he'd died. The day Tachyon had brought him back. Spector wondered if he might not live forever. At this point, he didn't really care. He stuck out his tongue. His reflection didn't. It smiled at him.

"Don't worry, Demise," said his face in the mirror. "You can still die." It laughed.

He backed into the bedroom. The air was cold. There was a loud, crackling sound. Spector ran for the living room. The bedroom door slammed in his face. He smelled ozone.

"Now, now, Demise. I only want to have a little chat." Spector recognized the voice now. He turned. The Astronomer's projected self was sitting on the bed. He was wearing a black robe sashed at the waist with a rope of human hair. His crippled body was straighter than usual, which meant his powers were charged up. He was covered in blood.

"What do you want?" Spector was afraid. The Astronomer was one of the few people his power didn't work on.

"Do you know what today is?"

"Wild Card Day. Everybody and his dog knows that." Spector picked a pair of brown corduroy pants off the floor.

"Yes. But it's also something else. It's Judgment Day." The Astronomer knotted his fingers together.

"Judgment Day?" He pulled his pants on. "What are you talking about?"

"Those bastards who ruined my plan. They intervened with our true destiny. They kept us from ruling the world." The Astronomer's eyes gleamed. There was a madness in them that even Spector hadn't seen before. "But there are other worlds. This one won't soon forget my parting shot at those fuckers who got in my way."

"Turtle. Tachyon. Fortunato. You're going after *those* guys?" Spector clapped his hands softly. "Good for you."

"By the end of the day they'll all be dead. And you, my dear Demise, are going to help me."

"Bullshit. I did your dirty work before, but not now. You fucking left me hanging out to dry, and I'm not going to give you another chance."

"I don't want to kill you, so I'll give you one chance to change your mind." A rainbow of colored light began to swirl around the Astronomer.

"Fuck off, man." Spector shook his fist. "You're not going to make a fool of me again."

"No? Then I'm afraid I'll have to make a corpse of you. Along with all the rest." The Astronomer shifted into a jackal's head. It opened its mouth; dark blood flowed steaming onto the carpeted floor. It howled. The building shook with sound.

Spector covered his ears and fell to the floor.

Fortunato called Caroline to come for Veronica. Caroline could take her to his mother's townhouse, the official business address for the escort agency. Caroline, and half a dozen of the other women, more or less lived there. He hustled Veronica into her clothes and then left her nodding out on the living room couch.

Brennan said, “Is she going to be all right?”

“I doubt it.”

“I know it’s none of my business, but weren’t you maybe a little hard on her?”

“It’s under control,” Fortunato said.

“Sure it is,” Brennan said. “I never said it wasn’t.”

They stood and looked at each other for a few seconds. As Yeoman, Brennan was probably the only one of the costumed vigilantes running loose in New York that Fortunato trusted. Partly because Brennan was still human, unaffected by the wild card virus. Partly because he and Fortunato had been through some serious shit together, inside a monstrous alien that some people called the Swarm.

The Astronomer called it TIAMAT, and he’d used a machine he called the Shakti device to bring it to Earth. Fortunato had smashed the machine himself, but he was too late. The alien had already arrived, and hundreds of thousands around the world had died because of it.

“What about the Astronomer?” Fortunato said.

“You know a guy they call the Walrus? Jube, the newsie?”

Fortunato shrugged. “Seen him around, I guess.”

“He saw the Astronomer in Jokertown early this morning. Told Chrysalis about it, she mentioned it to me.”

“What did it cost you?”

“Nothing. I know, it’s out of character. But even Chrysalis is afraid of this guy.”

“Where does this Walrus know the Astronomer from?”

“I don’t know.”

"So we've got a secondhand report by an unreliable witness and a cold trail?"

"Back off, man. I tried to phone. The operator told me it was off the hook. This isn't even my fight. I came here to help you out."

Fortunato looked at the Mirror of Hathor. It could take him all day to get it purified and get himself focused enough to try it again. Meanwhile, if the Astronomer *had* come out of his hole, it could be trouble.

"Yeah, okay. Let me take care of this other business and we'll go take a look."

By the time Fortunato had his street clothes on, Caroline had arrived. Even with her hair in short blond tangles, wearing an old sweatshirt and jeans, she made Fortunato want her.

She didn't look any older than she had seven years ago, when he'd first taken her on. She had a child's face and a compact, energetic body whose every muscle seemed to be under her voluntary control. Fortunato loved all his women, but Caroline was special. She'd learned everything he could teach her—etiquette, foreign languages, cooking, massage—but her spirit had never cracked. He'd never mastered her, and maybe for that reason she could still give him more pleasure in bed than any of the others.

He kissed her quickly when he let her in. He wished he could take her back into the bedroom and let her give him a shot of Tantric power. But there wasn't time.

"What do you want to do with her?" Caroline said.

"Does she have a date tonight?"

"It's Wild Card Day. Everybody has a date tonight. Mine should be over by midnight, and I may have to go out again if I get home too early."

"Keep an eye on her. Let her go out if she seems all

right. But keep her away from any more junk. I'll figure out the rest of it later."

She looked at Yeoman. "Is something up?"

"Nothing to worry about. I'll call you later." He kissed her again and watched her take Veronica down to the waiting cab. Then he looked at Brennan and said, "Let's go."

"Is that a lobster, or is that a lobster?" Gills asked. He held it up for Hiram's inspection, and the lobster waved its claws feebly. The pincers were banded shut and a few strands of seaweed draped the hard green shell.

"A lobster of distinction," Hiram Worchester agreed. "Are they all that large?"

"This is one of the small ones," Gills said. The joker had mottled greenish skin, and gill slits in his cheeks that pulled open when he smiled, showing the moist red flesh within. The gills didn't work, of course; if they had, the elderly fishmonger would have been an ace instead of a joker.

Outside, dawn light was washing over Fulton Street, but the fish market was already busy. Fishmongers and buyers haggled over prices, refrigerator trucks were being loaded, teamsters shouted curses at each other, and men in starched white aprons rolled barrels along the sidewalks. The smell of fish hung in the air like a perfume.

Hiram Worchester fancied himself a night owl, and on most days preferred to sleep in. But today was not most days. It was Wild Card Day, the day he closed his restaurant to the public and hosted the city's aces in a private party that had become a tradition, and special occasions made their own special demands, like getting out of bed when it was still dark outside.

Gills turned away, replaced the lobster in its barrel. "You want to see another one?" he asked, tossing aside a handful of the wet seaweed and extracting a second lobster for Hiram's inspection. It was larger than the first, and more lively. It moved its claws vigorously. "Look at 'im kick," Gills said. "Did I say fresh or did I say fresh?"

Hiram's smile was a quick flash of white teeth through the black of his spade-shaped beard. He was very particular about the food he served in Aces High, and never more so than for his Wild Card Dinner. "You never let me down," Hiram said. "These will do handsomely. Delivery by eleven, I assume?"

Gills nodded. The lobster waved its claws at Hiram and regarded him sourly. Perhaps it anticipated its fate. Gills put it back in the barrel.

"How's Michael?" Hiram asked. "Still at Dartmouth?"

"He loves it there," Gills said. "He's starting his junior year, and already he's telling me how to run the business." He put the top back on the barrel. "How many you need?"

Hiram anticipated feeding about one hundred and fifty persons, give or take a dozen—eighty-odd aces, each of whom would bring a spouse, a lover, a guest. But of course lobster would hardly be the *only* entrée. Even on this night of nights, Hiram Worchester liked to give his guests a choice. He had three alternatives planned, but these lobsters looked so splendid, undoubtedly they would be a popular choice, and it was better to have too many than too few.

The door opened behind him. He heard the bell ring.

"Sixty, I think," Hiram said, before he realized that Gills was no longer paying attention. The joker's oversized eyes were fixed on the door. Hiram turned.

There were three of them. Their jackets were dark green leather. Two looked normal. One barely topped five feet, with a narrow face and a pronounced swagger. The second was tall and wide, a rock-hard beer belly spilling over his skull-and-crossbones belt buckle. He'd shaved his skull. The leader was an obvious joker, a cyclops whose single eye peered out at the world through a monocle with a thick coke-bottle lens. That was strange; jokers and nats didn't often run together.

The cyclops took a length of chain out of the pocket of his jacket and began to wind it around his fist. The other two looked around Gills's establishment as if they owned the place. One began to kick at the sawdust with a heavy, scuffed-up boot.

"Excuse me," Gills said. "I have to . . . I . . . I'll be right back." He moved off toward the cyclops, abandoning Hiram for the moment. Across the room, two of his employees leaned close and began to whisper together. A third man, a feeble-minded joker who'd been moving the wet sawdust around with a push broom, gaped at the intruders and began to edge toward the back door.

Gills was expostulating to the cyclops, gesturing with his broad web-fingered hands, pleading in a low urgent tone. The youth stared down at him from that single implacable eye, his face cold and blank. He kept wrapping the chain around his hand as Gills talked to him.

Hiram frowned and turned away from the tableau. Trouble there, but it was none of his business, he had enough to think about today. He wandered down a sawdust-covered aisle to inspect a shipment of fresh tuna. The huge fish lay atop each other in rough-hewn wooden crates, their eyes fixed on him glassily. Blackened tuna, he thought. The inspiration brought a smile to his face. LeBarre was a genius at Cajun food. Not for tonight, that menu had been planned weeks ago, but blackened tuna would make an excellent addition to his regular bill of fare.

"Fuck that shit," the cyclops said loudly from across the room. "You shoulda thought of that a week ago."

"Please," Gills said in a thin, frightened voice. "Just a few more days . . ."

The cyclops put one booted foot up on a bin of fish, kicked, and sent it crashing over on its side. Whitefish spilled out all over the floor. "Please, don't," Gills repeated. His employees were no longer in sight.

Hiram turned and walked toward them, hands shoved casually into the pockets of his jacket. For such a huge man, his pace was surprisingly brisk. "Excuse me," he said to the cyclops. "Is there a problem here?"

The joker youth towered over Gills, who was a small man made even smaller by his twisted spine, but Hiram Worchester was another matter. Hiram stood six foot two, and most people took one look at his girth and guessed that he weighed around three hundred fifty pounds. They were off by about three hundred twenty pounds, but that was another story. The cyclops looked up at Hiram through his thick monocle, and smiled nastily. "Hey, Gills," he said, "how long you been selling whale?"

His companions, who had been standing by the door trying to look bored and dangerous simultaneously, drifted closer. "Look, it's the fucking Goodyear blimp," the short one said.

"Please, Hiram," Gills said, touching him gently on the arm. "I appreciate it, but . . . everything is fine here. These boys are . . . ah . . . friends of Michael's."

"I'm always pleased to meet friends of Michael's," Hiram said, staring at the cyclops. "I'm surprised, though. Michael always had such good manners, and his friends have none at all. Gills has a bad back, you know. You really ought to help him clean up these fish you knocked over."

Gills's face looked greener than usual. "I'll get it cleaned up," he said. "Chip and Jim can do it, don't . . . don't worry about it."

"Why don't you leave, lard ass?" the cyclops suggested. He glanced at the short kid. "Cheech, get the door for him. Help him squeeze his fat ass right through." Cheech stepped back and opened the door.

"Gills," Hiram said, "I believe we were discussing terms on these excellent lobsters."

The tall boy with the shaved skull spoke up for the first time. "Make 'im squeal, Eye," he said in a deep voice. "Make 'im squeal before you let 'im go."

Hiram Worchester looked at him with genuine distaste and a calm he did not really feel. He hated this sort of thing, but sometimes one was given no choice. "You're trying to intimidate me, but you're only making me angry. I doubt very much that you're actually friends of Michael's. I suggest you leave now, before this goes too far and someone gets hurt."

They all laughed. "Lex," Eye told the bald one, "it's too fuckin' hot in here. I'm sweating. Need some fresh air."

"I'll cool it right off," Lex said. He looked around, grabbed a small barrel in both hands, hoisted it above his head in a single smooth, powerful jerk, and took a step toward the big plate-glass windows that fronted on Fulton Street.

Hiram Worchester took his hands out of his pocket. At his side, his right hand curled into a tight, hard fist. A meaningless little tic, he knew; it was his mind that did it, not his hand, but the gesture was as much a part of him as his wild card power. For an instant, he could see the gravity waves shifting hazily around the barrel like heat shimmers rising from the pavement on a hot summer's day.

Then Lex staggered, his arms buckled, and a barrel of salt cod that suddenly weighed about three hundred pounds came crashing down on his head. His feet went out from under him, and he hit the floor hard. The barrel staves shattered, burying Lex under the fish. Very *heavy* fish.

His friends stared, uncomprehending at first. Hiram stepped briskly in front of Gills and pushed the fishmonger away. "Go phone the police," he said. Gills edged backward.

The short one, Cheech, tried to drag Lex out from under the shattered barrel. It was harder than it looked. The cyclops gaped, then looked sharply back at Hiram. "*You* did that," he blurted. "You're that Fatman guy."

"I loathe that nickname," Hiram said. He made a fist, and Eye's monocle grew heavier. It fell off his face and shattered on the floor. The cyclops screamed an obscenity and swung at Hiram's ample stomach with a chain-wrapped fist. Hiram dodged. He was a lot nimbler than he looked; his bulk varied, but he'd kept his weight at thirty pounds for years. Eye came after him, screeching. Hiram retreated, clenching his fist and making the joker heavier with every step, until his legs collapsed under his own weight and he lay there moaning.

Cheech was the last to make his move. "You ace fuck," he said. He held his hands out in front of him, palms flat, some kind of karate or kung fu or something. When he leapt, his metal-shod boot came pistoning toward Hiram's head.

Hiram dropped to the sawdust. Cheech leapt right over him, and kept going, weighing rather less than he had a moment ago. The force of his leap carried him into a wall, hard. He hit, rolled, tried to come up with a bounce, and discovered he was so heavy he couldn't get up at all.

Hiram rose and brushed the sawdust off his jacket. He was a mess. He'd have to go home and change before going on to Aces High. Gills edged up to him, shaking his head. "Did you get the police?" Hiram asked.

The old man nodded.

"Good. The gravity distortion is only temporary, you know. I can keep them pinned down until the police arrive, but it takes a lot out of me." He frowned. "It's not healthy for them either. All that weight is a terrible strain on the heart." Hiram glanced at his gold Rolex. It was past 7:30. "I really have to get to Aces High. Damn, I didn't need this nonsense, not today. How long did the police—"

Gills interrupted him. "Go. Just go." He pushed at the larger man with gentle, insistent hands. "I'll handle it, Hiram. Please, go."

"The police will want me to give a statement," Hiram said.

"No," Gills said. "I'll take care of it. Hiram, I know you meant well, but you shouldn't . . . I mean . . . well, you just don't understand. I can't press charges. Go, please. Stay out of it. It will be better."

"You can't be serious!" Hiram said. "These hoodlums—"

"Are my business," Gills finished for him. "Please, I ask you as a friend. Stay out of it. Go. You will get your lobsters, very fine lobsters, I promise."

"But—"

"Go!" Gills insisted.

His hoarse grunts and the beat of his groin against hers set a counterpoint to the ticking of the bright yellow dime-store "Baby Ben" alarm clock on the bedside table. Roulette pulled her topaz eyes from Stan's brown ones, watched the second hand sweeping smoothly across the face of the clock.

Time. The ticking of a clock, the wash of blood through her veins driven by the inexorable beating of her heart. Fragments of time. Fragments marking the passage of a life. Ultimately it came down to this. It respected neither wealth, nor power, nor saintliness. Sooner or later it came, and silenced that steady pulse. And she had her orders.

Roulette reached up, softly touched Stan's temple.

She drew breath—a gathering of will and power—but there was no release. It required hate, and all she felt was uncertainty. She lay back, and summoned an image of horror. *The agony of labor, knowing it would soon end, and she would hold her child, and all pain would be forgotten. The doctor's eyes widening in terror. Struggling up to gaze at the thing between her legs . . .*

Her taut belly went flaccid, and an added warmth washed through her vagina, an imitation of passion as the poisonous tide flowed free. Howler's eyes suddenly bulged, his mouth worked, and he recoiled from her, his rapidly swelling cock rasping harshly along the soft tissues of her vagina with his abrupt withdrawal. Hands wrapped protectively about his quivering discolored member, he gagged several times and emitted a choking scream. A glob of spittle ran over his chin in a thin thread, and the dresser mirror exploded in a crystal waterfall littering the bed with glass fragments. The baby Big Ben took the edge of the spreading wave of sound. Its crystal shattered, freezing the hands, and as the blow reached the clock's inner works the alarm gave a tinny, dispirited squawk as if it were complaining about its sudden and unfair demise.

Sound like a fist took Roulette across the right cheek raising a mottled bruise on the *café au lait* skin, coaxing a trickle of blood from her ear. Indrawn breath caught in her throat like a jagged block, and sickness filled her belly. Howler's agonized face hung above her, and she knew she was looking at death. His chest was heaving, lips skinned back from teeth, and a tide of blue-black was rising from his now completely black and swollen penis into his groin and belly.

The rumpled satin comforter gave no purchase to her flailing legs. She felt as if she were swimming on glass. With a final, desperate flounder, she got to her knees, and threw an arm around the ace's chest. Her other hand tangled in his sweat-matted hair, and she yanked his head around so he faced the wall separating bedroom from living room. A life-ending, time-stopping scream echoed to the fringes of the universe and back again, and the wall exploded. Plaster dust spun in lazy spirals, catching at the throat, and filling the nostrils. Rubble fanned across the living room floor, and the far wall was bulging. For an instant Roulette contemplated that sagging wall; pictured it falling, pictured the fat, lower-middle-class couple in the next apartment staring at the tableau she would present. Naked woman holding naked man—cock swollen to stallion proportions, whole body swelling as the poison exploded blood cells, the trail of the poison marked by blue-black discolorations.

Another convulsion shook Howler, but his throat had swollen, closing off the vocal chords. The sweat-drenched skin of his back was cold and clammy against her flattened breasts, and the stink of released bladder and bowel filled the room. Gagging, she pushed him away, crawled off the bed, and huddled in on herself on the floor by the bed.

Destruction at the Cloisters. *He* had implied it was Turtle who had crumbled the stone walls. . . . *But he lied!* He promised there would be no risk even though this was the first ace she had ever killed. *And he lied.* She touched a hand to her ear, and gazed in fascination at the congealed blood that stained her fingers. A sense of betrayal ate its way through to conscious thought, and resolved itself into anger. *He knew, and didn't warn me.* Had he wanted her to die here? But who then would kill Tachyon for him?

Sirens reminded her of her danger. She had been so immersed in contemplation of death and betrayal that she had forgotten reality. No one in lower Manhattan could have missed that death cry. She was running out of time. And if she wanted to survive, to attain her final goal, she too had to run. She pushed back her tangled hair, the tiny pearls and crystals braided into the long strands catching on her fingers, tugging at her scalp. She jammed stockings and garter belt into her purse, flung on her dress, and pushed her feet into high-heeled sandals.

A last glance around the shattered room to see if she had left any trace of her presence—aside from the obvious one, of course, the bloated body on the bed.

I always wanted to be special.

An inarticulate cry burst from her, and she ran for the fire escape. One spiked heel slipped through the iron grating underfoot, and with a curse she pulled off the shoes. Holding one in each hand she ran down the five flights to the first floor, and lowered the ladder to the filthy, garbage-strewn pavement of the alley. Glass from a hundred broken windows lay like a sparkling snowfall among rotting lettuce leaves, plastic six-pack dividers, stinking cans. It crunched underfoot as she reached the ground, and one splinter drove deep into her heel.

She whimpered, pulled it out, and worked on her shoes.

Tetanus shot, I'll need a tetanus shot. I haven't had one since that month Josiah and I spent in Peru.

The thought of her ex-husband set memory in motion. Jerking forward like a train gaining momentum. Images jostling and shattering like the frames of a nightmare film running at double speed . . . until no coherent pictures remained, just an undifferentiated blur of pain and grief and gut-burning fury culminating in a spewing sense of relief when she had released the tide, and Howler had died.

Out of the alley and onto the street. Trying to set the right tone. It would be suspicious to simply ignore the insurance company's nightmare and glazier's delight that surrounded her. Yet she could not bring herself to join the gaping jostling throng, many still in pajamas and bathrobes, who gathered in clumps and gawked at the glass-littered street and the parked cars with frosted or demolished windows. Better perhaps to ape a young working woman; interested but concerned with getting to work on time—

A police car shot down the street, braked suddenly as it passed her, jerking the two occupants like test-car dummies. Flat, bloodshot eyes raked over her, and she forced herself to face the cop's suspicious glance though fear was fluttering in her belly. It was a predominantly white neighborhood, and though she was dressed with understated elegance her dress was clearly for evening.

Hooker.

The thought read clearly on the bloated, pink face, and she felt a stir of resentment. Class of '70, Vassar, master's in economics. Not a prostitute, you asshole. But she was careful to keep her expression neutral.

A man ran out of Howler's apartment building, arms windmilling about his head, mouth opening and closing though no words could be heard over the cry of the sirens.

The cop, distracted, lost interest in Roulette. He growled something to his partner, and jerked his thumb toward the building. The car rolled on, and Roulette forced herself back into motion.

The fear was back. Fueled not by the presence of the tangible pursuers who gathered behind her, but by the baying of her soul hounds who loped easily at her flanks. They were waiting for the time when the doubt and horror and guilt that had been growing with every kill would overwhelm her, bear her down, and then they would move in and destroy her. They were there now—waiting. She could hear them. She hadn't been able to hear them before. She was going insane. And if she killed again, what would happen? But she had to. And to have Tachyon dead would make even madness bearable.

CHAPTER 3

8:00 a.m.

The stone lions guarding the staircase before the main entrance of the New York City Public Library might as well have taken the day off. The library was closed and the staircase was deserted.

Jennifer, having gone back to her apartment to have a light breakfast and to change into a conservative suit with a black skirt, black jacket, and white blouse, reached out and patted one on the side as she went by anyway, in seeming encouragement of a job well done. She let herself into the building with her key, and then locked the door again behind her. The soles of her shoes clicked loudly, echoing eerily in the library's vast antechamber.

"Morning, Miss Maloy," an old man wearing a rumpled uniform greeted her as she made her way through the cavernous central room back toward her desk near the first-floor stacks.

"Good morning, Hector."

"Not going to the parade?" The old man was one of the security guards. He liked to tell stories of when he'd seen Jetboy battling the zeppelins over Manhattan back when he was a cop and what it was like in the first few horrible moments of the new age, when the wild card virus had been released and the world had changed, suddenly and forever.

"Maybe later," she said. She liked the old man, but now was not the time to get caught up in his interminable reminiscences. "I have some work to do. A project I want to finish."

Old Hector clicked his tongue against his dentures and shook his head.

"You work too hard, Miss Maloy, a pretty young thing like you. You should get out more."

"I will. I just thought that today would be a good day to finish this project of mine. What with the library being closed and all."

"I get your hint. I get your hint," the old man said good-naturedly, moving off along the darkened row of tables. "Never saw a girl liked books so much and going out and having fun so little," he muttered half to himself.

Jennifer went back into the stacks, keeping an eye on Hector, making sure he was going on his desultory rounds. It wouldn't do, she told herself, to have him come upon one of the reference librarians poring over a catalog with a couple of books full of rare stamps on her desk. It wouldn't do at all.

The noise level inside the Crystal Palace was still low enough to listen in on individual conversations, but Spector wasn't interested in eavesdropping. He headed straight for the bar, sat down, and started drumming his fingers on the polished wood. Sascha, alone behind the bar, was busy making a brandy alexander for a blond woman in a tight red-and-white cotton dress. Sascha's eyeless face gave Spector the creeps.

"Hey," Spector said, just loudly enough to get Sascha's attention. "I need a double shot of Jack Black."

"I'll be with you in a minute."

Spector nodded and pushed his hair back out of his eyes. He was too scared to eat, but he could always drink. Shit, he thought, I should have agreed to whatever he wanted. That twisted old fuck can make mincemeat out of me. He put his hand over his mouth and tried to slow his ragged breathing.

He turned around, afraid that the Astronomer might be right behind him. Only a few people would have the balls to start something at the Crystal Palace, but the Astonomer wouldn't even think twice about it.

God, I really don't want that bastard after me. Maybe he'll be too busy with the others. Even the Astronomer will have trouble taking them all on.

"Your drink."

Spector jumped at Sascha's voice, then turned around. "Thanks." He fished in his pocket for a five and tossed the crumpled bill onto the bar. Sascha hesitated for a moment, then picked up the money and walked away.

Spector picked up the glass and downed the whiskey. Got to keep moving. Maybe he won't look for me in Brooklyn. He laughed softly to himself. Maybe the next President will be a joker.

The air was chill and calm as he stepped outside. He rubbed his palms together and walked quickly down the street, toward the nearest subway.

The first time she killed it had been by accident—if such a thing can ever be termed an accident—and even now she could excuse it because toads like Sully really shouldn't be allowed to breed and multiply.

She had just lost her job. Her fingers tightened, and sugar and stale doughnut crumbs pattered onto the plastic plate. It had been presented as a leave of absence, but she knew better. For weeks the whispers had haunted her; creeping about the corners of the office partitions, echoing in the washrooms, leaving a tangible mark on every face. *Poor thing . . . husband is divorcing her . . . Is it true? . . . she had . . . a monster?*

Several of her pregnant friends dropped her as if her very presence could mutate their child, and the fear was not helped by a disquieting rumor out of the CDC that two anomalous cases of the wild card virus had arisen that could only be explained if the disease was in fact contagious. Frank had been kind that day when he called her into his office, but very firm. Her presence in the office was affecting worker morale and productivity. And didn't she really need some time alone to come to grips with What Had Happened To Her? So why not take a little time?

Weeks later, money running low, and her spirits just as low, she found Sully Thornton at her door. He was a pathetic little toady who continually brayed about being one of Josiah's "business associates." Roulette had never particularly noticed him doing any business when he had been present at Smallwoods. Instead he had concentrated on lapping up all the free booze he could hold, and trying to press soggy drunken kisses on her whenever he caught her alone. She had slapped him once, and after a neighing titter that set his prominent Adam's apple to bobbing, he had boozily explained that he was just "emulatin' old grandpa Thornton, with his fascination for dusky women. Just runs in the blood." *Yeah,* she'd thought sourly, *like whuppin' on the boys, and fuckin' the mammies. Just comes natural.*

Sully had mouthed something about wanting to look her up because Josiah had treated her so bad, and could he buy her dinner, and he'd heard she'd lost her job, and did she need a "little loan?" She didn't miss the meaning, and despite her revulsion with the man she accepted. Being broke ruins a person's standards.

Late that night, as he'd lain groaning and panting atop her, she had remembered the bone-cracking release as her baby was born, and raised herself up on her elbows, and had seen . . . *No!* Then had come a release of another kind, and Sully had died.

Her eaters of the soul had begun to torment her within hours of Sully's death. And if Judas had not found her perhaps she would have ceased to deal in death. But the Astronomer's acehound did find her, and took her to the Cloisters, and the Astronomer had spoken to her hidden places, nurturing her festering hate, promising that she would have her final revenge, and that when the last kill was made he would give her peace—remove forever the memory of her child.

The Astronomer had used her sparingly, eager to keep her secret and very effective. And she was effective. Today marked the third kill she had made for her awful master, and each time it was worse. She gulped down some of the Sunshine Cafe's enamel-stripping coffee, trying to wash away the sick taste of death that lay on her tongue.

This time he would know. He would sense her guilt and

doubt, and react, and she was scared to disappoint—No. She was just scared. Terrified of him. Of his powers. Of his obsessive drive to destroy. First TIAMAT. Now those who had denied him his ultimate victory.

What if she just never went back?

No, without him there could be no final catharsis, no final release from the memory of monsters. He could have all the rest, but Tachyon was hers. The alien had destroyed her life. She would repay him by destroying his. That was her obsession, and it had wedded her to the Astronomer in an unholy union of hate and vengeance, and it was far stronger a bond than love.

"Lady, I don't rent tables by the hour," growled the proprietor of the Sunshine Cafe, who was living proof that the generators of cheerful advertising were under no obligation to follow it.

She tossed money onto the table, and decided to be grateful for the interruption rather than irritated. Her greasy-spoon haven had been removed. She had to go.

To face him.

Normally Hiram liked to ride through the city streets, to watch the ebb and flow of the human drama on the sidewalks of Manhattan through the frosted-glass windows of his Bentley, while his driver worried about gridlock and kamikaze cabs. But today Jokertown and surrounding neighborhoods would be chaos, as the jokers took to the streets and thousands of tourists flowed into the city for the parades, street fairs, fireworks, and other celebrations that marked Wild Card Day.

To avoid the crush, Hiram told Anthony to take the FDR

Drive, and even so the traffic was a horror. He would have preferred to return to his apartment to change, but there wasn't time. They went directly to the Empire State Building.

Velvet ropes had been hung in front of the express elevators to Aces High, and a tasteful gold-lettered sign said CLOSED FOR PRIVATE PARTY. Hiram hopped over the rope lightly, no feat at all for a man who weighed only thirty pounds, but it always raised a few eyebrows in the lobby. The elevator took him straight up to the restaurant's foyer.

As the doors opened, he heard his head chef shouting at someone. The saucier, no doubt; they were constantly arguing. A janitor was sweeping out the cloakroom as Hiram emerged from the elevator. "Make sure you empty the ashtrays, Smitty," Hiram told him. He paused a moment, looked around the room. The marble floor was gleaming, the couches had been freshly cleaned. All the walls were hung with framed photographs of celebrities: politicians, sports figures, sex symbols, socialites, writers, film stars, newsmen, and a myriad of aces. Most had scrawled warm personal inscriptions to Hiram across their likenesses. He stopped to straighten the picture of Senator Hartmann and the Howler that had been taken the night the senator had been reelected, then swept through the wide double doors into the restaurant itself.

Paul LeBarre's voice was much louder in here, even through the hubbub. Workmen were setting up round banquet tables for the party, and moving the everyday tables into storage. Cleaning crews were polishing the floors, the long curved bar, and the magnificent art deco chandeliers that gave Aces High so much of its ambience. The wide doors to the Sunset Terrace had been thrown open to air out the room, and a stiff New York wind was blowing.

Dimly, from far below, Hiram could hear the sounds of traffic and police sirens.

Curtis, his maître d' and good right arm, came up to Hiram Worchester with a dozen stiff pieces of posterboard under one arm. He was a tall slender black man with white hair. Tonight, in his tuxedo, he would look splendid, elegant, even a bit austere. Right now, dressed in a flannel shirt and a pair of worn dungarees, he just looked harried.

"The kitchen is in chaos," he announced briskly. "Paul insists that Miriam has ruined his special hollandaise, and he's threatening to throw her off the Sunset Terrace. We had a small fire in the kitchen, but it's out, no damage. The ice sculptures are late. Six of our waiters phoned in sick this morning. Carnival flu, I call it, complicated by the fact that no one ever tips at these private parties. A larger bonus might effect a sudden remission. The usual rumor about Golden Boy has made the rounds, and I've had three calls from guests anxious to let us know that if *he* was coming, they weren't. Oh, and Digger Downs phoned up to tell me that if he isn't admitted tonight, *Aces!* magazine will never mention the restaurant again. And how are you this morning, Hiram?"

Hiram sighed, ran a hand across his bald head in a nervous gesture left over from the days he'd had hair. "Tell Digger I'll let him in if his editor promises in writing that we'll never be mentioned in *Aces!* again. Get me six temp waiters—no, make that ten, they won't be as good as our regular people. I'm not worried about Paul. He hasn't thrown anyone out a window yet." He strode toward his office.

Curtis matched him pace for pace. "There's always a first time. What about Golden Boy?"

Hiram made a rude noise. "We get the same rumor every year, and Mr. Braun has yet to show up. If he ever does, I'll deal with the question of his dinner. Who's threatening to cancel?"

"Sparkle Johnny, Trump Card, and Pit Boss," Curtis said.

"Reassure Shawna and Lou," Hiram told him, "and tell Sparkle Johnny that Golden Boy is definitely going to be here. Are those the seating charts?"

Curtis handed them over. "I'll call Kelvin and check on the ice sculptures," he said as Hiram unlocked the door to his private office.

"Out the window!" Paul LeBarre was screaming in the kitchen. "All the way down you can think of the proper way to make hollandaise. Perhaps it will come to you, before you hit!"

Hiram winced. "Do that," he said. "And please have someone do me up a small breakfast. An omelet, I think. Tomato, onion, crumbled bacon, cheese."

"Cheddar?"

Hiram raised an eyebrow. "Of course. Four eggs. With *pomme frites* and a carafe of orange juice, a little Earl Grey. Are there biscuits?"

Curtis nodded.

"Good. Three, please. I'm weak with hunger." Using his powers always left him famished. Dr. Tachyon said it had something to do with energy loss. "Anthony will be back soon with a clean suit. I had a bit of an altercation down on Fulton Street. Send someone to the lobby to wait for it. If Anthony tries to bring it up, the Bentley will probably be towed." He closed the door.

A 26-inch color television was mounted in the wall above his desk. Hiram seated himself in a huge, custom-designed leather executive's chair that smelled like the inside of a very old and very exclusive British men's club, turned on his built-in back massager, spread the seating charts out across the black walnut, and flicked on the television with a jab at the remote control. Willard Scott and Peregrine appeared on the screen. Willard was wearing moose ears, for some reason. Peregrine was wearing as little as she could get away with. They were talking about the Jokertown parade. Hiram hit the mute button. He liked to keep the television on as he worked, a sort of video wallpaper that kept him plugged into the world, but the noise distracted him. After a final glance at Peregrine's admirable costume, he began reviewing the charts, initialing each in the lower right-hand corner after he'd looked it over.

By the time Curtis returned with his omelet, Hiram had finished the charts. "Two changes," he said. "Put Mistral over by the terrace. If it gets too windy, she can take care of it for us. Switch Tachy and Croyd. If we put Tachyon at the same table with Fortunato, we'll have innocents killed in the crossfire."

"Excellent," Curtis said. "Six tables for the at-the-doors?" Formal invitations were sent out annually to the Wild Card Day Dinner at Aces High, and RSVPs were expected, but there were aces who carefully kept their names secret, and others who'd yet to come out of the deck. The party was open to all of them, and each year the queue of those hoping to win admission by demonstrating an ace talent at the door grew longer and longer.

"Eight tables," Hiram said after a moment's reflection. "This is the fortieth anniversary, after all." He glanced up at the television screen again. "One more thing." He took back the top chart, made a notation. "There."

Curtis studied it. "Peregrine next to you. Very good, sir."

"I thought so," Hiram said, with a quiet smile. He felt rather pleased with himself.

"The ice sculptures will be delivered within the hour."

"Excellent. Notify me when they arrive."

Curtis closed the door behind him. Hiram leaned back in his chair, glanced up at the TV set, changed the channel. On the steps of Jetboy's Tomb, Linda Ellerbee was interviewing Xavier Desmond. He watched them mouth silent words for a minute. Then a news bulletin interrupted their conversation. Something about the Howler, whose picture flashed up on the screen, wearing his yellow fighting clothes. A nice fellow, but his color sense was almost as bad as Dr. Tachyon's.

Hiram frowned, and steepled his fingers thoughtfully. Everything was under control. The party would be a smashing success, the social occasion of the year. He ought to be feeling elated. Instead, he was troubled.

The business down at the Fulton Street Fish Market, that was it. He couldn't get if off his mind. Gills was in some kind of trouble. He needed help. Hiram was fond of the old joker. They'd been doing business for a decade, and Aces High had even catered his son's graduation.

Someone ought to find out what was going on, Hiram thought. Not him, of course; he was a restaurateur, not an adventurer. Still, he knew all the right people, and many of them owed him favors. Perhaps he ought to use his contacts.

Hiram found Dr. Tachyon's number on his Rolodex, picked up his telephone, punched out the number. He let it ring a long time. The Takisian was a notoriously late sleeper. Finally he gave up. Wild Card Day was always a trial for Tachyon. As often as not, it set him off on binges of guilt, self-pity, and cognac. This being the fortieth anniversary, the doctor's angst could be particularly acute. Oh, Dr. Tachyon would be on time for dinner, no doubt of that, but Hiram wanted to get someone working on this immediately.

He thought for a minute. His good friend Senator Hartmann would lend him the services of some Justice Department ace, undoubtedly, but involving the government was time-consuming and messy. Fortunato might help, but then again he might not.

He turned his Rolodex, looking at the names, and of course it was right there, on the very first card:

JAY ACKROYD
Confidential Investigations
& Sleight-of-Hand

Smiling, Hiram Worchester picked up the phone and dialed.

Ackroyd got it on the fifth ring. "It's too early," the PI complained. "Go away."

"Out of bed, Popinjay," Hiram said cheerfully, knowing it would irritate him. "The early bird gets the worm, and tonight you'll be solving for your supper, so to speak."

"It better be more than one supper, Hiram," Ackroyd said. "And don't call me Popinjay, dammit."

Each stockbook had ten pages and each page held about a hundred stamps with their Scott Postage Stamp Catalog numbers written in neatly below them, making them very easy to identify.

There were ten Ireland #38 (Great Britain #171, overprinted "Rialtar Sealadac na héineann 1922" in blue black ink), mint, catalog value $1,500 each. There were eight Denmark #1 (imperforate with yellow brown burelage), lightly canceled with four excellent margins, catalog value $1,300 each. There were twelve Japan #8 (native laid paper without gum), mint, catalog value $450 apiece. And on and on and on. All together there were 1,880 stamps in the stockbooks, cataloging, on the average, about $1,000 each, so that each stockbook held about a million dollars' worth of stamps. The third, book, though . . .

Jennifer flipped through the pages rapidly, but her mind was drawn from the mystery of the third book by the wealth in the other books on the cluttered desk before her.

Kien had put together quite a little collection. She didn't know much about philately, but a quick perusal of the pricing information in the front of the catalogs, and her general experience in the field of rare and collectable materials, told her that Kien had assembled the perfect collection for realizing maximum profit when it came time to sell.

The stamps he had gathered were rare, but not exceedingly rare. The really rare stamps were so well known that all extant examples of them were documented, but enough of these issues existed so that they were untraceable. They were rare enough to be, well, rare, and common enough so that their appearance on the market wouldn't cause a stir.

They were also rare enough so that—depending, of course, on how desperate he was at the time he liquidated his holdings—Kien could expect to get near catalog price for them when he wanted to turn them into something more negotiable.

A quick check of several selected issues in catalogs from previous years told her that they were also rare enough to increase in value every year. And if Kien played the proper cards when cashing them in he wouldn't have to pay taxes on them. Of course, a single stamp dealer would have a hard time coming up with enough cash to purchase the entire collection, but there were a lot of stamp dealers in any given large city.

Unfortunately, Jennifer reflected as she idly scanned the pages of stamps, she didn't have that option. She couldn't break up the collection piecemeal. She had to get rid of it at once, and she'd be fortunate if her fence would give her ten percent of value for them.

Still, ten percent would be nice. Two hundred thousand isn't bad for a morning's work.

She had a big balloon payment coming up on her apartment that had recently gone condo, and then there were her special projects. She took a small black book out of her purse and scanned her list of favorite charities, mostly small, poorly-funded centers for battered wives, deserted children, and abandoned animals. In the current age of government cutbacks private citizens had to do all they could to support worthy causes, and there were, Jennifer thought, an awful lot of worthy causes in the world.

Moisture was seeping from a long crack running diagonally across the wall of the tunnel. The entire weight of Manhattan seemed poised above her head, and she wondered for the hundredth useless time whether this rabbit warren of tunnels and tiny rooms would survive. Maybe her footsteps would be the final stress needed to bring down the crumbling lair. Fear pushed breath deep into her abdomen, and she hurried forward, moisture seeping in the sides of her sandals.

It seemed incredible to her that after the debacle in May when the aces of New York had stormed the Cloisters, killing a number of Masons and destroying the Shakti device, that the Astronomer had calmly returned to his old haunts and *no one had noticed.* True, there were only a handful of them left; Kafka, the Master himself, Roman, Kim Toy, Gresham, Imp and Insulin and her–saved because she'd chosen to spend that day at a concert in upstate New York. Perhaps the threat from the Swarm (only recently removed) could offer some explanation.

The tunnel debouched into a small room. Roulette entered, and felt her heel slide from beneath her as she hit the slick dark blood that lay in ever widening pools on the stone floor. It had been an energetic ritual, for bright blood also painted the walls. A garish red freckling here, flowing rivulets there, all washing across the sweating gray plaster, a modern art exhibition drawn in savagery. Dismembered limbs lay stacked like corded wood in a far corner, the head with its staring eyes placed like a melon on the top. She had been a pretty woman, her long dark hair caressing the jagged stump of her neck, crystal earrings flashing in the harsh light of a naked bulb that swung from a cord in the ceiling.

Still Life for a Madman, thought Roulette, and hysteria and revulsion pulled her throat taut.

Kafka, looking positively dadaesque as he doubled as a towel rack, hunched beside the Astronomer. Several fluffy towels with appliqué teddy bears hung over his chitinous, skeletal arms. His carapace was rattling, but whether with cold or fear Roulette couldn't tell.

Finally she forced her eyes to her master, who finished fastidiously wiping his hands on a towel and dropped it onto the floor at his feet. His eyes swam like enormous moons behind the thick lenses of his glasses, but he was vibrant, fairly crackling with energy, and she knew he was ready to begin the day's agenda. A blood feast now to prepare for the banquet to follow.

"Well?"

"Howler is dead."

"Excellent, my lovely dear. Excellent." He turned, and contemptuously pushed aside his wheelchair. Its wheels creaked mournfully as it rolled into a corner. "But tell me all. Every subtle nuance, every agonized grimace . . ."

"It wasn't very subtle," she said flatly, and pushed back her braided hair to reveal the bruise. "And I still can't hear very well out of my right ear."

He laughed, a deep-throated bass rumble that left her shaking with fury.

"I could have died! Doesn't that matter to you?"

"Not tremendously." His eyes were on her, and she writhed, unable to meet his gaze.

"You could have at least warned me," she cried, trying to find a safe place to rest her eyes, but everywhere she looked there was madness.

"I'm not your daddy. I assumed you had enough intelligence to do your own research."

"I'm not a professional killer. I don't *research.*"

Even Kafka emitted a whispering, panting chuckle that sounded like dry, dead hands being rubbed together, and the Astronomer threw back his head and roared, the tendons in his skinny neck standing out like twigs.

"Oh, my precious dear. Is that how you hide from your soul? You little fool. You should embrace the hate, lick it, eat it, revel in it. I am offering you a unique opportunity to find vengeance. To repay loss with pain. And after it's all over I'll give you the freedom you crave. You should thank me."

"I'm becoming a monster," Roulette murmured.

"Is this doubt I'm hearing? Then please quash it. Guilt is a most debilitating emotion. It makes you weak. You see, doubt can lead to betrayal, and you know how I deal with those who betray me. I'm giving you Tachyon, though I really want to kill him myself, so don't come bleating about how close you came to death, and how awful I am for making you kill. And don't even think about backing out. I haven't time to deal with the good doctor myself—I've even had to delegate Turtle to Imp and Insulin—so I would be very upset with you if I had to add Tachyon back into my agenda. The pleasure wouldn't outweigh the aggravation, believe me."

"I don't think you were motivated by generosity. I think you're afraid of him. That's why you're sending me to face him."

The words were gone, and she was a fool for uttering them for he was upon her, fingers closing like a vise about her jaw.

"Calling me a coward, my sweet pussy killer?" His face was set in a devil's grimace.

"No." She forced out the barely audible whisper.

"Good. I wouldn't want to think that you didn't respect me. *Now!* Tell me about Howler."

"No, I don't . . . I can't live it . . . again." She towered over him so she was gazing down on the top of his balding cranium covered only with a few straggling wisps of hair and patches of scabrous skin.

"Then live *this*!" And the rush of memory returned. The hideous misshapen thing that had lain between her legs. The net result of so many hours of painful labor. A monster so grotesque that even the nurses had hated to touch it.

"All right, all right! He was in . . . great pain."

"His face, what of his face? He must have been looking at you."

"He looked sad. Like a bewildered child who couldn't

understand why he was being hurt." Sobs lay like jagged glass in the back of her throat.

"And did you enjoy it?" His free hand closed about her left shoulder, and he forced her to her knees before him. She could feel the blood soaking through the hem of her skirt, sticking on the bare skin of her knees.

His eyes were on her again. There was no hope of lying.

"No." The tears spilled over, running in hot lines over her cheeks. "I didn't really know him. Just one night. But he was kind to me. And now he's dead and I'm afraid."

"Of what?"

"Of what I'm becoming. I'm afraid to go on . . ."

"My dear, you had best be afraid of what will happen if you don't go on. I own you, Roulette, and I will exact a terrible punishment if you fail me."

A shrill scream tore at her throat as she watched his hand go sliding into her chest, and felt the heavy pressure as he cupped her heart in his palm.

"One squeeze, Roulette, and you die." His hand drifted down, massaging her ovaries, sending waves of agony through her belly. "Don't make me kill you, Roulette. It would be such a waste." He removed his hand, and caressed her bruised cheek. "But I don't want to frighten you, my darling. I want to help you. To save and free your soul. You *will* go mad, Roulette, just as you fear, unless you achieve your final vengeance and purge your soul. Without that cleansing, my memory wipe will do you no good. Now go, find Tachyon, kill him, and you will be free."

"Free," she sighed. The Astronomer suddenly released his hold on her chin, and she fell forward, catching herself on her hands. She whimpered a bit as the now-congealing blood oozed between her fingers. *Even free from you*, she thought with an emotion that was neither love nor hate, but partook of both.

"Yes, my little love. Even from me." She squeezed her eyes shut, waiting for the blow or other punishment that had to follow. Moments passed and nothing happened. Cautiously she opened her eyes.

"And when will you . . ."

"Remove your past? When you report back to me, and tell me in painful detail"—his lips quirked at the little pun—"every moment of Tachyon's death."

"Yes . . . all right . . . I will."

Roulette pushed herself to her feet. With a jerk of the head the Astronomer indicated to Kafka to leave. The hideous little cockroach joker scurried to the door, and offered Roulette one of the remaining clean towels. She accepted gratefully.

"Will I find you here?"

"That depends on the time. My schedule's rather full today." He smirked, then stared consideringly at her. "You have served me well. Oh, why not? I've decided to take my more faithful followers with me when I leave." He wrapped a length of flexible tubing about his upper arm, and rubbed at the bulging vein.

"Leave?"

"Yes, I'm leaving this world which betrayed and cheated me."

"But how?"

"On Tachyon's ship."

"But you don't know how to fly a spaceship. Do you?" she added, suddenly doubtful. The range of his powers was awesome, maybe he could.

"This ship will fly, for it's an intelligent creature with a mind, and what has a mind I can control. We are set to rendezvous at three-thirty tomorrow morning. Be there and you can come. Provided of course you've killed Tachyon, and if your little recitation pleases me. Now, what do you say to that? I couldn't be any fairer," he added in a thoughtful tone as he considered his own magnanimity.

The little smile that pursed his mouth died, and his face twisted in a hideous grimace. *"Now go!"* he screamed, and spittle foamed in tiny white specks on his lips, and spattered on her face.

She went, running back down the damp tunnel, towel pressed to her lips. Kafka was still shuffling down the tunnel, and as she passed him, Roulette wondered how much he had overheard, if he constituted one of the "faithful," and what the Astronomer would do to him if he weren't and if he learned of Kafka's eavesdropping. For an instant their eyes met, and Roulette saw mirrored in the joker's the same fear and confusion and hopelessness and hate that she knew lay reflected in hers.

She touched him gently on the carapace. "Thank you for the towel, Kafka."

"You're welcome," he said with an odd formality that made his bizarre condition all the more ludicrous and heartbreaking. "Roulette," he added as she walked away. "Be careful. I would like to think that one of us came out of this with some semblance of normalcy and humanity intact."

"Well, it won't be me, but thanks for the concern."

CHAPTER 4

9:00 a.m.

Jennifer picked up the phone on her desk and dialed a number she'd used only half a dozen times in the past year, but had committed to memory. It rang three times before it was picked up and a rich, cultured voice with a Brooklyn accent still lurking in it said, "The Happy Hocker."

"Hello, Gruber."

The voice took on a new tone, deepening and becoming unctuous with unwanted solicitousness. "My dear Wraith." He called her by the nom de guerre Jennifer had adopted. "It's been a while. How have you been?"

"Fine." Jennifer kept her answers to a minimum. She didn't like Leon Gruber, though he continually let her know his all-too-evident feelings toward her. He was a pudgy, pasty-faced cokehead with a master's in fine arts from Columbia. He worked out of the pawnshop he'd inherited from his father—under, from what Jennifer had heard, rather suspicious circumstances. He was her fence. He never stopped hitting on her, despite the cold politeness with which she carried out all their transactions.

"Do you have something for me?" he asked.

He made the question sound salacious. Jennifer could almost see him licking his pouty lips.

"Postage stamps," she replied briefly.

"How much?" There was something of a sigh in his voice as he resigned himself to talking business.

"Nearly two million catalog."

There was a long silence, and when Gruber finally spoke his voice had changed again. There was something behind his words that Jennifer had never heard before, something that made him sound even more cold and calculating than usual.

"You do astonish me, my dear. Tell me, are these from a dealer's stock or a private party's collection?"

"None of your business."

"Well, we do like to keep our little secrets, don't we?"

"My secrets are my own," Jennifer said firmly, more than a little irritated. "If you're not interested in the stamps I can always find someone who is."

"Oh, I am interested. I am. I'm interested in everything about you, my dear Wraith." Jennifer grimaced at his words. She could almost imagine the scenes flickering through his coked-up brain. "You are a very, um, intriguing person. You appeared from out of nowhere and in less than a year became the city's finest thief. I feel very fortunate to be, um, associated with you and I'm very, very interested in the stamps. I have something on for this morning, though. I'm expecting some people. Can you come by elevenish? Perhaps we can do lunch after I take a look at the merchandise."

"Perhaps." There was no sense in antagonizing him before he looked at the stamps. "Eleven. I'll be there."

"I'll be waiting, dear."

His last sentence echoed oilily in Jennifer's ear as she hung up. There was more avid anticipation in it than was usual. She decided that she had to find a new fence. She couldn't take Gruber's leering comments much longer. Maybe he was sliding too deeply into his cocaine habit. He does so much of the stuff, Jennifer thought, one of these days his heart'll explode.

Fortunato checked his watch. He had to bring his arm up along his side and then across his chest to see it because of the crowds. It was a little after nine. When he looked up again the world was like a kaleidoscope. Shards of bright color surrounded him, shifting constantly into new patterns, unpredictable but not quite random.

When Caroline had said it was Wild Card Day it had meant nothing to him. He should have known better. Now he was trapped in the crowds with Brennan, committed. Every couple of minutes he thought again about breaking his rule about public displays. It would be nothing for him to levitate himself out of the crowd and sail back to the peace of his apartment.

Then he thought of the Astronomer, maybe just a few yards away, maybe on the verge of killing again and making himself that much stronger in the process.

Just ahead of them Hester Street met the Bowery, square in the middle of Jokertown. Police barricades blocked off the side streets, though there were so many tourists a car couldn't have gotten through if it wanted to. They mostly seemed to be dressed for a track meet, in shorts and running shoes and hideous T-shirts, except they were overweight and slung with cameras and had billed caps with moronic slogans on them.

"Look, there's one now," one of them said, pointing at Fortunato. The man's hat said EATING OUT IS FUN. Fortunato thought about turning the man's stomach inside out, leaving it hanging out of his mouth by the long tube of his esophagus, spilling his blood and drool and breakfast on the sidewalk.

Easy, he told himself. Just take it easy.

In typical joker fashion the parade had already gone to hell. The official floats were supposed to be lining up down at Canal, but the street was already full of unofficial entries, the most obvious of which was a twenty-foot-high latex phallus, pink and glistening, pointing up at about sixty degrees. It was mounted on a wooden platform, and three masked jokers were trying to push it through the crowds. The penis was forked and there was a sign hanging between the two heads that said FUCK THE NATS. A fourth joker stood on the platform, throwing what looked like used condoms into the crowd. Two knots of people were fighting their way toward the platform, one cops, the other outraged tourists.

"There he is." Brennan had to shout in Fortunato's ear to make himself heard. Fortunato turned and saw Jube sitting on top of his news kiosk, short, fat, his tusks glistening in the morning sunlight.

"Okay," Fortunato said. He used a little of his power to clear a space in front of the kiosk. He cupped his hands and called up to him. "Can you come down for a minute?"

Jube shrugged and started to clamber down. Fortunato reached up and took hold of a black, rubbery ankle to steady him. At the moment of contact Fortunato felt a weird vibration go through him. Jube looked down and their eyes locked. Fortunato read his thoughts involuntarily.

"Yes," Fortunato answered him. "Now I know." Jube was not human.

"I've seen you at the Crystal Palace," Jube said. "But we've never been formally introduced." He held out a hand. "How are you at keeping secrets?"

"I mostly mind my own business," Fortunato said. "Does Tachyon know about you?"

"No. Nobody does but you. I guess I just have to hope you don't come up with a good reason to give me away."

Jube's face went blank as Brennan walked up and said, "Chrysalis told me—"

"I saw the Astronomer." Jube's head, greasy black and covered with tufts of reddish hair, moved up and down. "About five this morning. I was picking up the *Enquirer*. Every Monday, you know." Fortunato cleared his throat impatiently. "He was in the back of a limo, headed down Second Avenue."

"How did you know it was him?" Fortunato asked. Jube hesitated and Fortunato made it an order. "Tell me the truth."

"I . . . went to some of their meetings. The Egyptian Masons. I thought they had . . . something I wanted."

A sudden crash made the alien jerk back in surprise. Fortunato turned around. Just across Hester a plate-glass window had exploded out onto the street. Four Oriental kids in blue satin jackets swarmed out of the store. The last one out smashed the glass of the door with a billy club. "You remember, old man!" the kid shouted. "You don't fuck with the Egrets, man!" They charged into the crowd and disappeared.

Brennan had the leather case open and the two halves of his bow together in a second and a half. Even so he had no chance for a shot. He put the bow away again and turned back to Fortunato. Fortunato hadn't moved.

"You weren't kidding," Jube said. "You really do mind your own business."

"I don't interfere where I don't know what's going on," Fortunato said. He was thinking about 1969, when his power had first appeared. For a few months there he'd been involved with a political underground movement, trying to stop the wholesale slaughter of jokers in Vietnam. Even then, with the issues as clear as they'd been, he'd felt uneasy about it. There had been a woman involved, and when she disappeared that had been the end of it for him. And since then he'd kept to himself. "If I wanted to be a cop, I'd be a cop."

He turned back to Jube. "I think you and me need to sit down and have a long talk sometime. When there's not so much going on. For right now, just keep your eyes open. If you see the Astronomer again, or anybody that you know is working for him, call Tachyon. He can get hold of me. All right?"

The alien nodded.

"And for Christ's sake," Fortunato said, "try to cheer up."

Spector walked slowly up the steps of the subway station, glancing in all directions. The Jack Daniel's hadn't helped. He'd seen the Astronomer kill before; he'd even been in on it several times. The old man could tear him to pieces faster than he could regenerate. He shuddered and stumbled on. Gruber's pawnshop was only a couple of blocks away.

Flatbush Avenue was quiet, almost deserted. A kid was

playing on a stoop, holding a jet in one hand and a blimp in the other. He smashed the plane into the side of the blimp and yelled, "I can't die yet, I haven't seen *The Jolson Story.*"

Spector shook his head. He didn't understand why anyone considered Jetboy a hero. The little shit had tried to stop the virus from being released over New York, but he fucked up, failed. For that he got a statue and the adoration of millions.

"Jetboy was a loser," he yelled at the kid.

The boy stared at him, then picked up his toys and scrambled inside.

Spector reached inside his gray suit and pulled out his death's-head mask. He slipped it on when he was across the street from the Happy Hocker.

Spector crossed the street quickly and tried the door. It was locked. Spector banged loudly on it several times and waited. No sound. He tried again. This time there were heavy hurried footfalls. He heard the lock click and the door opened a crack.

"I'm busy right now. Come back later," Gruber said.

"You've got coke on your lapel," Spector said, pointing at the tailored tweed suit. He put his foot in the door. "It's Spector. I need to buy something."

Gruber opened the door and closed it quickly when Spector was inside. "Buying? That's a bit unusual. Well, what do you need?"

"An automatic pistol and a flak jacket." Spector looked around at the dimly lit clutter. The place smelled of disuse and Gruber's cologne. "How do you ever find anything in here?"

"All the important business is transacted in back." Gruber opened the cage and walked into the back room. He was fat and soft. Spector could have hated him just for that.

He followed the little man, bringing his pain into focus.

Gruber opened a cabinet and pulled out a pistol. "Ingram Mac-11 with shoulder holster. I'd want eight hundred from a normal customer, but you can take it out in trade. You will have something soon for me, I hope."

Spector took the Ingram and looked it over. The gun was well-oiled and had a nice heft. "Sure. No flak jacket?"

"Sorry."

Spector had hoped the jacket might help if the Astronomer tried to tear out his heart. Just his luck; it was an item Gruber normally had around. "What about bullets?"

"Right here," Gruber said, handing him an unopened box. "Why do you need a gun? I mean, being an ace and all it just seems, um, unnecessary."

Spector noticed that Gruber was careful not to meet his eyes. He grabbed the fat man by the ears and pulled him close. Gruber tried to gouge Spector's eyes with one hand and pulled a .22 automatic with the other. Spector took hold of Gruber's gun hand and pointed it at the fence's stomach. There were two shots, both into Gruber's abdomen. Spector knocked the gun away; he knew that Gruber would be a long time dying from the gunshot wounds. Spector pulled Gruber's head around, forcing their eyes close.

"No," said Gruber, shutting his eyes. Spector punched Gruber in the throat, knocking him to the floor. He straddled the fat man and pinned his arms.

"Don't kill me. Please, no."

"You're dead already." Spector grabbed Gruber's eyelids and pulled them up. Gruber screamed, but it was too late. Their eyes locked.

Spector was the only person who had drawn the Black Queen and lived to tell about it. Unfortunately, the memory of his death was always there. He turned it loose on Gruber, projecting his agony into the man's body, convincing him that he was dying. Gruber's pudgy flesh believed. His eyes rolled up into his head and he gasped. Spector felt him turn to dead weight and let go.

He looked at the desktop. Gruber had written one word on a notepad. *Stamps.* He shrugged and turned away.

Spector put on the holster and slid the Ingram into it. If he ran into the Astronomer it might help, then again it might not. He closed and locked the cage door, donned his mask, and left through the back.

Stupid! How much more of an idiot could I have been? Jack thought as he fought his way downtown through the throngs. His anger with himself still burned savagely. He scanned what he could see of Eighth Avenue ahead of him. Where was the girl with the man wearing the purple suit and the dapper fedora?

He hadn't called Cordelia's mother yet. Elouette would just have to wait, impatient or not. Jack had made the one phone call he thought might do some good. If Bagabond and her animals could just sight his niece . . . He'd take care of the rest. His tongue felt rough, sliding across teeth that were slightly more profuse, sharper, and longer than were normal. He tried to damp the anger. Time enough for that later.

Control. Obviously he had some now. At first, upon exiting the Port Authority, he'd searched at random, fighting his way first one direction through the crowds, then another. Then the human level of his mind started to calm the urgent reptile brain. Set up a grid. Don't repeat a line of search. Try downtown. Consider Fortunato a lead. He didn't *know* that the guy he supposed was a pimp was one of Fortunato's freelance talent scouts; in fact, he didn't know if the man even *used* that kind of scavenging talent; but it was worth a try. The man with Cordelia would find it easier to fall in with the flow of the crowds down toward Jokertown. Eighth was less crowded right now than the other avenues. Eventually Jack would have to worry about a good crosstown route. But for now, he went on his hunch.

It paid off.

He came up to the intersection of 38th Street. Suddenly he saw, across the street, a familiar fedora bobbing a bit as though the wearer were looking about himself confusedly. He also saw the back of a head, a quick glimpse of a fall of shining black hair. The fedora moved toward the black hair. The young woman with the black hair moved farther away. She was running.

Fedora pursued.

Jack, staring after them, started off the curb. A hand grabbed his shoulder, roughly tugging him back. A honking yellow cab nearly took off his toes and latent snout.

"Watch it, bub," said a husky joker standing beside him. "Cabbies don't give a shit. Not today. Not never."

By now, the intersection was full of traffic. The last cabs to make it through had done so. Now there were vehicles lined up in either direction. No one seemed worried about automatic $25 tickets for gridlocking.

"Never a cop when you need one," somebody said.

Jack made it across the intersection like a good broken-field runner. The Jets'd be proud, he thought irrelevantly. This season, they could use him. On the other side of 38th, he realized that neither the fedora nor Cordelia was in sight.

Damn it. Sooner or later, he thought, striking downtown

again. He looked around for one of Bagabond's birds, a cat, a squirrel, anything.

Never a pigeon when you need one.

Having chosen her clothing from the collection of tattered and dirty mismatched coats, pants, and shirts she kept at Jack's, Bagabond jammed a Greek fisherman's cap on her stringy hair and left the cats behind as she made her way up to ground level through the tunnels that bypassed Jack's home. Agile from years of moving through the underground, she used the eyes of the rats who lived in the tunnels to show her the path. The floor-level view she gained from their perspective was enough to avoid most obstacles. She had spent days underground without using her own eyes. It was best to remove herself as much as possible from contact with the mass of people who crawled on the surface as her creatures crawled in their tunnels and burrows.

Bagabond grasped the rungs of a ladder to the world above her and climbed. Shifting the manhole cover slightly upward, she looked around and saw only a sleeping derelict in the alley. She climbed out, replaced the cover, and limped toward the crowds at the mouth of the alley. Long ago she had found the most direct route to Rosemary Muldoon's office in the district attorney's complex. Today, though, the streets were crowded with revelers. Many wore grotesque masks; some were in full costume. Bagabond felt anger at these "normal" people. The virus that had given her a means of survival had also removed her from this human world. Sometimes she regretted it, most of the time she did not. It took no effort to curse the crowd and clear a path to the Justice Center.

Somebody whistled, appreciative by the sound of it. She didn't glance around. It wouldn't be at her.

Before the security guard noticed her, Bagabond joined a crowd of people waiting for the elevator. Keeping the crowd of three-piece suits between her and the guard, she walked with lowered head and sidelong glances to the stairs. It took several minutes to walk up to the eighth floor but she hated the elevator.

Instead of the usual receptionist, who knew that she was an old client of Rosemary's from her days with Social Services, the front desk was manned by a handsome, black-haired man in a brown suit. He was having trouble with the phone as she walked up.

"Damn! Lost another one. Whoever created hold buttons should be shot. Don't you agree?" He spoke without looking up from the phone console whose buttons he was punching. "Even though I know that's no attitude for a lawyer." He finally looked up and his face registered surprise for just a moment. "Hello. What can I do for you?" He smiled at the bag lady. "Do you want this floor? This is the DA's office. What are you looking for?"

"Rosemary." Bagabond kept her head down and her voice weak and rough.

"Rosemary? I'm new here, but the only Rosemary here—I think—is Rosemary Muldoon. She's an assistant district attorney." He turned to look dubiously down at the phone console. "Well, I could try to buzz her, but . . ."

"Rosemary." The derelict's voice was stronger and angry. When he looked up again, he met, for a mere second, a pair of sharp and clear black eyes.

"I'll do my best." The phone rang. "Paul Goldberg. District attorney's office. May I help you?"

Bagabond started toward a door behind Goldberg, but it opened as she reached for the knob.

The woman behind the door was petite, about three inches shorter than Bagabond. The bag lady knew that because they had once been obliged to exchange clothes. Rosemary's eyes varied from dark brown to hazel, depending on her mood. Today they were dark and intense.

"Hello there. Good to see you. Go right in. I'll be back in a moment." Rosemary Muldoon held the door for the bag lady. Before she entered the office, Bagabond looked back at the receptionist's desk. Rosemary nodded. "Paul, call that temporary service again. Tell them if someone doesn't show up in fifteen minutes, we're calling another service. This is ridiculous."

"Yes, Ms. Muldoon. I hope I didn't offend your client." He smiled apologetically at the bag lady, who shook her head once, sharply.

"My *friend*, Paul," Rosemary said. "Hold my calls, will you, please?"

The man behind the desk sighed and nodded. "Of course, Ms. Muldoon. I look forward to seeing you again, Miss," he said to Bagabond. He was already reaching for a ringing phone as Bagabond stared at him again, then turned and limped into Rosemary's office.

"Donnis is on vacation and things are a mess." Rosemary shut the door and walked over to the walnut desk. "Here we are, understaffed, and our newest addition has to answer phones instead of working on the caseload. He's decorative, though." Rosemary perched on the side of her desk. "They offered me new carpet to replace this ghastly green shag. I took another staff attorney instead."

"Good choice." Bagabond sat down on the edge of an

old straight chair. She took off her hat and brushed the hair out of her face.

"How's Jack?" Rosemary reached out and took the cap from Bagabond. Putting it on, she looked inquiringly at Bagabond, who shook her head.

"Doesn't go with the tweed." Bagabond sat back carefully, as if worried the chair would collapse. "Okay, I guess. We're not talking all that much right now. I just got a call from him before I came over. He's out hunting a niece who ran away to New York City."

Rosemary raised an eyebrow.

"Her name's Cordelia Chaisson. Sixteen. Country girl from Louisiana. Jack says she's real pretty—tall, slender, black hair, dark brown eyes. That's all he told me. He sounded pretty upset."

"I'll put the word out in the station houses," said Rosemary. "That much I can do. Too many kids run away to the city." She took a fountain pen out of the desk set by her hip.

Bagabond nodded her appreciation. "How's life off the street?"

"Who says I'm off the street? With this job, I never leave." Rosemary sighed and continued to play with the fountain pen. It was obvious she had other things on her mind. "Things are getting worse with the Family. The Butcher—remember Don Frederico?—is killing anyone who threatens his authority. It's no way to run the Gambione Family. We're no longer completely in control in Jokertown. Somebody's setting the jokers against us, the Family. They're just being used, of course."

"The jokers are always getting used. Either they're the great downtrodden minority of this century, or else they're a plague to be eradicated." Bagabond fixed her with wide black eyes.

Rosemary continued, "They get something when they pay protection to the Gambiones. That's one tradition that even the Butcher doesn't dare abandon." She gestured with the pen. "I keep thinking that if my father had just had a son, to take over the Gambiones, this wouldn't be happening. Maybe that S.O.B. Butcher will have a nice accident. Slip in the bathtub or something."

"He always was bad news." Bagabond smiled humorlessly up at Rosemary. "Even in our brief acquaintance, I can't say that he made a good impression. If I hear anything, I'll let you know. I usually avoid Jokertown, but the rats like it down there. Lots of food."

"I don't want details, please." Rosemary shivered. "You want to know what else is making my life interesting? First thing I hear this morning is that there're some valuable notebooks on the street. I don't even know whose they are, but the Egrets want them. If the Egrets want them, so do I. You really do hear the strangest things, so if you find out anything about this, I would appreciate it." Rosemary wouldn't meet Bagabond's dark gaze. "I feel as if I'm using you, Suzanne, but you know things no one else does. Thanks."

"I have a lot of eyes and ears." Bagabond looked out the window behind Rosemary's shoulder. "You are a friend. I only have one other—human. I want to help."

"I wish Jack wasn't such an idiot," Rosemary said. "What is *wrong* with that boy?" She shook her head in sympathy. "Have you thought of maybe looking elsewhere?"

"Maybe at the mission?" Bagabond combed the hair back across her face with her fingers and jammed the cap down on her head. She stood up and spread the ratty paisley skirt she wore over a pair of chinos. "Or perhaps the singles bars. I could start a new fashion trend."

"I'm sorry." Rosemary slid off the desk and touched Bagabond's shoulder. Bagabond swung away from her hand.

"I've been alone for years. I'll survive. Besides, the cats would be happier." Bagabond showed her teeth, white and sharp. "I'll be in touch."

Rosemary opened the door and walked with her to the front desk.

"I've got court in twenty minutes. Just call me if you need anything, dear." The stooped and limping bag lady nodded her lowered head and walked away. As she passed the receptionist's area, Goldberg looked up.

"Hope to see you again soon. Have a nice day."

As he said the last words, the bag lady turned her head to stare at him.

"Yeah, I don't believe I said that either." He grinned and shrugged in apology, and the phone rang again. " 'Bye."

Making her way slowly down the stairs, Bagabond wondered if Jack had found Cordelia yet. Missing girls, missing notebooks. Everyone was looking for something. She wasn't. It was the advantage of having nothing to lose.

The jokers started all looking alike.

So did the normals dressed and made up as jokers.

Jack blinked confusedly. Trying to survey *all* the faces he was encountering was akin to scanning more than about six rows of book spines in the Strand. After a while, the colors, the sizes, the titles, all began to look the same. He saw black hair—never the *right* black hair. He saw fedoras, panamas, snap-brims, nothing was exactly right.

At the corner of West 10th, he nearly collided with a kid heading east. "Watch it, faggot," the young man said.

Jack stared at him in surprise.

"You can't fool me," said the kid. "Don't even try."

Jack started to step around him, since it was obvious the kid wasn't going to move. Punk, he thought. Real street punk—not costume punk with mohawk and makeup.

Shorter than Jack, the kid was as skinny as a ferret. Face hollowed, eyes the color of rainwater, there was a tight, springloaded look about him. "Just watch it," he said again.

As Jack moved past, he was jostled by a passerby. Recovering his balance, he brushed the kid's elbow with his hand. The young man recoiled, his hands coming up in what looked to Jack like a martial arts stance.

"Don't touch me, fairy," said the kid.

They stared at each other for several seconds. Then Jack nodded, stepped back, and turned to go. He didn't look back, but had the feeling that the kid was staring after him with those clear, mean, psychopathically intense eyes.

The Crystal Palace smelled like any other bar in the morning—like stale smoke and spilled beer and disinfectant. Fortunato found Chrysalis in a dark corner of the club, where her transparent skin made her nearly invisible. He and Brennan sat down across from her.

"You got the message, then," she said in her phony English-public-school accent.

"I got it," Fortunato said. "But the trail's cold. The Astronomer could be anywhere by now. I was hoping you might have something else for me."

"Perhaps. You know a yo-yo calls himself 'Demise'?"

"Yes," Fortunato said. His fingernails dug uselessly at the urethane finish on the table.

"He was in about an hour ago. Sascha got a reading off him, loud and clear. 'He's going to fucking kill me. That twisted old fuck.' "

"Meaning the Astronomer."

"Right you are. This Demise seemed completely round the bend. Had quite a lot on his mind, Sascha said."

"You mean there's more," Fortunato said.

"Yes, but the next bit's going to cost you."

"Cash or favors?"

"Blunt this morning, aren't we? Well, I'm inclined to say favors. And in honor of the holiday, I'll even extend you a line of credit."

"You know I'm good for it," Fortunato said. "Sooner or later."

"I don't like charging for bad news, in any event. The other line Sascha heard was, 'Maybe he'll be too busy with the others.' "

"Christ," Fortunato said.

Brennan looked at him. "You think he's going on some kind of killing spree."

"The only thing that surprises me is that it took him this long. He must have been waiting for Wild Card Day out of some fucked-up sense of drama or something. Was there anything else?"

"Not about the Astronomer. But there is another matter. This is perhaps more in your bailiwick, Yeoman. I got a call this morning advising me to keep my eyes open for a certain stolen book. Three books, actually. Two of them are stock-books with rare postal stamps in them. It was the third the caller seemed most interested in. It's the size of a regular schoolboy's notebook, blue in color, with a bamboo pattern on it."

"So who was the caller?" Brennan asked.

"Unimportant. What interests me is the group he seems to belong to. It took me a bit of time and a bit of influence, but I came up with a name."

"What's your price?" Brennan said.

"Information for information. I think if we should put our heads together on this, we'd both benefit. But you mustn't hold out on me. I'll know it if you do."

"Agreed."

"Does the name 'Shadow Fist Society' mean anything to you?"

Brennan shook his head. "Not much. I've heard the name in Chinatown. That's all."

"All right," Chrysalis said. "Suppose I mentioned a name high in the organization. He's known as 'Loophole.' Mean anything to either of you?"

Fortunato shook his head. Brennan was looking at the table. "Yeah," Brennan said. "I've heard of him. His real name's something-or-other Latham. As in Latham, Strauss, the law firm. The story is that nobody knows if the wild card virus destroyed all his human feelings, or if he's just a very, very good lawyer."

Chrysalis nodded. "A fair trade. Shall we go another round?"

"You first," Brennan said.

"By sheerest coincidence I got another call this morning. From a man named Gruber. He's a broker–pawn, rather than stock, I'm afraid. He was concerned about some stock-books full of stamps an ace tried to sell him this morning. Called, apparently, Wraith. Works as a thief. She's just a girl, and she's quite a bit over her head in this. Anyone who found those books would be in a position of enormous power."

"Or end up dead," Brennan said.

"Pray go on," Chrysalis said. "I'm all ears."

"You've probably guessed the rest," Brennan said. "Maybe you don't want to mention the name. It's a dangerous name. Therefore very valuable."

"Say it," Chrysalis said.

"Kien," Brennan said. "I'm convinced Loophole is working for Kien. Something must have happened, something big. If Loophole is that desperate for the book it must be something of Kien's, something really important. Something damaging. And if the Shadow Fist Society *is* Kien, they could be everywhere." He stood up. "This is where we part ways, my friend."

Fortunato took his hand. "Thanks. If I find out anything about those books I'll let you know."

"Good luck," Brennan said. By the time he hit the front door he was running.

Chrysalis leaned across the table. "This 'Demise,' is he valuable to you, then?"

"If he can take me to the Astronomer, he is."

"Why can't you use your powers to find this Astronomer for yourself?"

"They're no good against him. He's got me jammed, like they used to jam radar with tinfoil. I couldn't even see him if he was standing right over there." He pointed and Chrysalis, her eyes suddenly afraid, turned slowly to follow his finger.

"No," she said. "No one there."

Fortunato was no longer looking at her. He was building up the image of a tall, grotesquely thin man with brown hair and a ravaged face. If Demise was close enough, within a few blocks, Fortunato could find him just by concentrating.

He opened his eyes.

"Canal Street," he said. "The subway."

CHAPTER 5

10:00 a.m.

By the time he got into the crooked, winding streets of the West Village, Jack had started to wonder whether he should cross over toward the East Side and Jokertown or continue down toward what was clearly the center of action in the city today, Jetboy's Tomb.

At least he was in more familiar territory now. Spotting a familiar facade on Greenwich, he fumbled in his breast pocket and found the creased color snapshot Elouette had sent him the previous Christmas. Obviously Cordelia had blossomed, but the likeness would suffice.

The bar was called the Young Man's Fancy. It was a sort of social were-creature. From its opening first thing in the morning, it was a solid blue-collar, working-class joint. Then, about six in the evening, it underwent a shift switch and utter sea change. All night, Young Man's Fancy was a gay bar. Whatever its guise, the Fancy was one of the oldest businesses in the Village.

Jack took the three steps in one and swung open the door. It was dark inside, and his eyes took their time adjusting. He crossed the width of the rectangular room, hearing peanut shells crunch under his size-elevens.

The bartender looked up from polishing a tray of Bud glasses. "Help you?"

"Maybe you were looking out the window this morning," said Jack. He held up the photograph. "You see her?"

"You a cop?"

Jack shook his head.

"Didn't think so." The bartender scrutinized the picture. "Mighty pretty girl. Your woman?"

Jack shook his head again. "Niece."

"Right," said the bartender. He scrutinized Jack more closely. "Ain't I seen you in here about six?"

"Probably," said Jack. "I come here. The girl in the picture—have you seen her this morning?"

The bartender squinted thoughtfully. "Nope." He looked appraisingly at Jack. "Reckon she really is your niece, huh? Lost, strayed, or stolen?"

"Stolen." Jack scribbled a number on a Hamms napkin. Bagabond had given him Rosemary's direct office line. "Do me a favor, okay? You see her, whether she's alone or with someone else, leave a message here." He headed for the door. "Appreciate it," he said back over his shoulder.

"Gotcha," said the bartender. "Day or night, anything for a customer."

She had the cabbie drop her at Freakers. The club was jumping even at 10:20 in the morning, and the doorman who handed her out of the cab looked as if he were already two or three sheets to the wind. His soft white fur was rumpled, and his red eyes were both bleary and bright at the same time. He indicated the door to the club, but Roulette merely shook her head, and headed off toward the Crystal Palace.

And nearly jumped out of her skin when the double doors crashed open, and a long line of conga-dancing jokers came undulating into the street from between the neon thighs of the six-breasted stripper that adorned and formed the club's door. Leading the line was a beautiful-faced woman who was having no trouble with the sinuous curves of the dance, since from the neck down she had the body of a iridescent snake. Her tail, which ended in an incongruous tuft of feathers, was uplifted, and the joker immediately behind her in the line had a firm grip on the tip.

He wasn't wearing a mask, but he was one of the few. The rest of the swaying, yelling, shouting crowd wore a variety of dominos from elaborate feathered, jeweled, and sequined creations to hideous visages that were worse than the deformities they hid—perhaps.

At the tail end of the line clung a few nats looking both excited and self-conscious, and a touch belligerent, as if daring the jokers who inhabited the Bowery—and provided a wealth of skin-crawling, spine-tingling entertainment for the tourists—to object.

For a moment Roulette hated the thrill seekers with their bland, normal faces and smug security. *I hope it is catching,* came the vicious thought. *God damn you all.* But the thought was really meant for Josiah. Josiah, who had sworn to love and care for her, and instead had abandoned her when she most needed him. Apparently white liberal guilt wasn't enough to deal with a woman who had the wild card virus. Might be catching. And she could imagine her former mother-in-law seated in prissy splendor at her Newport mansion sipping tea and discussing how *no matter how much you worked with one of those "black" girls it so often went to naught. Many times they were simply too badly warped and scarred both mentally and physically by the white man's oppression to enter white society. Wasn't it a shame. Sigh.*

But she probably burnt the sheets and had every piece of furniture in the house re-covered after Josiah divorced me. Sanctimonious, hypocritical bitch!

Roulette realized that she had been walking blindly, shouldering past the throngs that filled the streets of Jokertown. The sound of hammers and staple guns echoed in the already sultry morning air, shouts of greeting and insult from the jokers busy setting up booths for the day-long party, the smell of cooking (good and bad) wafting over the exhaust-laden air. Overhead a small private plane droned by pulling a long banner that read JOKERS INTO ACES. RESULTS GUARANTEED. CALL 555-9448.

On another corner the Church of Jesus Christ Joker had a booth already up and running, handing out literature to anyone who could be stopped. Their results were guaranteed too, but in the afterlife. Beset on all sides, thought Roulette, charlatans for the here and the hereafter. Hopeless hope. Well, my people can tell you all about that, and it never gets any easier until there's some new and even more unpopular minority to take your place. And I can't conceive of a more unpopular and hideous minority than the jokers ever arising, you poor bastards.

There was a barricade across Henry Street. It wasn't legal, but Chrysalis was a major figure in Jokertown, and the area precinct had reason to be grateful to the owner of the Crystal Palace. More than one tough case had been solved because of her intervention, so the chief wasn't about to raise a stink over a few traffic snarls once a year. Chrysalis also had control of street decorations, so Henry Street projected an image of tasteful pride rather than the garish shock value that held sway on other streets. Roulette slipped past the barricade, and started down the street. To her right, and for about half the length of the block, there was an empty lot filled with piles of rubble, a reminder of the Jokertown riot back in '76. Waist-high weeds and a few hardy saplings thrust up through the brick and plaster mounds. Several of the piles had dark openings like yawning little mouths, and she wondered if the place had become a haven for animals. She couldn't picture the fastidious Chrysalis allowing a rat warren to grow up next door to her bar. As she watched, there was a gleam from deep in the hole that soon resolved itself into a pair of bright eyes surrounded by hair. But it wasn't the shy muzzle of an animal that peered from the burrow. It was human—sort of.

With a gasp Roulette ducked her head and hurried on, passing Arachne, whose eight slender legs caught at the line of silk extruding from her bulbous body and wove it swiftly into one of her famous spider-silk shawls. Her daughter was busy in their booth hanging out an array of delicately dyed scarves and shawls. Most nats would never have purchased one of the trembling, almost transparent scraps of fabric if they'd seen it being created, but Arachne made a good living supplying the scarves to Saks and Neiman-Marcus. Roulette owned one, a delicate peach-colored creation that looked like she had thrown a sunset over her dark shoulders. If she had known Arachne was going to be on Henry Street she would have worn it to show the woman that she at least did not mind the source, and that she honored the artistry.

There was a low rumbling that gained in speed and intensity, and ended with a crashing *boom* as Elmo, the Palace's resident bouncer, rolled another metal keg of beer out the front door and into the street where it joined its brethren like a rotund cue slamming into a setup of stumpy balls. The bouncer, who looked rather like a beer keg himself, flexed his shoulders in satisfaction, and headed back for another one.

Kids darted up and down the pavement chasing a battered soccer ball while at the far end of the block an impromptu baseball game had begun. Ghetto blasters throbbed out a cacophony of conflicting music: soul, rock, country, classical. Children cried and mothers called, but this madness had a sense of serenity and security; a feeling of family. Nowhere did she sense that desperate and nerve-stretching drive to *have fun* that had gripped the dancing throng outside Freakers. These people, as hideous as many of them were, were at peace with themselves.

Roulette tore her eyes from the gang of playing urchins, and forced herself to scan the crowd for a distinctive, tiny, redheaded figure. Thirty minutes ago she had stopped at the Jokertown clinic only to be told by Tachyon's very cool, very elegant, very beautiful, and very disapproving chief of surgery that the *good* doctor was not present, but could no doubt be found making house calls at any one of a number of bars. Roulette had tried Ernie's and Wally's and the Funhouse with no luck, and now the Crystal Palace . . .

And she found him.

Seated at a small table among many other small tables that had been squeezed onto the sidewalk out front of the Palace. Brandy snifter held lightly between long, slender fingers, glass tilting softly so the amber liquid flowed gracefully about the sides. Another glass figure standing at his left shoulder, but this one filled with the bone and viscera that form a human being, long nails painted an iridescent pink, a dusting of silver-blue glitter across one unseen cheek. Chrysalis herself.

Roulette had reached the moment. She hadn't thought beyond simply finding the Takisian, but now having found him what did she do? Faint? Sprain an ankle? She knew—as did most of the world—of the alien's fascination with beautiful women, but there were lots of beautiful women in New York, and what if he'd already found a companion for the day? And if he hadn't, how could she insure that he picked her? Beauty she had, but not the skills that usually accompanied it. She had never mastered the art of flirting. And in that moment she felt a surge of relief. She would walk past; if he noticed . . . well, so be it. He was meant to meet his fate. If not . . . She tried not to think of the wizened little man lurking in his damp lair.

She focused her eyes on the barricade, and began to count her steps, noting how the crepe-rubber soles of her shoes seemed to spring away from the concrete, and the way her slacks whispered against her ankles, and the brush of her braided hair against—

"I think you're a fool." Chrysalis bit off the words in her clipped British way. "Every year you start out here, having your first brandy of the day, remain sober long enough to get through your speech, begin soaking up beer at the game, maintain your liquid diet right through Hiram's dinner, and then to put a perfect cap on the day, you end up back here, blind drunk, guilty, and miserable. Why don't you take my advice and—"

"And every year you give me the same advice," Tachyon said in lilting counterpoint.

"Go to Miami," they concluded in chorus.

Tachyon's smile faded. "How could I leave? This dreadful news about Howler, and not a clue as to his murderer."

"And you're not a cop. Leave it to the professionals." A stubborn shake of his head. "Tachy, it's not necessary for you to take part in this annual celebration of the grotesque. Jokertown knows you care. We won't hate you for being absent for one out of three hundred and sixty-five days."

"But not this day. I have to be here." His throat worked at gulping down another large swallow of the brandy. "It's my penance." His voice husky, perhaps, from the effects of the brandy.

"You're a fool," Chrysalis said again softly, and gave his shoulder a hard squeeze with one transparent hand.

Roulette, staring in fascination at the white finger bones against the deep ruby material of Tachyon's coat, had a dislocating image of Death capering beside the man. Slowly she brought her hand up before her face, and studied it. The way the tendons shifted beneath the *café au lait* skin, the half-moons of pale white beneath the buffed nails, the tiny scar on the index finger where she had cut herself during a cooking lesson when she was only six. Then looked back to Chrysalis now disappearing through the door of the Palace, and thought, I should look like her, I'm Death.

Cool touch against the bruised skin of her face. An anchor. She gasped, and her eyes flew open and she looked down into the concerned pale lilac eyes of the Takisian.

"Madam, are you all right? You looked like you were about to faint."

"Yes . . . no . . . I'm fine," she babbled.

The strength of the arm about her waist was at odds with his delicate features. "Here, sit down."

The metal edge of the chair caught at the back of her knees, and she sprawled, and realized how close she had been to fainting. The brandy snifter was pressed into her hands.

"No."

"It's an accepted if somewhat old-fashioned remedy for faintness."

Her wits were returning, and she straightened in the chair. "And I'm old-fashioned enough to consider it far too early in the day for brandy."

She watched in astonishment as a wave of red washed across his thin face, and the red lashes lowered to hide the chagrin in those purple eyes. Tachyon hurriedly removed the glass, and set it well away from both of them as if abjuring the alcohol.

"You're right. Chrysalis is right. It's far too early in the day for me to be imbibing. What would you like?"

"Some fruit juice. I . . . I just realized I haven't had anything but coffee today."

"Well, that clearly won't do, and can be easily rectified. A moment please." He bounded from his chair and hurried into the Palace.

And Roulette rested her head on a hand, and tried to readjust her thinking. Or perhaps truly thought for the first time. The man who had ruined her life had been a hazy outline. For one thing she hadn't expected him to be quite so tiny, or to have a smile of such sweetness, or a quaint courtesy that seemed more appropriate to an eighteenth-century drawing room.

And Hitler loved children and small animals, she reminded herself. Her eyes settled on one of the ballplayers, a small boy whose bloated body rested on narrow webbed feet, and whose flipper arms flapped in excitement as the ball was pitched. *The crime is too monstrous, and his death will ease not only my suffering.*

He was back, depositing a glass of orange juice before her. He watched while she sipped, tipped back in the chair, booted feet propped on the table. He seemed comfortable with the silence which was not a thing she was accustomed to in men. Most seemed to need a constant babble from the women around them as if in reassurance of their importance.

"Better?"

"Much."

The front legs of the chair crashed down. "Since introductions would now seem in order . . . I'm Dr. Tachyon."

"Roulette Brown-Roxbury."

"Roulette," he repeated, giving it its French pronunciation. "Unusual name."

She twirled the glass, leaving a circle of condensation on the table. "There's a story behind it." She glanced over, and found his eyes resting with unsettling interest on her face. "My mother was allergic to most birth control devices, so my parents settled for the rhythm method. Dad said it was like playing Russian roulette, and when the inevitable happened they decided to call me Roulette."

"Charming. Names should say something, about the person, or about their background. They're like stories that get added to with each successive generation. But I've said something to offend you."

Roulette forced her features back into an expression of calm. "No, not at all."

She returned to her contemplation of the condensation ring, and silence settled softly over them, making the cries of the children and the pounding of hammers all the louder.

"Doctor . . ."

"Madam . . ."

They both began together, and fell back into their chairs

embarrassed. "Please." She gestured toward him. "Go ahead."

"I was wondering what brought you into Jokertown on this day. You lack the guilty curiosity or the morbid hunger that motivates most normals."

"I've come to journey a bit farther in despair," she heard herself say, and that darker part of her soul cursed her for a fool. What man would want to spend the day with a morbid and lachrymose woman?

His hand closed over hers, tightening about the fingers, and pain seemed to flow between them. "Then, let us journey together. If you would like," he added quickly as if fearful to offend. "This day is . . . difficult . . . for me. It would be easier in your company."

"I have no comfort to give."

"I ask for none. Only for your company." His fingers brushed lightly across her bruised cheek. "And perhaps, if you wish, I might comfort you."

"Perhaps." And in her secret place Death reveled . . . just a little.

People crushed into him from all directions. The sidewalks were jammed with costumed jokers and rubbernecking nats. He moved the same speed and direction as the crowd, letting it carry him along. There was no point in calling attention to himself. The Astronomer could be anywhere, and usually was.

Spector didn't need to be at Times Square for over an hour. He didn't want to show up early; it might make him appear overeager. The Jokertown parade was the safest place he could think of to kill time.

In the street a band started playing "Jokertown Strutters Ball." Spector was beginning to feel claustrophobic. He picked his way toward the edge of the crowd. A three-eyed mime wearing white tights blocked his path and signaled him to stop. Spector tensed. The mime frowned in an exaggerated manner, then stepped aside and motioned him past. Spector gave him a hard elbow in the stomach. He smiled as the joker doubled over. He hated mimes.

Spector was thankful for his constant pain. It distracted him enough that he couldn't focus on the smell of hundreds of sweating jokers. By the end of the day plenty of nats would be green from the dead-fish scent.

Spector looked at his digital watch. He'd taken it from a young broker he'd killed in the financial district the week before. It was only a little past ten-thirty. The day, like the parade, was crawling slowly by. He hadn't been this afraid since the first time he'd met the Astronomer. The old man had told him they'd rule the world. That he'd be a top dog in the new order. It was all bullshit. The local aces had stepped in and ruined everything. At least the Astronomer was going to get them, too. I hope he makes it last when he's doing Tachyon, Spector thought.

He reached the edge of the crowd and ducked into an alley. Garbage was littered about in large piles. Three steps in he heard the howl. Spector stopped and looked up. The Astronomer, smiling, was floating down toward him.

"I told you what would happen, Demise. You had your chance." The Astronomer howled again, a throaty, inhuman bellow.

Spector turned and ran back into the crowd, pushing past people, knocking them down. He ignored their threats and curses and fought his way into the street. He dodged through the startled band members, then ran past a crepe float of the Turtle and into the mass of people on the other side. He was afraid to look back.

A policeman grabbed him by the arm. Spector kneed him in the crotch and pulled away. People all around him were screaming. He could barely breathe.

"I'm right behind you." The Astronomer's voice was close.

Spector turned. The Astronomer was hovering by the policeman, who had raised his pistol to fire. Blue light leapt from the Astronomer's right hand, connecting with the weapon. The gun exploded, showering the policeman and spectators with shrapnel. More screams.

Spector tripped over a trash basket and fell hard to the concrete sidewalk, skinning his hands. He stood slowly, his knees wobbling. He felt hands grip his shoulders, fingers digging powerfully into his flesh. He couldn't pull away.

"No." Spector's voice sounded just like Gruber's had earlier.

The Astronomer let go with one hand and grabbed the top of his head. "Look at me when I speak to you, Demise."

Spector felt his head being spun around. There was a stab of unbearable pain, a snap, and his mouth filled with blood. The Astronomer grinned at him. "It's Judgment Day."

Noise ran through the crowd behind them. The Astronomer turned away, distracted by something, dropping Spector like a sack of garbage.

His body was paralyzed; he couldn't break the fall. Spector landed face first on the sidewalk, smashing his mouth and nose. He watched the pool of blood widen around his open mouth. It was time to die, again. At least he wouldn't have to see or feel what was going to happen to him.

♥♦♠♣

Side by side and bumper to bumper, the floats took up a block and a half of Center Street south of Canal. Fortunato could see Des, the elephant-faced joker, done up in chicken wire and flowers. There was Dr. Tod's blimp and Jetboy's plane behind it, complete with floral speed lines. A clear plastic balloon of Chrysalis floated overhead.

This was deep Jokertown and there weren't so many tourists here. The tourists that came this far down didn't bring their kids. Drivers in coveralls stood by the floats, smoking and talking to each other. The worst of the crowd seemed to all be moving the same way as Fortunato, toward something that was happening up ahead.

Half a block away he could see the lines of power in the air. Like heat waves, shimmering, distorting everything around them. It was a signature that wasn't really a signature, a set of psychic eraser marks. He'd seen them for the first time seventeen years ago, in a dead boy's room not far from here, where women had been brutally cut to pieces as part of a conspiracy that ended with the great, devouring monstrosity of TIAMAT orbiting the sun.

He was lightheaded and his pulse was going crazy. He realized that he was scared, really, honest-to-Christ terrified, for the first time in seventeen years.

He sent a wedge of power out in front of him and ran toward the place where the lines came together. People spun away on both sides of him, shouting at him but unable to touch him.

Demise screamed. Even over the noise of the crowd Fortunato could hear the crunch of mangled bone and cartilage and the thud of a body hitting the sidewalk.

As he broke through the wall of people, they were already turning, trying to get away. Somebody dragged away a wounded cop, his right hand burned black, his face pocked with blood. There was a ten-foot circle of sidewalk, empty except for Demise.

Demise lay on his back, the lapels of his gray suit and the open collar of his scruffy shirt exposed. His head was turned completely around, his face flat against the pavement. Blood ran out of his mouth and nose.

A man in the crowd was screaming. "There! He's right over there! He's getting away! Stop him, for God's sake!"

He was pointing at nothing at all. All Fortunato could see was a blur of faces, like he was trying to look too far to one side, even though he was staring straight ahead.

Jamming me, he thought. He focused his power and slowed time, until the man's voice and the moans of shock and disgust around him dropped to a subsonic rumble. A tornado of psychic energy hung in the frozen chaos around him, Demise's power, Fortunato's own, the viral energy of the jokers. It was hopeless.

He let go and time came up to speed. There was nothing he could do. Demise was dead. It was not much of a loss.

Most of what he knew about Demise was second- or third-hand, picked up from cops and bystanders after the riot at the Cloisters. He was a loser, a middle-class failure who'd caught the wild card and died of it in Tachyon's clinic. Tachyon brought him back and Demise never forgave him for it.

He'd come back a projecting telepath, so they said, and what he could project was the memory of his own death, strongly enough to kill with it. For a while he'd sat at the Astronomer's right hand, until Fortunato and the others had destroyed their base at the Cloisters and Fortunato had blasted their Shakti device into atoms.

He'd have done the same for Demise and the Astronomer if he'd been able. But now Demise seemed inconsequential. From a sense of wounded aesthetics Fortunato got on one knee and twisted Demise's head the right way around. He was about to walk away when Demise said, "Thanks. I needed that."

Fortunato turned back, his skin crawling. Demise squatted on his heels, rubbing the swollen purple lumps in his neck where blood vessels had burst. Already the bruises were turning yellow, healing as Fortunato watched.

Demise smiled. His mouth was a little too long and thin, and it came up too high on one side. The smile was full of terror and the man's hands shook so hard he held them up and laughed at them. "Didn't know about that little trick, did you? I got my little black message I can send and I got this other thing, too. Even the Astronomer didn't know about it. I can heal, brother." He hacked up a gob of blood and it was a solid brown crust by the time it hit the sidewalk.

"Then he thinks you're dead," Fortunato said.

"Christ, I hope so. Not that he wouldn't have gone ahead and ripped my heart out, just to be sure, if you hadn't shown up. Son of a bitch even told me he was going to do it. If I had stayed in Brooklyn maybe I could have kept out of his way." He coughed up another lump. "If the dog hadn't stopped to piss he would've caught the rabbit."

"Why does he want you dead?"

"Thinks I sold him out. All it was, after that shit at the Cloisters, I started thinking another line of work might be healthier." Demise stared at him. There was a spark back there. Fortunato could see it. If not genius, at least some craft and cunning. Most people wouldn't see it because people didn't spend much time looking into Demise's eyes. One way or another.

Behind the spark was something else. Fortunato had seen it before, seventeen years ago, when he brought a dead boy back to life. It was the black despair of having looked at death too closely.

"In fact," Demise said, "I'm surprised he didn't take you out while he was here. Unless he's saving you for dessert."

"Dessert?"

"This is it, man. Judgment Day, he calls it. I'm gonna die, you're gonna die, every one of you fuckers that hit him at the Cloisters is gonna die, and it's all coming down today. With all this other shit going down in Jokertown he doesn't have to worry about cops or anybody else getting in his way."

Fortunato had a sudden hunch, a convergence of invisible power lines. "You know anything about some stolen books? Or a man named Kien?"

"You ask a lot of questions."

"I just saved your life."

"No. No to the books, no to whatever-his-name-was."

He was telling the truth, but Fortunato still felt the connection. "A man named Loophole, or Latham?"

"Sorry. No dice."

Fortunato started to turn away. "Hey, listen," Demise said. "I didn't mean to get snippy. Maybe you could hide me out for a while? Just till this time tomorrow?"

"Why tomorrow?"

"Just the way the man was talking. 'Parting shot' and shit like that. I got a real strong sense that by tomorrow morning you can color me gone. So what do you say? Got someplace to stash me?"

"Don't push your luck," Fortunato said.

Demise shrugged. The gesture was a little stiff, but otherwise his neck looked almost normal. "I guess I better turn up something on my own, then, hadn't I?"

The ice sculptures arrived at half past ten, in a refrigerated truck that had fought its way through the holiday crowds from the artist's loft in SoHo. Hiram went down to the lobby to make certain that there were no mishaps as the life-size sculptures were transported up the service elevator. The artist, a rugged-looking joker with bone-white skin and colorless eyes who called himself Kelvin Frost, was most comfortable at temperatures around thirty below, and never left the frigid comforts of his studio. But he was a genius in ice—or "ephemeral art," as Frost and the critics preferred to call it.

When the sculptures were safely stored in the Aces High walk-in freezer, Hiram relaxed enough to look them over. Frost had not disappointed. His detail was as astonishing as ever, and his work had something else as well—a poignancy, a human quality that might even be called warmth, if warmth could exist in ice. Hiram sensed something forlorn and doomed in the way Jetboy stood there, looking up at the sky, every inch the hero and yet somehow a lost boy too. Dr. Tachyon pondered like Rodin's *The Thinker*, but instead of a rock, he sat upon an icy globe. Cyclone's cloak billowed out so you could almost feel the winds skirling about him, and the Howler stood with legs braced and fists clenched at his side, his mouth open as if he'd been caught in the act of screaming down a wall.

Peregrine looked as though she'd been caught in some

other act. Her sculpture was a recumbent nude, resting languidly on one elbow, her wings half-spread behind her, every feather rendered in exquisite detail. A sly, sweet smile lit that famous face. The whole effect was magnificently erotic. Hiram found himself wondering if she'd posed for him. It was not unlike her.

But Frost's masterpiece, Hiram thought, was the Turtle. How to bring humanity to a man who'd never once shown his face to the world, whose public persona was a massive armored shell studded with camera lenses? The artist had risen to that challenge: the shell was there, every seam and rivet, but atop it, in miniature, Frost had carved a myriad of other figures. Hiram walked around the sculpture, admiring, picking out detail. There were the Four Aces at some Last Supper, Golden Boy looking much like Judas. Elsewhere a dozen jokers struggled up the curve of the shell, as if climbing some impossible mountain. There was Fortunato, surrounded by writhing naked women, and there a figure with a hundred blurred faces who seemed to be deep in sleep. From every angle, the piece unveiled new treasures.

"Kind of a shame it's going to melt, isn't it?" Jay Ackroyd said from behind him.

Hiram turned. "The artist doesn't think so. Frost maintains that all art is ephemeral, that ultimately it will all be gone, Picasso and Rembrandt and Van Gogh, the Sistine Chapel and the Mona Lisa, whatever you care to name, in the end it will be gone to dust. Ice art is therefore more honest, because it celebrates its transitory nature instead of denying it."

"Real good," the detective said in a flat voice. "But no one ever chipped a piece off the Pietà to put in their drink." He glanced over at Peregrine. "I should have been an artist.

Girls always take off their clothes for artists. Can we get out of here? I forgot to bring my fur muumuu."

Hiram locked the freezer and escorted Ackroyd back to his office. The detective was a nondescript sort of fellow, which was probably an asset in his profession. Mid-forties, slender, just under medium height, carefully combed brown hair, quick brown eyes, an elusive smile. You'd never look at him twice on the street, and if you did, you'd never be sure if you'd seen him before. This morning he wore brown loafers with tassels, a brown suit obviously bought off the rack, and a dress shirt open at the collar. Hiram had asked him once why he didn't wear ties. "Prone to soup stains," Ackroyd had replied.

"Well?" Hiram asked, when he was safely ensconced behind his desk. He glanced up at his muted television. A color graphic was showing sound waves coming out of the mouth of a yellow stick man and knocking down a wall. Then they cut to an on-the-scene reporter speaking into the camera. Behind him, a dozen police cars cordoned off a brick building. The street was covered with shards of broken glass, winking in the sunlight. The camera panned slowly over rows of shattered windows and the cracked windshields of nearby parked cars.

"It was no big thing," Ackroyd said. "I nosed around the fish market for a hour and got the general idea fast enough. You've got your basic protection racket going down."

"I see," Hiram said.

"The waterfront draws crooks like a picnic draws ants, that's no secret. Smuggling, drugs, the rackets, you name it. Opportunities abound. Your friend Gills, along with most of the other small businessmen, paid the mob a percentage off the top, and in return the mob provided protection and occasional help with the police or the unions."

"The *mob?*" Hiram said. "Jay, this sounds suitably melodramatic, but I had the impression that the mob was made up of ethnic gentlemen partial to pinstripes, black shirts, and white ties. The hoodlums who were troubling Gills lacked even that rudimentary fashion sense. And one of them was a joker. Has the Mafia taken to recruiting jokers?"

"No," Ackroyd said. "That's the trouble. The East River waterfront belongs to the Gambione Family, but the Gambiones have been losing their grip for years now. They've already lost Jokertown to the Demon Princes and the other joker gangs, and a Chinatown gang called the Egrets or Snowbirds or something like that has run them right out of Chinatown. Harlem got taken away a long time ago, and the bulk of the city's drug traffic no longer flows through Gambione hands. But they still controlled the waterfront. Until now." He leaned forward. "Now there's competition. They're offering new and improved protection at a much higher price. Maybe too high for your friend."

"His son is in college," Hiram said thoughtfully. "The tuition is quite substantial, I believe. So what I witnessed this morning was a little, ah, dunning?"

"Bingo," Ackroyd said.

"If Gills and his fellow merchants have been paying the Gambiones for protection, why aren't they receiving it?"

"Two weeks ago, a body was found hanging from a meat-hook in a warehouse two blocks from Fulton Street. A gentleman by the name of Dominick Santarello. He was ID'd by fingerprints, his face having been beaten into ground round. A colleague of Santarello's, one Angelo Casanovista, turned up dead in a barrel of pickled herring a week prior. His head was not in the barrel with him. The word on the streets is that the new guys have something the Gambiones don't—an ace. Or at least a joker who can pass for an ace in a bad light. These things do tend to get exaggerated, but I'm told he's seven feet tall, inhumanly strong, and ugly enough to make you wet your pants. He goes by the charming *nom de guerre* of Bludgeon. The Gambiones are overmatched, I'd say." He shrugged.

Hiram Worchester was aghast. "And what about the police?"

"Gills is afraid. One of his friends tried talking to the police, and his body turned up with a flounder shoved down his throat. Literally. The cops are investigating."

"This is intolerable," Hiram said. "Gills is a good man, an honest man. He deserves better than to have to live in this kind of fear. What can I do to help?"

"Lend him the money to make his payment," Ackroyd suggested with a cynical smile.

"You can't be serious!" Hiram objected.

The detective shrugged. "Better idea—hire me to be his full-time bodyguard. Does he have a nubile daughter, by any chance?" When Hiram didn't respond, Ackroyd got up and slid his hands into his jacket pocket. "All right. There might be something to be done. I'll work on it. Chrysalis might be able to tell me something useful, if the price is right."

Hiram nodded and rose behind his desk. "Fine," he said. "Excellent. Keep me posted." Ackroyd turned to go. "One more thing," Hiram said. Jay turned back, raised an eyebrow. "This Bludgeon sounds, ah, ill-tempered to say the least. Don't do anything too dangerous. Be careful."

Jay Ackroyd smiled. "If Bludgeon gives me any trouble, I'll dazzle him with magic," he said. He made a gun out of his fingers, three fingers folded back, index finger pointed at Hiram, thumb up straight like a hammer.

"Don't you dare," Hiram Worchester told him. "Not if

you want to eat tonight." Ackroyd laughed, and slid his hand back into his pocket, and sauntered out.

Hiram glanced back at his television scene. They were running an interview with the Howler. The interviewer was Walter Cronkite. A ten-year-old clip, Hiram realized, from the Great Jokertown Riot of 1976. He changed the channel, hoping to see some coverage from Jokertown and Jetboy's Tomb, and perhaps get another glimpse of Peregrine. Instead he got Bill Moyers, doing a commentary in front of a large still photograph of the Howler. The Howler seemed to be much in the news this morning, Hiram thought. He was curious.

He turned on the sound.

CHAPTER 6

11:00 a.m.

A parade in Jokertown was always a unique experience. No need to create some fantastic creature out of wire and flowers and paper. No, here the jokers could provide all the grotesquerie required with just their miserable bodies. There was no Joker Queen either. Several years ago they had tried to introduce the notion, Tachyon explained as he guided Roulette through the crowds, but he had been so revolted by the notion that the planners had dropped the idea. There were a number of politically active jokers who hadn't forgiven him yet.

Sara Roosevelt Park had been cordoned off, and was filled with belching, grinding flatbed trucks all carrying fantastic scenes on their utilitarian backs. Off to the west a knot of sweating cops were demolishing a vast, double-headed phallus. Roulette noticed that a number of men in the crowd looked away each time a crowbar bit deep into the latex. To the west the Joker Moose Lodge Bagpipe Band was tuning up. The braying of the pipes sounded harsh in the still, sultry air.

"Are you the parade's grand master?" Roulette asked with more acid than she'd intended.

"No," Tachyon snapped back, and she found herself staring at his rigid back as he scanned the crowd.

A portly joker, his nose replaced by a long trunk ending in several tiny fingers, broke from the edges of the crowd like a calving iceberg, and chugged toward Tachyon.

"All set?" he asked, thrusting out a hand.

"All set. Des, may I introduce Roulette Brown-Roxbury. Roulette, Xavier Desmond, owner of the Funhouse, and one of Jokertown's most sterling citizens."

"Some would argue that that's an oxymoron."

"My, we're crabby today," Tachyon teased, with a touch of acid.

A look passed between the two men, and Roulette realized that theirs was a complex relationship. They were friends, they respected one another, but something lay between them, a memory of ancient pain.

This flash of cattiness had an unusual effect. Rather than strengthening her desire to kill the man it somehow made him all the more charming. He was not perfect, or even perfectly evil. Just "human," and therefore understandable, and she cursed the insight, for it is easier to hate in the abstract.

Des glanced at his watch. "Running late as usual."

"I just hope delays and the heat don't conduce to any shall we say . . . incidents." He tugged on his upper lip. "I can't help but think of '76 when I see all these police."

"There was a strange feel on that day. Mercifully we've never felt it since."

"Well, I'd best mingle." He caught up both of Roulette's

hands, and pressed a quick kiss onto each. "I will be back to collect you before we get under way."

"Are you sure I should be with you? Maybe we could just meet for lunch afterward, or something . . ." Her voice trailed away.

"No, no. I need the support."

"Difficult situation."

"I beg your pardon?" Roulette pulled her eyes from Tachyon's fast-vanishing form.

"If he doesn't take part in the parade he's accused of showing contempt for the jokers, and favoring the aces. When he does join in—which he's done for the past five years—he's accused of being a heartless parasite, living off the misery of the jokers he helped create. A little tin-plated king of his own freak kingdom."

Her eyes roved the park. Sno-cone vendors hawking through the crowd, police with sweat stains in the pits and front of shirts, Tachyon like a tiny redheaded, red-clad devil in the midst of a Dantesque scene as jokers doubled for demons. Just do the job, and get out of this. That was all she wanted now.

Somehow she had to pry him loose, seek the privacy of a hotel or apartment, and make the kill. She couldn't cut him out yet. His sense of duty would keep him in this freak parade, and he was a featured speaker at the tomb. Her thoughts propelled her, carried her across the park toward the Takisian, while behind her Des frowned over her abrupt departure.

Perhaps a sudden indisposition? *Stupid!* All that would get her was a bed at the Jokertown clinic. Definitely the wrong bed. Perhaps a—*Use your goddamn body! Most men's brains seemed to be lodged in their penises!*

His welcoming smile embraced her. "Ah, I think you

must be a telepath. I was just coming for you."

"Were you?" she heard herself reply, but the voice seemed to be coming from a long distance. "I hope you'll continue to come for me." Her arm slid around his neck, and molding her body to his, she pressed a kiss onto his mouth.

For an instant there was withdrawal. Had she overplayed the moment? Then their tongues met, and all restraint was swept away. His tongue teased, thrust past the barrier of her teeth. His hand, hot against the nape of her neck, pulled her closer. A chorus of appreciative catcalls rose around them, and they broke apart.

"Well," Tachyon gusted, and, pulling a handkerchief from a pocket, patted briskly at his forehead.

She snuggled in close, and pulled his arm through hers. "I was very sad earlier. You've changed all that, and I wanted to thank you."

"Madam . . . Roulette, thank me anytime you wish."

A chauffeur, tail lashing at the ankles of his boots, held open the door of a large gray Lincoln.

"Ah, Riggs, punctual as always. I often wonder how you tolerate me, for I am so notoriously unpunctual."

"I've learned to bear with it." His voice was like soft velvet, and his luminescent green cat's eyes seemed lit from behind with amusement.

"Riggs, this is Roulette Brown-Roxbury. She is our guest for the day." A pinch to her fingers. "And I hope into the night."

Riggs touched the bill of his cap. "Ma'am."

"So, you employ jokers," she remarked as she slid across the leather upholstery.

"Of course." And the reply struck her as smug. "Riggs's reflexes and night vision are far superior to an ordinary human's. I'm very grateful to have my safety in his capable hands."

The lead float was nosing majestically onto the Bowery. Behind it P.S 235's marching band swung into a snappy rendition of the "Pineapple Rag."

Senator Hartmann's open car was next in the line. An ace jogged beside the limo. At least Roulette presumed he was an ace. Most normal secret-service agents didn't run about dressed in white form-fitting jumpsuits complete with black hood covering face and head.

Hartmann beamed and waved, every inch an elder statesman. Someone in the crowd lining the street shouted out, "How about '88, Senator?"

"Suggest it. I'm ready," Hartmann called back, and grinned as the laughter and cheers rippled through the throng.

Two more floats, the mounted patrol, then Riggs put the big Lincoln in gear, and they rolled out at a steady ten miles per hour.

"Why not an open car?" Roulette asked, and from overhead a whining answered as the sun roof slid back.

"I may have lived on Earth for forty years, but I'm still a Takisian. I'm damned if I'm riding in an open car for anyone. And on Wild Card Day my enemies as well as my friends are abroad."

Fifteen minutes later, and he dropped back onto the seat fanning himself with his handkerchief. "Dreadful weather."

"Here." She had been exploring while he had perched on the roof and waved to the crowd, and had discovered the bar.

"Dubonnet on ice. What an elegant lifesaver you are. Are you joining me this time?"

"Yes."

She moved in close, her thigh pressing against his. They each took a thoughtful sip, then she ran one long nail down his cheek, noting the way his sideburns lay in red-gold whorls against his white, white skin. She paused, and inspected the small isosceles-shaped scar on his pointed chin.

"What happened?"

"Combat training. Sedjur and my father agreed we should leave it as a reminder to move more quickly next time." And his face closed down while tears of grief blurred his lilac eyes.

It was the moment. She cupped his face between her hands, and kissed him, her lips coaxing the rigidity out of his mouth. A tear splashed warmly on her hand, as she licked the tiny point of moisture away.

"Why so sad?"

"Because Sedjur is dead, and my father, were he aware, would like to be. I think memory is a curse."

"Yes, so do I." Her hand slid down the satiny fabric of his waistcoat, and gripped his waistband. His gasp played counterpoint to the rasp of the zipper. "So let's explore sensation and the moment, and forget memories."

She had him free now, and was gently rolling his penis between the palms of her hands. He stiffened instantly, his back arching, and beads of sweat broke across his brow and upper lip.

"By the Ideal, woman, what are you doing?"

She gave him a Mona Lisa smile, took him in her mouth, and gave gentle suction. One hand shot out and hit the control, raising the window between them and Riggs. He moaned as her tongue teased at the underside of his glans.

"Have mercy," he groaned, one hand twisting in her braids.

"All right." She drew back.

"The Ideal, you leave me like this?"

"Then let's go somewhere."

"The speech."

"Afterwards."

"Oh God!"

The subway car's metal wheels squealed as they pulled into Times Square. The doors hissed open and Spector got up, feeling better than he had all morning. The Astronomer had to figure he was dead, and the old man was having a very busy day. There wouldn't be any time for second thoughts about him.

He dug dried blood out from between his teeth with a fingernail and slipped through the standing passengers toward the door. A surge of people entering the car pushed him back; he shoulder-cut his way through them and out onto the platform in front of a couple trying to enter the car. The doors closed.

"Hey, man, you made us miss the train." The man was young and Hispanic with a snap-brim hat and purple pinstripe suit. A girl was holding onto the sleeve of his sealskin coat. He pushed Spector back and shook his head. "You goddamn space case. Can't go anywhere in this town without running into jerks. Don't worry, baby. There'll be another along a few minutes."

Spector was looking at the girl. She was tall and slender, with dark hair and eyes. She was wearing a heavy metal T-shirt with the name FERRIC JAGGER on the front. The pimp was carrying a soft-sided floral-print suitcase that was obviously hers. There was something about her that demanded attention. Spector could have some real fun with this one.

Not sex, he didn't do that. He'd liked killing girls with the Astronomer, though. It was the only thing that got Spector off anymore. It would be a real charge to feel the life go out of this little number.

"Hey, man, what you lookin' at?" The pimp pushed him again, hard.

Spector's hatred and pain clawed their way out. He stared hard into the pimp's eyes. The other man made a soft sound as the air went out of him and he collapsed onto the platform. People nearby looked uncomprehending at the body for a few moments, then voices began to call out for a doctor.

He tugged at his mustache, happy at the pimp's death. The girl was staring down at the body, but there were no screams. Not yet.

He pulled the suitcase from the pimp's hand and smiled at the girl. "New in town? I can show you a thing or two. Local sights, whatever you want."

She pulled the suitcase from him and turned away. She didn't say a word.

Spector saw a transit cop moving in. He sifted into the crowd. It was a shame about the girl, but, overall, things were beginning to look a little brighter.

The Happy Hocker Pawnshop was in the Flatbush section of Brooklyn, on Washington Avenue and Sullivan Street. Jennifer took a cab to within a few blocks of the address and walked the rest of the way. It was located among other small, family-run businesses, including a delicatessen, a clothing store, a shoestore, and a small pizzeria. Everything but the deli was closed and the street around the pawnshop was virtually deserted, but down a couple of blocks and across the street a large crowd was gathered outside Ebbets Field for the Dodgers' annual Wild Card Day game. According to the sign across the main gate the Dodgers were playing the Los Angeles Stars. The teams were old rivals, and since the Dodgers were in the midst of another close pennant race, it looked like the crowd already streaming into the stadium would stretch the seating capacity of the old ballpark to its limit.

Jennifer glanced at her wristwatch. It was a few minutes after eleven. Tom Seaver, who'd been pitching for the Dodgers for almost all of Jennifer's life, was scheduled to go against Fernando Valenzuela, the Stars' young Mexican hurler. There was still time to get tickets, and watching the ballgame would be a more pleasant way to spend the afternoon than lunching with Gruber.

She peered through the dusty window of the pawnshop. If she hadn't known better, she'd have thought that it was closed along with most of the other small stores on the block. But Gruber had never broken an appointment with her before.

She tried the front door. It was unlocked, and she went in. Inside the pawnshop it was dark and still. Its narrow aisles and tall shelves crammed with unwanted merchandise, most of which had been around since the time of Gruber's father, always gave Jennifer a touch of claustrophobia. Guitars with broken strings, televisions with burned-out tubes, toaster ovens with frayed electrical cords, stained and torn coats and shirts and dresses, crowded the shelves in the dingy room, the ink on their pawntags faded to illegibility.

The only light in the room came from a naked bulb dangling from electrical wires in the cage behind the counter, Gruber's customary lair. But Gruber wasn't there.

She called out his name, but her words echoed hollowly and she had a sudden feeling of wrongness. She walked closer to the cage and the sole of her right shoe stuck in something tacky, like a blob of chewed-out gum. She looked down.

A puddle of thick, rich liquid flowed out from one of the aisles. She took a step forward and peered around the edge of the shelving into the aisle, and stared.

It was Gruber. His pale, soft face was frozen into a rictus of intense horror. His pale, soft hands were clutched tightly to his stomach, but they hadn't prevented his blood from running out and collecting around him in a sticky, shallow pool.

Jennifer hung over a low counter that was filled with cheap jewelry and cheaper guns and lost her breakfast. She leaned shakily against the glass counter after vomiting up everything in her stomach, letting it take her weight.

After a moment or two of utter blankness she wiped her lips and forced herself to look back at what was left of Gruber. It was the first body she'd ever seen. She stared in fascinated horror, thinking she ought to do something, but not knowing what.

"It'sss her."

A hissing, sibilant voice sounded behind her, starting her heart jumping like that of an aerobic instructor on speed. She whirled around in a half-crouch and stared at the three men who had silently entered the shop through the back entrance.

Two were norms, or looked to be. The third was a joker, a tall, slim man who looked like a lizard walking on two legs. He was the one who had spoken. Jennifer stared at him and his long, forked tongue rolled out of his mouth again and flickered at her.

"Ssshe'sss the one," he hissed. "Get her."

"Christ," one of the others muttered. "She killed him."

The two norms looked at each other uneasily and Jennifer's brain finally began to work again.

She recognized the reptilian joker. He had been in Kien's condo, he had shown up when the joker in the jar started screaming. How'd he trace her here? She glanced at Gruber's corpse. Gruber was a possibility, but she'd never be able to ask him if he'd turned her in. But how would he have known she'd stolen the stuff from Kien?

This was no time to worry about it. The men with the reptiloid had just about convinced themselves to tackle her. They approached her slowly, pistols out, while the joker stood by watching.

Jennifer ghosted.

She stepped out of her clothes, conserving only the bikini that she normally wore and the small bag that had the books in it. She glanced back over her shoulder as she stepped through a shelf crammed with hocked junk. The two norms stared at her with open mouths, the joker cursed with a hissing sibilance.

She kept going through the shelves, the wall, and the alley between the pawnshop and the next building, leaving the men far behind. She caught her breath, metaphorically, and then solidified. She was in the clothing store.

She grabbed a pair of jeans, a blouse, and sneakers, threw them on, stopped to take two twenties from her bag and put them into the cash register, and then fled through the front door.

Kien's men were nowhere in sight. They were, she suspected, baffled by her disappearance, but she couldn't count on their bewilderment to last for very long.

She looked down the street. To the right was Ebbets Field, still filling with baseball fans. To the left was Prospect Park with an inviting offer of greenery and isolation. Somehow, though, she felt like being around other people. She'd be safe around people. No one could try to kill her. She'd have time to think things out.

She ran down the street and joined the end of the line filing into the stadium just as Kien's men came around the far end of the block, shaking their heads in exasperated anger.

They crowded into Hiram's office, all of them. The cleaning crew, the dishwashers, the kitchen staff, even the electrician who'd come up to fix the faulty wiring in one of the chandeliers. They sat in the chairs, on the floor, on the desk and cabinets. Many stood. No one said a word. Even Paul LeBarre was silent. All eyes were on the television. Geraldo Rivera was interviewing one of the Howler's sisters. Hiram hadn't known the Howler had a sister. It turned out he had four of them.

It was like the day Kennedy had been shot, he thought, or the Day of the Wild Card, the first one, forty years ago, when Jetboy had died and the world had changed forever.

The newscast cut to a police press conference. Hiram listened, and felt sick.

"Jesus." That was Peter Chou, the slim quiet man who was in charge of Aces High security, Peter who collected depression glass and black belts in assorted martial arts, and who never raised his voice or used profanity. "Jesus fucking

Christ," he said now. "Nerve toxin. Jesus fucking Christ."

"It don't make sense," one of the dishwashers said. "Man, it don't make no fucking *sense*, man, that fucker could scream down *walls*, I saw him do it, man, I saw him."

Then everybody started talking at once.

Curtis tapped Hiram's shoulder, gave him a questioning look and nodded toward the door. Hiram rose and followed him. The floor seemed cavernous and empty now with everyone jammed into Hiram's office.

"Outside," Hiram said. They went out onto the Sunset Terrace, and stood looking down over the city. The Empire State's public observation deck was on the floor above them, and above that was the old mooring mast that had once been intended for zeppelins, but except for that, there was no higher spot in New York City, or the world. The sun shone down brightly, and Hiram found himself wondering if the sky had looked as blue to Jetboy on the day he died.

"The dinner," Curtis said simply. "Do we go ahead, or cancel?"

"We go on," Hiram said, without hesitating.

"Very good, sir," Curtis said. His tone was carefully neutral, neither approving nor disapproving.

But Hiram felt he needed to explain. He put his hands up against the stone parapet, gazed off blindly to the west. "My father," he said. His voice sounded strange and halting, even to himself. "He was, ah, a robust man. As large as myself, in his later years. He was a man of, ah, healthy appetites."

"British, wasn't he?" Curtis said.

Hiram nodded. "He fought at Dunkirk. After the war he married a WAC and came to America. A male war bride, he called himself, not that he wore white. He'd always add that, and my mother would always blush, and he would laugh.

God, but that man could laugh. He *roared*. He did everything in a large way. Food, liquor, even his women. He had a dozen mistresses. My mother didn't seem to mind, although she would have preferred a tad more discretion. He was a loud man, my father."

Hiram looked at Curtis. "He died when I was twelve. The funeral was . . . well, the sort of function my father would have loathed. If he hadn't been dead he never would have attended. It was grim, and pious, and so *quiet*. I kept expecting my father to sit up in the casket and tell a joke. There was weeping and whispering, but no laughter, nothing to eat or drink. I hated every second of it."

"I see," Curtis said.

"I have it in my will, you know," Hiram said. "A certain sum has been set aside, a rather handsome sum I might add, and when I die, Aces High will open its doors to my friends and family, and the food and drink will keep flowing until the money is gone, and perhaps there will be laughter. Perhaps. I don't know Howler's wishes in that regard, but I do know that he could eat and drink with the best of them, and he was the only man I ever knew who laughed louder than my father."

Curtis smiled. "He shattered several thousand dollars' worth of crystal with one of his laughs, as I recall."

Hiram smiled. "And wasn't the least bit abashed, either. Tachyon was the one who'd made the witticism, and of course he felt so guilty I didn't see his face for almost three months." Hiram clapped a hand on Curtis's shoulder. "No. I cannot believe that Howler would have wanted us to cancel the party. We go on. Most definitely."

"The ice sculpture?" Curtis reminded him gently.

"We will display it," Hiram said firmly. "We're not going to try and pretend that Howler never existed. The sculpture will remind us that . . . that one of us is missing tonight." Somewhere far below, a horn was blaring. A man was dead, an ace, one of the fortunate handful, but the city went on as always, and as always someone was late for something. Hiram shivered. "Let's get it done, then." They went back inside.

Peter Chou was crossing the floor in their direction. "You have a phone call," he said to Hiram.

"Thank you," Hiram said. He went back into his office. "I know all of you are interested in the news," he told his staff. "So am I. But in a few hours, we'll be feeding a hundred and fifty-odd people. We'll pipe in the latest bulletins, rest assured. Now let's get back to work."

One by one they filed out. Paul LeBarre put a hand on Hiram's shoulder before shuffling past. On television, Senator Hartmann stood in front of Jetboy's Tomb, promising a full SCARE investigation of the Howler's murder. Hiram nodded, touched the mute button, and picked up his phone.

At first he didn't recognize the voice, and the fragmentary words, spoken with so much difficulty, didn't seem to make much sense. The man kept apologizing, over and over, and he was saying something about gasoline, and Hiram couldn't seem to focus on any of it. "What are you talking about?"

"Lops . . . lobsters," the voice said.

"What?" Hiram said. He sat bolt upright. "Gills, is this you?" It certainly didn't sound like him.

"Sorry . . . sorry, Hiram." He began to wheeze. Then someone took the phone away from him.

"Good morning, Fatboy," said a voice strange and shrill, a voice like a razor blade scratching down a blackboard. "Gills don't talk so good. He's still spitting out teeth." Hiram heard someone laugh in the background. "What fishface is trying to tell you is that we just got done marinating your fucking lobsters in fucking gasoline, and if you want 'em you can fucking well come down here and pick 'em up yourself, 'cause his fucking truck is on fire." Another laugh. "Now listen good, asshole, I don't care if you are a fuckin' uptown ace, you cuntface, you fuck around with me, this is what you get. You listening?"

There was a moment of dead air, and then a scream, and a sharp sound like a bone breaking.

"Hear that, cuntface?" the razor-blade voice said. Hiram didn't reply. *"Did you fucking hear it?"* the voice screamed.

"Yes," Hiram said.

"Have a nice day," the voice said, followed by a click.

Hiram slowly returned the phone to its cradle. The day could not possibly get any worse, he thought.

Then the phone rang again.

Fortunato picked up the phone and dialed a Brooklyn extension. As soon as he was sitting down, the cat got in his lap and began kneading the legs of his jeans. The phone rang twice and a woman answered. "Hello, is Arnie there?" he asked. He could have sent his astral body, but he was already running on about half a charge and it was time to save his strength.

"No, this is his mother. May I help?"

"My name is Fortunato—"

"Oh, heavenly days. I've heard Arnie talk about you forever. He'll just *die* when he finds out you called and he wasn't home."

"If you could just tell me where he is, ma'am, I'll try and find him myself."

"Oh, he's headed for Jetboy's Tomb. His father takes him down there every Wild Card Day. They left about an hour ago. I don't know if you'll be able to find him in all those crowds. He's not in any trouble, is he?"

"No, ma'am, nothing like that. I'm sure I'll be able to find him."

"Oh, that's right. I guess you do have your ways, don't you? It's just that I'm a little nervous, what with the Howler and all."

"The Howler?"

"Oh, you haven't heard. Oh dear. They found the Howler just a little while ago. He was murdered. Some kind of nerve poison or something. It was just on the TV."

Fortunato hung up. He'd written the list on paper, just to focus his thoughts. The aces who had been at the Cloisters. Kid Dinosaur. Tachyon. Peregrine. The Turtle. Modular Man. The Howler. Jumpin' Jack Flash. Water Lily.

He crossed the Howler's name off the list. So it was true, he thought. It wasn't just Demise's raving. It was happening, had already started.

Of the ones that were left, Flash and the Turtle could take care of themselves. Tachyon couldn't, but that was Tachyon's problem.

He called Hiram at Aces High. He didn't think Hiram would be on the Astronomer's hit list; he'd only been involved peripherally with the TIAMAT business and hadn't been at the Cloisters at all. Still he deserved a warning.

He told the story as simply as he could, and then said, "Listen, there's something you can do if you're willing. I need a command post. Somewhere safe to bring the ones I find, and somewhere for people to leave messages."

"Of course. Nobody would attack Aces High. It would be insane."

"Right," Fortunato said. "But just in case. Do you have some way of getting hold of that android? Modular Man?"

"I think he gave me some kind of signal thing once. I could probably find him if I had to."

"Just flatter him a little. I think that should do it. If not, you could subtly suggest that there'll be women there. If necessary, he can have one of mine. Just call and have one sent over, on the house." He hung up before Hiram could change his mind.

So what next? Try to find a kid he barely remembered out of thousands at Jetboy's Tomb? Or move on down the list?

No. The Kid was reckless and stupid and had just enough power to get himself in real trouble. It had to be the Kid.

The game was almost sold out. Only bleacher seats were left by the time Jennifer got to the ticket window, but that was fine with her. She just wanted to sit down in the warm sun, let the reassuring sounds of the crowd wash over her, and think.

She paid for her ticket, and some atavistic sense made her turn around and look behind. There was a man, moderately tall, slimly but strongly built, dark-haired, dark-eyed. He seemed to be watching her intently, but he looked away the moment after their eyes met.

Her gaze lingered on him for a moment. He wore jeans, a T-shirt, and dark running shoes. The muscularity of his lithe build struck her, then she was carried along the wave of ticket-buyers into the stadium.

Had he really been looking at her, or was she just getting paranoid? She let out a deep breath. It was probably her clothes that made him stare. She hadn't exactly had time to try on the clothing she'd taken. The pants were short and tight across her behind and the pullover shirt was also short, leaving a couple of inches of her midriff peeking out. That was it. Her clothes. She was getting paranoid, picking out strangers in a crowd, thinking they were menacing her.

Not that she didn't have a reason to be paranoid. After all, there were people after her. Now she just had to figure out why, and, more importantly, how.

Spector was tired of waiting. His anonymous contact had said eleven-thirty, and it was already several minutes past that. Maybe they hadn't been satisfied with the way he'd handled Gruber. It wasn't his fault the idiot had pulled a gun. They couldn't have been stupid enough to think the bullets did it.

He leaned against the statue of George M. Cohan and cracked his knuckles. He was aware of the bulge the Ingram was making in his coat. Most of the cops were in Jokertown, but the rest of the city had to be covered, too. It might be good to dump the gun, now that the Astronomer was off his tail. Then again, you never knew when an automatic pistol might come in handy.

The crowd waiting in line for Broadway show tickets was smaller than usual. Spector had never been to one; they seemed stupid and overpriced. He used to come over from Jersey on New Year's Eve to watch the ball drop at midnight. It was one of the few times he felt like a part of something bigger than just him.

The neon signs around the Square were washed out and

dull during the day. If his connection didn't show up soon, he might pick up a whore for some fun. Seeing the tombstones rolled up in some cheap hooker's eyes would give him a few moments' relief from the pain. It wouldn't be great, like the girl in the subway, but it would be distraction. God, he had wanted to kill her. At least hurt her enough to get a reaction out of her. Better to just get drunk and watch the ball game on television, though. A low profile for the rest of the day was not an entirely bad idea.

"Fuck it," he said, walking away from the statue. "Those Shadow Fist boys are going to have to do better than this."

"Don't go away mad," said a deep, nasty voice from behind.

Spector turned. There was a joker a few paces behind him, closing the distance with slow, measured strides. There was dried blood smeared on his shirt. He had a single eye set in the center of his forehead.

"You're late."

"It's been a busy morning. Had a little business to attend to down at the waterfront." The cyclops made a fist, showing his badly bruised knuckles. "You must be Spector."

"Right. So tell me something."

"It's like this." He looked over his shoulder. "The Gambiones are having dinner at the Haiphong Lily tonight. Family meeting, you know. The don is in the way. He has to be taken care of. That's where you come in."

"Tonight, huh? What's the job pay?"

"Five grand."

Spector ran his tongue around his teeth, cleaning away more dried blood. He figured this punk had been given a ceiling amount by someone higher up and could keep the rest for himself. The joker didn't have the brains to snow a six-year-old. "No way. Do it yourself."

"Okay, okay. Seven-five."

"Ten, or get somebody else. We're not talking about an easy target here. This is the don you want iced." Spector took a step back and looked away. He wanted to push this guy hard, so the organization wouldn't take him for a fool.

The joker put his hands on his hips. "You got it."

"I'll want two of that right now." Spector extended his hand.

"What? Right here? You've got to be kidding." He glanced around again, this time in melodramatic fashion.

Spector had to bite his tongue to keep from laughing. This moron needed acting lessons *and* the brains to use them. "They wouldn't send you here with just change in your pocket. Now pay up, or find me somebody who will." Spector liked leaning on the punk a little, watching him squirm.

The cyclops pulled a thick brown envelope from his coat and shoved it in Spector's face. "Just to show we trust you."

Spector tucked the envelope in his coat pocket and smiled. "I won't even count it. Yet. Now, what time is dinner for our friend the don?"

"Around eight, so you'll need to get there a little before. You can eat pretty well, now," he said, tapping the envelope in Spector's pocket.

"When do I get the rest?"

"Tomorrow night. We'll let you know where." He leaned in close. His breath stank of decay. "By the way, if you happen to hear anything about some missing stockbooks, let me know." He pulled out a small spiral notebook and pen, then wrote a phone number on the top sheet. "You can reach me here for the next few hours," he said, tearing out the sheet and handing it to Spector. "It's the Bowery Wild

Card Dime Museum. I do security work there in my spare time."

"You keep an eye on the place, right?"

The cyclops ignored his joke. "Hey, you have to have a legit job for tax reasons. That's what the boss says. Looks suspicious otherwise."

"Sure. Sure. What did you say your name was? Just in case?"

"Eye."

"And if I can't get hold of you?"

"Call the Twisted Dragon. Ask for Danny Mao. Tell him you were born in the year of the fire horse. He'll take it from there."

"How would you like to come with me tonight? Just so you'll be completely sure the contract was filled." Spector put his arm around the joker and walked him down the sidewalk.

Eye shrugged him off. "Just do your fucking job. And keep your faggot hands off."

"Pleasure doing business." Spector watched him walk away. There was time to hit a bar and watch the game before he went to work. The Dodgers had better fucking win today or the don would have plenty of company.

CHAPTER 7

12:00 Noon

The Dodgers were taking batting practice when Jennifer found her seat in the bleachers. The late summer sun was soothing on her bare arms and face. She closed her eyes and listened to the friendly sounds of the stadium, the call of the vendors, the conversation of the fans, the unmistakable crack of bat hitting ball.

She suddenly realized that it'd been two years since she'd been to a ball game, two years since her father had died. Her father had loved the Dodgers and he'd taken her to many games. She wasn't that big a fan herself, but she'd always been happy to accompany him. It was a good excuse to get out into the sunshine or the cool evening air.

She remembered, in fact, the first Wild Card Day game her father had taken her to. It had been in 1969, the Dodgers against the Cardinals. The proud Dodger franchise had fallen on hard times in the mid-1960s, finishing at or near the bottom of the league for five straight years, but in 1969 the incomparable Pete Reiser, who had been in center field for the Dodgers that day in 1946 when the Wild Card virus had rained down from the sky, had come out of retirement to manage his old team. When Reiser played for the Dodgers they'd been a collection of glorious names. In 1969 they were a bunch of castoffs, never-has-beens, and untried rookies. Reiser, the center fielder nonpareil of the '40s and '50s, the man who had made the most hits, scored the most runs, and compiled the highest batting average in history, took a ragamuffin team that had finished last in 1968 and led them to first place with a miraculous combination of managerial insight and inspiration.

Tom Seaver, Brooklyn's only bona fide star, had pitched on that day in 1969, and beat Bob Gibson, 2-0. The Dodgers' runs had come, she remembered, on solo home runs by the elderly third baseman, Ed "The Glider" Charles. That game had clinched the division flag for the Dodgers, and they went on to beat Milwaukee in the National League's first divisional playoffs, and then demolished the vaunted Baltimore Orioles in the World Series.

Memories of the exultation of that day, when an entire city had roared a collective shout of glee, brought a smile to her face. It had been a rare moment, and, looking back, she wished that she'd been old enough to appreciate the absolute and pure joy, untainted by any other emotion or thought. She'd rarely experienced that feeling since, and never with tens of thousands of other people.

The loud crack of a bat meeting a ball brought her back to the present, and she wiped the smile off her face. These reminiscences weren't doing any good. Fleeing the perilous present by taking refuge in pleasant memories of the past was no way, she realized, to solve anything. Men were after her, and she had to figure out why. Well, actually she knew why. Obviously they wanted the books back. But how had they tracked her down so quickly? And why did they kill Gruber? No, that's not right. They thought *she* had killed Gruber. She hadn't. If they hadn't, and she knew that she hadn't, who had?

Something strange was going on and Jennifer was caught in the middle of it. She suppressed a shiver. Suddenly the sunlight wasn't as warm. The people around her didn't seem as innocent. Kien's men had tracked her to the Happy Hocker. They could very well track her here. Any one of these "Dodger fans" sitting around her could be a killer.

She glanced around and froze when her worst fear seemed to be confirmed. Out of the corner of her eye she saw the dark-haired man who had been watching her in the ticket line. He was sitting two rows behind her and to her right. He was pretending to be looking at his scorecard, but he was also surreptitiously studying her.

He could be the killer. At the very least he must be an agent of Kien's. Jennifer looked firmly ahead. What to do? She could, of course, go to the police. But then she'd have to admit that she was Wraith, the daring thief who'd made the front page of even the staid *New York Times*. They could probably protect her from Kien's men, but she'd end up doing hard time for the string of burglaries she'd committed.

She clenched her teeth as she saw from the corner of her eye that the man was moving toward her.

What to do? What to do? The frantic refrain ran through her mind, keeping pace with the pounding of her racing heart. Nothing, she told herself. Be calm. Do nothing. Deny everything. He can't do anything to me with all these people around.

Darryl Strawberry, the young right fielder obtained two years ago in a trade with the lowly Cubs, was putting on a show in the batting cage. Everyone's eyes were on him as he whacked balls into and over the bleachers in right, left, and center field. No one was looking at her and the man.

Fear knotted her insides as he set a large hand lightly on her shoulder and said, in an unexpectedly soft voice, "Wraith," and she utterly and totally panicked at his use of her alias and ghosted, leaving him with an astonished look on his face as he stared at her pants and shoes lying in a crumpled heap before her bleacher seat, and holding her shirt in his right hand.

She heard him blurt "Wait!" and then she was gone, sinking through the structure of the bleachers like a stone ghost.

An officious security officer waved the limo to a position behind the bunting-hung stands. Riggs opened the door, and his expression gave new meaning to cat and canary. Tachyon, his color already heightened by her ministrations and the heat of the day, turned an even more fiery red, and said in an urgent undertone, "We will be leaving as soon as my speech is over."

"Very good, Doctor. Will we then be going to Ebbets Field as planned?"

"No!" Tachyon added something explosive in his own language, and, tucking Roulette's arm beneath his, escorted her up the back stairs and onto the stands. A large group of dignitaries were already assembled in a semicircle around the podium. She saw Hartmann looking peevish while the mayor of New York hung over the back of his chair and agitated for support for his upcoming gubernatorial race. The ace in the white jumpsuit, hood now thrown back, hovered solicitously nearby. He was staring glassily into the crowd at a nubile teenager whose breasts strained at her halter top, and Roulette noticed that his face didn't quite come together. The eyes weren't quite level, and the nose seemed to blossom like a wisted tuber above a too-small mouth and chin. He looked like an artist's clay model the artist had gotten bored with before completing the bust.

Seated in the second row of chairs was a distinguished-looking Oriental. Periodically he jotted quick notes in a leather-bound book, and Roulette noticed that the gold fountain pen left a trail of gold ink. She made a face over the affectation, considering how often money did not translate into class or taste. The man's dark eyes lifted from the book, and stared with frightened intensity at a silver-haired man whose tailoring screamed "lawyer." This man seemed to be looking for an opening to interrupt the unending flow from Koch and speak to Hartmann.

At the far end of the front row sat a major rock-and-roll figure whose "Joker Aid" concerts had raised several million dollars—none of which had yet reached Jokertown. Roulette gave a cynical smile. From her days at the UN she knew in just how many ways money could be channeled and skimmed. Tachyon and his clinic would be lucky if they ever saw $10,000. . . .

Her thoughts drew up short. The Takisian's voice penetrated her black study. "Roulette, here."

She glanced about confused, focused on the folding metal chair, seated herself.

"My God, Mrs. Brown-Roxbury! What are you doing here?" She stared into Senator Hartmann's pale brown eyes. He gave an embarrassed cough. "Oh damn, that sounded rather rude, didn't it? I'm just so surprised and delighted to see you. Mr. Love told me you had left the UN, and I was sorry to hear it."

"The UN? What is this talk of the UN? You worked there?" broke in Tachyon. "Senator, good to see you." The men shook hands across her.

Roulette opened her mouth, and shut it again as Hartmann took over the conversation for her. "Yes, Mrs. Brown-Roxbury was an economist with the United Nations Development Program."

"Not that we ever managed to develop a damn thing," she replied mechanically.

Hartmann laughed. "That's my Roulette. You always did give 'em hell up there."

"Mrs.?"

"Don't panic, I'm divorced."

Hartmann went nattering on about the "wonderful work being done by the IMF and the World Bank" while overhead the striped awning, erected to give some relief from the sun, snapped and popped in the wind. It created an odd punctuation to his sentences.

"Yes," *pop* "the electrification pro" *snap* "ject in Zaire is a" *pop* "classic example of the fine work. . . ."

A discreet cough interrupted the flow. "Senator."

"Yes, what is it?"

"St. John Latham, with Latham, Strauss." Latham leaned in close, his pale eyes expressionless. "My client." A hand indicated the Oriental gentleman, and Hartmann slewed around to look.

"General Kien, how the hell are you? I didn't see you come sneaking up here. You should have said something."

Kien slid the notebook into his coat pocket, rose, and shook the senator's outstretched hand. "I didn't wish to disturb you."

"Nonsense, I always have time for one of my staunchest supporters."

Latham's pale, expressionless eyes shifted to Kien, back to the senator. "That being the case, Senator. . . . The general has suffered a severe loss this morning. Several very valuable books of stamps were stolen from his safe, and the police are having little success in recovering them." The lawyer eyed Tachyon, but the alien showed no inclination to move. With a shrug he continued. "In fact, they don't seem to give a damn. I pressed them, and was told that given the other problems attendant on Wild Card Day they haven't got time to worry about a simple burglary."

"Outrageous. I'm afraid I don't have a lot of pull with New York's finest, nor would I want to tread on Mayor Koch's territory." A quick smile to the mayor still hovering hopefully on the outskirts of the conversation. Hartmann's eyes slid thoughtfully across the ace. "Still. . . . Allow me to offer you Mr. Ray, my faithful Justice Department watchdog."

Kien tensed, and exchanged a glance with his expressionless attorney. Roulette wondered if the lawyer's face ever displayed anything other than cold calculation.

"That would be fine—"

"Sir," Ray interrupted. "My job is to guard you, and meaning no offense, you're a hell of a lot more important than some stamps."

"Thank you for your concern, Billy, but your job is whatever the hell I tell you it is, and I'm telling you to help Mr. Latham." The senator didn't seem so charming now. The ace shrugged and capitulated.

"Thank you, Senator," Kien murmured softly, and he and Latham faded back through the chairs, drawing Billy Ray with them.

"Now, where were we?" The smile was pinned firmly back into place. "Oh, I remember, talking about your tremendous contributions."

Roulette pressed her shoulder urgently against Tachyon's, with a display of that disconcerting sensitivity he understood.

"Ah, Senator, I see someone with whom I must speak. Adieu for the moment. Madam, will you walk?" He rose, offered his arm to Roulette, and they moved quickly to the other side of the stand.

A tide of humanity lapped at the edge of the stand, and stretched away in a great undulating wave, filling the square before Jetboy's Tomb. Behind them loomed the tomb itself, huge flanged wings reaching to heaven. Through the tall narrow windows she could see the full-size replica of the JB-1 suspended from the ceiling. And out front the twenty-foot-tall Jetboy stared aloofly over the heads of the crowd.

"Curious little drama we witnessed," remarked Tachyon.

"Yes."

He leaned back, looking up at her. "And you don't like the senator. Why?"

"Because I suspect he has an interest in the companies backing that multi-million-dollar boondoggle he was discussing with such relish."

"It sounded like it would help the people in Zaire."

"Hardly. It's been designed so no power can be siphoned off to provide services to the people living along its 1,100-mile line. It's basically a billion-dollar project to give money to that thug Mobutu, and to line the pockets of various large international corporations, and to make vast amounts of money in the form of interest for a number of large Western banks. It does fuck-all for the people of Zaire who will continue to live at a subsistence level despite one of the greatest repositories of mineral wealth on the continent."

"Roulette, you're wonderful."

She spun to face him. "If you're about to tell me how beautiful I am when I'm in a passion I'll slug you off this stand!"

He held up his hands. "No, no, I do admire the passion, and you are very beautiful, but you care, you're so interested . . . you remind me of another woman." The rather tangled sentence trailed away, and he seemed to be looking at some picture that had nothing to do with the holiday crowds that stretched away before them.

Roulette, staring idly out, suddenly gasped as the shadow of a pterodactyl rippled over the people. She glanced up, and sure enough, a pterodactyl was winging its way toward them. Tachyon, alerted by her indrawn breath, sighed, and made shooing motions with his hands. The prehistoric creature came on, the alien grabbed her about the waist, and pulled her back beneath the awning just as several small pterodactyl turds pattered onto the stand.

"Kid," Tachyon shouted. "Next time I catch you I'm going to beat you."

Koch was beckoning, so they returned to their chairs. Ten minutes later a cute-faced kid with several inexpertly covered pimples on his chin, and dressed in jeans and a T-shirt, wiggled through the front row of the crowd, and waved impudently up at the Takisian.

"Hey, Tachy, here I am."

"Well, at least you're dressed."

"I thought ahead. Left my clothes in the plane." A hand shot out indicating the tomb. "Thought you were going to beat me."

"I may yet."

"Bet you can't."

Koch was tapping the mike with a forefinger, sending booming, thrumming pops echoing across the square. Roulette, glancing between boy and alien, saw the human's eyes widen in alarm. Tachyon, with a guilty glance to Koch, darted to the edge of the stand. The Kid turned, bent, and obligingly presented his posterior to the doctor, who gave him a quick but gentle kick in the seat.

"Kid, stay out of trouble."

"No fair. Disgusting Alien Powers Used to Abuse Little Kid," he said in a tone indicative of a headline from the *National Informer.*

"Juvenile Delinquent Uses Ace Powers to Aggravate City."

"Aggravate? Can't I at least terrorize?"

"Maybe when you're older." Koch was glaring at the pair. "Now shoo. I have to be dignified now."

"Good luck." And with a flip of the hand he vanished back into the crowd.

"Who is he?"

"Kid Dinosaur. He's very bright, but unfortunately at that awkward age between boy and man which means he's something of a monster. He drives the aces mad for he's always underfoot. It must be very trying to his parents to be raising an ace, but children are such a delight–"

"Hey, you're on," Roulette said, interrupting the babble.

"Oh, by the Ideal, thank you." Leaning in close he said with a wink, "And then we can leave."

She thought he presented a rather comic figure. Tiny little man, head just topping the podium, red satin suit, and long red hair like a punk Lord Fauntleroy. She noticed that he had no notes, and wondered if an extemporaneous speech was quite wise. Then he lifted his head, and began, and comedy was replaced by dignity, and a wealth of caring.

"I always find it a little difficult to think what to say on this day. Are we celebrating, and if so what? Or are we honoring and remembering? And if so who do we honor, and what do we remember as a guard against future mistakes? You will hear a great deal today about Jetboy, and the Turtle, and Cyclone, and a hundred other aces," He waved at the great green shell where it hovered over the crowd. "And yes, even about me. But I don't think that's fair, and I'm going to talk about other people. About Shiner, who gave a home to an abandoned child, and Jubel, who can always spare a dime for some other joker down on his luck, and Des, who's done more to get parks built and schools improved in Jokertown than any other person.

"I speak about the jokers because I think they can offer a lesson and an example to other people. Their sufferings, mental, physical, and emotional, match anything experienced in human history, and they've tried a number of methods to cope with their isolation ranging from quiet fortitude as they were abused by police, and other public officials, to violence culminating in the events of 1976, and now a new approach. A sense of self-reliance, and sharing that has allowed them to build, within the confines of our so-called Jokertown, a true community.

"I point out the various accomplishments of these remarkable people because there is a new mood in this country which I find fearsome. There is once again an attempt to delineate what is 'American,' to despise and discriminate against those who exist on the periphery of this fairy-tale 'majority.' And it is a fairy tale. Each person is an utterly unique individual. There is no 'consensus of opinion,' no 'right way' to do things. There are only people who, no matter how hideous and twisted on the outside, are internally driven by the same hopes and dreams and aspirations that drive all of us.

"I suppose what I really want to say on this Wild Card Day, 1986 is 'Be kind.' For adversity comes from many sources, not just from alien virus brought across light-years, and there may come a time when all of us, 'nats,' 'aces,' and jokers alike, will need that kind word, that offer of help, that sense of community that the jokers so wonderfully represent. Thank you."

The applause was thunderous, but Tachyon looked unhappy as he walked back to her.

"Very noble, but how do you think it will play?" Roulette asked as he scooped his hat off the chair.

Her arm was once more pulled through his, and he urged her toward the back stairs. "Some people will compare me to Mother Theresa, and others will say I am a self-serving son of a bitch."

"And you, what do you say?"

"That I'm neither. Just a man trying to live with honor, and to embrace whatever happiness is given me." They were standing by the limo, and Tachyon suddenly wrapped his arms about her waist, and buried his face in her bosom. "And I'm glad you are here to be embraced."

Furiously she cast him off, and backed away until brought up short by the back of the car. "Don't look to me for comfort. I have none for anybody. I told you that already. And what do you need it for, anyway? You're the saint of Jokertown. The big shot with a private limo, as much a star as any of the aces."

"Yes, yes, and yes! But I am also consumed with guilt, devoured by a failure that gathers every year on September fifteenth to haunt me! God, how I hate this day." His fists slammed onto the top of the car, and Riggs drifted away to stare in fascination at the cuff of his uniform coat. Tachyon's shoulders shook for several seconds, then he dashed a hand across his eyes, and turned back to face her. "All right, you have no comfort for me. I accept that. You said you were on a pilgrimage of despair. So am I. So let us at least journey together, and if we can't comfort we can at least share."

"Fine." She climbed into the car, and rested her head against the window.

And maybe I can do something. I can free you from your guilt, and by destroying you perhaps find my own peace.

Jennifer pulled herself through an endless expanse of concrete and steel, looking for a place where she could solidify and take a much-needed breather. She felt lightheaded, even for a specter, and it was getting hard to concentrate. She had an overwhelming urge to simply drift, to float disembodied like a cloud and forget all her worries, all the danger that was dogging her footsteps like a snarling Doberman.

But she couldn't give in to that urge. If she did she'd lose all being and become an attenuated will-o'-the-wisp, floating mindlessly until the random forces of Brownian movement scattered her to all corners of the Earth.

It was hard to work up the urgency to make herself move faster, but Jennifer succeeded, pulling herself through the last of the bleacher supports. She found herself in a carpeted corridor lit by overhead fluorescent lamps, and immediately solidified and leaned shakily against the corridor wall. She still felt distant and disoriented and her head swam with vertigo. It had been close, but she'd solidified in time. She realized that she had to be careful about using her powers for a time, until she was certain that her system hadn't been overtaxed.

Now, Jennifer thought, if she could only orient herself, she'd get the hell out. The only problem was, she'd never been in the bowels of Ebbets Field before, and she had no idea where she was.

There was a double door at one end of the corridor. In the opposite direction the corridor branched. She had to go one way or the other, and Jennifer chose the doors. Unfortunately they were blank, with no windows set in them.

Well, she thought, if anyone questioned her she'd simply say she'd gotten lost. Although why she was wearing only a bikini might be hard to explain.

She took a deep breath, let it out noisily, and pushed the doors open. She took a step into a large, well-lit, richly carpeted room, and froze. The murmur of a dozen conversations gradually died down as all eyes in the room turned toward her.

I don't believe it, she told herself. She closed her eyes, but when she opened them a moment later everyone was still there, staring. I don't believe I just walked into the Dodgers' locker room.

Twenty men were in the room. Some were playing cards in small groups, some were talking. Hernandez, the first baseman, was sitting by his locker doing his customary pregame crossword puzzle. Pete Reiser himself, sixtyish, gray-haired but still lean and arrow straight, was standing in front of Seaver's locker, talking with the pitcher and the Dodgers' Cuban pitching coach, Fidel Castro. Some of the players still had their practice jerseys on, some had started to change to their game uniforms. Some hadn't gotten very far in the change.

Jennifer, feeling the pressure of all those eyes on her, felt she should say something, but when she opened her mouth no words would come.

"Uh . . ." She tried again. "Uh . . . good luck today."

A small metallic snuff box slipped out of the hand of Thurman Munson, veteran Dodger catcher and team captain, and the sudden sound it made as it clattered against the stool in front of his locker broke the spell that seemed to hold everyone.

A dozen players spoke at once, from Reiser's strident, "How the hell did you get in here?" to half a dozen variations on, "Jeez, nice body" and "Great outfit."

Jennifer, mortified, forgot her earlier worries and ghosted through the nearest wall into a small room with a drug cabinet, a couple of empty padded tables, a bunch of incomprehensible machines, and a dripping Dwight Gooden climbing naked out of the whirlpool.

"Hey!" he said as she went by.

"Great game yesterday," Jennifer said, smiling weakly. He slid back into the whirlpool, ducking down so the water came up to his chin, and stared in disbelief as she passed though the wall next to the whirlpool.

Great body, too, Jennifer told herself, sneaking a final peek before she vanished.

As a capo working for Rosemary's father, Don Carlo Gambione, Don Frederico "the Butcher" Macellaio had once ordered Bagabond's death. Bagabond had not forgotten. Standing beside an oak in a nearly deserted Central Park, she started toward Central Park West and was glad most of New York appeared to be down at Jetboy's Tomb. She felt conspicuous in the brown tweed business suit and high heels she'd scavenged from one of her subterranean stashes. But this way none of the normal denizens of the park could possibly recognize her. A few of the street people had seen too much over the years; it was best to be . . . discreet. She slid her aching left foot out of the shoe and stood, weight on her right leg, as she watched Don Frederico exit his exclusive apartment building. The sheltering canopy said The Luxor. Dressed in an expensively tailored black suit, the Butcher crossed the sidewalk to a white Cadillac stretch limousine.

He was flanked by two guards in dark glasses and unbuttoned suit jackets. Getting into the car, Don Frederico snatched the door out of his chauffeur's hand and slammed it. The driver paused for a fraction of a second before turning sharply around and getting into the car. One of the guards got into the front seat beside the driver, while the other appeared to scan the sidewalk and Central Park West in both directions.

The limousine pulled out and crossed against horn-blowing traffic to enter the park at the West Drive. With disbelief, Rosemary had once told her about the don's habits. It was always the same route. The don was either very stupid or very self-assured. A show of power. Knowing the limo would drive across the Transverse, then exit onto 65th and cruise past Temple Emanu-El to the Butcher's favorite restaurant, Aronica's, Bagabond walked at an oblique angle through the park. She mentally summoned a flock of pigeons and nearly a hundred squirrels. They waited at the stone bridge near the middle of the drive.

As Bagabond walked across the park to meet them, a

large gray cat, one of the black's and calico's offspring, dropped out of a lightning-warped maple tree to block her path.

The gray was one of the few kittens at least as intelligent as his parents. He had refused to join Bagabond's group of animals when he understood how Bagabond used the creatures to her advantage, sometimes without caring about the effect on the animals' lives. The gray had chosen to live apart in a section of Central Park Bagabond used only infrequently. He resented her presence.

Now Bagabond told him she would not be there long. The cat imaged dead bodies scattered across the landscape. Bagabond stiffened and told him to leave her. He turned and trotted a few yards away, before he turned and spat at her. She reached out with her mind to attack, but stopped before she burned out his brain. The gray disappeared into a stand of maples. Clenching her fists, Bagabond stood watching the cat.

Then she was abruptly aware of the progress of the don's car. A peregrine, escaped from a would-be urban falconer, was Bagabond's eye, following the Butcher's car as it cruised through the park. There were no colors, but the perception of movement caught her consciousness as the falcon's eyes roamed across the park. She brought him gliding back around to follow the Butcher's car. According to Rosemary's file, Don Frederico Macellaio used this daily drive to order the deaths of his opponents from his armored, surveillance-proof car. Bagabond leaned back against a broad tree trunk, kicked off her shoes, and concentrated on directing her animals.

As she began the mental routine of organizing and directing the birds and animals she had summoned, Bagabond realized that the gray was hiding among the maples and observing her. She warned him off, but he responded with an image of himself marking the trees to show his territory. She ignored him as the don's car drew closer to the spot she had chosen.

She found she was nervous at the car's approach. The gray had broken her concentration. He had a gift for making her think in ways she normally avoided. The Butcher was Rosemary's enemy as well as her own. She had learned from the animals themselves to kill or be killed. The Butcher was a threat that had to be removed. Besides, it would please Rosemary. It was obvious to Bagabond that Rosemary was too worried about too many things. Her concern with the Gambiones had become consuming. With a new don, she could relax and spend more time with Bagabond. Bagabond wanted that enough to disturb the rhythms and lives of her creatures. *To kill them.*

She closed the gray out of her mind and sent *pain* down the connection joining them. The gray yowled as she felt the energy hit him.

The part of her mind that was organizing the birds had completed that task. The flocks of pigeons temporarily roosted in the trees around the bridge. For an instant, there was an unnatural stillness.

Breaking out of the trees, gleaming as the sun hit the finish, the limousine proceeded around the corner on its stately way. The mirrored windshield reflected the tree branches overhead.

A lone pigeon wheeled free of the flock and, at Bagabond's command, sent itself soaring high into the sky. Then it hurled itself down at the limousine's windshield as though intending to land on one of the phantom trees. Blood splattered the white paint of the hood. The driver braked and seemed to hesitate for an instant before continuing.

Bagabond watched the scene in fragments seen through the eyes of the hawk now behind the car and the pigeons above and before the limousine. Her own eyes were wide and staring, but the other visions overwhelmed her human sight. She damped the pain of the pigeon in the same way she removed from her consciousness the constant deaths she normally experienced.

Overhead, a hundred birds stopped cooing as she took them over completely. The avian wave swept down toward the car, covering it in a cloak of blood and feathers. The limousine's brakes shrieked as the driver attempted a panic-stop before his blindness wrecked the car.

Keeping more of the pigeons in reserve, Bagabond shifted her attention to the hordes of squirrels gathered in the lower branches of the oaks and maples lining the road. As she directed a battalion of squirrels toward the swerving car, pain careened across her own mind. Her first thought was that either the black or the calico was in trouble. But tracing their individual patterns within her awareness of the city's wild ones told her that the cats were well. *The gray.* He deliberately was inflicting pain on himself, trying to destroy her concentration. Bagabond reprimanded him mentally, sending waves of emotional chill, stunning his rebellion.

Only a few seconds had passed. But the driver was close to regaining control when the roadway become a moving carpet of squirrels. The driver had accelerated to escape the birds. Bagabond sent the animals under the wheels of the car. The shrieks of the dying squirrels mixed with the sound of abused brakes. The heavy car's momentum carried it across the massed rodents. Their blood greased the road and the limousine skidded sideways. Now the doors and side panels were streaked and spattered with blood.

Bagabond's head snapped to the side as feedback from the gray flooded her mind. This time he was not satisfied with distraction; now he tried to disperse the animals, using Bagabond as a focus. Her anger streamed out, knocking him unconscious. She might have killed him, but her attention was needed at the bridge.

The driver had overcorrected for the skid and sent the car into a spin. The right wheels struck the low guardrail, bending it out. The mass of the car's armor-plate sent it crashing through the retaining wall and over the side. Streaks of white paint remained on the metal and concrete. One wheel cover was slung free. It preceded the limousine over the edge, skimming slowly through the air like a Frisbee. The automobile wasn't so fortunate.

Time, for Bagabond, seemed to stop as she watched the car roll over in the air. One part of her was ending the lives of the birds and squirrels injured in the attack. Another part considered the murder and wondered if it was worth the cost to help a friend and take revenge.

The vehicle plunged to the jogging path. It landed hard on the concrete trail, crushing the roof of the passenger compartment flush with the body. The car rocked to a halt and burst into a *whuffing* ball of flame.

Sacrificing a few animals to feed others had been nothing compared to this carnage she saw as she looked around at the bridge. Bodies were scattered everywhere. She felt a pain she had not experienced since first learning to distance the lives of her animals from her own. Maybe the gray had been right to attempt to stop her. The side of her mind she considered human was happy for her success, eager to find out Rosemary's reaction. The animal side wanted to reject what she had done.

Abruptly, Bagabond realized that the remaining creatures waited patiently for her instructions. The dark cloud of pigeons rose into the sky and dispersed in all directions. No one saw the undulating mass of squirrels break apart and run for the wooded sections of the park. Bagabond was already hidden by the trees and walking toward the subway entrance at Columbus Circle.

Before she could cross 59th Street, the recovered gray confronted her with the image of what she had done, an image that changed into a picture of *her* lying bloody and broken on the ground.

Bagabond paused, staggered by the final realization of what she had done. This was not an occasional sacrifice for food or her own protection. She had used the animals she had always protected, in her own war, to achieve a goal that had meaning only to her. She had betrayed a trust she had held since she came back from the hospital. Bagabond felt sick. It was not the gray's doing. She hoped Rosemary was worth it.

Rosemary waited, if unknowingly. Before checking in with her, Bagabond would go by Jack's home to check for messages about his missing niece, Cordelia. Maybe now there would be time to help him.

Bagabond walked down the steps into the subway station and used one of the tokens the raccoon had proved so adept at stealing. Taking the Number 1 local downtown, she ignored the admiring glances she attracted from her male fellow passengers.

CHAPTER 8

1:00 p.m.

The street was still crowded with late-arriving fans, souvenir sellers, and ticket scalpers. Somehow Jennifer managed to slip through the outer wall of the stadium without anyone noticing, but on the street she attracted a fair amount of attention. Heads turned and wolf whistles followed her down the street, but she barely noticed. She moved quickly, watching out for the men who had tried to grab her in the Happy Hocker and the man who had followed her into the stadium, but none of them seemed to be around. She spotted an empty taxi, flagged it down and told the driver, "Manhattan."

She settled down to think as the taxi carried her back to more familiar territory. Events around her were moving with incomprehensible speed and violence. Kien must really want his stamps back, she thought. Unless it was the other book . . .

She glanced at her purse, a small leather bag closed by

a simple drawstring. It had the stolen books and a few dollars she carried for emergencies like this, but nothing else. No wallet, no identification. The whole thing was going sour. Feeling eyes upon her, she looked up into the mirror and caught the cab driver staring at her. He looked away and Jennifer tried to sink further back into the stained and worn upholstery of the cab's back seat. She had to find some decent clothes somewhere. As it was she looked as if she were dressed for a Rio de Janeiro carnival.

Maybe, she thought, she'd better call it all off and return the books. They'd already cost Gruber his life—though for the life of her she couldn't figure out who had killed him—and given her a few too many close brushes with violence.

She'd have to contact Kien. That'd be easy, but the details of the exchange might be tricky to work out. Also, she didn't want to come out of this thing entirely empty-handed.

She looked out the window of the cab pensively, and, struck by sudden inspiration, called out, "Stop, stop right here!"

The driver took her at her word and slammed on the brakes, bringing the taxi to a screeching halt. She could hear tires squeal behind them as she leaped out and tossed some crumpled bills onto the front seat.

"Thanks," she said breathlessly, and turned and ran up the street.

"My pleasure," the cabbie said with a bemused expression, watching her bikini-clad form with appreciation as she ran up to the front of the Famous Bowery Wild Card Dime Museum.

"Jack! Jack, it is you, am I not right?"

A familiar voice, *any* familiar voice in the Village's circus atmosphere today was a shock. Jack turned and saw a handsome man, half a head taller than he, looking down at him.

"Hello, Jean-Jacques," Jack said. Jean-Jacques had arrived from Senegal six years ago. He worked part of the time as a waiter at the Simba on Sixth Avenue at Eighth, and the rest of the time as a tutor for foreign students learning English at the New School. Jack had never seen a man with more striking features. "Listen," he said to the other. "I need some help." He took out Cordelia's snapshot.

Jean-Jacques nodded, but seemed distracted. "Anything, my friend. Anything at all."

Jack knew there was something wrong. "What is it?"

"Nothing to be of concern." Jean-Jacques looked away toward the pedestrians moving briskly past them. The early afternoon sun shone on his skin so that the deep black shone almost blue.

"I doubt that." Jack put a hand on the man's shoulder, conscious of the warm vitality radiating through the bright pattern. "Tell me."

Jean-Jacques looked back at Jack, his penetrating gaze meeting Jack's eyes. "It is the retrovirus," he said. "It is the killer. I have just been to see my doctor. The diagnosis was unfortunately positive." He sighed. "Quite positive."

"Retrovirus?" said Jack. "You mean the wild card—"

"No." Jean-Jacques interrupted him. "The surer killer." The word seemed to stick in his throat. "AIDS."

"Mother of Jesus," said Jack. "I am sorry." He started closer to Jean-Jacques, caught himself for just a second, then went ahead and embraced the man. "I'm very sorry."

Jean-Jacques gently pushed Jack away. "I understand,"

he said simply. "You are not the first I have told. Already they are treating me like one of the damnable jokers." He shut his eyes sadly, then opened them and said, "Don't worry, old friend. You are all right. I know who it was." He shut his eyes again. "And I know *when* it was." His head began to shake slightly and Jack again embraced him. This time, Jean-Jacques did not push him immediately away.

"I think you are on a mission," Jean-Jacques said. "Tell me what you are seeking, and if I can help, I shall."

Jack hesitated, then told him about Cordelia. The Senegalese inspected the photograph. "A very beautiful young lady." He glanced at Jack. "You share the same eyes." Then he handed back the picture. "Go," he said. "Continue your search. As I said, if I observe anything that could be of use to you, I will let you know."

There was nothing more to say, but Jack remained there beside Jean-Jacques.

"Go," Jean-Jacques repeated. He smiled slightly. "Good fortune." Then he turned on his heel and was gone.

"This is your important stop?" Roulette asked, eyeing the decaying wall of a riverfront warehouse. Tachyon had dismissed Riggs several blocks away, and a brisk sweat-raising walk had ended here.

He glanced back over his shoulder as his slender hands opened the large shiny padlock. His expression was one of suppressed excitement and mischief, rather like a little boy about to show off his collection of tadpoles. And she suddenly realized that he *was* very young. Because of mutation and their obsession with the life sciences, the Takisian life span was vastly longer than the human. Tachyon at eightysomething was a graybeard by Earth standards, but only verging on manhood by Takisian norms. It explained a lot.

The door swung open on well-oiled hinges, and he waved her through. Her sharp retreat brought her up hard against his chest.

"Don't be afraid."

"My God, what?" She glanced cautiously at the glowing monstrosity squatting in the center of the empty, echoing room. It looked rather like a wentletrap seashell, but the tips of its gray spines were set with glowing amber and purple lights. It also seemed to be resting in a glittering whirlpool, for dust was spiraling in toward the creature.

"The ship."

"What?"

"Your ship," she amended quickly.

"Yes, *Baby.*"

"Baby?"

"Uh huh." Tachyon's lilac eyes rested lovingly on the ship, and Roulette's shields (painstakingly erected by the Astronomer) responded to a nearby telepathic communication.

"She's frustrated. She tried to say hello to you, but you have shields." He cocked his head to one side, seriously regarding her. "Strange. Most humans . . ." A quick shake of the head. "Well, come inside."

"I . . . I'd rather not."

"She won't hurt you."

"It's not that."

"What then?"

She hunched her shoulders and walked toward the ship, though it felt like a betrayal. Sometime early tomorrow morning the Astronomer would seize this living vessel, and pilot her far away.

The ship obligingly opened her lock, and they entered the control room. The inner walls and floor of the ship glowed like polished mother-of-pearl, casting opalescent light across the large canopy bed that dominated the room. Tachyon chuckled.

"Your expression is priceless. You see, unlike most of my kind I vowed I would die in bed. This seemed to be a way to ensure it."

The rest of the furniture had a fragile beauty, and it was clear from the width of the chair seats that Takisians were smaller than humans. Unless this furniture had been made for Tachyon's personal use.

The alien took her gently by the shoulders, and indicated the wall. Flowing silver script gleamed.

Greetings, Roolete.

Tachyon smiled, and shook his head.

Roulette.

"Her spelling isn't so good yet. She just started this when I had some other friends aboard. She's picking up a knowledge of written English by a low-level drain. I'm indulgent so I let her get away with it."

"It's unbelievable."

She seated herself on the bed while Tachyon unearthed a pair of crystal goblets from a chest which seemed to be an extrusion of the ship herself.

Another message flitted across the wall while the alien's back was turned.

You are honored. There was something peevish about the message.

"Cut it out, Baby," warned Tachyon.

Apology.

"Accepted," Roulette said, feeling like an idiot.

Tachyon splashed a dollop of brandy into each glass

from his hip flask. Two bright spots of color were burning on his cheeks. "You are the first woman I've ever brought here. So she is curious, hopeful, and a little resentful."

"She loves you."

"Yes, and I her." He brushed his palm across one curving wall.

"Why hopeful?" She took a sip of cognac.

"Despite being a little jealous she wants to see me marry, and sire children. Pedigree, continuance, is very important to the ships. Over the centuries they've absorbed our obsession with ancestor worship, and she considers me a failure. I keep telling her I have a lot of time left. Especially since I now live on Earth." He joined her on the bed.

"I've read a great deal about you, but I've never seen this mentioned. Of course it's logical you would have a ship, how else would you have gotten here?"

"I try to keep it very quiet. When I was trying to recover her from the government I raised a great to-do about *Baby*. Now I'm more cautious, and fortunately people's memories are short. Unfortunately she gets lonely so I come as often as I can. She misses her own kind too. They are essentially herd creatures, and this kind of isolation is not good for her."

"Why don't you live in her, then?"

"I want a social life, and I also want to keep her secret. Those two goals rather conflict. So I compromise. I live nearby, I visit often, and sometimes I take her out. According to Sister Magdalene at the South Street mission I'm doing a positive service. She's had several derelicts take the pledge after spotting us."

She laughed, leaned down, and kissed him where he reclined against the cushions. He caught the top button of her blouse in trembling fingers, and from the corner of her eye she could see his erection straining at the satin material of his breeches. She jerked away, and swiftly rebuttoned her blouse.

"I'm sorry, but I thought you . . . we–"

"Not here! I couldn't perform with an audience." She also wondered what would be the ship's reaction if she killed Tachyon within *Baby*'s skin. Roulette doubted she'd leave the ship alive.

The Famous Bowery Wild Card Dime Museum (Admission Only $2) was closed, probably because its manager realized that most people would be taking advantage of the day's free entertainment.

That was, Jennifer thought, just fine. She went down a side alley and, making sure no one was watching, slipped through the wall. It was difficult. It took some moments of concentration and then she had to fight her way through the brickwork as if she were solid and the bricks were a viscous, unyielding liquid. Her body was getting tired and she knew that she shouldn't ghost for a while, but she had to get this done and then maybe she could think about resting.

She finally made it through and found herself in a small dark room with a series of dimly glowing glass bottles set along one wall like a bank of aquariums in a pet store. Floating in the tanks were pathetic little corpses, little embalmed "Monstrous Joker Babies" as the sign above the exhibit proclaimed. There were maybe thirty of them. Most had little of humanity about them and Jennifer was thankful, in a way, that they had experienced for so short a time the cruelty of the world.

She hurried from the room and found herself in the section of the museum devoted to large displays that were life-sized dioramas. It was eerily quiet and dark with the displays' lighting and sound effects turned off, and quite disconcerting to be the only living thing about.

She went by a scene depicting Jokertown burning, commemorating, as it were, the Great Jokertown Riot of 1976. There was, now only mildly shocking to modern tastes, an older tableau showing a purported Jokertown orgy. A sign in front of a curtained-off area said to watch for the latest addition to the entertaining yet informative displays, Earth vs. The Swarm.

Jennifer went on past the dioramas into the long hallway beyond and entered the museum's Hall of Fame, or, in some instances, Infamy.

Lifelike wax figures of prominent aces and jokers clustered in groups or stood alone in the hallway. Jetboy looked young and handsome, his scarf blowing out behind him in an unfelt, perhaps divine wind, his eyes squinting slightly as if he were staring into a gentle sun. The Four Aces—Black Eagle, Brain Trust, the Envoy, and Golden Boy—stood in a group, three of them together, one isolated by the slightly turned backs, the slightly averted faces of his fellow aces. Dr. Tachyon was resplendent in an outfit that a small card at his feet said had been donated by him to the museum. And there were others. Peregrine maintaining, Jennifer had to admit, her smoldering sensuality even when graven in wax, Cyclone, Hiram Worchester's astonishing bulk apparently floating lightly over his pedestal, Chrysalis with invisible flesh and visible organs caged by her skeleton . . .

Jennifer looked them over carefully. Tachyon, she decided, would be the one. She stepped over the velvet rope and approached the waxen statue. She towered over it by half a foot and its waxen features were as delicate as her own. Moved by an irresistible impulse, she ran her hand down the rich fabric of his peach-colored waistcoat. It had a fine, soft feel to it. She could almost believe that the card was telling the truth and the outfit had once belonged to Tachyon himself.

She caught herself and looked around guiltily. The hallway, of course, was deserted. She summoned all her will, reached out, and put the bag through the chest of the wax figure. She withdrew her hand and left the bag snug in Tachyon's chest, the two stockbooks of stamps and the mysterious volume safely hidden away until her return.

Now she had to get in touch with Kien. It might take some doing. She couldn't simply look him up in the phone book.

She left the Hall of Fame with one last jealous glance at the Peregrine figure, pondering her next move. She never noticed the eye watching from a curtained doorway at the other end of the hallway.

The worst of it, Fortunato thought, was having to listen to the goddamned politicians. There were a dozen of them on stage, including Mayor Koch and Senator Hartmann. Tachyon, the bastard, was already gone, cozied up to a gorgeous black woman with plaited hair.

Hartmann was at the podium. "The time has come for acceptance. A time for peace, as the biblical poet said. Not only for peace between nations, but peace within ourselves. A time to look into our own hearts, human and joker and ace alike. A time not to *forget* the past, but to be able to look back at it and say, this is where I have been, and I am not ashamed. But my duty now is to the future. Thank you very much."

A police helicopter circled overhead. As Fortunato glanced up he saw the Turtle's shell float slowly over the park and then pass out of sight again.

Fortunato knew roughly where the kid was. This close to him he could get a vague image of what the kid saw, and he could triangulate off Hartmann as he sat down at the edge of the stage.

There. Fifteen or twenty yards away, wearing clothes, for once, which meant he'd come in his human form and stayed that way. The kid slouched against a light pole, a good fifteen or twenty feet away from an older version of himself, clearly his father.

The kid looked around at all the suits and high heels as they offered Hartmann dignified, minimal applause. One side of his mouth turned up in disgust. Fortunato knew how the kid felt. Maybe once there'd been some sincere feeling in these ceremonies, but now it was a case of the bored leading the boring. Nobody came to self-serving political speeches except the people who needed to be seen there, the ones making some kind of political statement themselves by showing up.

And those few who really did care. The starstruck kids who still had some illusions about personal power, who still believed in that sharp, clean line between good and evil and wanted to wage war across it.

Fortunato saw the wild card as a kind of Aladdin's lamp of the unconscious. The virus rewrote DNA to match what it read in the back of the mind. If your luck was bad it transcribed a nightmare, and if you lived through it you were a joker. But sometimes it hit a vein of the pure stuff, like Arnie's love for dinosaurs and comic books and aces.

And even though it made a bit of a joke out of him, it let him live his dreams out on the street.

The joke was a law of nature, the conservation of mass. Arnie could turn into any dinosaur he could visualize, but his mass remained the same. If he was a tyrannosaur he was a three-foot-high tyrannosaur. Okay for a kid, but he was already thirteen or fourteen, full of adolescent juice and delusions of immortality.

"Hey," Fortunato shouted at him. "Hey, kid!"

Arnie turned to look at him.

The kid's arm came off.

It flopped like the muscles had grown their own brain, and then it was sailing through the air and bouncing across the pavement. Fortunato and the kid both stood there for an instant, not comprehending. And then blood began to fountain out of the ragged flap of flesh and the air smelled like a butcher shop.

The kid started to change. Even with an arm gone his instincts were good. His remaining arm shrank and grew scales. His thighs began to swell and his stomach shrank.

Fortunato reached out with his power and tried to stop time. The people around him slowed but the blood pumped undiminished from the kid's arm socket.

The Astronomer, Fortunato thought. Shielding the kid from the power that could save him.

Fortunato tried to run toward him. It was like running in a nightmare, the air thick as wet cement, draining his strength.

The kid was losing too much blood. It puddled around his tennis shoes, soaked the cuffs of his jeans. He couldn't finish the change. His left hand had grown a huge, scythe-shaped claw and he slashed futilely in front of him with it. His face was still human except for a bulging lower jaw.

The eyes flashed from shock to rage to fear and finally to helplessness.

A handful of flesh came out of the kid's throat. The blood from his shoulder slowed as his neck began to spurt.

The kid collapsed. His weirdly jointed legs and the beginnings of a long, stiff tail kept him from falling more than halfway. His chest opened and his heart fell out onto the concrete. The heart seemed to shiver in the sunlight, fibrillating spasmodically for no more than a second before it lay still.

And then there was a little man, maybe a couple of inches over five feet tall, standing next to the kid's distorted corpse. He had an ankle-length black robe that was soaked and spattered with blood. His head was too big for his body and he wore thick glasses.

Fortunato had seen him twice before. Once was inside an Egyptian Masonic temple in Jokertown, seven years before. Fortunato had been looking out through the eyes of a woman he loved, a woman named Eileen who was now dead.

The second time was when Fortunato had led the attack on the Cloisters. Which had led to the Howler being dead, and to this death, right here in front of him.

"I waited for you," the Astronomer said. "I was beginning to think you wouldn't come and I'd have to start without you." His voice had an ugly singsong rhythm.

Fortunato couldn't get within twenty feet of him. "Why the kid? For Christ's sake, why the kid?"

"I wanted you to know," the Astronomer said. "I'm not fucking around any more." He sniffed his blood-drenched fingers. "You're all going to die. Between now and four A.M. Be sure and set your watches." He glanced up at the podium, his eyes moving as if he was looking for somebody that wasn't there. He nodded to himself and smiled.

"Four A.M.?" Fortunato was shouting. He leaned into the force field that straitjacketed him. "Why four A.M.? What happens then?"

Then the field was gone and he staggered forward, off-balance. The Astronomer was gone. Time sped up around him. He was unable to look away as the kid's father saw the mangled ruin of his son and began to scream.

Spector emptied his beer mug and stifled a belch. The Bottomless Pit, located between 27th and 28th Streets a half-block west of Chelsea Park, was far enough off the beaten track to avoid a crush of tourists. The place had a reputation for violence that kept most of the locals away. There were only two other people sitting at the bar, although all the tables were occupied. The only light in the bar area came from the neon beer signs and the television. He heard billiard balls smacking together in the back room.

"You want another?" the bartender asked. He was tall, with curly blond hair and a bodybuilder's physique.

"Sure." Spector was a little light-headed. His fingers and toes were getting numb. It was about time. He'd been drinking on and off all day. The Astronomer was off his back, so he could lie low here, get drunk, and watch the game when it came on. That would just about fill the time until he had to go to the Haiphong Lily.

The bartender drew a beer and set it down on the scratched, pitted wood. Someone had carved "Joyce + whoever I say" into the surface. Spector picked up the beer, enjoying the cold glass on his skin. As usual, the pain was chewing him up inside. Maybe, if everything went well tonight, he'd cap off the evening by killing some tourists. He'd never go to jail for it. That was the beauty of his power. The cops had hauled him in once, but the case had been thrown out in the preliminary hearing. There was never any physical evidence to prove he'd killed his victims.

"And now, for a special report from Channel Nine reporter Carl Thomas, live, at Jetboy's Tomb." Spector looked up at the television.

The young black reporter paused, put a finger to his ear, and nodded. People standing in the crowd behind him leaned around and waved their arms, trying to get into the shot. "This is Carl Thomas reporting. Yet another story in what is already the most violent Wild Card Day in ten years. Apparently, a psychopathic ace killer is roaming the streets. His latest victim is a young boy who had the power to turn himself into a small dinosaur. There is no official word from the police indicating whether the boy's death is related to the earlier killing of the Howler. However, based on eyewitness accounts, this is the second such attack today by the same person. This morning in Jokertown a man fitting the suspect's description assaulted what we hope was only his first such victim, twisting his head completely around. Luckily, Fortunato intervened and healed the victim with his ace powers. Sadly, he was unable to do anything to save the boy. This is Carl Thomas, Channel Nine News, at Jetboy's Tomb."

"Fuck." Spector reached for his beer and knocked it over. Foam spread slowly over the bar. "They have to come on the goddamn TV about that. Couldn't have kept their ugly mouths shut."

". . . that terrible tragedy. In an apparently unrelated incident Frederico Macellaio was killed in an automobile accident earlier this afternoon. Macellaio, also known as 'the

Butcher' and reputed to be a major figure in the city's underworld, was dead at the scene."

"It's just not my fucking day," Spector muttered.

He pulled out his wallet and motioned to the bartender, but the man was looking at the door. Spector turned. There were three punks standing just inside the doorway. They all had black hair cut like Moe of the Three Stooges. The words BEDTIME BOYS were emblazoned in red on the backs of their leather jackets. Each carried a fiberglass skateboard. The leader, who was a head shorter than the other two, wore mirrored sunglasses.

"Shake everybody down," said the little boss, blowing on his fingertips.

Spector's barstool creaked loudly as he swiveled to face them. He was worried about the kid with shades; his power was no good unless his victim's eyes were visible. The other two he could handle.

"Nice of you to get that out for us," said one of the stooges, eyeing Spector's wallet. "Hand it over."

Spector shoved his wallet back into his pants pocket. "Fuck off, you little shit. While you still can."

"Feed 'im his teeth, Billy," said the leader. "It'll save time with everybody else."

Billy whipped the board around his body a couple of times, then swung it up into an attack position. It reminded Spector of the Chinese bench fighters he'd seen in kung fu movies. These guys obviously knew what they were doing. He'd have to take them out in a hurry. He locked eyes with Billy. Spector's death flowed into him. Billy fell face first into the bar-rail.

"Shit, get him, Romeo." The little punk was still directing traffic.

Romeo looked at Billy's body, then at Spector. Mistake. Five seconds later he was dead on the floor.

Spector sensed movement and raised his arm, reaching for the Ingram with his other hand. The skateboard slammed into his forearm, jolting him hard enough to knock him over and send the gun flying. He bounced off a table and landed on the floor. The gun was several feet away. The punk dropped his skateboard and grabbed the pistol. He centered it on Spector's chest and smiled. A cue ball caught him in the side of the head as he pulled the trigger.

Spector rolled as the bullets tore up the table and floor. He felt bits of wood dig through his clothes and into his flesh. He crawled to the remaining Bedtime Boy. The kid sat up and shook his head. The sunglasses were gone.

"Good-bye," Spector said.

The punk met his eyes and gasped, then keeled over.

Spector grabbed the Ingram and holstered it, then stood. The bartender was looking at him, afraid but annoyed. Nobody was talking.

"Some people got no manners at all. These boys are doing the big sleep now. Serves them right," Spector said, rubbing his arm.

The bartender gestured tentatively toward the door.

"Don't worry. I'm gone."

"Hey, tough guy. Throw us back our cue ball." A short, well-built man in a white tank top pointed at Spector's feet.

He picked up the ball and tossed it back. "Nice shot."

The bartender coughed.

Spector walked out into the sunlit street, reaching inside his shirt to tug the splinters out. The fight with the skateboard punks had momentarily made him forget about the Astronomer. He sucked air in through his clenched teeth. With Butcher dead, the job was probably off. Couldn't hurt to find out, though. He pulled a quarter from his pants pocket.

He found a pay phone just down the street from the Bottomless Pit. There was no answer at the Dime Museum, so Spector called the Twisted Dragon and asked for Danny Mao. After waiting for a few moments a young Oriental came on the line.

"Danny Mao. Who's this?" The voice was smooth and assured, with only a trace of accent.

"My name's Spector. I was born in the year of the fire horse. I need to get in touch with one of your people. Guy with a Boston accent, sharp, careful."

There was a brief pause. "Mr. Spector, I'm not familiar with you. Who gave you my number?"

"A joker named Eye. Look, I was contacted this morning about a job. Things have changed, I have to find out what he wants done. Can you help me or not?"

"Possibly, but he's a very busy man, particularly today. Perhaps I can have him contact you later."

"Fine. I'll take the notebooks to someone else." He figured the lie would get Mao's attention.

"Ah, I see. Where are you now?"

Mao had bitten hard. The notebooks must be even more important than Spector had originally guessed. "You just give me the number, or I'll make sure the word goes around that you held up delivery on these babies."

"Call 555-4301. It's his private line. You'd better not be jerking us around . . ."

Spector hung up on Mao in midsentence. A chic young couple was standing behind him, obviously waiting to use the phone. He stared at the woman, grabbed his crotch, and licked his lips. They hurried away. Spector dropped another quarter into the slot and punched in the number.

He answered on the first ring. "Latham."

It was the person who'd called that morning. No question. The only Latham he was aware of was a big-cheese lawyer. "This is Spector. Have you heard about Butcher?"

"Of course. His death does alter a few things." Latham didn't act surprised to hear from him. There was the sound of fingers on a keyboard.

"So everything's off, right?"

"Let me see. I think it would be best for you to have dinner at the Haiphong Lily in any case. The Gambione Family is extremely vulnerable right now. I don't think they could stand to lose any more leadership. It could destroy the Family entirely."

"So; you want as many senior members killed as possible. Right?" Spector looked around to make sure no one was in hearing distance.

"Yes. We might be able to work out a bonus situation for you based on how many you neutralize."

"Fine. Eye said you'd set it up for me to get in with no trouble. Is that right?"

"I'm sure that's the case. By the way, who gave you my private number?"

"Smooth punk named Mao." Spector hoped they gave the kid bamboo shoots under the fingernails.

"I see. Thank you, Mr. Spector. We'll be in touch. Good hunting."

Spector hung up the phone. The quarter dropped into the change box. He looked up and down the street; if the Astronomer got hold of him there wouldn't be a bonus. There wouldn't even be a tomorrow.

Out on the street again, Jennifer took stock of her situation. She wasn't wearing much in the way of clothes. She had no shoes. She'd spent her last dime on the taxi that brought her back to Manhattan. What to do next?

Before she could make up her mind, though, things were decided for her.

They came out of nowhere. Two men emerged from the pedestrians milling around her, gripped either arm, and hustled her down the street.

"Make a sound and you'll die," one whispered to her, and she swallowed the instinctive scream welling in her throat.

The crossed the street and went into a small park across from the Dime Museum. There were three other men there, waiting. One of them was the reptilian joker she'd first seen in Kien's condominium.

"The booksssss," he hissed, coming close to Jennifer. "Where are they?"

She flinched backward from the long forked tongue that lolled from his mouth.

"I-I don't have them on me."

"I can ssssee that." He stared without blinking at her bikini-clad figure. "Where are they?"

"If I told you then you wouldn't need me."

The reptilian joker grinned, dripping saliva from the overlong incisors that hung down from his upper jaw. He leaned forward and his tongue flickered caressingly over Jennifer's face. She flinched backward at the warm, wet touch of it. The joker stooped and his tongue slipped down the column of her throat, between her breasts, then up again and down her bare arms. It rasped sensuously on her forearm and Jennifer shivered, half in fear, half in delight. The man gripping her right arm held it stiffly at the wrist, and the joker licked her palm before she could close it into a fist. The tongue lingered on her hand, then the joker straightened himself and pulled his tongue back into his mouth.

"We don't need you anyway," he hissed. "You tasssste of the alien, Tachyon." His eyes narrowed. "Why did you give him the book?"

The card hadn't lied, Jennifer thought. The suit had once belonged to Tachyon and this joker had somehow gotten his scent off it. She couldn't deny his accusation, but she didn't want to tell them that she'd put the books in the statue, either. She had to come up with a good story, but she wasn't a very good liar.

"Uh . . ."

"Tell me."

The joker's fingers had thick, sharp nails. He ran them across the bare skin of Jennifer's chest, not hard enough to draw blood, but hard enough to leave red welts with their passing.

"Uh–"

The tree behind them blew up. Blew right up, showering them with leaves and fragments of branches. The shock waves from the explosion knocked Jennifer and the men holding her to the ground. One let go of her arm and she kneed the other one three times. She wasn't sure if she hit his stomach or groin, but whatever she hit was tender enough to make him scream and let her go. She rolled away and looked wildly around, as the thugs were doing.

"There!"

One of them pointed across the street. A man stared back at them. His features were concealed by a hood. He was of average height, rather nicely built. Nothing about him really stood out, though, except for the bow he held. It was a high-tech piece of machinery with funny curves and multiple strings and what looked like small pulleys attached to it. He was calmly nocking another arrow while people on his side of the street also noticed him and started to run about like a flock of panicked chickens.

The reptiloid seemed to recognize him. He hissed hatefully as the man brought his bow to bear, but a bus going down the street suddenly blocked his aim.

The thugs were scattering and Jennifer took this as a propitious time to do some vanishing of her own. She ran deeper into the park, thanking her lucky stars for the man's intervention.

How did he fit into this? she wondered. What could he want? She wondered if he was the crazed Bow and Arrow Vigilante that the papers had been full of the last few months. He must be. New York City was a strange place, but she doubted that there could be two people running around shooting at things with a bow and arrow.

And she realized something else as she cut through a copse of trees, wincing as she stepped on a sharp stone. She had seen him before. Even though he now wore a hood, she recognized him by his clothes and by his build as the man who had accosted her in the bleachers of Ebbets Field.

Why was he following her? What did *he* want?

CHAPTER 9

2:00 p.m.

It was two o'clock before Bagabond was able to return to Rosemary's office. Both the streets and the subways were swollen by the masked and made-up revelers. Once she had seen an alligator snout in the crowd but, even as she turned toward it, she realized it was papier-mâché—not Jack. It had deeply disturbed her. Bagabond had always felt self-pity at the changes in her life caused by the virus. Jack and his often-uncontrollable shape-shifting taught her that there were worse fates than experiencing the deaths, births, and pain of every wild creature in the city.

She leaned against the wall and considered the horrible fates of the jokers, never able to escape into hiding because of deformities too hideous or life-threatening to be hidden. Trapped in the isolation of their own betraying bodies. Bagabond shivered violently, closed her eyes for a moment, and reached out to the black and the calico, her oldest companions. They were safe. The thought warmed her.

A slight tug alerted her. She reached down for her camouflage-fabric purse as she sent a wave of hate and threat at the man attempting to snatch her handbag. Startled at her reaction and disoriented by the alien feeling in his head, the tentacled-joker-masked purse snatcher retreated into the crowd.

She rarely attempted to use her ability on humans; she was never sure what its effect, if any, would be. Still uncomfortable in her heels, Bagabond pushed off from the wall and entered the surging flow of the crowd as it, and she, moved toward Jetboy's Tomb and the Justice Center.

By the time she reached the Justice Center, much of the crowd had diverted into Jokertown, Jetboy's Tomb, or Chinatown. Bagabond walked into the district attorney's building. She felt less at home in the business-suit costume than she did in rags, and it was more difficult to walk with head raised confidently. Getting out on Rosemary's floor, she realized that Paul Goldberg was no longer on phone duty. Bagabond nodded to the current receptionist and walked back toward Rosemary's office. As she did, Goldberg walked out of an adjacent office, arms filled with legal references, nearly colliding with Bagabond.

"Christ! Sorry." Goldberg attempted to juggle the books, succeeding with all but the top one which Bagabond neatly caught. "Thanks," he said. "You okay?"

"Fine. You were released from the phones, I take it." Bagabond carefully placed the book on top of the stack beneath Goldberg's chin.

"You caught my act?" Goldberg grinned, then looked puzzled. "I can't believe I don't remember seeing you."

"You were distracted. Is Ms. Muldoon in?" Bagabond gestured toward Rosemary's office.

"If you thought this morning was distracting, you'll love

this afternoon. All hell's broken loose." He shifted the books slightly to the right. "So, if you get a chance, say good-bye before you leave. You'll be a breath of sanity."

"We'll see." She reached out and steadied the top volume.

"Goldberg! Where are those goddamn casebooks?" The rough disembodied voice was distinctly impatient.

"*Never* keep Mrs. Chavez waiting." He trapped the first book with his chin and began trotting down the hall. "Later, I hope."

Bagabond turned to watch him leave. Looking back toward Rosemary's office, Bagabond saw her leaning against the doorframe, smiling.

"Making a conquest, Ms. Melotti?" Rosemary waved Bagabond inside her office.

Bagabond shook her head, realizing angrily that she was blushing.

"Uh huh. Why the outfit?" Rosemary closed the door behind her. "Have a seat."

"Business." Bagabond sat down and kicked off her shoes with an inaudible sigh.

"Does that translate to 'I really don't want to know'?" Rosemary received only a bland stare from Bagabond. She continued, "The Butcher's dead. 'Car accident.' I can't say I'm tremendously distraught, but I'm not buying the accident theory. Know anything about it? Happened in Central Park a little after twelve noon." Rosemary sat on the edge of her desk and leaned back, stretching her neck and arching her spine. "As resident expert on the Families, everybody's been asking me about it. I was hoping maybe a squirrel or one of the cats saw something . . ."

"Sorry. Their memories are much too short for—" Bagabond gasped and broke off. "Jack!" Her body spasmed.

"Suzanne, what's going on? Should I call a doctor?" Rosemary grasped Bagabond's hand only to have it jerked away. Bagabond saw *the end of her snout, a bright flash of flame; she saw a hand holding a packet of small books wrapped in clear plastic, another hand waving the pistol; another flash–*

She still looked sixteen to Fortunato, though she was obviously old enough to be serving drinks. She wore jeans, sneakers, and T-shirt under her apron, and her red-brown hair was pinned up in a loose mess on top of her head. She had a row of dishes lined up on one arm and a fat tourist grabbing the other. The tourist was shouting at her about something and she was starting to sweat.

Her sweat was an event. Water began to condense out of the air all around her. The fat tourist looked up, trying to figure out how it could be raining inside.

"Jane," Fortunato said quietly.

She whirled around, eyes as wide as a gazelle's. "You!" she said, and the dishes hit the floor.

"Relax," Fortunato said. "For god's sake."

She pushed her hair off her forehead. "You wouldn't believe the day I've had."

"Yes," Fortunato said, "I would. I want you to not ask any questions, just come with me, right now. Forget your purse or sweater or whatever."

Obviously she didn't like the idea. She looked at him for a couple of seconds. She must have seen something there, seen the urgency in his eyes. "Uh . . . okay. But this had better be important. If this is some stunt, I'm not going to be amused."

"It's life or death. Literally."

She nodded, and wadded her apron into a ball. "Okay then." She threw the apron in a heap with the broken dishes. "This job really sucked anyway."

The fat tourist stood up. "Hey, what the hell is going on around here? You her pimp or something, buddy?"

Fortunato never got a chance to react. The girl gave the fat man a look of pure hatred and the light drizzle pattering around him turned into a sudden five-second torrent that soaked him to the skin.

"Let's get out of here," Water Lily said.

"Good Lord, and how many times have you been robbed?" she exclaimed as her eyes roved about the immaculate living room with its plush white carpet, maroon vertical blinds, white baby grand piano, and maroon sectional sofa.

"Too many. I do wish you humans would have the sense to legalize narcotics. It would make life so much simpler for so many people."

"Some of us *humans* wish that too. It would make such a nice cash crop for developing nations," she answered, drifting over to fondle the petals of an elaborate gardenia-and-orchid bouquet resting atop the glass coffee table. The air conditioner chattered away, pouring cold air into the room, making it less than comfortable.

The gardenias breathed their fragrance into the room mingling with the smell of coffee, which still lingered from the morning, and the pungent scent of incense. The rest of the table was swept clean but for a large photo book. *All Those Girls in Love With Horses* by Robert Vavra. Roulette rested the book in her lap, and turned the pages.

"And which do you love? The girls or the horses?"

"Which do you think?" Tachyon responded with an impish smile. He was playing back his phone messages, most of which seemed to be from women. The final message ended, and he switched off the machine and unplugged the phone. "So we can have at least a few hours of privacy." She found herself unable to meet the hunger in his gaze, and she dropped her eyes back to the book.

"Would you like a drink?"

"No thanks."

Tension filled the room, forming almost-tangible lines between them. Agitated, Roulette rose and roamed about the room. Two walls were covered by floor-to-ceiling bookshelves with works in several different languages, and in an alcove formed by an outthrust of the wall and flanked by two windows was what could only be described as an altar. A low table covered by an embroidered gray cloth held a simple but profoundly beautiful flower arrangement, a single candle, a small knife, and a tiny Hopi seed pot holding a long, thin incense stick.

"Is this really for . . ."

"For worship?" he said, turning from the small efficiency kitchen where he was pouring himself a drink. "Yes. That's that ancestor business I told you about."

That opened a whole set of disturbing memories: singing in the choir at the Methodist church back home, her mother rehearsing the angels for the Christmas pageant, her head bobbing energetically as she pounded out the melody on their old piano, and the children's voices like piping crickets filling the house. Being frightened by a hell-and-damnation sermon by a visiting missionary, and clinging to her father for comfort.

She flung herself to the piano, seating herself on the cushioned bench. A violin, its smooth golden curves softly reflecting back the light from a brace of track lights, lay on the piano. And for the first time she found some disorder in this perfect room. A jumble of scores and music sheets marched across the stand. Roulette frowned and leaned in, studying the notation on one of the hand-scored pieces. The notes seemed to be in the familiar positions, but there were odd notations in the clefs. The piano cover fell back with a thud, and she sight-read through the music.

She was very aware when Tachyon came up behind her, for the sense of tingling magnetism increased, and the delicate scent he favored washed over her. Ice tinkled in the glass as he attempted to clap.

"Bravo, you are quite accomplished."

"I should be, my mother's a music teacher."

"Where?"

"Philadelphia public school system."

There was a slight pause, then the Takisian asked, "What did you think?"

"Very Mozartian."

A tiny line appeared between Tachyon's arching brows, and he closed his eyes as if in pain. "What a blow."

"I beg your pardon?"

"No artist likes to be told they are derivative."

"Oh, I'm sorry—"

He held up a small hand. Grinned. "Even when they know it's true."

She turned back, and shuffled the sheets, and went on to the second page. "Derivative or not, it's pretty."

"Thank you, I'm glad my small effort pleased you, but let us play a true master. I so rarely find someone I can—" he paused, and shot her a glance alight with mischief

"*—jam* with." He flipped quickly through the piles of music, and pulled out Beethoven's Sonata for Violin and Piano in F, the so-called *Spring* sonata.

She watched, held by the way his small, elegant hands caressed the polished surface of the violin, tightening a string here, plucking a single quivering note from another. "Which do you prefer?" she asked, indicating the piano and the violin.

"I can't choose. I am partial to this." Another stroke to the wood of the violin. "For it kept me on the edge of the gutter rather than in it for a number of years."

"Pardon?"

"Old history. Shall we tune?"

The A hung trembling in the room matched by a floating tone from the violin.

"Good God, what is that? A Stradivarius?"

"Don't I wish. No, it's a Nagyvary."

"Oh, that chemist in Texas who thinks he discovered the secret of the Cremona school."

The violin dropped from his chin, and he smiled down at her. "What a delight you are. Is there nothing on which you're not informed?"

"I daresay a thousand things," she replied dryly.

His lips pressed against the corner of her mouth, drifted down her neck, the breath puffing gently and warmly across her skin.

"Shall we play?" And she noticed with embarrassment and anger the catch in her voice.

They began in perfect unison, the violin singing the first held note then gliding into the elegant ornamentation. She echoed the phrase, and time ceased and reality withdrew. Twenty minutes of perfect harmony and graceful genius. Twenty minutes without word or thought or worry. A perfect moment. Tachyon stood transported; eyes closed, lashes brushing at his high cheekbones, metallic red hair curling across the violin, joy on his narrow face.

Roulette laid her hands in her lap, stared down at the keys while Tachyon, also remaining silent, placed the violin in its case. Moments later his hands touched her shoulders, resting like nervous birds, as though frightened to remain.

"Roulette, you make me feel . . . well, something that I haven't felt for many, many years. I'm very glad you came walking down Henry Street today. Perhaps there was even a reason for it."

She watched with rather distant interest as her fingers tightened about each other, knuckles whitening with strain. "You're looking for significance again."

"I thought you only warned me against looking for comfort."

"Well, add significance to it." She lifted a corner of the numbing blanket with which she had covered her emotions, and found panic throbbing in time to her rushing heartbeats. She probed at her soul, and found a bleeding wound. *Fear, hate, guilt, regret, hopelessness.*

She blamed him.

"Let's go to bed." And she was startled by the flatness of the words when they masked so much anguish.

It would have been quicker to travel crosstown underground. Jack had clattered down the steps at the West 4th Street station. One level, two levels, three. Few people other than maintenance workers went down to the fourth level. He went through an anonymous steel door and entered an eastwest maintenance tunnel. In their little cages, the dim safety bulbs shed a brittle yellow glow, casting islands of illumination along the passageway. Jack's shoes scuffed in dirt.

It was exhilarating to be able to stride along without having to account for endless numbers of slower pedestrians getting in his way. Jack checked his watch, and then looked at it again, unbelieving. It was only a little after two. It seemed as if he'd been searching the city for Cordelia for days. More to the point, he'd completely lost track of time. He wondered if maybe he was squandering his time now. Maybe he should be calling Rosemary, checking with Bagabond, phoning the police, *anything*... He should have been watching instead of thinking.

When he swung around a dogleg in the passage and slammed into someone coming the other way at a dead run, he had, at first, only the briefest impression of a dark figure. He glimpsed one huge eye centered in the other's face, a monocle glittering in the dim light—

"Son of a bitch!" said the other person, raising one hand toward Jack. Red flame erupted from the fist, a rolling wave of painful sound crashed against Jack's ears, and he heard something buzz past his head, spanging against the concrete wall of the corridor. Cement chips sprayed the side of his face. There was no pain yet.

"Hey!" Jack yelled. He dropped to the floor of the tunnel and the epinephrines took over. Now it was all instinctual. All the pent tension of the long day, the frustration of his search, his intermittent desire to *kill* something, flashed into critical mass. Also he was hungry. Very hungry.

"Bastard. Get away from me! You die!" The dark figure drew down with the pistol. Another shot. Jack saw the sparks where the bullet hit a steel stanchion.

"What the hell you doin'?" Jack cried. "Aaaaaahhh!"

said the reptile brain, flooded with welcomed hormones. Jack felt his body elongate, the vestigial tail extending and swelling, clothing ripping, his snout springing forth before his eyes. The rows of teeth sprang up faster than anything sowed by Cadmus.

His claws scrabbled for purchase on the hardpacked earthen floor. He hissed with anticipation.

Hungry, he thought. There was anger, too. But mostly hunger.

The man with the pistol backed into the corner of the dogleg. He held something shiny in his other hand. He stared unbelievingly at the alligator. “Get the fuck away!”

Jaws scissoring open wide, the alligator lunged forward. Brief thunder rolled as the pistol flashed and a bullet nicked the creature’s armored hide above one front leg. The jaws slammed closed with incredible force as the man screamed and thrust his hands out in a hopeless attempt to fend off the beast. The pistol skittered away, lost in the darkness. The plastic-wrapped package went into the alligator’s mouth. Along with the hand that held it. Along with part of an arm, the man’s shoulder, and his face. His bubbling screams stopped in a matter of seconds.

Glass shattered as the monocle spun away and smashed against the tunnel wall.

The alligator wrenched his jaws away from the remains of the corpse. There was no chewing. The food went down his gullet where the powerful enzymes would take care of assuaging his hunger. He opened his jaws again to roar a challenge.

No one and nothing answered him. The alligator swung his head heavily from one side of the corridor to the other. On some deep level, he remembered that food was not his only priority this day.

He started forward into the darkness. There was something he had to *do*.

"A cab?" Water Lily said. "I thought we were in a hurry."

"It'll get the job done," Fortunato said. "We don't want any grandstand moves. Not today."

The cab pulled over and they got in. "Empire State Building," Fortunato told the driver. He leaned back in the seat. "We don't need to make targets of ourselves."

"It's the Astronomer, isn't it?"

"He just killed Kid Dinosaur. Tore him to pieces. He would have killed Demise, but Demise was tougher than anybody knew. You probably heard about the Howler. So it's . . ."

He broke it off. Jane had stopped listening somewhere in the middle. "Kid Dinosaur?" she said.

Fortunato nodded.

"Jesus." She stared straight ahead. Water—not tears—beaded up on her cheeks. Fortunato couldn't tell if she was going to cry for real or start ripping up the cab's upholstery. Finally she said, "All right." The words came out small and strangled. She tried again. "All right. Count me in. Where do we start?"

This isn't working, Fortunato thought. She's not going to go weak and helpless on you. She's gotten too tough for that. What do you do when they don't want your protection?

"Um," he said. "How about a bodyguard assignment?"

"What, are you serious? Guarding who?"

"I was thinking of Hiram Worchester."

"Oh. That fat guy?"

"He identified the Astronomer's coins. He could be in danger too."

"Oh, all right," she said. "For now."

An establishment as celebrated and unique as Aces High drew its share of trouble, and Hiram had long ago resigned himself to the unfortunate necessity of security, but he insisted that it be discreet. Peter Chou's men (and women) were quick, efficient, highly skilled, and very unobtrusive. When it came to dealing with drunks, holdup men, and leapers, no one was better. But the Astronomer was more than they'd been trained to handle.

Modular Man was about as unobtrusive as a joker in Idaho. The android had a certain male-model handsomeness, although his prefab features were without either character lines or hair. He wore a skullcap to conceal the radar dome built into his head. Twin grenade launchers were mounted on rotating pivots set in the synthetic flesh of his shoulders.

The shoulder modules popped right out, and normally Hiram insisted that Modular Man check his armament at the door. But today was not the day for normalcy. When the android landed on the balcony and was ushered into his office, Hiram asked him straight out what sort of weaponry he was equipped with.

"The left module fires tear-gas canisters, and the right is loaded with smoke bombs," Mod Man said. "The smoke will not affect my radar, of course, but will blind any potential adversary. The tear gas—"

"I know what tear gas does," Hiram said curtly. "Your

creator is assuming the Astronomer has to breathe. Let's hope he's correct."

"I could exchange the grenade launcher for an armor-piercing 20mm cannon," Modular Man said cheerfully.

Hiram made a choking sound. "If you even *think* about firing a cannon inside my restaurant, you'll never set foot in here again."

"It's more like a large machine gun, actually."

"Nonetheless," Hiram said firmly.

"Would you like me to patrol the perimeter?"

"I'd like you to sit at the end of the bar and stay out of the way," Hiram told him. "There's still a great deal of work to be done. The guests will begin arriving around seven for cocktails. If anything's going to happen, it should happen well before that."

He escorted the android out to the bar and left him in the company of a bottle of single-malt Scotch. On the way to his office, Curtis accosted him. "The lobster was the only thing they bothered to destroy," he reported. "Some of Gills's employees are cleaning up the damage. The ones who didn't run away. Gills was taken to the Jokertown clinic."

"Find out who's in charge, and tell them I want the tuna," Hiram said. "As much as he has. We'll do blackened tuna tonight instead of lobster."

"Paul will not be amused," Curtis said.

Hiram paused at the door to his office. "Let him scream. Then let him cook. If he refuses, I'll do it myself. I'm not unfamiliar with Cajun cuisine." He paused thoughtfully. "Alligator has an interesting taste. You don't suppose that Gills might have . . . no, that's too much to ask. Oh, and offer a premium price for that tuna. If I hadn't interfered this morning, none of this would have happened."

"You shouldn't blame yourself," Curtis said.

"Why not?" Hiram asked. He snorted. "I remember when I was first diagnosed, back in 1971. After Tachyon assured me that I wasn't going to die, that I'd been gifted with extraordinary powers instead, I determined that I must use those powers for the public good. Absurd, I know, but it was the tenor of the times. I tell you, Curtis, heroism is a ludicrous career choice, although not half so ludicrous as I was in my costume." He paused thoughtfully, and flicked a piece of lint off the swell of his vest. "It was well-tailored," he said, "but ludicrous nonetheless. At any rate, my physique was distinctive, masked or no, and my abortive experiment in semi-professional adventuring ended abruptly when a gossip columnist accurately divined my identity. I'm not a modest man, Curtis, but food is what I'm best at. Gills would be a lot better off if I'd remembered that this morning." He turned away before Curtis could reply, and shut the office door behind him.

His lunch was waiting on his desk: three thick-cut pork chops grilled with onion and basil, a side of pasta salad, steamed broccoli with grated romano cheese, and a piece of the famous Aces High cheesecake. Hiram sat down and contemplated it.

A newspaper lay next to his untouched lunch platter. The *Daily News* had already gotten out an extra, and Anthony had brought up a copy with Hiram's tux. The picture spread across the front of the tabloid had been taken at Jetboy's Tomb by some amateur photographer. Hiram supposed that it was a great news photo, but he could scarcely look at it.

He found himself averting his eyes from Kid Dinosaur's mutilated body, and looking at the faces in the background. Their emotions were plain to read: horror, hysteria, anguish, shock. Some just seemed baffled; others stared with unwholesome fascination. In the right-hand corner was a pretty blonde who couldn't have been more than eighteen, laughing, no doubt amused by some witticism from the boy whose arm she clung to, as yet oblivious to the horror a few feet away. How did she feel when she looked around, the laughter still fresh on her lips? How would she feel when she saw this picture, her laugh frozen there for all time?

His lunch was growing cold, but Hiram had no appetite. Kid Dinosaur had been a constant nuisance to the proprietor of Aces High. He remembered one hot summer night when a pteranodon had swooped in through the open terrace doors and buzzed the diners. Drinks were spilled, plates were dropped, the dessert cart tipped over, and a half-dozen indignant customers left without paying their bills. Hiram had put an end to the incident by making the creature too heavy to stay aloft, and reprimanding him in no uncertain terms. From all reports, the boy had been cowed for almost a week.

When the phone rang, Hiram grabbed it quickly. "What?" he demanded brusquely. He was in no mood for conversation.

"Me, Hiram," Jay Ackroyd said.

Hiram had almost forgotten about the detective. "Where are you?" he demanded.

"At the moment I'm at a pay phone outside the men's room of the Crystal Palace, being eyed by a joker who looks like a cross between a douche bag and a saber-toothed tiger. I think he wants to use the phone, so I'll get right to the point. Chrysalis knows something."

"Chrysalis knows a good many things," Hiram said.

"Real good," Ackroyd replied. "Your friend Bludgeon isn't independent. Him and his whole scam are part of something, something a lot bigger. Chrysalis knows who and what, but the price she quoted for the information was way out of my budget. Maybe not out of yours, though. I'm bringing her up tonight, you can talk to her yourself."

"You're bringing her *here*?" Hiram said. "Jay, she's a joker, not an ace."

"I'm an ace," Ackroyd reminded him, "and she's my date. Don't worry, I made her promise to cover her tits. A shame, though. They're nice tits, even if they are invisible. Just pretend she's really British and you'll get on great."

"Fine," Hiram said. "And while you've been arranging your social calendar and studying Chrysalis's breasts, Bludgeon put Gills in the hospital and destroyed my lobsters."

"I know," Ackroyd said.

Hiram was astonished. "How could you possibly know?"

"I dropped by Fulton Street before I went to see Chrysalis, figured maybe I'd see Gills, charm him with a few magic tricks, pull a coin out of his gills, and see if he'd talk to me. I got suspicious right off when I saw a truck burning in the alley. This seven-foot-tall guy was going out as I was coming in. He looked a lot like the guy waiting for the phone, only ugly. I made a citizen's arrest. He's in the Tombs."

"God," Hiram exclaimed. "Jay, this is the first good news I've heard all day. Thank you, and good work. You'll get a month of free dinners for this."

"Appetizers included, I hope. The thing's not done, though. Bludgeon's locked up for the moment, but sooner or later someone's going to notice him hollering in there, and then they'll count heads and let him go, unless we can get him charged with something. Can you go downtown and do the honors?"

Hiram felt in a terrible bind. "I . . . Jay, I want to, but I can't possibly leave now."

"A crisis with the *pâté de foie gras*?"

"Fortunato is going to be bringing some people by. I need to, ah, stay. Besides, I've never laid eyes on Bludgeon. Gills was the one they assaulted. Have him prefer charges."

"He's terrified, Hiram."

"If we put Bludgeon away, he has nothing to be terrified of. Tell him that. He can't let them get away with this."

Ackroyd sighed. "All right. I'll go talk to him. Hell. On days like this, I wish I could pop myself around. Do you have any idea what the traffic's like out there?"

Spector stared across the Hudson River toward the Jersey shore. He'd grown up in Teaneck. As long as he could remember he'd hated New Yorkers. Hated them for their contemptuous comments and unending supply of Jersey jokes. They really thought they were better, just by living a few miles away. Every New Yorker he killed was a little revenge for the way he'd always been treated by them.

The Astronomer knew he was alive by now. The old man was probably too busy to watch TV himself, but had plenty of flunkies to dish him the information. Spector could only hope that the other aces on the hit list were more important than he was. Hell, there was even a chance the Astronomer would buy it. They'd kicked his ass before. If he could manage to stay out of the way, Spector might be able to read everybody else's obit in the *Times* tomorrow.

The West Side Highway was behind him, already crawling with cars. The docks were busy; working guys still had to eat. They couldn't take the damn day off to gawk around.

Spector looked back into Manhattan. The Windhaven Tower building was directly across the highway. The apartments in it were exclusive and pricey. The architecture was like something out of a thirties sci-fi pulp, including an open lobby all the way to the top of the building. He followed the unbroken silver line of the tower all the way up. He squinted. There was something, someone, up there.

A man in a hang glider pushed off the edge of the roof, twenty stories up. He dived for a few seconds, then leveled off and headed out toward the river.

"Cops are gonna put your ass in jail when they catch you, buddy." Spector hated heights, and shuddered as he thought of falling off a building like that, wings or no. He turned back toward Jersey.

There was something coming toward the city from across the river. It was several hundred feet up and moving fast. He recognized the familiar shell. "Turtle. So the Astronomer hasn't gotten you yet."

Spector liked the Turtle about as much as he liked the other aces who'd raided the Cloisters, which was not at all. He straightened his shoulders and rubbed his mouth, feeling suddenly vulnerable. If the Astronomer tried to take the Turtle now, he didn't want to be anywhere close.

The Turtle slowed down and hovered over the river. A couple of private boats were cruising around nearby bobbing a little in the light chop, but they didn't seem to be in any kind of trouble. The Turtle began to wobble slightly; the hang glider banked and moved directly toward him. Spector wanted to run, but curiosity held him where he was. The hang glider moved straight and fast toward the Turtle. It was less than a hundred feet away. There was a sound like glass being cut and then a loud pop; the glider veered away. Spector recognized the noise and knew the Turtle was in trouble. One of the last aces the Astronomer had lured in was a Puerto Rican kid who he called Imp. He could generate an electromagnetic pulse that neutralized all electricity within fifty yards or so. The cameras and other equipment on the Turtle's shell were so much junk now.

Imp maneuvered his glider back over the Turtle. The wind was slowing him down, making him climb. Longshoremen were setting down their crates, looking out at the river. Moments later the shell was covered in an explosion of orange flame. Napalm. The boom echoed off the water. As the flames began to die down, Spector could see that parts of the shell were on fire. The Turtle began to wobble even more, and fell toward the river. There was a loud slap and hiss as the shell struck the water. One of the nearby boats steered toward the Turtle. The shell floated for a second, then sank fast, like there were pulleys at the bottom of the river dragging it down. There was nothing left but a little steam on the surface of the river.

"Jesus. Who would've thought it could be so easy." Spector felt his skin tighten. It was a safe bet that the Astronomer had watched the Turtle go down, just like he had. The other aces weren't going to be much help. The Astronomer was knocking them off one by one. They'd only beaten him before because they'd been organized and had taken the old man by surprise. It was the other way around today. Spector heard approaching sirens. He turned and ran.

"We saw it on TV," Hiram told Fortunato. "First the Howler, then the Kid. It was dreadful, unbelievable." Fortunato nodded, uncomfortable in the crowded office. Hiram's chef was there, his bouncer, a couple of the waiters.

Modular Man came over from where he'd been leaning by the window. "Hello," he said to Jane. "I don't know if you remember me. Modular Man? You can call me Mod Man for short."

Jane nodded to him, brushing him off. "You don't need me here," she said to Fortunato. "You're trying to hide me someplace where I'll be out of your hair."

"That's not true," Fortunato lied. "You've seen the Astronomer. You know more than anybody how powerful he is. The only hope we have is strength in numbers. All of us, together, in one place."

"All of us? You included?"

"I have to find the others. This is my karma, okay? My responsibility."

"You don't have to do it alone, you know. It's not a crime to let somebody help you." Fortunato didn't say anything. "I . . . oh, hell. Why am I wasting my breath? But one thing. If you leave me here, and somebody dies, or gets hurt, that I could have saved, I'm not going to let you forget it. Understand?"

"I can live with that," Fortunato said.

Hiram followed him into the hall. "Uh, Fortunato? Can I see you a second?" Fortunato nodded and Hiram shut the door. "I got a call a few minutes ago. From a Lieutenant Altobelli, NYPD. Looking for you."

"What did he have?"

"He wouldn't say, but he said he needed you at the Cloisters, ASAP."

"Okay, well, that's next then."

"Fortunato?"

"What?"

"What about Tachyon?"

"What about him?"

"Isn't the Astronomer after him too?"

"Fuck him."

"Would it be okay if I at least *warned* him?"

"I don't care," Fortunato said. "Just as long as you don't do anything stupid and don't go off and leave the people I'm bringing here. I'm counting on you, man. Don't fuck up."

"Right," Hiram said cheerlessly.

Fortunato's elevator came. He pressed I and jiggled the Door Close button.

The smell of hot pretzels made Spector's stomach rumble. Other than a few peanuts at the Bottomless Pit, he hadn't eaten all day. He walked over to the stand. The vendor was a short, middle-aged man in a light blue shirt and black beltless pants. He smiled at Spector, showing crooked yellow teeth. He wore a button that said PRETZEL VENDORS KNOW HOW TO GET TWISTED

"What can I do for you?"

"Give me a pretzel. Make it two."

The vendor pulled out the pretzels and wrapped them absent-mindedly. "Boy, I'll tell you. It would be fine by me if every day was Wild Card Day. I could retire and play the horses."

Spector took the pretzels and paid him. The vendor had the kind of dim, simple-minded dreams only losers have. Spector was beyond even having dreams anymore. He just killed people and occasionally wondered why it didn't bother him more.

He took a large bite of the pretzel. It was warm and chewy. This would fill him up until he ate at the Haiphong Lily.

A wave of nausea and dizziness hit him in midstride.

He dropped the pretzels and fell to his knees. Darkness was creeping in around the edge of his vision.

"You sick or something, mister?" he heard someone ask.

He saw the limousine pull up next to him. A mirrored window lowered slowly. The Astronomer smiled at him. Spector doubled over and pressed his face to the cold concrete. He didn't have the strength to move. He closed his eyes, fighting for breath. He could still smell the pretzels.

A car door slammed. He felt hands lifting him just as he passed out.

Fortunato introduced her as Water Lily, but she told Hiram she'd prefer to be called Jane. "I know how you feel," he said, with one of his most charming smiles. "They used to call me Fatman." She seemed shy and sweet, but the way she was dressed would simply not do. Blue jeans had their place, but it was not in Aces High, and her sneakers were unbearably ratty. "A droll fellow, that one," Hiram said conversationally, indicating the smirking likeness of Jumpin' Jack Flash on her faded T-shirt.

"Will he be here tonight?" Jane asked him.

"I'm afraid not," Hiram said. "He received an invitation via Dr. Tachyon, of course, but sent his regrets. He did say a friend of his might attend, whatever that means. Come with me, if you please. It's a madhouse out here right now."

Hiram escorted Jane through the din of the restaurant to the relative sanity of his office, and buzzed for Anthony. When the chauffeur arrived, he introduced him to Jane and said, "Give him your sizes."

"Sizes?" She seemed confused.

"The dinner tonight is a formal affair," Hiram explained,

"and there's no reason a lovely young lady like yourself shouldn't look her best. It will have to be off the rack, I'm afraid, we can't have you leaving to go shopping. Fortunato insists that we all stay together, and I think his tactical instincts are sound." He turned to Anthony. "Something in blue or green, I think. Off the shoulder. With hose and accessories. Are you comfortable in high heels, Jane, or would you prefer to wear flats?"

"Wait a minute," she said, her eyes wide and apprehensive. "I can't afford a lot of expensive clothing."

"Heels," Hiram said. "Definitely. You have lovely legs. Aces High will take care of everything." He smiled. "Don't worry, I'll find a way to deduct it. I have an extraordinary accountant."

She shook her head. "No. I'm sorry, I can't let you do that."

Hiram was nonplussed. "Why ever not?" he said.

"I can't accept a lot of expensive clothing from you as a gift. I can't. I *won't.*"

"My dear," Hiram said uncertainly. "You put me at a loss. Mind you, I don't enforce a *rigid* dress code at the dinner, but it would be a shame if—"

Anthony spoke up unexpectedly. "Perhaps the lady would accept the clothing as a loan." Both Hiram and Jane turned to look at him in surprise. "If I may be so bold to suggest it."

"I couldn't," she said. "Even as a loan. I quit my job this afternoon, and even if I get another one, I'd never be able to pay you back waiting tables."

Hiram stroked his beard thoughtfully, and smiled. "You might," he said, "if the tables were at Aces High. Not tonight, of course, but starting tomorrow, when we reopen to the public. I promise you, the tips are excellent, and we can always use a good worker."

Jane seemed to think it over for a moment. "All right. I'll do that. You can take what I owe you out of my pay." She looked at Hiram evenly, with a ghost of a smile.

"Excellent," Hiram said. "Now, I'm afraid I've got work to attend to. If you're hungry, find Curtis and he'll have them bring you some lunch."

Hiram found himself staring at the closed door after Jane had gone. She was far too young for him, but she was lovely, with an air of innocence about her that he found very erotic. She reminded him of Eileen Carter, who had been almost as young as Jane when she and Hiram had first met, years ago. Innocence and strength; a potent combination. The girl would be lucky indeed if the blend didn't get her killed.

He frowned, made a small reflexive fist, and thought about the dead. An adolescent boy with delusions of glory, and a big man all in yellow whose shout could crack stone. And Eileen. He must never forget Eileen.

That had been a long time ago, seven years now, since Fortunato had come to him with a shiny blood-red penny and Hiram had given him her name, never dreaming that he was sealing her death warrant. Afterward, Hiram had scarcely been able to believe it. Dead? Eileen dead? She helped identify a rare coin, and for that she is *dead?*

Eileen had been his lover years before the virus had taken him for its own. That was over by the time she had gotten involved with Fortunato, but she had still meant a good deal to him. The pimp had bedded her and then gotten her killed, involved her in something she had no more business in than Hiram.

The night that Fortunato had broken the news had been

one of the worst nights of his life. As he had listened to Fortunato go on about Masons, Hiram could taste the bile in the back of his throat, could feel the rage rising in him. He had never used his spore-given ability to kill, but that night he had come close. He had flexed and unflexed his fingers, watched the gravity waves shimmer about the tall black man with the almond-shaped eyes and the bulging forehead, and wondered just how much weight Fortunato could stand. Five hundred pounds? A thousand? Two thousand? Would his heart burst before or after those long, wiry legs shattered under the weight of his body? Hiram could find out. Just make a fist, a tight hard fist.

He hadn't done it, of course. Hadn't done it because he realized something, as he listened to Fortunato's voice. It was nothing the man said; he was not the sort to make such admissions. Yet it was in his tone, and in the look of those dark eyes snug in their epicanthic folds: Fortunato had loved her too. Had perhaps loved her more than Hiram, who had his father's large appetites and wandering eye. And so he'd relaxed his half-made fist, and instead of hate, Hiram had felt a strange bond to the sharp-tongued sorcerer-pimp.

Afterward, he had tried to put it all behind him. He made no pretensions to heroism, whatever powers he might have. Crimes were the domain of the police, justice a matter for gods; his business was feeding people well, and making them a bit happier for a few hours.

But as he remembered Eileen and Kid Dinosaur and the Howler, and worried about Gills and sweet young Water Lily and Dr. Tachyon and the other names on the Astronomer's death list, Hiram Worchester could feel the rage building once again, the way it had risen inside him that night in 1979.

This Astronomer was an old, old man, Fortunato said.

He probably wouldn't be able to take very much weight at all.

Hiram regarded his cold luncheon plate for a moment, and then lifted his knife and fork and methodically began to eat.

Spector kept his eyes closed when he came to. He knew he was in the Astronomer's limo. He could feel a person sitting on either side of him. The one on the left had bony elbows; the old man, he figured.

"Don't play possum on me, Demise. It won't do you any good." The Astronomer jabbed his elbow into Spector's ribs.

He opened his eyes. There was a middle-aged woman on his right. Her facial features looked like a caricature of someone beautiful, and she wore no makeup. Her dress was white cotton with padded shoulders and a narrow waist. She avoided looking directly at him.

"Nothing to say? But then you never were the talkative type." The Astronomer put a hand on his left arm. "I trust I have your undivided attention."

Spector looked into the Astronomer's dilated eyes. He tried his power; maybe this time it would work. No go. He slid his hand inside his coat, reaching for the Ingram. Both the gun and holster were gone.

The old man shook his head. "I took it away. It's pathetic, your being reduced to carrying a gun. You're lucky I found you again."

"The Turtle's dead, isn't he?"

"Yes." The Astronomer rubbed his palms together. "It's so easy when you know what's going to happen and they don't."

"How'd you set it up?" Spector asked.

"Our good friend Captain Black arranged to send out a misleading distress signal over the police band." The Astronomer put a finger to his wrinkled forehead. "You just have to outthink your enemies. That's all."

"Imp was lucky to get that close." Spector pushed back into the soft upholstery and sighed. He didn't have any cards left to play.

"Hardly luck. Turtle was having blood-sugar problems, right, my dear?"

"Rather severe ones," the woman said. "Even worse than what I did to Mr. Spector."

"Demise, my dear. Call him Demise." The Astronomer tightened his grip on Spector's arm. "Say hello to Insulin, Demise. She's my new star pupil."

"Hello, sugar," he said sarcastically. She still wouldn't look at him. "I'm alive. You must want me for something if I'm still alive. Who do you want me to kill?"

"All that's being taken care of by my more trustworthy associates. No, I'm keeping you alive for another reason. This Fortunato—" the Astronomer made a fist with his free hand, "I want him to suffer before I kill him. He has women. You and I are going to entertain some of them tonight. You always did enjoy that, didn't you, Demise?"

"Yeah. What time?" Spector didn't believe it was going to be this easy. The old man still had hold of his arm.

"Late. Very late."

"Fine."

"Still, I must punish you for trying to hide from me. You need to be reminded of your place."

"No," he said, trying to pull away.

The Astronomer grabbed his arm with both hands and twisted. The bones in Spector's forearm snapped; grinding pain shot up his arm into his shoulder. He clawed at the old man, tearing flesh from his cheeks and knocking his glasses off. The Astronomer held the broken bones together at an oblique angle.

"Any power you have, Demise, I can use against you. I can brainwipe everything but the memory of your death, and I can mutilate you until you look like something from a joker's worst nightmare."

Spector could feel the bones knitting together. His arm looked like a third, frozen joint had been added to it. He tried to pull away, but the Astronomer held him fast.

"I think he's all better now, Insulin. He won't cross us again." The Astronomer turned his arm loose.

"Look what you fucking did to me," Spector screamed.

The Astronomer picked up his glasses and propped them back on his nose. "There are much worse things waiting if you disappoint me again. Driver, stop the car."

The limo pulled over to the curb. Insulin opened the door. She looked at his twisted arm and smiled.

Wait'll he gets pissed at you, Spector thought, crawling over her and stepping out onto the sidewalk. I hope he turns you inside out.

"Tonight. Be ready. I'll come for you when it's time," the Astronomer said. Insulin closed the door. The limo pulled out into the traffic.

Spector looked up. People were pointing at him, laughing like it was some kind of joke. Others turned away. The Pan Am Building was a few blocks away, down Park Avenue. They would have to drop him in the middle of midtown. He rubbed his arm; he couldn't rotate his wrist anymore.

A helicopter took off from the top of the Pan Am Building. Spector wished he was on it, then shook his head. There was no place on the planet where anyone was safe from the Astronomer. He walked quickly down the street, wishing he had time to kill each and every person who looked at him funny.

CHAPTER 10

3:00 p.m.

The bedroom continued the maroon motif, but with highlights in gray rather than white. More books, more flowers, and on the dresser the photo of a sad-eyed woman in the dress of the 1940s. An enormous walk-in closet filled with clothes, a riot of color. Tachyon, seated in a chair by the window, eased off one high-heeled boot. The air conditioner set the crystal and silver wind chime above his head to ringing.

"Let me." She knelt before him, and pulled off the second boot noting how small his feet were, contrasting it with Josiah's size-twelves.

"I should be undressing you."

She dropped the boot. "How about we move things along, and undress ourselves."

"I am either flattered that you're so eager, or worried because you're simply anxious to have the deed done."

Her fingers froze on the buttons of her blouse, and she

watched in the mirror while the color drained from her face leaving behind that strange gray quality that affects black skin. She hurriedly stripped off her clothes, and stared at the slender reflection in the glass. The crystals in her braids gave back the light, sparkling against the ebony hair.

"Madam, you are beautiful." He made an ivory and carnelian figure next to her. His head with its tumbled red curls just topping her shoulder.

Her lips skinned back from her teeth in a travesty of a smile. "Come on. I'll thank you in bed."

The mattress gurgled and swayed as they settled beneath the coverlet. He reached for her, then rolled away and unplugged the bedside phone. With a wink and a leer he snuggled against her, his hands and lips played expertly across her body finding the pleasure points, dissolving her nerves into a wash of sensation. This time it was not an obligation to be bitterly endured. He was an accomplished lover, seeming almost to worship her with his body. His fingers swept aside the moisture-matted hair of her mons, and his tongue teased along the lips of her, tantalizing her clitoris. She tangled a hand in his hair, and pulled him closer. For a moment past and future were forgotten in the all-enveloping sensation of the moment.

He wriggled up the length of her, his penis hot, stiff, and moist against her thigh. The head of his cock probed like a nuzzling foal at her mons; she sighed, spread wide welcoming him. But he continued to tease, his arms rigid on either side of her body, teeth worrying at her nipples, the maddening almost-penetration a hot presence against her clit. She growled, and jerked him down to her, capturing his mouth as he slid smoothly into her.

And she sensed several things simultaneously: the feather-like brush of his mind sliding harmlessly off the shields that had been erected by the Astronomer to prevent just this sort of penetration, and the surging weight of the poison advancing like a questing hunting dog with tiny half starts and halts, waiting for permission.

A permission that she withheld, justifying the decision in a half-formed thought that she would toy with him, promise him love, so the betrayal would be all the more devastating for him. Her arms and legs twined about him, and she met each thrust with an uplift of the hips. His cries were punctuated with gently murmured endearments, but she bit back any sound, as if by silence she could deny the pleasure. He came, semen fountaining within her, gave a harsh cry, and collapsed across her chest, crushing her bosoms between them.

"Roulette, I think you're an ace." The words punctuated by pants.

"No!" She pushed him aside, and he lay blinking bemusedly up at her.

"Your shields are not the inchoate shields formed by normals. These are very sophisticated."

She knelt, swaying on the bed, hands clenched between her thighs, the sweat growing clammy on her bare skin. "I can't explain it."

"If you will permit me to probe I might be able to explain it."

"No, no! It frightens me. I don't want you to! I won't let you!" The shrill tones drilled through her, sending a stabbing pain behind her eyes.

"All right. All right." His hands soothed her as one would a restive horse. "Your body and mind are yours to command. I would never violate you."

She flung herself down next to him, burying her face against his side, tasting the salt sweat, inhaling the scent of man, and sex and aftershave. "Hold me. I don't want to think anymore."

"Hush, hush. You're safe with me."

And he again stared in confusion as her laughter filled the room, mad splinters of sound that seemed to cut at her throat, and fill her chest with pain.

"Suzanne!"

"I'm cool. It's okay." Bagabond had sat back and taken a deep breath. "So strong . . ."

"What is it?" Rosemary's voice had been filled with genuine concern.

Bagabond looked back at her. "He's got the books—I think. The notebooks."

"Jack? How?" Rosemary spread her hands in confusion.

"He ate them."

"Then, they're mine." Rosemary's eyes shone and she bit her lip in thought.

The conversation stopped abruptly as four men walked into the office and Rosemary was pulled into a quick conference with the NYPD's Organized Crime Task Force on where hot spots were likely to develop. To Bagabond, the men were cyphers, administrative types.

With the police already spread thin, no one needed a major gang war. It was all too possible, according to Rosemary. The other Families were likely to strike at the Gambiones, but they would move slowly, testing for the Gambiones' strength and leadership. The Immaculate Egrets were the greatest danger, outdistancing the Colombians, the bikers, and even the Mexican Herrera family. The Egrets were not known for caution, restraint, or patience. If the

Gambiones did not reestablish their power very quickly, they would be destroyed. None of the men liked the Gambiones, but they all feared the alternative.

While Rosemary discussed the reaction of the Five Families, Bagabond sat quietly on her chair in a corner behind Rosemary's desk. Eyes closed, allowing the conversation to weave around her, she tracked Sewer Jack. He had retreated to the tunnels where he felt safest, but every time Bagabond attempted to influence him to stop moving, he resisted. Although the alligator did not understand precisely why he searched or for what, he kept looking. Tracing the quest further into his brain, Bagabond found that the alligator had made a connection between Cordelia and a particularly tasty bit of food. Discovering that, Bagabond nearly lost contact as the humor of it overcame a portion of her concentration. Wait until she told Jack. Bringing herself back into sync with the reptile, she moved through his brain and carefully changed a few of the neurochemical connections between his legs and his brain, modifying the resistance in the neurons. This done, the alligator moved virtually in slow motion.

Bagabond blinked and brought Rosemary's office back into focus, beginning with the portrait of Fiorello La Guardia on the far wall. The men had left. Rosemary sat at her desk, reviewing a file.

"Welcome back to the real world." Rosemary closed the file. "So where's Jack?"

"Somewhere under the Bowery, as best I can tell." She blinked. "Do you really think it is—the real world?"

Rosemary looked out the window. "It's the only one I have." She looked back at Bagabond. "Did you catch much of that conversation?" At Bagabond's shrug, she continued, "I'm supposed to contact my 'sources' and find out what's happening now. After that, I want to go get those books. I'll figure out what I'm going to do with them when I get them." She picked up the phone and began punching buttons.

Bagabond watched silently.

"Max, this is Rosa Maria Gambione," Rosemary said into the receiver. "I heard there was trouble today, Don Frederico . . ." She reached out and placed the phone on the speaker.

". . . long time since you last called, Maria."

"Yes, it has been a long time. But I am still a Gambione."

"Don Frederico has passed on," Max said after a pause. "Perhaps an accident, perhaps the damned—excuse me, Maria—Chinamen. I do miss your father, Maria. This never would have happened if he were still with us."

"My father was a good don, Max. Is there someone in line to become the new don?"

"No, the Butcher—excuse me, Maria—thought he would live forever."

"What will happen with the Family?"

Bagabond looked up sharply at Rosemary. The assistant DA's tone held more than intellectual concern, and she looked worried. Her hands were curled, the knuckles livid.

"There is a meeting tonight at eight at the Haiphong Lily—the younger capos find it amusing to meet there, and the food is good. The capos will decide who will be the next don. Forgive my impertinence, but I hope they choose more wisely this time."

"I'm sure they will, Max."

"Maria, if you give me your phone number, I could let you know what happens."

"No, no, I'm never at home and I hate answering machines."

"I can't believe that a nice girl like you hasn't found a

husband yet. You can't mourn Lombardo Lucchese forever, you know. Don't let that tragedy ruin your life."

"Thank you, Max. I'm not. You know how picky I am. My father's daughter."

"Yes, you are. Strong and smart like him. Please don't be such a stranger, Rosa Maria. We all miss you."

Bagabond's eyes widened as she listened to Rosemary's conversation. Rosemary picked up a ballpoint from her deak and threw it at her.

"Take care, Max. I'll speak to you soon. Ciao."

"Ciao, Maria."

The phone squealed when Rosemary switched off the speaker.

"And what's so funny, Suzanne?"

" 'Oh, Max, I'm just too busy being a district attorney to have a family.' They really don't know?"

"Suzanne Melotti, God will get you for that. Of course they don't know. Rosemary Muldoon is black Irish and doesn't look a thing like Maria Gambione, the only twentieth-century Madonna. I haven't seen any of them in person since my mother's funeral years ago, and I wore a wig, veil, and no makeup for that." Rosemary shook her head. "Why would they make the connection? Everybody around here just figures I read the right books in school and somehow know the right people to be an expert on the Families. They also allow me the factor of good luck."

"God already has." Bagabond leaned back in her chair and tilted her head to one side. "You really are worried about the Gambiones' welfare, aren't you? The Gambiones are still your family."

"If the balance of power shifts, we'll have a disaster." Rosemary stood up.

"Bullshit. Let's go get Jack."

Rosemary opened her mouth to reply, but the phone beeped at her and the disembodied receptionist's voice spoke. "Ms. Muldoon, I've got a problem here. Sergeant Fitz-Gerald is calling from the Tombs. It seems that someone, um, 'teleported,' I think he said, an alleged criminal into the Tombs."

"Mother of God, why today!" Rosemary stared at the phone as if she wanted it to explode. "Patricia, isn't Tomlinson on call this afternoon?"

"Well, yes, Ms. Muldoon, that's what my sheet says. But he's still out to a late lunch and everyone else I've tried is either in conference or away from their desk."

"I'll just bet they're in conference." Rosemary sighed and sat down again. "I'll take it."

Bagabond didn't believe Rosemary's protests of uninvolvement with the Gambiones. The books had become an excuse for Rosemary to be reunited with her real family. It angered Bagabond that she had been maneuvered into aiding Rosemary in that goal. It also made her jealous of Rosemary's past.

Bagabond blocked out the office and tracked down Jack, still treading his reptilian path toward his prey. It took time to scan for him, even at his current slow pace. When she located him, she returned to the office to find Rosemary watching her balefully.

"Sergeant FitzGerald, soon to be Officer FitzGerald, is hysterical. He is also incoherent. I've got to get down there now. Why don't you come along and we'll leave from there?" Bagabond nodded at her as Rosemary reached for the intercom. "Patricia, try and find Goldberg for me. Tell him to meet me at the elevator." Rosemary grabbed her jacket off the back of the chair. "Let's go before anything else happens. I want to make this quick."

"Why him?" Bagabond put her shoes back on and winced. She walked through the door Rosemary held open for her.

"Your buddy, Goldberg? Because he's new and he's got to learn how to handle this sort of thing. And besides, I *like* spreading misery around. Come on."

Goldberg waited at the elevator, apparently nervously watching for Rosemary. He nodded at Bagabond as the pair walked up.

"Suzanne, I believe you've met Paul Goldberg." Rosemary waved at Bagabond. "Paul, Suzanne Melotti, a friend and associate of mine."

"I'm pleased to meet you officially, Ms. Melotti." He smiled at her. "I hope I wasn't too abrupt earlier."

"No." Bagabond punched the Down button.

"Um, good. Good." Paul turned to Rosemary. "Ms. Muldoon, may I ask why I'm here?" He spread his hands and looked inquisitive.

"Today is *not* a good day to give me straight lines, Paul." Rosemary glanced at Bagabond, who was watching the floor numbers change. "I'll tell you on the way."

"Yes, ma'am," said Paul.

Altobelli met Fortunato at the barricades across the south entrance to Fort Tryon Park. The barricades had been up so long, what with the kid gangs and then the damage the aces had done rooting out the Masons, they'd become permanent fixtures.

There were cops everywhere. As one paddywagon pulled away another crawled up to take its place. They were down to the dregs now, skinny, underage kids in jeans and T-shirts, handcuffed and sweaty, some of them bleeding from the face and hands. Altobelli shook his head. He was short, graying at the temples, thin except around the middle.

"PC's idea," he said. The police commissioner had been on the radio all last week, taking a hard line about Wild Card Day. "Nice, huh? Of all the fuckin' times to pull this kind of stunt. If we'd been on the streets where we were supposed to be, instead of up here kickin' a few kids' asses, maybe we could have saved the Howler or that kid. Not to mention the Turtle."

"What?"

"It just come over the wire," Altobelli said. "Couldn't fuckin' believe it myself. Couple of punk aces took him out with some sort of scrambler or somethin'. Then they napalmed the poor bastard. Went into the Hudson. They're dragging for the shell. No sign yet."

"Jesus. The Turtle." If they can get him, Fortunato thought, then we're all finished. There's no hope for any of us.

I'm going to die, he thought.

In a way losing all hope made it easier. Now it was just a question of grace under pressure. Saving what he could and letting the rest go.

Sometime, he thought, before four o'clock, you're going to get your shot. What you have to do is wait for it. Be ready. Don't even think about saving yourself, because you're already lost. What you have to do is kill him. Whatever it costs you, you have to kill him, or die trying.

His hands were shaking. Not fear, not really. More like sick, helpless rage. He made them into fists. He was squeezing so tight he thought he was going to hurt himself. Before he knew he was going to do it he had turned around and put his fist through the back window of one of the squad cars. Chunks of safety glass rolled across the back seat like uncut jewels.

"Jesus Christ, Fortunato!" Altobelli ran to the car and then looked back at Fortunato's hand. "You okay?"

"Yeah."

"Christ, how am I gonna explain this window?"

"Say one of the kids did it. I don't care." He flexed his fingers, went through a couple of calming mantras in his head. "Forget the window, okay, Altobelli? Tell me why you wanted me here."

"Gangs," Altobelli said, turning reluctantly from the car. "Nobody went to the Cloisters after you guys trashed the place, so the kids moved back in. PC thinks to grab some headlines from the jokers by rounding up the kids. Only what happens, there's all these tunnels under the place. And there's bodies down in there."

"Show me."

Altobelli took him past the barricades to an EMS wagon. There were two bodies on gurneys, side by side. Fortunato pulled the first sheet down. It was one of the kids, with long black hair and a rolled-up bandanna around his head. He looked vaguely familiar. There was a wad of cotton where his throat should have been. "He was some kind of runner for the Masons," Fortunato said. "That's all I know."

Altobelli nodded him to the next body. This one had been handsome when he was alive—bright golden hair, sharp nose and chin. He'd been there at the Jokertown lockup, the night Eileen died. He'd decided Fortunato wasn't worth killing.

"Roman," Fortunato said. "I think his name was Roman. He was one of them. He was in jail last I heard. Must have got out on bail or something."

"There were half a dozen other kids—we already carted

'em off. Parts of either two or three girls, it's hard to say which. The ME can sort that out. Hookers, probably." He glanced up quickly. "No offense. And something else that looked like it had been a wooden statue, except it was mostly splinters when we found it. The weird thing was, it had clothes on."

"Probably another ace," Fortunato said. "Some kind of wood man or something."

"There's one more," Altobelli said. "This one's still alive."

He searched through the garbage that littered the alleyway for something heavy. Spector was tired and unsteady. It was probably some kind of hangover from what that Insulin bitch had done to him.

The Astronomer had to be using up power fast. That was the only reason Spector was still alive. The Astronomer needed him to help recharge his powers, which he'd do later with Fortunato's girls. When they got together to off somebody, there was something about the way Spector killed people that made it easier for the Astronomer to eat their energy, or whatever the hell it was he did to get his power. The Astronomer always channeled some of the juice to him. It made Spector feel great, and not many things could anymore. He might have a chance to kill the old bastard before then if the Astronomer was weak enough. Otherwise, the Astronomer would get charged to the limit and then nobody could stop him.

He dug into a dumpster and pulled out a broken marble paperweight. It was shaped like a rearing horse, only the head was gone. Spector knelt down and set his mangled arm against the asphalt. He positioned the paperweight over where the bones had been broken and practiced bringing it down several times, then raised his arm as high as he could. He closed his eyes and pictured the Astronomer's head under his raised hand. Spector brought the paperweight down as hard as he could. There was a snap. He ground his teeth together to keep from screaming and did it again. Another snap. He dropped the headless horse and pulled his bones into line. After a minute or two he let go. His arm was fairly straight, but he still couldn't rotate his wrist. The bones were knobbed and didn't slide over each other the way they should.

Spector shakily stood up, his arm hanging limply at his side. He hurt even worse than usual and his suit, the only one he owned, was a mess. He walked slowly down the alley toward the street, hoping that this was as bad as it would get.

Fortunato stepped carefully over the heavy power cables the cops had strung up in the tunnels. There were arc lights every few feet. The walls were slick and cratered with tiny bubbles. Fortunato guessed that one of the Masonic aces must have drilled them with some kind of heat power.

The main chamber was thirty feet across. There was a battered Persian rug on the floor; somebody had ground out their cigarettes on it. The furniture was cheap vinyl junk that had spent some time in the rain.

Plainclothes cops in latex gloves were gathering up bits and pieces and putting them in ziplock bags. One of them had just picked up a disposable plastic syringe. Fortunato took the man's wrist and bent over to sniff the needle. The cop stared at him.

"Heroin," Fortunato said.

"Been a lot of it around," the cop said. "Cheap as dirt these days."

Fortunato nodded, thinking about Veronica. She could be on the street right now, tying off, raising the bright blue vein inside her elbow . . .

"Over here," Altobelli said. "I don't know what the fuck he is."

Fortunato recognized him from Water Lily's description. He was one of the nightmares, a weird little genius who'd rebuilt the Shakti device for the Astronomer. His fear and hatred of cockroaches had turned him into one.

"Kafka," Fortunato said. "That's what they call you, isn't it?"

"Not," the man said, "to my face. As a rule." He sat on a tobacco-colored couch in the corner. The parts of him that weren't covered by a white lab coat were the same brown color as the couch—skinny legs with spikes coming out the back, hands like tweezers, a flat, noseless face, with nothing but lumps where the eyes should have been.

Fortunato stood in front of him. All he felt was cold. "Where is he?"

"I don't know," Kafka said.

"Why aren't you dead like the others?"

The faceless head swiveled toward him. "Give me time. I'm sure I will be. Some of those . . . *children* . . . outside were having some sport with me. By the time I got here I heard screaming. I hid in a back tunnel."

"Did you hear anything else?"

"He told someone else—a woman—to meet him at a

warehouse when she was done. There was something about a ship."

"What kind of ship?"

"I don't know."

"Who was he talking to?"

"I never knew her name. I only saw her once or twice. Besides, my eyes are nearly useless. I could try to describe her smell to you."

Fortunato shook his head. "Is there anything else? Anything at all?"

Kafka thought for another few seconds. "He said something about four o'clock. That was all I heard."

Demise had said it was all going to happen by four A.M. A yacht? Fortunato wondered. Some kind of cruise ship? Not likely. Nothing that traveled on water could take him far enough fast enough to keep Fortunato from finding him.

Which meant a spaceship. But where in hell would the Astronomer be able to come up with a spaceship?

"Have them cremate me, will you?" Kafka said. "I hate this body. I hate the idea of it being around after me."

"You ain't dead yet," Altobelli said. "For Christ's sake."

"As good as," Kafka said. "As good as."

On the way back out Fortunato said, "He's right, you know. The Astronomer is going to come after him. You need a guard around him at all times. Like SWAT guys with M16s."

"You're serious, aren't you?"

"He got the Turtle," Fortunato said.

"All right. You got it. Procedure in a case like this, the perp goes to the Jokertown lockup. That's Captain Black's turf. But I'll keep a detail of my own guys with him. We've got enough shit on our faces for one day."

They came back up into daylight. "Now look," Altobelli

said. “You be careful. You see this Astronomer character, you call for backup, you understand?”

“Right, Lieutenant.”

“Sure you will,” Altobelli said. “Sure you will.”

CHAPTER 11

4.00 p.m.

Electrochemical neutral responses diminished, body slowed to a dreamlike slow motion, the alligator moved among the tunnels deep below the Bowery. The reptile brain wasn't aware of it, but he was moving vaguely in the direction of Stuyvesant Square. The creature that only sometimes was Jack Robicheaux sought food, wide-nostriled snout casting from side to side as he sought to sense the location of a particularly delectable morsel. The morsel had dark brown eyes and glossy black hair. The alligator's mind fixed on that image.

The creature padded through pools of cold radiance shed by the low-wattage trouble lights fixed to the tunnel walls. The sort of maintenance crew Jack Robicheaux sometimes bossed had presumably left the system on, despite not planning to return to work until after the holiday weekend. The city would foot the electricity bill. No one cared.

The alligator turned a corner and entered a much older

section of passage. The floor was slab stone rather than concrete. The ceiling lowered. The creature felt the welcome increase of humidity as his feet plopped down now in brackish pools.

His unblinking eyes passed incuriously across years of graffiti vandals had scrawled and spray-painted on the stone walls. Near a narrow branching tunnel, someone with considerable time had incised letters in the rock: CROATOAN.

The alligator didn't care. He responded only to his basic drives and forged ahead against the awful inertia that tugged him back at every step. Hunger. Still so hungry . . . So needful.

The dark shallow water now covered the entire passageway. The alligator welcomed it, hoping on a primal level that the level would deepen until the reptile could start to swim. The powerful tail switched slowly with anticipation.

His ears detected unfamiliar sounds and he halted jerkily. Prey? He wasn't sure. *Anything* could be prey ordinarily, but there was something about the noises . . . He heard the scrabbling of a multitude of claws on stone, a hissing sibilance of almost-voices.

They came upon him from around the next bend. There were at least two dozen of them, most tiny, as small as the web-span of his foot. Others were larger, and a few, the leaders, perhaps a quarter the size of his twelve-foot bulk.

The larger alligator slowly opened his jaws and bellowed a challenge.

The smaller reptiles stopped in a semicircle around him, their eyes glittering in the trouble-light glare. Their damp hides shone moistly, the mossy green most pronounced in the smaller ones. The skins of the larger, older alligators held an overlay of hoary whiteness, a dark-bred pallor.

The pack started to hiss and grumble as one, and started forward. Hundreds of sharp teeth shone bright as polished bone.

The larger alligator looked at them and roared again. These *could* be food, but he didn't want them to be. They were something else. They were as he, even if their forms were much smaller. He closed his jaws and waited for them.

The smaller ones reached him first, scuttling up, rearing on their tails and hind legs, and rubbing against his own muscled feet. The hisses, some low and rumbling, most high and sharp, filled the tunnel.

They surrounded him only a short time, the smaller, more agile alligators gamboling about, while the larger reptiles nuzzled against their bigger brother. The larger alligator felt something alien, something puzzling, disturbing on all levels. It was not hunger. It was something like the opposite.

Then the pack left him, the smaller members again merrily circling a few times before rejoining their comrades down the tunnel and around the next bend. The sound of claws ticking on wet stone receded, as did the scent of other reptiles.

The larger alligator hesitated then in his single-minded course. Something tugged at him, urging the creature to turn in the passage and follow after the smaller reptiles, to be part of something bigger, something different from what he already was.

Then the sounds and scents faded, and all the alligator heard was dripping water. He turned back to the darkness of the tunnel ahead and again lifted one foot heavily after the other. The hunger he sought to assuage was somehow more than mere appetite, and right now, he knew there was nothing more important than pursuing the image in his head.

Jennifer, spending two hours on the street, alone, with no money, no shoes, and very little in the way of clothes, was learning what it meant to be hunted. She was afraid to stay for very long in any one place, afraid that the reptilian joker would track her down again, yet she was afraid to go to anyone for help. She was afraid to return to her apartment in case they'd track her there and discover her real identity, but, with late afternoon coming and night not too far behind, she was afraid to remain out on the street. She had already ignored half a dozen indecent proposals and that could only get worse with the coming of night. She wanted to take some positive action, but she was feeling too harried, too much the hare in the game of hound and hare, to come up with a decent plan.

She needed a haven, a place of peace and safety where she could take a breather, rest her sore feet, and, above all, think. The sign in front of a small brick-and-stone building on Orchard Street made her pause. This, she thought, was exactly what she needed.

It was a church. The sign in front said Our Lady of Perpetual Misery. It looked Catholic. Jennifer had been brought up as a Protestant, but her family hadn't been very religious and she herself harbored no deep religious feelings. None, at any rate, that would prevent her from seeking refuge in a Catholic church.

She hurried up the worn stone steps and through the large wooden double doors that opened up into a small vestibule. She stepped inside the vestibule, looked at the doors leading into the nave, and stared.

The vestibule itself was a small windowless room with flagstone paving. Wooden benches stood along its side walls with coat hooks, now all empty, above them. The closed double doors leading into the church nave were also wooden. A scene had been painted on them in a naive style that would have been beautiful if the subject matter hadn't been so grotesque.

The central figure was a crucified Christ, but a Christ like Jennifer had never seen. He—Jennifer thought of Him as He, though she wasn't exactly sure if the pronoun applied in this case—was naked but for a scrap of linen draped around his loins. He had an extra set of shriveled arms sprouting from his rib cage and an extra head on his shoulders. Both heads had aesthetically lean features. One was bearded and masculine, the other was smooth-cheeked and feminine. Blood trickled down both faces because of the crowns of thorns that each head wore. Four pairs of breasts ran down the front of the Christ's body, each pair smaller than the one above. There was a gaping red wound running blood onto the lowest breast on the figure's right side. The Christ was not crucified upon a cross, but rather upon a twisting helix, a convoluted ladder, or, Jennifer realized, a representation of DNA.

There were other figures in the background of the scene, subordinate to the Christ figure. One was a slight, lean figure dressed in gaudy clothes that resembled Dr. Tachyon. But like the Roman god Janus this Tachyon had two faces. One was serene and angelic in profile. It smiled sweetly and had an expression of benevolent kindness. The other was the leering face of a demon, bestial and angry, dripping saliva from an open mouth ringed with sharp teeth. The Tachyon figure held an unburning sun in his right hand, the side of the angel face. In the left he held jagged lightning.

There were other figures whose antecedents were somewhat less clear to Jennifer. A smiling Madonna with feathered wings nursed one head of a baby Christ figure at each breast, a goat-legged man wearing a white laboratory coat carried what looked like a microscope while cavorting in a dance, a man with golden skin and a look of perpetual shame and sorrow on his handsome features juggled an arcing shower of silver coins.

Inscribed above the tableau were the words: Our Lady of Perpetual Misery. Below that, in slightly smaller letters, was Church of Jesus Christ, Joker.

Jennifer pursed her lips. She had heard a little about this offshoot of orthodox Catholicism that had been embraced by many jokers who had a religious bent. The Catholic hierarchy, of course, wanted nothing to do with the Church of Jesus Christ, Joker, and considered it heresy. It wasn't exactly an underground religion, but nobody who wasn't a joker knew much about it, especially the secret rites that were rumored to be carried on in subterranean crypts that weren't as accessible to the public as the churches themselves were.

This was not the time, Jennifer decided, for theological exploration. She was about to turn and leave the church when a sudden sound, a sort of grasping, sucking, squishy noise, came from the other side of the doors leading into the nave. She froze and the image of Jesus Christ, Joker, split down the middle as the doors swung open. A figure stood there, vaguely illuminated by the banks of candles that were burning within the nave. It was large and bulky, the height of a normal man and twice as broad, and covered completely by a voluminous cassock that hung to the floor.

The figure's hands were hidden in flowing sleeves and Jennifer could barely make out a glabrous, dead-gray face in the shadow of the gown's hood. The face was round and oily looking with two large, bright eyes covered by nictitating membranes that were constantly blinking. The face had no nose, but a cluster of tendrils hung where the nose should be, twitching and rustling, covering the joker's mouth like some kind of weird, unkempt mustache.

Jennifer stared, swallowed hard.

The figure took another step into the vestibule and she heard again the faint squishy sound, like suckers on stone. The joker had a strange musty smell to him, as of the sea, or of things that lived in it.

He regarded Jennifer with his bright, solemn eyes, and when he spoke his voice was somewhat muffled by the tentacular tendrils that covered his mouth, but Jennifer could understand his words clearly.

"Welcome to Our Lady of Perpetual Misery. My name is Father Squid."

The nictitating membranes on Father Squid's eyes slipped back and forth rapidly over his protruding orbs, although the eyes themselves remained open and staring. He smiled, maybe, behind the fall of tentacles that masked his mouth. At least his cheeks rose and his voice took on an even more gentle, kindly tone.

"Don't be afraid of me, or any you would find within these walls, my child. I perceive that you may be in need of help. I would endeavor to assist you, if I only knew what you needed."

The priest's words spoken in plodding sentences calmed Jennifer immediately. Somehow she couldn't be afraid of someone who said things like "I would endeavor to assist you."

"Well, um, Father, I guess I do need help. I'm not sure that you could help me, though."

"Perhaps," Father Squid said, "perhaps not. However, I'm sure that your coming to Our Lady Of Perpetual Misery was no accident. Perhaps our Lord guided you to our door. Perhaps you should simply tell me your story."

Why not? Jennifer suddenly thought. Perhaps he really could see a way out of this mess.

"All right," she began, then fell silent again. Father Squid nodded, as if he could read the hesitation on her face.

"Do not worry, my child. Everything you tell me will be held in the strictest confidence." He opened the door and pointed into the nave. His hand, taken outside the voluminous sleeves of his cassock for the first time, was large and gray with long, attenuated fingers. Jennifer could see faint circular depressions, like vestigial suckers, impressed all over its palm. "The confessional is within. The priest-penitent bond is well known and universally respected. Everything said there shall be privy between us."

Jennifer nodded. The priest-penitent bond was as strong as that between lawyer and client and, in fact, was less easily broken. If the priest was trustworthy, that is. She looked at the large, solemn-faced joker and decided she trusted him.

Father Squid held open the door and stood aside as she entered Our Lady of Perpetual Misery, Church of Jesus Christ, Joker.

Bagabond shivered as the trio walked through the heavy deco doors at the entrance to the Tombs. "I can see why they call it the Tombs," she said.

Paul shook his head. "Goes back more than a century to the first prison they built on this site. This is the third. Originally the building really did look like an Egyptian tomb."

"I still don't like it."

He touched her on the shoulder. "I know. I may be a criminal lawyer, but I hate jails too. They make me feel like a trapped animal." He spoke quietly. Rosemary, moving briskly ahead of them toward the desk sergeant, apparently didn't hear.

"Most animals are free, unless enslaved by a human." Bagabond looked at him directly. Paul flinched at her stare.

"True."

Bagabond looked past him. "I think Rosemary wants you." The assistant DA had turned away from the desk and was waving at Paul.

Flicking her consciousness through a wino rocking on a lobby bench, a man who was no longer humanly aware, Bagabond watched the expression on Paul's face change from confusion to thoughtfulness, and then to interest. She followed Paul up to Rosemary as the assistant DA argued with the desk sergeant.

Rosemary was unhappy. "You *can't* have lost him. This guy was *teleported* into a cell. How many people teleport into here every day?" Rosemary glared at the bald officer sitting above her. The cop glowered back.

"If he teleported in, he wouldn't come through this desk," said the sergeant. "He don't come through this desk, he ain't got no paperwork. No paperwork, no way to trace him. He's here, we got no record." The officer leaned back in his overburdened and creaking chair, and smiled down at Rosemary. "Ya gotta follow procedure." He tucked his many chins against his barrel chest and looked pleased with himself.

Rosemary grabbed the edge of his desk with both hands and took a deep breath.

Before she could speak, Paul said, “I believe his name is Bludgeon, *the* Bludgeon.” He interjected the information into the conversation in an obvious attempt to keep his boss from either apoplexy or killing the desk sergeant. Rosemary swung around to stare at him with wide, angry eyes. “Large, muscular build,” Paul continued. “Somewhat like your own.”

“Nothin’ comes to mind.” The sergeant grinned widely as Paul turned to Rosemary, shrugging in resignation. She turned back toward the sergeant.

Voice tightly controlled, she said, “Perhaps you could find an officer for me.”

“Lots of ’em around.” The sergeant gestured at the room around them where a number of people, both police and those under arrest, had stopped their own conversations to listen to the exchange.

Rosemary closed her eyes and clenched her teeth. Wearily she said, “Where might I find Sgt. Juan FitzGerald?”

“Juan,” said the desk sergeant, as though pondering a lengthy list. “Why dinya say so? Juan’s down in Block C. Can you find your way, or should I assign an officer to hold your hand in the dark?”

“I *know* the way.” Rosemary stalked toward the first gate leading down into the cellblocks. Paul and Bagabond trailed her. The corners of Bagabond’s eyes crinkled in amusement.

“What’s so funny?” Paul glanced apprehensively at Rosemary’s back.

“What she puts up with. I would have ripped his throat

out." Bagabond spoke matter-of-factly. Utterly sincerely.

Paul looked confused for a moment and then smiled. "Nah, too many witnesses. Besides, no throat, no information." He nodded to himself. "What you want to do is invite him to one of these stairwells and then break his kneecaps."

Bagabond stopped and looked at him with respect for the first time. "Right on, Mr. Goldberg. I like that."

"I'm glad. The name's Paul."

"Suzanne," she said. "You can call me Suzanne."

"Will you two come on?" said Rosemary from ahead of them. "I'm not holding this elevator forever. Conduct your romance on your own time." She stared at them, apparently realizing how flat her joke was falling. Paul and Bagabond exchanged self-conscious glances. "Right." Rosemary got into the car first and punched the floor button.

At Block C, they underwent a cursory search before walking through the peeling, tan-painted steel gate. Turning a corner in the cellblock, the three of them halted at the sight of the hulking giant nearly filling the entire corridor from one dull green wall to the other. His back was to them.

Bagabond uttered a small *miaow* of alarm, and both Rosemary and Paul looked at her.

"The things I do for this city." Rosemary started forward. "Rosemary Muldoon, district attorney's office. What's happening here?"

The giant maneuvered to face her. Two men standing beyond him started to speak too.

"My client–"

"This *gentleman*–"

"I want *out*!"

"Hold on!" Rosemary cut them all off. "FitzGerald, talk to me," she said to the uniformed officer. "You other two, hold that thought and stay right where you are."

The lawyer in the light gray Armani suit spoke loudly enough for Rosemary and the others to hear as she passed, "NYU, I'd venture to guess." There was no mistaking the tone.

Rosemary pulled the six-foot Puerto Rican officer down the hall.

Bagabond glanced at Paul and nodded toward Bludgeon. "Keep an eye on him."

"Great." Paul smiled at the lawyer and the towering man beside him. He stuck out his hand. "Paul Goldberg, DA's office. How's it going?"

Bagabond followed Rosemary.

"Just what is going on?" the assistant DA said to Fitz-Gerald. "Who's the snappy dresser?"

"He says he's from Latham, Strauss." The officer looked abashed at Rosemary's expression of disgust and disbelief.

"Not bad for an oversized punk." She nodded. "What exactly happened?"

"This Bludgeon just popped in. Had to be Popinjay—Jay Ackroyd."

"I've heard the name." Rosemary shrugged. "This city doesn't need any more vigilante do-gooders."

"Well, he's done it before, no problem. He comes in and files charges later. But this time, he never showed. I read Bludgeon his rights and let him make his phone call." Fitz-Gerald gestured at the dapper man examining the gold clasp of his briefcase. "Then twenty minutes ago, that guy shows up."

"Wonderful." Hand over her mouth, Rosemary stared at the ceiling as if waiting for inspiration.

The lawyer came up to them. "Excuse me, but my client would like to leave now." The shade of his Armani was the precise gray of his hair. He had an unctuous smile.

"Well, Mr. . . ."

"Tulley, ma'am. Simon Tulley."

"Mr. Tulley. There are a number of serious charges against your client." Rosemary shook her head in concern.

"Oh?" said Tulley. "I was not aware that there were *any* charges against him."

"I don't think it would be in the public interest to release Mr. Bludgeon without thoroughly investigating this matter."

Bagabond nodded in agreement.

Tulley frowned past Rosemary at Bagabond. "And who is this lovely lady?"

"An associate. Ms. Melotti." Rosemary looked at Bagabond and then quickly back at Tulley. Bludgeon's lawyer extended his hand. Bagabond stared down at it as if inspecting a piece of rotting meat.

"Charmed, I'm sure." Tulley took a breath and shifted his attention back to Rosemary. "I don't want to bring up false arrest as a potential problem, Ms. Muldoon, but you should seriously evaluate your position."

"Mr. Tulley, as you so astutely have pointed out, your client has not been officially arrested yet."

"False imprisonment, then. I am beginning to lose my patience." Tulley looked down his long, aristocratic nose at Rosemary. "Where are the charge sheets?"

"The paperwork is undoubtedly a little slow today—the holiday and all. I've just had a little problem with that myself." Rosemary shifted her hands and smiled innocently at Tulley. "I do have to consider the community's welfare."

"And I am here to protect my client's. We are leaving now." Tulley showed his teeth and pranced back toward Bludgeon.

"Tulley—" Rosemary started toward them.

"Show me a witness. Show me a witness's *statement.*

No? Then he's mine or I'll file against the city." Tulley possessively grasped Bludgeon's arm. The giant grinned at Rosemary and Bagabond.

" 'Bye, now," he said to them in a high-pitched voice ill-suited to his size. "I'll see you again. Real soon, I hope." Bludgeon watched for the women's response. When he failed to get one, he glared and preceded Tulley to the gate. FitzGerald flattened himself against the wall as they passed.

Rosemary looked at Paul and laughed bitterly. "Say to yourself, 'I love the Bill of Rights' three times." She lifted her right hand and massaged her temples. "You two go ahead. I want to ask FitzGerald a couple things. I'll meet you out front."

Bagabond and Paul were silent in the elevator. Paul looked depressed. Walking out into the sunlight was like coming up from deep water into the air. The lawyer sat down on one of the worn marble steps.

"I worked in corporate law for years—mergers, takeovers, leveraged buyouts, the whole routine. Then I decided I wanted to make a difference, to contribute. Payback, you know? So I got a job here." He rapped the stone with his knuckles. "Some difference, huh? We're trapped by our own strengths."

"I realized that a long time ago." Bagabond shrugged and watched the yellow torrent of passing cabs. Idly, she shifted a portion of her consciousness into the pigeons sitting on the roof of the Tombs and looked out across the crowds.

"But you've just got to give something back. There's a responsibility." Paul looked up at the woman staring blindly into the sky.

Bagabond started. "You're the second person today to

say that to me." A pigeon swooped down almost to her shoulder, but she guided it away before it could land. "Maybe you're right."

Paul hesitated, then said, "I realize this is abrupt, but I have to say something."

The woman focused her attention on him.

"You're the most intriguing person I've met in this city . . ."

"Rosemary will be thrilled," Bagabond said.

"Rose—Ms. Muldoon is my boss. Besides, she isn't my type. A bit too conventional." Paul stood up and faced her.

"I'm not conventional?" Bagabond was amused, wondering how "different" he thought she was.

"No offense, please. I was wondering if we could have dinner sometime." The attorney watched people scale the steps behind her left shoulder. "Sorry. You make me very nervous."

"Thanks, but I work most nights." Bagabond was confused. A part of her actually wanted to do this.

"Okay, then. What about breakfast?"

"Breakfast?"

"Sure. I run six miles really early, about five. Then I go home and get ready for work. If I feel like it, I go get a big breakfast before coming in. It ruins the roadwork, but tastes great." He smiled at her and cocked his head a little to one side. "Join me one day—just for the breakfast?"

"All right." Bagabond nodded and then hesitantly smiled. For the first time, the smile was reflected in her eyes as well. "Yes, I might like that."

"How about tomorrow?"

She stared at him, once again without expression.

"Don't tell me you have another date," Paul said.

"What time?"

"Seven. I can pick you up—"

"I'll meet you. Where?" Bagabond concentrated on suppressing the thought that she was making a *big* mistake.

"The market, at Greenwich and Seventh."

"You two look deep in thought." Rosemary strode down the steps. "I know that Popinjay was trying to help, but there are times I wish aces wouldn't get involved. It would make my life simpler. Yours too, Paul." She shook her head ruefully. "Paul, go on back to the office. Work with Chavez. Suzanne and I have some business to take care of."

"See you later," he said to Bagabond, shaking hands with her.

As the two women watched Paul walk back toward the DA's building, Rosemary looked at Bagabond speculatively. "He likes you, you know. Of course Jack's a union man and undoubtedly makes a lot more money, but Paul has certain attractions." Rosemary cocked her head and narrowed her eyes. "Great ass."

"Twentieth-century Madonna?"

"*That* was a *long* time ago." She changed the subject. "Where's Jack?"

"Let's go someplace quiet where I can concentrate. I need an alley." Bagabond started to walk toward the corner.

"An alley," said Rosemary. "You hang out in the classiest places. Didn't anyone ever tell you to stay out of Manhattan alleys?" She caught up with Bagabond and they crossed Lafayette Street. "Places like that, people can get killed."

The darkness in the confessional was somehow soothing. The air in the box smelled even more strongly of the sea and Father Squid's bulk was a comforting presence on the other side of the frosted glass window. He made small sighing sounds as he considered Jennifer's story.

"I believe that I know of the joker who is accosting you," the priest finally said. "He is not of my children, but there are few jokers who have not come by at least once or twice to hear the Word. He goes by the name Wyrm. His reputation is not of the best." Father Squid fell into a meditative silence that lasted for some minutes. "I am perplexed, but perhaps understanding will come. Come." He rose to his feet, swept back the heavy drapery that curtained his side of the confessional, and stepped out of the box. Jennifer followed. "I must make some inquiries." He held up a broad, spatulate hand and wiggled his long fingers to silence the question he saw on Jennifer's face. "Never fear. I shall be most subtle and circumspect. Make yourself comfortable. Rest. You are as safe here as if you were in your own home. Perhaps infinitely safer if your suspicions are correct."

His cheeks bunched again as if he were smiling, and Jennifer nodded. She watched as Father Squid waddled off, making faint squishing sounds on the flagstone flooring as he went with ponderous dignity to the rear of the church.

Roulette was approaching climax, and she tried to resist, the effort causing her thighs to cramp and nausea to wash about the tendrils of fire that filled her belly and groin. Tachyon with that *damnable* sensitivity fixed his pale eyes on her, and slowed his thrusts, his hands caressing her breasts, sweeping down her sides.

Release!

And as quickly as the command was given it was withdrawn. The tide sank back, growling its frustration in a voice that was the Astronomer's.

Her mind and body were once more in harmony, no longer rent by her fear and indecision. Her passion rose, and she rocked in a frenzied rhythm, matching each thrust of his small, compact body.

The shrill ring of the front bell tore through the apartment. Beneath her hands she felt his muscles tighten and leap, and his cock slid free.

"Damn, damn, damn," he whispered, urgently trying to fit himself once more into her. She reached down to help, and their hands bumped and tangled, sliding on the slick skin of his penis.

Ring.

He was finally in, but the ringing persisted, and he lay flaccid and inert atop her.

He sighed, briefly closed his eyes, and said, "I think the moment is ruined."

"Yes."

"Shall I answer the door?"

"I don't think they'll go away otherwise."

"Wait here."

He rose, and shrugged into an elaborate brocade dressing gown of black silk shot through with threads of silver and red. It was too long, and the hem whispered across the smoke-gray carpet. He was careful to close the bedroom door behind him, and she wondered if that was to protect her reputation or his.

Folding her arms beneath her head, she stared up at the ceiling and listened to the sounds of muffled conversation from the front room. A strange thumping sound followed by a crash brought her upright in the bed, sheet slithering to her waist.

And with a harsh rasp the bedroom window was forced up, and the delicate fabric blinds kicked aside. Roulette screamed, and the foot was withdrawn only to be replaced by the head and shoulders of a man. The wind chime rang wildly as he caught it. She came off the bed, bolting for the door, but in two strides he had caught her by the hair and thrown her into the dresser. She yelped as the beveled edge slammed into her side. Grimly she grasped a silver-backed hairbrush, and gave the intruder a ringing blow between the eyes as he moved in on her. He bellowed, and as if in answer a second man entered through the window. This one carried a gun.

Being naked and armed only with a hairbrush, she decided to opt for prudence. With a little shrug she dropped her inadequate weapon, and raised her eyebrows inquiringly.

"Get in the other room," the second man ordered while her assailant gingerly rubbed his head and then inspected the damage in the mirror.

"May I put on some clothes?"

"Get her something."

The man abandoned the mirror, but continued rubbing as he stepped into the closet and then emerged with one of Tachyon's coats. It was too small, and she felt the shoulder seams split as she forced it on.

Both the men were Orientals. Chinese, she guessed from the high planes of their faces, and their size. Of the four men who stood threateningly over Tachyon in the front room two were Chinese, the other two jokers. The tall reptilian joker wasn't too bad, but his four-foot-tall companion sent a cold shudder across her bare skin, and the hair on the back of her neck tried to climb for cover. Roulette had a horror of flying, stinging insects, and now she was faced with a human wasp. The body of the creature was vaguely humanoid, but the face was a triangular wedge complete with multifaceted eyes, and between the legs hung a long stinger. Transparent wings beat a frantic tattoo, filling the room with a low buzz.

A nervous little laugh erupted from her. "My God, when mysterious East meets homegrown grotesque, does that give us joker slavery?" she inquired brightly, and staggered as a hard blow from behind took her between the shoulder blades.

Tachyon came off the coach like a compact, redheaded whirlwind, dodged a blow from the left, and wriggled out of a second man's grasp. There was a blur of motion, and the wasp jabbed its stinger into the back of Tach's knee. The reptilian joker's lips skinned back in a grimace of pleasure as the Takisian cried in agony and collapsed.

"It won't kill you, Tachyon. Jusst hurtsss like hell. And he's got unlimited sssstings sssso don't try it again."

The tall joker in a show of strength caught Tachyon by the nape of the neck, and set him on his feet. The alien touched the inflamed and swollen skin at the back of his knee, eyed the .38 pressed against Roulette's throat, and the fighting tension leached from his body.

It was an outlandish picture they presented. Four burly Chinese in satin jackets and mirrored sunglasses; some with guns drawn, others with (what the sensational press called) suspicious bulges under their arms. A joker perched like an obscene bug on the back of the couch, and the reptile leaning nonchalantly against the piano, cleaning his long, sharp nails with a switchblade. Then there was Tachyon, tiny and rumpled, his hair tangling on his shoulders, gown gaping to reveal his pale chest, and the head of his cock peeking like a shy bird between the folds of material.

The joker by the piano gestured, and two of his men swung out straight-back chairs from the dining room table. "Dr. Tachyon, please, sssssit down. Then we can talk. Tommy." One of the Chinese glanced up, alert, quivering like a dog on a scent. "Please tie the good doctor. I wouldn't want him trying anything sssstupid. Then I might have to hurt the lady."

Roulette and Tachyon were hustled to the chairs, and he gave her a concerned glance. She smiled with a confidence she didn't feel, and said, "What a blow. Betrayed by popular culture yet again."

"I don't understand."

"In the Fu Manchu books the yellow peril is always mysterious and exotic. Spoils it when the goons have names like 'Tommy,' and speak with flat Brooklyn accents."

Snake-face's long forked tongue lolled out, and he eyed her with hostility. "You want exotic, jussst keep it up, and I'll let the bosss handle you. He'll give you all the exotic you can ssstomach."

Tachyon sat with relaxed elegance, but his lips were white and Roulette realized that the sting was still paining him. Tommy finished binding him to the chair with the belt of his dressing gown, and tilting back his head Tachyon drawled, "Of course, I am delighted to have your company, but might I know to what I owe this singular pleasure?"

Snake-face pulled out a chair with his foot, and straddled the seat, arms folded across the back. Roulette was free, but one of the thugs had placed a hand on her shoulder, and she was very aware of all those guns, and if there was one thing she had learned from her police-officer father it was *Don't fuck with a gun.*

"Tachy, we've come for the book."

The alien's coppery, upswept brows climbed toward his

bangs. "My good man, I have something in excess of a thousand volumes in this apartment. To which book do you refer?"

"Hit him," came the flat reply.

Tommy swung, there was a sound like a dull axe biting into wood, and Tachyon spat out a mouthful of blood. Roulette noticed he was careful to aim the sticky glob onto the lap of his gown, and thus protect the white carpet.

"The book."

"I'm not a lending library."

This time Tommy moved to the front, gathered a fold of the gown in a fist, hauled Tachyon up against his bonds, and gave him several hard backhands. The Chinese was wearing a number of rings, and Roulette bit back a squeak as the metal dug into the alabaster skin. When he finished, the alien's lip had split, his nose was bleeding, and one eye was blackening.

"Hiram will no doubt refuse me entrance tonight," he murmured around his rapidly swelling lip. "He does so like a gentleman to be *point de vice*."

The forked tongue unrolled and flicked caressingly across Tachyon's face licking up the blood. "Tachy, maybe you don't underssstand. I'm going to have that book if I have to take you apart to get it."

Tachyon dropped the affected, maddening tone, and said bluntly, "I truly don't know what you're talking about. What book?"

The joker stared implacably back at him. "It was ssstolen, I know you have it, and I'm going to get it back."

The alien sighed. "Very well, please, search my home, but I assure you I have no stolen book."

"Ssssearch it, tear the place apart." Tachyon winced. "But tie her first. We don't want to be distracted."

Tommy pulled a thin cord from his pocket, and quickly bound her hand and foot to the chair. They scattered and began to ransack the apartment. The wasp continued to sit on the couch buzzing and chittering to itself. A cascade of books tumbled from an upper shelf hitting and shattering a delicate celadon bowl as they fell. Pain and anger flickered deep in Tachyon's eyes, but his voice was level, almost conversational, as he said, "Twice in as many months. This is quite beyond everything. I can forgive the swarmling, it was a mindless monster and so destroyed without thought, but these thugs . . ."

"I thought you had powers. He–someone told me you did." Roulette said in a low voice.

"I do."

"Then, why didn't you use them?"

"I began to, then I heard you scream, and I realized there were more than four. I can control three humans," he whispered, "but the hold is weak, and if I should also have to fight . . ." He turned the full force of his beautiful eyes on her. "I was afraid you would be hurt if my powers proved less strong, or my reflexes less quick than pride would like me to admit. And that wasp is damnably fast." An aggrieved grumble.

"So what do we do?"

"Wait, and pray for an opportunity. I wish you didn't have shields," he added fretfully. "I could keep contact with you telepathically. Ah well, no good mourning for a fled ship."

"Shhh."

"Yellow really isn't your color, my dear," he said, responding quickly to her warning. One of their captors gave them a suspicious glance as he walked past, and Roulette said pettishly for his benefit, "I don't need a commentary on taste from *you*. You're the one who picked this cat-vomit yellow."

The Chinese's mouth spread in a wide grin that displayed a good deal of pink gum and a gold-capped tooth, and he passed into the kitchen alcove.

Tachyon cast her a rueful glance. "Cat vomit? I'd always thought it to be a particularly lovely shade of lemon." Roulette laughed, and the alien gave her an approving look. "Good girl, we'll get out of this yet."

"What a team," she replied dryly.

CHAPTER 12

5:00 p.m.

The dark current swept around his legs and the alligator welcomed it. The pulsing water had started to rise only a short time before; first just a film creeping across the rocky floor of the tunnel, then a succession of gradually higher waves. Now the water lapped around his belly, a quartet of small eddies tugging at his legs where the haunches creased into his armored sides.

The alligator's tail swung back and forth ponderously, impatiently. He wanted the water to float him away from the hard floor and to give him the buoyancy he needed for true swimming. The water meant freedom.

But the level rose no further, and so the alligator plodded on. Various objects, chunks of a variety of substances, nudged against him. He nuzzled some of them with his snout before they were swept away in the current.

The scents were largely unpleasant. There was nothing

there worth the devouring. Lumps of something soft batted against him and were gone.

He briefly detected meat, but it was carrion and he had no taste for that now. Instead of snapping up the ragged object, the alligator forged on. Something alive and delectable still lay ahead of him. He knew that, and, knowing it, forced his nearly insatiable hunger into abeyance.

Under his feet, through his ears and nostrils, through the very wave action of the current, he could feel the pulse of the city. Now it beat in time with his own body.

He ignored the slight pain in his belly. It was as nothing compared to his appetite.

Ahead and behind, the dark tunnel stretched on forever.

He had been trying to reach Tachyon for two hours now, and Hiram was growing concerned.

Everyone agreed that the little alien had left Jetboy's Tomb soon after completing his speech, in the company of an attractive black woman. But where had they gone? His home phone did not answer, and down at the Jokertown clinic, Troll insisted he hadn't seen the doctor all day. Tachyon was probably out somewhere drinking, but where? Hiram had called all of his usual haunts one after the other, had even tried Freakers and the Chaos Club and the Twisted Dragon on the off chance that the Takisian might have decided to drown his guilt on unfamiliar turf. No one had seen Tachyon since the early afternoon, when he left the ceremonies at the Tomb.

Fortunato might not have cared, but Hiram was growing concerned. Had the Astronomer already gotten to Tachyon? Was there another name to add to the list of the dead?

There was a tightness in the pit of his stomach that no amount of food would cure. Restless, uneasy, unhappy, Hiram Worchester got to his feet and strode out into his restaurant. The doors would be opening in less than two hours. Nearly every ace who counted would be arriving, and he devoutly hoped that Dr. Tachyon would be among them. By then, the worst would be over. Even the Astronomer was not insane enough to attack the kind of power that would be assembled at Aces High in two more hours.

Hiram strode to the long, curving bar. The wood gleamed, and the mirror was spotless and brilliant with reflected light. A quartet of bartenders in sky-blue shirts were tapping into fresh kegs of Guinness Stout, New Amsterdam, and Amstel Light. Modular Man was way down on the last stool, drinking a rusty nail. The android liked to experiment.

"I detect no sign of any hostile presence," Mod Man said.

Hiram nodded absently. "Keep watching," he said. He headed for the kitchen with long light strides, still thinking about Tachyon. He must be at home, nothing else made sense. But if he were home, why not answer his phone? Because he was *dead,* whispered some dark part of Hiram's brain, and he could almost see the small alien lying on his carpet, blood seeping through his long red hair and staining his hideous clothing.

In the immense kitchen, the whirring of the great ceiling fans filled the room with a steady throbbing hum as they struggled with the heat from the ovens. Paul LeBarre was in a corner with his spices, mixing his own Cajun blackening powder for the tuna, and roaring his displeasure at anyone who tried to see what he was doing. Rows of potatoes Hiram covered a dozen long trays, cut and seasoned and ready for baking, and six fat suckling pigs were being dressed and prepared. Prep cooks were washing vegetables and slicing them with slim, sharp knives, and the pastry chef was fretting over a triple-chocolate sour-cream torte fresh from the oven. Hiram surveyed it all, tried a taste of the sour cherry sauce being prepared for the pork, exchanged a few words with his saucier, and escaped every bit as restless as when he'd entered.

What if Tachyon *wasn't* dead yet? What if he were just dying? Someone needed to check on him. But Fortunato had warned Hiram not to leave, hadn't he? If he went over to Tachyon's apartment and the Astronomer attacked Aces High in his absence, and perhaps even killed someone, he would never be able to live with himself. But how could he live with himself if he stayed here and Dr. Tachyon died as a result?

Aces High occupied the entire floor, its dining areas terraced so all the customers might enjoy the magnificent views its altitude afforded in all directions. The kitchen, storage lockers, freezer, rest rooms, service elevator, and offices were in the center. Hiram made the grand circuit, supervising everything, nodding to his staff, his mind a long way off.

The temporary waiters were clustered around one of the tables, listening to his captain explain how things were done at Aces High. They looked a motley crew in their jeans and shoddy jackets and Dodger windbreakers, but once in tuxes and blue silk shirts, they'd look as good as his regulars. Elsewhere, linen carts were making the rounds as teams of busboys unfolded crisp clean tablecloths across the round banquet tables. Curtis was talking to the wine steward.

Off by a window he saw Water Lily, standing by herself and staring out at the gold reflections off the top of the Chrysler Building. She wore a floor-length blue satin gown that left her right shoulder bare. She looked very lovely and somehow sad. Hiram started toward her, but there was something in her eyes that made him hesitate to intrude on her. He paused a moment, then turned and left.

Peter Chou had a small office next to Hiram's, in the center of the floor, but instead of one television screen in the wall, he had a dozen. Hiram entered without knocking. "Are we secure?" he asked.

Peter looked at him with cool brown eyes. "I've added a few men," he said. "No one will get in without us noticing, believe me." He gestured at the screens. "The monitors are all working, and so is the metal detector in the main door. I'll have six men on the floor instead of three. We're as secure as we're going to get, at least against human beings."

"Excellent. I have to go out for a little while. I'll try to be back as quickly as possible, but it may take longer than I anticipate. Wait till I've left, then bring Modular Man and Water Lily into your office. Explain our security system to them. Explain the system in great detail. Keep them in here, with you, together, for as long as possible, preferably until I return."

Chou nodded.

Hiram went to the foyer, pressed the elevator button, rocked back on his heel for a moment, then pressed the button again, as if that would make the elevator come more quickly. When the doors finally opened, he rushed to board, and almost slammed into Popinjay getting out.

"You!" Hiram exclaimed. "Excellent, just the man I hoped to see. Come with me, we're going to see Dr. Tachyon."

Ackroyd stepped back inside the elevator. Hiram pushed for the lobby, and they began their descent. "How did it go with Gills?" Hiram asked.

"Not real good," Popinjay said. "By the time I talked Gills around, Bludgeon was out again. He's got good lawyers. I think they're going to sue me." His mouth twisted in a half-smile. "You too, probably. Gills was afraid to go home. I popped him back to my sister's place, he ought to be safe there, and we'll know where to find him if we need him."

"Damnation! Can't we get rid of even one of the bad guys? I don't know what this city is coming to!"

Ackroyd shrugged. "Why are we visiting Tachyon?"

Hiram gave him a glum look. "I'm afraid," he said, "that he might be dead."

Bagabond leaned forward, away from the brick wall of the alley. She steadied herself with a dumpster. The alley smelled of recent garbage. Rosemary was looking around a bit apprehensively. "Relax. We're alone."

"You don't get to read all the crime reports I do," Rosemary said. "You haven't seen the photos detectives snap in places like this. You haven't had to go to the morgue to check out—"

"Quiet," said Bagabond.

"Get him?"

"He's uptown from us, and a ways to the east. I'd guess about Stuyvesant Square. Underground, of course."

"I don't think anyone would even notice today," Rosemary said. "Does he still have the books?"

"As far as I can tell. He doesn't really remember or notice what's in his gut. It's the *absence* that makes the difference. But there's no reason the packet shouldn't still be there."

Rosemary took a step toward the mouth of the alley. "It's quite a ways, especially today. We'd better get started if we're going to make it back to the Haiphong Lily by eight." She smiled ruefully at Bagabond. "*Then* I'll figure out what I'm going to do."

Bagabond frowned. "Jack's still moving, but so slowly we can connect with him easily. We should take the subway. Cabs'll be a mess." She saw Rosemary tense, but didn't comment. Then she grinned. "I've never known an animal to be so constantly hungry as that alligator. I just hope he doesn't connect with *us*."

Rosemary's eyebrows rose.

"He's too worried about his niece for that," Bagabond said. "He just doesn't know it on the surface level of that reptile brain." She shook her head, thinking about appetites, and led the way out of the alley and into the loud, holiday crowds.

They entered the chaos of chants, exotic food carts, screams, and rock 'n' roll.

"The book'sss not here, Tachy. Where isss the book?" The explosive silibants indicated the joker's fast-vanishing patience.

"Almost a thousand books, and they can't find one that suits them. I call it churlish, and a reflection upon my taste."

"Or theirs," offered Roulette.

Tachyon snapped his head back to face Snake-face, the sudden gesture forestalling the blow. "I don't know about this ephemeral book. You say it was given to me. No one has given me a book this day. I have spent the past six hours in this lady's company. Did anyone give me a book?"

"No."

"You've got it." The tongue once more played across the alien's face and down his chest. "I tasted it on her, and if I have to take the nigger apart to get it, I will." A blunt forefinger tipped with a fantastically thick and sharp nail drove into her shoulder, and Roulette stifled a cry. What was coming was going to be a lot worse than a finger jabbing into a numb, aching shoulder, and she'd better be prepared.

"All right, I'll be reasonable. The book isn't here. I put it in a safe place."

"And you're going to take usss there."

"Yes, but you have to let her go."

"No, I think ssshe'll come along."

"Then, no book."

"Then, I redesign her face."

The doorbell rang.

There was a sudden shifting of their captors. Guns touched reassuringly, Tommy starting for the door then dropping back, Snaky jumping for Tachyon, but the alien had also seen the possibilities, and sang out, "Yes, one moment please."

"Fuck you, I ought to break your ssscrawny neck," hissed the joker, his hand closing around the doctor's throat.

"Better let him answer the door instead," whispered Roulette since Tachyon's face was suffusing with blood, and he didn't seem capable of answering for himself. "Otherwise they'll know something's wrong, and come back with help."

"We'll wait it out. It may be the paperboy, or the Mormonssss."

But it was neither. A man's voice, deep, bass, cultured, but bearing a thread of strain and agitation, called, "Tach? I must speak with you. Is everything all right?"

"Tell him yesss."

"Yesss," Tachyon obligingly mimicked, then coughed trying to ease the soreness in his throat.

"Who isss thisss man?"

"Hiram Worchester."

"Okay, you can answer the door, but get rid of him fasst."

"Better clean his face," Roulette offered in the same flat tone she'd maintained since the beginning of this nightmare. She was both pleased and bemused by her control. Inwardly she was a shrieking mess.

"Do it."

A handkerchief was thrust at her, while Tommy untied her. Within seconds the tips of her fingers began to burn as the blood flowed back into her hands.

"Tach?"

"Coming," he replied as Roulette dipped the cloth into the vase on the coffee table and quickly began wiping away the worst of the gore from his face.

"The right side's not too bad," she whispered. "But don't let him see that shiner." The left eye was so badly damaged that it had swollen completely shut.

"I'll be careful," he said in a carefully neutral tone, but his right eye seemed feverishly bright, the gaze intent. She again felt that cloud kiss about the edges of her mind. And she understood, or least hoped or thought she understood. This might be their chance. She gave his hand a quick squeeze and was rewarded by a flash of that sweet smile, somewhat marred now by the split and swollen lip.

Two of their captors took up a position on the wall beside the door, one behind and slightly to the left of Tachyon, gun pressed into the alien's kidneys. Tommy laid a hand on Roulette's right shoulder. The reptilian joker indicated the kitchen with a jerk of the head, and wasp flitted away. The droning of his wings lessened in intensity. Tachyon barely cracked the door, peeped out.

"Hiram."

"What on earth took you so long?"

"I'm entertaining." A subtle stress on the final word.

"You unplugged your phone. We've been trying to get in touch with you for hours."

The joker laid a hand over Tachyon's, trying to force the door shut, but Tachyon threw himself backward, pulling it open. The alien went sprawling, and the portly and impeccably dressed Hiram came willy-nilly into the room.

"Hey," said a second man as he stepped through the door, then snapped his mouth shut as a gun was thrust into his side. Snake-face quietly closed the door.

"Good God, Tachyon, what is all this?"

"What does it look like, Hiram?" He scrambled to his feet, and sent a sour look about the room.

Two of the Chinese moved in, and briskly searched the newcomers.

"They're clean."

"What do we do now?" whined Tommy.

"Ssshut up."

The smaller man gave a golliwog's grin, thrust a hand into his pocket, and pointed with his forefinger. "Okay! Everybody freeze, I've got you covered."

Even Tachyon looked disgusted, and someone said, "Fuck off, asshole, I just frisked you down."

The man shrugged, removed his hand, studied the finger for a long moment, then pointed it at the joker and said "Pop!" Snake-face vanished.

Two of the Chinese clutched their heads, and collapsed with a sigh. "Hiram, *look out!*" bellowed Tachyon.

The big man hesitated for an instant, then belly-flopped

between sofa and coffee table as Tommy let go with his .45 right next to Roulette's ear. There was an earsplitting *boom*, and the delicate bowl on the coffee table shattered, sending a cascade of water and blossoms across Hiram's back, and leaving a single gardenia perched forlornly on the curve of his ample rump.

At Tachyon's yell Hiram's companion stepped backward, opened the door, and vanished into the hall. The Chinese immediately behind the alien raised his gun, then formed a snoring puddle on the floor.

Tachyon pivoted to face Tommy. It was a face-off, Tachyon's power versus the jerk of a finger on a trigger. Which would be faster? Roulette seized the empty chair beside her, and slammed it into Tommy's shins. He howled, dropped the gun, and went for her, arms outstretched like a drunk trying to embrace an elusive lover. Roulette danced back, poking at him with the chair.

There was a buzz like a thousand angry bees, and Wasp came blitzing out of the kitchen. Hiram, heaving off the floor like a breaching whale, tightened his fist, and the joker slammed into the floor, wings folding like an origami figure.

Tommy grasped a leg of the chair, and for an instant they played tug-of-war as Roulette tried to keep a grip on her inadequate defense. His free hand groped at his back, and he pulled free a knife. Roulette abandoned her defense of the chair, and ran, screaming. He caught her by the hair, and swung her across his body. She never knew whether he meant to use her as a hostage, or to kill her out of hand, for suddenly his face went slack, and he let out a loud "Ooof." The arm across her chest felt like a steel girder, and they both collapsed in a heap. She struggled free though it felt like he weighed several tons. This was more than her overset nerves could stand. The screams that had been tearing at her throat subsided into hysterical laughter, and degenerated from there into hiccuping sobs.

"Hush, hush." Gentle hands stroked her hair, wiped away the tears, held her close. "You're quite safe now. It's all over." She laid her head on Tachyon's shoulder, and drew a shaky breath.

"What the devil is going on here?" Hiram exploded in aggrieved accents.

Tachyon righted a chair, eased Roulette into it. "Hiram, my deepest thanks, yours was a timely arrival."

"Who are these men?"

"Damned if I know. They wanted a book."

Worchester's brown eyes goggled, and he stared suspiciously at his friend as if suspecting inebriation.

Hiram's companion thrust his head around the door. "Should we call the police?"

Tachyon stepped to meet him, extended a hand. "My thanks to you as well, but what did you do to . . . ?" He made a helpless gesture at the space that a few seconds before had contained Snake-face.

The man in the brown suit shrugged. "I'm a projecting teleport. Point my fingers, and pop, they're gone."

"Where? Where has he gone?"

"The men's room at Freakers."

"The men's room at–"

He shrugged. "I can only send people to some place I know."

"Wish you had known the Tombs."

"Oh, I do, but . . ." He shuffled his feet, stared at the ceiling, glanced at Hiram, looked back to Tachyon. "I already sent one guy there today, and the cops are pissed. I didn't want any more trouble."

"So we've lost him, and I'll never know what book."

"I'd say that's the least of our worries today," Hiram said.

"Why?"

"If certain people would show more responsibility, and not unplug their phones, they wouldn't have to ask."

"Don't be testy."

"Tachyon, I've had a rather difficult day . . ."

"I've had better myself."

They stared in silence at each other, then Worchester sighed, and ran a hand across his bald pate, and smoothed down his full beard. Tachyon smiled, and said in a softer tone, "Shall we try again?" He tightened the belt on his robe, seated himself on the arm of the sofa. "Now, what brought you here?"

"Excuse me, but what about these . . . these . . . goons?" asked Roulette.

"You needn't worry, they will sleep for a good many hours."

"And him?" She pointed at the wasp.

"He weighs about six hundred pounds," Hiram answered. "I doubt he'll go anywhere."

"Oh," she said faintly.

"The Astronomer's raging through the city," Hiram said. "I was afraid he might have gotten to you already. You know about the Howler, of course. Kid Dinosaur's dead, too, torn to pieces at Jetboy's Tomb, and the Turtle was attacked and reportedly crashed into the Hudson. He hasn't been seen since."

Worchester caught the slight doctor as he swayed, and eased him onto the couch. "Brandy," he snapped, and Roulette forced tension back into her weak knees, and obeyed. "I apologize for putting it so baldly, but there's no good way to deliver news like that."

"I cannot believe . . . the *Turtle*, you say? And that child!" Tachyon covered his face with his hands.

In a few brutal words Worchester appraised them of the events at the Tomb.

Roulette didn't notice when Hiram lifted the glass from her slack fingers. She was seeing a pointed-faced kid, cute despite the wash of pimples across his chin, teasing his elders. She wondered what his dreams and goals had been, and she felt anguish for his parents. A sound that was both an agonized cry and a sob tore from her, and she went down into darkness.

Unfortunately it was not empty. Within waited the twisted body of *her* child, and the burning eyes of her master.

Fortunato got as far as a middle-aged woman guarding the entrance to the NBC sound stages. He could see the skating rink at Rockefeller Plaza through the huge window to his right. He couldn't get any sense of Peregrine being in the building, but she was an ace and it was possible she could block him somehow.

"I'm sorry, sir, but we simply can't give out that kind of information about our performers."

Fortunato locked eyes with her. "Page her," he said.

Her hand moved involuntarily to the phone, then hesitated. "She's not in the building. Letterman's doing her show tonight."

"Tell me where she is."

The woman shook her head. Her tightly permed red hair followed her every move. "I can't." She looked like she was about to cry. "She had some important dinner to go to tonight. That's why she's not here for the taping."

"All right," Fortunato said. "Thank you. You've been very helpful." The woman smiled tentatively.

Fortunato leaned his head against the elevator doors as he dropped back down to street level. They still hadn't found the Turtle's body. Peregrine's apartment was empty. Nobody had seen Jumpin' Jack Flash in weeks.

The game had been going on for seventeen years, and now it was down to the last twelve hours. He's beating the shit out of me, Fortunato thought. The only time I ever hurt him was when I broke that fucking machine and stopped TIAMAT.

He was exhausted. Up all night with the Mirror of Hathor, chasing around uselessly ever since. You have to turn it around, he told himself. Strike back at him, hurt him.

He wanted it so bad he could taste it.

But how could he even find someone that he couldn't see?

How?

CHAPTER 13

6:00 p.m.

Spector decided to go ahead and hit the Gambiones for Latham and his Shadow Fist friends. He had to operate on the assumption that he'd find a way to keep the Astronomer from killing him. If he could manage that, his new connections might mean some big jobs in the very near future.

He didn't like spending money on clothes, but there was no way he could go into the Haiphong Lily with blood spattered all over his suit. He'd decided on this clothing store because it didn't look like much from the outside. It didn't look like much from the inside, either. There were no fancy dressing rooms and too much dust on the floor. It was his kind of place. Spector slid a dark brown coat off the rack and pulled it on. He walked over to the mirror and winced. He looked like a man in a fudgsicle.

"Can I help you, sir?" The clerk was short with tufts of curly red hair on the sides of his head and a white cloth tape measure draped around his neck.

Spector struggled out of the coat; his arm was still bothering him. His sweat-soaked shirt clung to him. "I need a suit. Brown's not my color. Got anything in gray?"

The clerk walked over to the rack and started poking though the suits. He was muttering to himself and shaking his head.

Spector made sure no one was looking, then pulled a few hundred-dollar bills out of his brown envelope.

The little man turned around, holding an ash-gray suit. "Mm. This has possibilities, I think. Is this yours?" He pointed to Spector's old coat, which was lying on a straight-back chair. The clerk looked close and ran his hands over the material. "What's this all over? Bloodstains?"

"It's fake blood. I was down in Jokertown earlier. Pretty wild down there." Spector took the gray jacket and put it on. It was a little large, but fit him well in the shoulders. "I'll take it."

"What? Don't you want to try on the pants?" The clerk blinked and stood up straight.

"That's why I've got a belt. How much is it?" He draped the pants over his good arm.

"With alterations, two hundred and fifty dollars. Nice material, though. Worth every penny. You can't get workmanship like this often anymore."

"I don't need any alterations," Spector said. The clerk opened his mouth to speak, but Spector raised a finger. "I've got an aunt in Jersey who loves to do this kind of stuff. So how much?"

"Two-twenty."

Spector handed him the money and picked up his other coat, feeling for the envelope to make sure it was still there. He looked in the mirror again. Not bad, he thought. You may be the best dressed killer at the Haiphong Lily tonight.

He dropped his old pants and stepped into the new ones. They were big on him, but he'd manage.

The clerk returned with Spector's receipt and change. "Here you go, sir. Let us know if you change your mind about those alterations. I can promise you the finest fit in town."

Spector took the money and thrust it into his pocket. "Sure." The bell over the doorway tinkled as he opened it to step outside. "An angel just got his wings." He cleaned out the pockets of his old suit as he walked down the street, then dumped it into the first trash can he saw.

The alligator had a waking dream—or at least as much of a dream as reptiles have.

He was no longer here in the tunnel deep below the pulsating city. He was someplace else, somewhere warmer and lighter, where the water was hospitable and frequently full of live, darting food. The reptile ghosted along the bayou, most of his body concealed below the surface, with nostrils and orbital ridges protruding up out of the water and cutting small wakes.

After a time, he entered a place where the trees seemed to grow upside down, their gnarled roots twisting in dense wooden knots above the water. Above him, the canopy of interlaced branches blocked most of the sun. Shadows increasingly dappled his back as he slid along.

Sounds came to him, amplified by the water. He recognized the patterns—food, though food that sometimes could injure him if he were incautious. He homed in on the vibrations.

Around the curve of a deeper channel, beyond an

almost-impenetrable copse of cypress, he saw the pirogue. The two men in it did not see him, busy as they were, poking long poles into the plaited jumble of wood at water-level.

More sounds came. The man wearing a cap said, "She got' be in dere someplace, Jake."

The other man shouted so loud, the alligator had to contract its hearing openings. "Bitch, you come outta dere! This your grand-uncle speakin', Delia."

"You tell her, Snake Jake," said the first man.

"I tell you, girl—I don' wan' hurt you." He chuckled. "Leastways, nothin' you won' like."

The alligator swept remorselessly toward the pirogue. There was no debate, nothing but intent. He did what he did because of what he was and who *they* were.

He slid deeper and came up beneath the boat, lifting the prow high into the bayou shadows. The two men yelled and plunged into the water. The alligator did not care who was first. He would have them both.

His jaws stretched wide, teeth ready to rend—

—and he was back in the dark tunnel below the city.

The alligator mindlessly placed one foot in front of the other, continuing his imponderable, slow-motion odyssey. The dream stayed as vivid as reality in his mind. So much as he could consider the issue, he didn't know whether the dream was something that had happened once, or was something that *would* happen.

Either way was fine. It didn't matter.

Using the set of keys Jack had given her years before, Bagabond opened yet another gray metal door, revealing a set of steps descending into darkness. She reached down to pick up the soft bundle she had laid at her feet.

"How much farther?" Those were the only words Rosemary had spoken since they had entered the subway system at Chambers Street.

"Down these stairs and a few hundred yards along a tunnel—I think." Bagabond closed and locked the door behind them. The metal clinked dully. "What's bothering you?"

"Nothing."

"Don't give me that," said Bagabond. "It must be pretty heavy to keep you from talking."

Rosemary took an audible breath. "Ever since my father . . . died, and C. C.—I hate subways, tunnels, all of this. It's fifteen years ago, but that night is still a blur and I . . . don't want . . . to remember." The words ran down like clockwork exhausting a mainspring.

"But you want the books," Bagabond said practically, grasping Rosemary by the shoulder and pulling her around to face her. In the dim yellow light, the attorney's eyes were black shadows. Bagabond probed Rosemary for weakness.

The attorney took another deep breath. "I'm here. I'm going on. But you can't stop me from thinking what this place did to C. C." Rosemary shrugged away from Bagabond. "Don't worry about it, all right?"

"I don't think I'm the one who's worried."

Rosemary's foot was on the first step when the two women heard the muffled chuffing sounds of the alligator, followed by a growl. Rosemary's lips paled as she set her mouth tightly. Bagabond nodded to herself with satisfaction. "That's Jack."

Rosemary lagged Bagabond perceptibly as they approached the alligator. At their approach, the reptile stopped and swung his heavy head toward them, eyes glittering in the cold light of the tunnel. He roared a challenge that made both women wince as the sound crashed and reverberated against the stone walls.

"Stay here. I'll call you when it's finished." Bagabond sloshed toward Sewer Jack, gently moving inside his head now. Heedless of her clothing, she knelt in the tunnel muck and stroked the alligator's lower jaw as she mentally reached further inside for the key to Jack Robicheaux. Finding the spark of humanity deep within the reptile brain, she cradled it, fanning it, drawing it out, calming both the proto-human synapses and the distinctly reptile brain. As the alligator mind receded, Bagabond withdrew and watched as the long armored tail grew smaller and the snout diminished. The short legs of the animal elongated into the arms and legs of a man.

The naked man now lying on the tunnel floor gasped and cried out in pain as he wrapped his arms around his stomach. His face and hands grew gray-green, again lapped with scales, as the process began to reverse itself.

"Jack! It's Bagabond. Control it!" She spoke sharply, taking the man's hand tightly between her own. She moved with him as Jack rolled onto his back, panting hoarsely. Bagabond tried to penetrate back into his head, but now was blocked by the human intelligence there. Jack opened his eyes and looked directly into hers. He convulsed once, but took a deep breath and lay back. Although livid, the texture of his skin was normal again. His breathing slowed to a normal rate.

Running a hand across his face, Jack grimaced. "I know I always ask this, but it's important–where am I?" He glanced down at Bagabond's hand and released it, looking away self-consciously.

"Try Stuyvesant Square," said Bagabond. "Maybe a

hundred feet below it. It's about six at night." She reached across him in one unconscious motion and pushed the damp black hair back off his face. "Here are some clothes. I got them out of your cache at Union Square." Bagabond handed him the bundle she had been carrying. "Rosemary's here, a little ways up the tunnel."

"I assume there's a reason you're both here." Jack stiffly got up, one hand to his belly, the other holding his forehead. "I feel like shit." He painfully pulled on the chinos and work shirt.

"It's something you ate," Bagabond said laconically. "That pain in your gut–it's no tin can. It's books. Very important books."

"So I ate a librarian? Wonderful." Jack ran his fingers through his matted hair and looked up at the ceiling of the passage. "My card's expired anyway."

Bagabond shook her head. "From what I saw, you ate a thief. The thief just happened to be carrying notebooks that every criminal in the city would kill any twenty grandmothers for."

"And I want those notebooks so I can find out why." Rosemary walked up to them, her usual poise regained. "There's a meeting of the Gambione Family in a couple hours. If I have those books, I think I can stop a bloodbath."

"So ask me if I care," said Jack. He grimaced. "My niece has been wandering around New York City for almost twelve hours. By now she could be dog food. That's *my* problem. I'm going to find her. *Then* we'll discuss your precious books." Jack winced, doubling over, as he started to walk back toward the steps.

"Robicheaux, I can make your life miserable!" Rosemary started to follow him.

"Shut *up*, Rosemary," Bagabond said. "Jack, there's one

more thing you should know." Her voice was flat and it stopped him. "It's not just the Mafia looking for these things. They're the sweethearts. The others are using jokers, maybe aces too. If you hit the street knowing what's inside you, you're a dead man before you can whistle up a cab. Some telepath'll pick it up and they'll gut you like a pig. Then what about Cordelia?" She let several moments go by. "I can't protect *you* out there, but I can look for Cordelia while you're out of sight. And mind."

"So how long?" Jack tried to straighten, but gasped again in pain.

"Rosemary?" Bagabond took Jack's arm and supported him.

"Two hours, outside. That will get the books to the meeting. That's all I want." Rosemary stared at Sewer Jack and waited.

He met her eyes. "You got two hours, lady. That's all. And if Bagabond can't find Cordelia, I want your people on it. Every cop in the borough. Deal?" Jack swayed against Bagabond, putting one hand out to the wall.

Rosemary smiled. "Deal."

Time seemed to flow differently within the confines of the small church. Perhaps it was the quiet darkness lit only by flickering votive candles and a few fluorescent lamps, perhaps it was the reverent silence of the parishioners praying in the pews. Whatever the cause, the peace and tranquility she'd found within the small church had gone a long way toward calming her distraught nerves. Jennifer began to take her safety for granted, and her mind wandered. She studied the bizarre symbolism in the stained glass windows above the equally strange dioramas depicting Jesus Christ Joker's twelve stations of the cross, but soon wearied of their obtuse theology. Her stomach growled with discontent and she looked toward the altar, wondering what was keeping Father Squid.

The parishioners praying silently around her were all jokers, though the deformities of some were more obvious than others. There was a bearded triclops, a pretty, shapely woman with a glossy pelt covering every visible inch of exposed skin, and a sweet-faced altar boy who moved jerkily, but carefully, about the altar, rearranging things and replenishing the stock of wine and wafers.

Jennifer heard the sound of a soft footstep behind her, and whirled around, an image of Wyrm and the memory of his tongue rasping her skin leaping into her mind. She relaxed when she saw that it wasn't the reptilian joker creeping up behind her, but just a girl who was as startled by Jennifer's sudden movement as Jennifer had been by her quiet approach.

"I-I'm sorry," she said. "I didn't mean to scare you."

She was a tall, slender, very beautiful teenager with very black, very glossy hair, and dark brown eyes. She wore worn jeans and a faded sweatshirt with the name of the rock band Ferric Jagger imprinted upon it in washed-out letters. She wore no makeup and only a single piece of jewelry, a silver ear stud in the shape of an alligator. The gator's eyes were small green gems. Her voice was soft and melodic and had a pleasingly exotic drawl to it that Jennifer had never heard before. She was carrying an old suitcase covered in faded floral-print cloth.

"That's all right," Jennifer said, smiling reassuringly. "I'm just a little jumpy."

"I've been watching you for a while," the teenager said

in her elusive accents, "and noticed that, um, maybe you could use a sweater or, um, something else, it being so chilly in here and all." She stopped, smiled shyly, and then added quickly, as if afraid she'd offended Jennifer, "Unless you want to dress, that is, have a reason for wearing that swimming suit to church."

Jennifer smiled again, touched by the girl's offer. She was obviously new in town, probably *very* new in town, maybe even a runaway or in some kind of trouble. Yet she was considerate enough to approach Jennifer and offer help.

"That'd be very kind," Jennifer said, "if it wouldn't put you out too much."

The girl shook her head, set her suitcase on the flagstone paving of the floor, and opened it.

"Wouldn't put me out at all," she said, rummaging through her bag. "Here, try this."

It was a large, faded sweatshirt that said TULANE in worn letters. Jennifer slipped it on and smiled at the girl gratefully.

"Thanks." She hesitated a moment, then went on. "My name is Jennifer. I've got . . . some things . . . to take care of right now, but later, if you need something, a place to sleep or something—"

"I can take care of myself."

"So can I," Jennifer pointed out, hoping it was true, "but it's nice to have someone to rely on, every now and then."

The girl nodded, returning Jennifer's smile, and Jennifer gave her her phone number as the young altar boy with tousled blond hair, a cherubic face, and a joker deformity hidden under his distorted cassock approached them with slow and lurching steps.

"Father Squid would like to see you," he told Jennifer.

Jennifer nodded, and turned back to the girl. "What's your name?"

"Cordelia."

"Thanks for the sweatshirt, Cordelia. Be sure to give me a call."

Cordelia nodded and Jennifer followed the boy into the private rooms in the back that had been set aside for the priest to prepare for mass and conduct church business.

He led her to a small, sparsely furnished, unpretentious little room. Father Squid was sitting in a huge old chair behind a cluttered desk. He watched Jennifer unblinkingly as she entered, as did the man who sat in the plain wooden chair in front of the priest's desk.

"I have discovered from a reliable source that this man has been searching for you for some time. You have something he wants. In return he offers you his protection." Father Squid rose ponderously to his feet. "I have it on good authority that you can trust him explicitly. I don't know his name, but his *nom de guerre* is Yeoman."

It was the man she had first seen in the stadium, the man who had later, perhaps inadvertently, rescued her from Wyrm. He wore the same clothes and hood. A flat rectangular case was on the floor by his feet. There was speculation in his dark eyes as he gazed steadily at Jennifer.

Father Squid watched them watch each other, then edged around his desk carefully.

"You two doubtless have much of mutual interest to discuss and there is work for me to accomplish as well, so I shall leave you." He gave Jennifer a long, kindly look. "Good luck, my child. Perhaps one day you will come to visit us again."

"I shall, Father."

He nodded once at the man he called Yeoman and left

the room with ponderous dignity, closing the door behind himself. Jennifer decided that if she didn't have to return the stamps to Kien that the father would find a sizable donation in his poor box. She owed him that much, even if his attempt to help her didn't fully work out.

Jennifer felt Yeoman's eyes on her and she turned and met the weight of their steady gaze.

"Kien's diary," he said. His voice was low and powerful. Jennifer sensed a quivering tenseness about him, as if he was barely holding himself in check. "Do you have it?"

So that's what the third book was. A diary. She opened her mouth, then shut it, wondering if she could afford to tell him the truth.

Yeoman's intensity frightened Jennifer a little, but the fear combined with her hunger and weariness and resentfulness at being pushed around all day made her answer back in a hard voice that surprised even her, "I know what you look like, so you might as well take off that mask. I don't like talking to people who look like they have something to hide."

The man sat back in his chair and scowled. "I'll keep it on for now."

His features, as Jennifer remembered, were sharp and harsh, with frown lines on his forehead and around his mouth, and there was a vibrating tenseness about him that his mask couldn't conceal.

"You're called Wraith?" he asked unexpectedly. Jennifer nodded. "You're a thief. A good one, from what I've heard. You broke into the apartment of a man named Kien early this morning and removed some valuable items from a wall safe."

"How do you know all that?"

"A crystal lady told me," he said, looking a little pleased

by Jennifer's look of irritated incomprehension. "A lot of people are looking for you, you know. They want the things you stole."

"Well," Jennifer said noncommittally, "the stamps are very valuable."

Yeoman leaned forward in his chair and rested his chin in the palm of a large, strong-looking hand. He stared at her intently. Jennifer looked back defiantly, until he sighed and spoke again.

"You really don't know, do you?" She shook her head, trying to hide a rising excitement. Yeoman evidently knew the answers to some of her most pressing questions. "To hell with the stamps. No one gives a damn about them. Everyone's after the other book you took, Kien's personal diary. It details all the corruption and rot he's had his filthy hands in since he's come to New York."

"I thought he was a businessman. Owns restaurants and laundromats and things."

"He does," Yeoman said, "but only as a masquerade, and to explain his wealth. He's into everything that's dirty—drugs, prostitution, protection, gambling. He's into it all. The information contained in that diary would probably put him away for a very long time."

"Are you trying to recover it for him?"

Yeoman's lips were pressed into a hard, tight line. Knots of muscle jumped in his jaw. "No." The word that escaped from between his clenched lips was hard, flat, and cold enough to make Jennifer suppress a shiver.

"And you don't care about the stamps?"

He shook his head. His eyes had captured hers. She felt as if she were a sparrow held in the grip of a massive, now calm, but potentially destructive giant. It was a frightening yet somehow exhilarating feeling.

"Okayyy," she said slowly. "You don't care about the stamps. I don't care about this diary. I think that we can come to an understanding."

Yeoman smiled and again Jennifer suppressed a shiver.

"Then you do have it."

"Well, I know where it is." She fell silent for a moment, considering. She didn't know this Yeoman from Adam. She knew that he was behind the recent spate of bow and arrow killings, since notes signed Yeoman had been scrawled on many of the crime scenes. Father Squid said he could be trusted, but then she didn't know Father Squid, either. He waited patiently as this all ran through her mind, as if aware that she was trying to resolve an internal dilemma. He wasn't acting like a murderous maniac. He was manifestly a dangerous man, but the dangerous aura that hung about him was like a spice, an alluring scent. A sudden resolve struck her, sparked by an equally strong impulse.

"I'll tell you where the book is," she said, "if you answer two questions."

"What?" There was genuine puzzlement on Yeoman's face and in his voice.

"How'd you trace me to Ebbets Field?"

"Simple." He grinned wolfishly. "Your fence turned you in. He heard the word that Kien had put out on the streets about the books, but he didn't know how to contact Kien directly. He had to go through a third party, an information broker who's a . . . friend . . . of mine. She put him in touch with Kien, but she also told me about it. I got to his shop just in time to see you leave one of the stores next to the pawnshop, go down the street and join the ticket line in front of the ballpark. I just followed you inside."

"That makes sense . . . I guess. Now, my second question." She smiled sweetly. "What's your name?"

Jennifer herself barely understood why she asked him that, knowing only that she wanted them to interact on a personal level, not as anonymous masked figures.

He drew back in his chair, frowned at her. "I could make you tell me where the diary is."

Jennifer pulled the sweatshirt more tightly around her. Her throat was suddenly dry with the realization that she was reading in dangerous, potentially fatal waters.

"I know you could," she said in a small voice. "But you wouldn't."

"What in the world makes you say that?"

She shrugged slim shoulders. "I just know you wouldn't."

He stared at her a moment longer, but she wouldn't drop her gaze. He growled something inarticulate like an irate bear, and then said in an angry voice, "Brennan."

Jennifer nodded, obscurely relieved that she had been correct. Not that she had really been in danger. Her powers had certainly rejuvenated by now, and if he had attacked her all he would have had to do was ghost.

"Good," she said. "The books are with Dr. Tachyon."

"Tachyon?" Brennan asked in obvious astonishment.

"Actually," she smiled, "in his wax figure in the Bowery Dime Museum."

"Not a bad hiding place," Brennan said after a moment of reflection. "Kien's men are still looking for you–once Wyrm tastes a scent he can follow it anywhere, as long as traces of it remain on his tongue–so I'll take you to a safe place and then go after the books. I'll keep the diary, you can have the others."

"I'll go with you–"

"No." The word was as hard and sharp as the edge of a

guillotine blade. Jennifer knew there'd be no arguing with him about this.

"Well, if you're going to take me someplace, make it a place with food. I feel like I haven't eaten in a week."

Brennan thought for a moment, then nodded. He reached into a back pocket of his jeans and took out a playing card, an ace of spades, borrowed a pen from Father Squid's desk, and scrawled a note on the face of the card. He put the pen back and passed the card to Jennifer.

"Hiram Worchester is throwing an aces-only party in his restaurant, Aces High. You should be safe there and there'll also be plenty to eat. You've heard of Fortunato?" Jennifer nodded. "Give this to him."

Jennifer glanced at the note he'd written on the card. It was short and to the point: *Watch over her. Y.* She looked up at Brennan, respect in her eyes. She'd heard a little about the shadowy ace, Fortunato. Not much, as he wasn't one to seek publicity, but the fact that Brennan was on personal terms with him was an interesting development. She wondered if he were an ace himself, and what ability the virus had given him.

"Or Tachyon, if Fortunato's not there. Whatever you do, though, stay away from Captain Trips—the tall, skinny hippie—and the dancer known as Fantasy. I'm not sure about them. Not sure at all."

She pondered his advice for a moment, then nodded. If she was to trust him, she'd trust him all the way.

"I don't want to be a bother, but could we stop for some clothes? I'd hate to go to Aces High dressed like this."

"The father told me about the state of your, um, dress." He reached down into the case on the floor by his feet and took out a bundle of clothes. "I hope they fit." He looked at her critically. "You're taller than I first thought."

He studiously looked all about the office while Jennifer stood, pulled the sweatshirt off, and got into a pair of jeans and a dark pullover sweater. She put on the socks Brennan had brought her and looked up from lacing the running shoes to see him gazing at her intently. There was also a mask among the clothing. She stuffed it into the back pocket of her jeans and stood up. The shirt and shoes fit fine, though the jeans were a little short and hugged her slim figure tightly. She folded the sweatshirt neatly and left it on the priest's desk with a short explicatory note.

"Right." Brennan stood and hefted his case. "First stop, Empire State Building." He smiled in satisfaction. "If you're not going to be safe in a room full of aces you wouldn't be safe anywhere."

Upstairs in his mother's brownstone, in the comfortable luxury of the upper West Side, Fortunato closed his eyes. Miranda straightened his black tie with skillful fingers. She was in her late forties now, heavier than she should have been if she was still a geisha, wearing tailored Chanel instead of low-cut ready-to-wear. She'd become his mother's business manager ten years ago and hadn't turned a trick since.

"You look bad," she said. "Is Veronica not working out?"

"No," Fortunato said. "I don't think she's going to make it."

"I never understood her. All she wants is to be married and have kids and put them in day-care, to have a husband she never sees, to have servants and cars and money. I keep asking myself what I did wrong."

"It's not you. It's the whole country. Greed is very chic these days."

She touched his lips and the skin tingled. "You're very tired."

"Exhausted."

"I used to know the cure for that." She was standing very close. He could smell her perfume and the sweetness of her skin. She read the willingness in his face and said, "Lie down."

He stretched out across the bed. She took off her jacket and skirt. Fortunato reached for his tie and she said, "Don't move."

She took the rest of her clothes off. She was still graceful enough to get out of her panty hose without breaking the mood. Her bra had left lines around her chest and over her shoulders and there was dark stubble under her arms.

She got onto the bed and straddled Fortunato and began to touch herself. She started with her forehead and let her fingers trickle down her cheeks and back up to where her ears met her jawline. Goose bumps came up on her neck. She swayed forward until her full, sagging breasts were inches from his face. He leaned up to kiss them and she pulled away. "No," she said. "I told you to hold still."

She brushed her broad, dark nipples with her fingertips until they tightened and thrust out at him. Then she brushed lightly over her belly and buried her left hand in her pubic hair. With her right she touched Fortunato's lips again. He licked her fingers and arched his back.

She moved up the bed on her knees and lowered herself onto his mouth. "Gently," she said. "It's been a long time."

As he licked and probed with his tongue she gradually began to melt and open to him. She took hold of the brass railing of the bed and slowly moved against him, her breath coming faster, her heavy thighs pressing against the sides of his head.

Then her body stiffened and she let out a tiny, hoarse scream and he drank the power from her, hungrily, gratefully. He felt it tingling through his body and hardly noticed as she bent to kiss him lightly on the mouth. "You taste like me," she said. "Take care, Fortunato."

She picked up her clothes and was gone.

Fortunato came downstairs to find a circle of beautiful women around the couch in the sitting room. In the middle sat a tall, striking girl in jeans and a long-sleeved T-shirt.

"Ichiko," Fortunato said, using his mother's geisha name. "What's the deal?"

"Ellroy found her in Jokertown," Ichiko said. Like Miranda, she'd put on weight in the last ten years. She was tall anyway, and now she looked positively Anglo-Saxon. She wore a black cotton sweater and skirt with a red-and-black silk blouse. The top three buttons were undone. She moved across the room to Fortunato without sound or visible effort. "She was coming out of the Church of Jesus Christ Joker and looked like she was about to get in trouble with one of Gambione's scouts. Ellroy offered her a ride." She shrugged. "Here she is."

"She's beautiful."

"Yes," Ichiko said. "She is."

"Okay," Fortunato said to the others. "Break it up. Don't you ladies have places you're supposed to be?" They moved off, one at a time, Caroline stopping to slip one arm around his waist as she passed. Then he was alone with her. "I'm Fortunato," he said.

"Cordelia." She didn't stand up, but held her hand out to him. Fortunato took it for a second and then sat down next to her. "I appreciate the rescue," she said. Her voice was deep, a little breathless, very Southern. Sexy.

"Do you know where you are?"

"Ellroy told me a little. He said there were no obligations, but I could hang around for an interview if I wanted."

"And?"

"I'm still here, aren't I?"

She was flirtatious, but she seemed terribly young. "I'll have to ask you some personal kind of things."

"Like am I a virgin, you mean?"

"For instance."

"No. I had a regular boyfriend back in Atelier Parish. And—well, you know what they say about virgins from Louisiana. They're just the girls without any close male kin." She laughed but Fortunato didn't.

"We need to talk some more," he said. "Do you have dinner plans?"

" 'Dinner plans?' Not hardly! But from the way you're dressed I can't see myself going anywhere with you."

Fortunato looked at his watch. "We can find you some thing here to wear. How soon could you be ready?"

CHAPTER 14

7:00 p.m.

When his barber finished trimming his beard and swept away the apron, Hiram Worchester rose majestically from his chair, shrugged into a perfectly-tailored tuxedo jacket, and surveyed himself in the mirror. His shirt was silk, of the deepest, purest blue. His accessories were all silver. Blue and silver were the Aces High colors. “Very good, Henry,” Hiram said. He tipped the barber handsomely.

Curtis waited just outside his office door. Beyond, his restaurant was ready. Waiters and bartenders stood at their stations. Kelvin Frost’s astonishing ice sculptures had been moved out onto the floor, each one surrounded by a moat of crushed ice dotted with bottles of Dom Pérignon. Tables of hot and cold hors d’oeuvres were scattered throughout the restaurant, to keep the guests from clumping. The musicians stood poised by their instruments. Overhead, the glittering art-deco chandeliers shone softly. The beginnings of a magnificent red-gold sunset were visible to the west.

Hiram smiled, "Open the doors," he told Curtis.

A dozen people were already waiting in the foyer when the doors were opened. Hiram bowed to the women and kissed their hands, gave each man a firm handshake, performed the necessary introductions, and pointed them all toward the bar. The early birds tended to be obscure minor aces, insecure of their status and excited by Hiram's invitation. A few, only recently out of the deck, had never been to Aces High before, but Hiram treated them all like long-lost friends. The major aces tended to be fashionably late.

The first uninvited guest was a tall blond college student who looked uncomfortable in his rented dinner jacket. "What do I have to do to get in, guess your weight?" he asked when Curtis called Hiram over to pass on his admission.

"No," Hiram said, smiling. "That got a bit old, I'm afraid. But I see you've read your *Wild Card Chic.*"

"You bet. So what does it take to get in?"

"Show me proof that you've got an ace power," Hiram said.

"Right here?" The boy looked around uneasily.

"Is there a problem? What is your power, if I might be so bold?"

The boy cleared his throat. "It's kind of hard to—"

His date giggled. "He gets itsy-bitsy," she announced in a loud, clear voice.

The college boy turned a bright shade of red. "Yeah, uh, I compress the molecules of my body, I guess, to make myself smaller. I can, uh, shrink down till I'm six inches tall." He tried keeping his voice low, but it had gotten very quiet. "My mass stays the same," he added defensively.

"That's some power, kid," Wallace Larabee opined loudly from the buffet, where he stood holding a tiny buckwheat pancake that sagged dangerously under the weight of the caviar he'd piled atop it. "Whooeee, I'm sure scared."

Hiram wouldn't have thought it possible for the boy to turn a deeper red, but he did. "Don't mind Wallace," Hiram said. "He nearly ruined our 1978 get-together when he demonstrated *his* power, and he knows I'll throw him out if he ever does it again. They call him the Human Skunk."

There was general laughter, Larabee turned away to load up another pancake, and the boy seemed a bit less mortified. "Well," he said, "the only thing is, when I do it, I, uh, well, it's like this, I shrink, but my clothes don't."

Hiram understood. "Curtis," he said, "take him back to my office, and see if he can do what he claims."

Curtis smiled. "This way, please."

When they reemerged a few moments later, the maître d' gave a slight nod, the assembled guests broke into applause, and the boy turned red again. "Welcome to Aces High," Hiram said. "I didn't catch your name."

"Frank Beaumont," the college boy replied.

"But I call him Itsy-Bitsy," his girlfriend volunteered.

"Gretchen!" Frank hissed.

"You have my word, I'll take that secret to my grave," Hiram promised. He caught the eye of a passing waiter. "Soft drinks, or are you old enough to enjoy some champagne?" he asked Frank and Gretchen. "Please remember, the room is full of telepaths."

They settled for soft drinks.

The street in front of the Empire State Building's Fifth Avenue entrance was a madhouse. Paparazzi and celebrity watchers and ace groupies formed a milling gauntlet that scrutinized anyone who tried to enter. Jennifer and Brennan watched from across the street as limos pulled up to the red carpet that had been rolled out from the building's foyer to the curb and ace after ace was greeted by popping flashbulbs and squeals of delight.

Peregrine arrived in her chauffeured Rolls. She wore a backless, strapless black velvet dress that was slit in the front to her navel. She smiled graciously at the milling crowd, but kept her wings curled closely to her body, having dealt with feather-snatching souvenir seekers in the past. Tachyon arrived in a limo. His companion was a gorgeous black woman who wore a gown almost as low cut as Peregrine's.

"I'll have to leave you here," Brennan said as a cab pulled up and deposited a man in a white skintight suit.

"Be careful," Jennifer said.

Brennan smiled. "It'll be a piece of cake. Remember, stay away from Fantasy and Captain Trips. They may be in Kien's pocket."

Jennifer nodded.

"One more thing. I can't imagine anything dangerous happening in there, but, just in case something goes wrong and you have to leave, I want to set up a meeting place so we don't have to chase each other all over the city again." Brennan thought for a moment. "Times Square, the corner of 43rd and Seventh."

"Fine," Jennifer said. She wanted to warn him to be careful again, but that was silly. Things were under control, and the adventure was almost over. She felt, she realized, a little regret mixed in with her relief.

Brennan lifted a hand in salute and she waved. She watched him fade silently into the shadows, then put on her mask, turned, and crossed the street.

♥♦♠♣

"Have you heard about the Turtle?" Hiram asked, almost the second Fortunato came through the door.

"Not since this afternoon. Have they found the shell yet?"

Hiram shook his head. "Nothing. I still can't believe it. It's—" He suddenly noticed Cordelia. She'd cleaned up nicely and Ichiko had found her something white and clinging. "My dear. Please excuse my rudeness. I'm Hiram Worchester, proprietor of this establishment."

"Cordelia," Fortunato said. Hiram bent over her hand. Fortunato waited him out. "What about Jane? Is she all right?"

Hiram pointed to the bar. "She hasn't been out of my sight all afternoon. His either," he added, pointing to the android next to her.

Fortunato nodded, saw the bottle of unblended Scotch by Modular Man's right hand. "Is he drunk?"

"I heard that," Modular Man said, with great dignity. "I am an android and incapable of becoming intoxicated in any conventional human sense." He made an artificial throat-clearing noise. "I *have* initiated a subroutine which somewhat randomizes my thought processes, simulating the effects of alcohol, but it will be overridden at any sign of danger. I assure you I am *not* drunk." He turned back to Water Lily, who was staring into a Shirley Temple and nursing her impatience. "Now, where were we?"

"Fortunato?" Water Lily said.

"Hang on," Fortunato said. "Just another couple of minutes." He could see Peregrine across the room. He turned back to Hiram and said, "Would you show Cordelia around for me? There's something I need to take care of."

"I'd be delighted."

The knot of men around Peregrine saw him coming and drifted away. By the time he got to her it was just the two of them.

She wore long gloves with her gown, which left plenty of room for her broad, muscular shoulders and the big brown-and-white wings that came out of her back. It was cut so low that she must have glued it on.

In her spiked heels she was just over six feet tall. Her brown hair had been styled with a deliberate artlessness that took up several cubic feet around her head. Her nose and cheekbones were so sharply cut they looked like the product of sculpture rather than genetics.

Her eyes were such a vivid shade of blue that Fortunato suspected contact lenses. But the expression in them took him a little by surprise. The eyes glittered like they were about to squint shut with laughter, and one side of her mouth twisted up in an ironic smile.

"My name is Fortunato," he said.

"So I hear." She looked him up and down, slowly. Miranda had left him with a lingering taste of musk and a clearly visible erection. Peregrine's smile grew wider. "Hiram said you've been looking for me?"

"I think you could be in very serious danger."

"Well, not at the moment, maybe, but I could see it as a distinct possibility."

"I'm afraid I'm serious. The Howler and Kid Dinosaur are already dead. The Astronomer killed them both this morning. Not to mention about ten or fifteen of his former associates. The Turtle is missing and probably dead. You and Tachyon and Water Lily are the next most obvious targets."

"Wait a minute, wait a minute. I'm getting the picture.

You're the only one that can save me, right? So after dinner you should come back to the penthouse with me and guard my body, right? As in all night long?"

"I promise you—"

"I'm a little disappointed, Fortunato. After everything I've heard, I'd hoped for something, well, a bit more romantic. Not this kind of lame approach. Original, mind you." She reached out and patted his cheek. "But very lame."

She walked away smiling.

Fortunato let her go. At least she was here now, where she would be safe.

He looked for Cordelia and spotted her talking to an Arab in a circus costume. The Arab was trying, with some success, to see down the front of her dress.

She had talent, Fortunato thought. She could play a man like a fish, seemed smart and funny and not prohibitively fussy. If he took her on, it would be up to him to break her in. It was the kind of job he normally looked forward to, but in this case he had doubts. She seemed so goddamn innocent.

There was a commotion at the door. Hiram was pumping Tachyon's arm, overdoing the genial host bit. Next to Tachyon was the woman Fortunato had seen him with at Jetboy's Tomb. The woman glanced his way for a second and Fortunato recognized her. She did freelance outcall, and she was very expensive. Expensive the way blowfish was expensive in Japan, because every man who went with her risked his life. Every so often, supposedly at random, she secreted a deadly poison when she climaxed. Her nickname on the street was Russian Roulette.

Tachyon would be okay, Fortunato thought. He didn't see much chance the little alien fruitcake would be able to make a woman like that come.

"Are you certain you wish to be here?"

Silk slithered as her leg thrust through the slit in her skirt, and she stepped from the limousine, Tachyon's hand a steady prop.

"Are you sure *you* want to be here? You're the one who got his face danced on."

A dismissing gesture with one small hand. "It's nothing. And I would not like to disappoint Hiram after he was so obliging as to rescue us."

"Okay."

"But you've had a very terrifying experience, and I wouldn't want—"

"Doctor, we're here now, and I really don't see what's to be gained by continuing to discuss the matter on the sidewalk in front of several hundred gawking tourists."

She swept through the front doors of the Empire State Building, thoroughly bored, and thoroughly irritated by his harping. Tachyon had been concerned while he dressed for dinner, attentive when they'd returned to her apartment so she could change from her neat slacks into the white silk evening gown she now wore, solicitous as they drove, and she was ready to kill him. And the irony was not lost on her. For even as he had fussed and cosseted, all her thoughts were obsessed with the fact that he yet lived. She had spent eight hours in his company, helped rescue him from kidnappers, and still hadn't killed him.

Later, there is still time.

The lobby was crowded with reporters. They lay like a seething lake before the elevators, and when Tachyon entered they become a tsunami rushing forward to accost him.

Microphones thrust rapier-like into their faces, a babble of overlapping questions—"Any comment on the death of Kid Dinosaur, and the Howler?" "Are you working with the authorities on this case?" "What's this about *you* being kidnapped?"—blended with the whine of high-powered cameras. Tachyon, looking thunderous, waved them away, and when that failed, shouldered through them toward the express elevator.

A handsome man in a rumpled gray suit pushed up close to Roulette, and she shied back.

"Hey, Tachy, givin' our eyes a rest or what, or just trying to match your lady love?" The reporter's eyes swept ironically across the white breeches, tunic, and cloak, and white boots, the heels inset with moonstones, and ended on the small white velvet hat with a moonstone and silver brooch pinned to its upturned brim.

"Digger, step aside."

"Who's the new ace? Hey, babe, what's your power?"

"I'm not an ace, let me be." Agitation made her breath ragged, and she looked away from those too-piercing eyes.

"Tachyon," Digger said, tone suddenly very serious. "May I speak with you?"

"Not now, Digger."

"It's important."

"Tachyon, please get me out of this crowd." Her fingers plucked at his sleeve, and he pulled his attention from the journalist.

"See me at my office."

The elevator doors sighed closed behind them, and her heart began to slow. "I've never known Digger to be wrong. Are you quite sure—"

"I am *not* an ace!" She jerked his hand from her bare shoulder. "How many times do I have to tell you!"

"I'm sorry." His tone was low, the hurt evident in his lilac eyes.

"Don't! Don't be sorry, don't be solicitous, don't care!"

He moved to the far side of the elevator, and they completed the ride in silence. The elevator deposited them in the large outer lobby of Aces High. Roulette glanced about, curiosity submerging agitation. She had never been to the restaurant. Josiah had considered the entire ace/joker phenomenon vulgar and more than a little frightening (witness his response when he discovered that he too carried the alien virus), and had avoided this ace mecca.

Celebrity photographs lined the walls, and in the center of the room stood Hiram, smiling, urbane, polite, but implacable in his refusal to allow the tall scarecrow figure in the purple Uncle Sam suit to enter his restaurant.

"But I'm, like, a friend of Starshine's," the gangling blond hippie was protesting, "and Jumpin' Jack Flash too, man."

"I'm sure you are," Hiram said. He went on to gently explain that well-known aces had a great many friends, far more than the restaurant's seating capacity, and while Aces High would be delighted to have the Captain's patronage on any other night of the year, tonight was a *private* party; he was sure that the Captain would understand.

Tachyon grasped the situation in an instant, and put a hand on Hiram's broad shoulder. "I know what it looks like," he said, "but Captain Trips really *is* an ace, and a good man too. I'll vouch for him, Hiram."

Hiram looked surprised, then relented. "Well, of course, if you say so, Doctor." He turned to Trips. "Please accept my apologies. We get a great many would-be gatecrashers and, ah, ace groupies, often wearing outlandish costumes, so when someone cannot demonstrate an ace talent, we . . . I'm sure you understand."

"Yeah, sure, man," Trips said. "It's cool. Thanks, Doc." He put on his hat and entered the restaurant.

"Just because you're wearing a mask doesn't mean you can just waltz in, lady," the big man wearing a tuxedo in the foyer of Aces High told Jennifer.

She smiled at him, ghosted her arm, and put it through the wall. She wanted to do something more box-office, like sink through the floor, but didn't want to have to dress again in front of all the people waiting to enter the restaurant.

"Yeah, okay." The man in the tuxedo waved her in, looking faintly bored.

Aces High was a dream. Jennifer felt small, insignificant, and decidedly underdressed. She wished that Brennan had brought her an evening gown rather than jeans, but realized with a sigh that that would have required supernatural foresight on Brennan's part.

There were over a hundred people in the main dining area, drinking cocktails, nibbling on delicious-looking hors d'oeuvres, and talking in small groups and large parties. Jennifer headed for the buffet table, her stomach rumbling at the sight of so much food. There was pâté de foie gras, caviar, slices of Danish ham, twelve kinds of cheese, and a half-dozen varieties of bread and crackers. She spread pâté on a cracker and looked around the room, feeling like a celebrity hound as she watched scores of famous people pass by her.

Hiram Worchester, Fatman, looked harried. Probably the

strain of orchestrating the dinner, Jennifer thought. She recognized Fortunato, even though he was an ace who had never sought publicity. He was talking to Peregrine. He looked earnest, she looked amused. She felt the playing card that she'd tucked into her back pocket, but was hesitant to go up to him and present it. It looked like he had his own worries, and besides, she could take care of herself.

She snagged a glass of champagne from a tray of a waiter circulating around the room, and drained it, washing down pâté de foie gras and cracker.

"I knew it, I just knew it." The voice was masculine and drawling, with an undercurrent of excitement in it. "I just knew she'd show up here."

Jennifer turned, champagne glass in one hand and half a cracker smeared with pâté in the other. Hiram was standing behind her. With him was the man she had seen get out of the cab, the man in the white battle suit.

"Are you talking to me?"

"You bet your sweet butt, honey," the man in white said. There was something wrong with his face. He looked her over with an annoying intentness that made Jennifer feel naked, but that was only part of what made Jennifer feel uncomfortable. His features, individually, were all right, perhaps even handsome, but taken together were utterly unmatched. His nose was too long, his chin too small. One of his intense green eyes was higher than the other. His jaw was canted, as if it had been broken and then healed crookedly. He licked his lips in an agitated, excited manner.

Hiram sighed. "Are you sure, Mr. Ray?"

"She's the one, I know she is. I knew she couldn't stay away from this goddamn party. Damn if I wasn't right."

"Very well then. Do your duty." He sighed again and made wringing motions with his hands, as if he were washing them of the matter. The man he called Ray nodded, then turned to Jennifer.

"My name's Billy Ray. I'm a federal agent and I'd like to see some ID."

"Why?" Jennifer asked with a sinking feeling.

"You look like someone who robbed the home of a prominent citizen this morning."

Jennifer looked at the fragment of cracker she still held in her hand. She hadn't even begun to take the edge off her appetite.

"Damn," she said, and the cracker and champagne glass slipped through her hands as she ghosted through the floor.

Ray moved like a cat on speed. He leaped upon her, but only grasped her shirt which was crumpling to the floor.

"Ah, Jesus, Worchester," Jennifer heard him say before she slipped entirely through the floor, "you should've let me coldcock the bitch."

Tachyon's small form had vanished into the milling aces in search of alcohol. Alcohol she badly needed. The rumble of voices, the tinkle of ice in crystal glasses, and the energetic efforts of a small combo all combined to form a drill that was digging ever deeper into her head.

Ice sculptures of various of the more prominent aces dotted the room. Peregrine had taken up a position near her statue, and her beautiful wings threatened to overset the frozen replica.

Captain Trips, a glass of fruit juice clutched in a bony hand, tried to negotiate the room, but his amazing stovepipe hat kept tumbling to the floor. The Harlem Hammer, looking decidedly uncomfortable in his best suit, retrieved the hat.

The contrast between the immensely powerful black ace, his bald pate shining under the lights, and the weedy Captain was startling.

The Professor and Ice-Blue Sibyl lounged near the bar. Sibyl with her blue, sexless naked body could have doubled for one of the ice sculptures. She even gave up a faint chill to those standing near her. Her companion created a stir by his own peculiar sense of style. With his whiskers, balding head, wire-rimmed spectacles, and belching pipe, he looked like someone's kindly old uncle. But no uncle of Roulette's would ever have worn a sky-blue tux with scuffed sandals.

Fantasy, the ABT's prima ballerina and one of New York's more public aces, waved a rose before Pit Boss's nose while Trump Card looked on indulgently.

So many, and which of you will survive this night? Not many, I think, with my master seeking you.

The problem with being a genial host was the necessity to be polite to boors. Hiram sipped at a champagne glass full of Vernors ginger ale (he liked to have a drink in hand, to promote the atmosphere of conviviality, but he had too many responsibilities to allow himself to get tipsy) and tried to feign a great interest in what Cap'n Trips was saying.

"I mean, it's like *elitist*, man, this whole dinner, on a day like this it ought to be aces and jokers all getting together, like for brotherhood," the gangling hippie with the long blond hair and weedy goatee told him.

The Aces High staff had barred a dozen groupies and pretenders, including the fishwoman with her bowl of telepathic goldfish, an elderly gentleman in a cape who time-traveled in his sleep, and a two-hundred-pound teenaged girl who wore only pasties and a G-string and claimed to be immortal. That one was tough to disprove, admittedly, but Hiram had turned her away nonetheless. He found himself wishing he'd been similarly resolute with Trips, whose powers seemed equally elusive, if in fact he had any at all. If only Dr. Tachyon had not arrived just when he did . . .

Hiram sighed. It was spilt milk now. He'd admitted the Captain, and a few minutes later, while making his rounds of the party, mingling and smiling, he'd made a second mistake and asked Trips how he was enjoying himself. Since then he'd been trapped by the ice sculpture of Peregrine, while the tall man in the purple Uncle Sam suit explained earnestly that, like alcohol was *poison*, man, and he really ought to be serving some tofu and sprouts because the body is like a temple, you know, and wasn't the whole idea of the Wild Card Dinner like, uh, politically incorrect.

It was no wonder Dr. Tachyon had vouched for him, Hiram thought, gazing at Trips's prominent Adam's apple and purple top hat: they obviously shopped at the same boutique. Hiram's smile was so frozen he hoped that frost wasn't forming in his beard. His attention wandered across the room and he noticed a number of diners taking their drinks out onto the balcony, where the sun was sinking behind New Jersey, turning the sky a deep, robust red. That gave Hiram an inspiration. "It looks to be a magnificent sunset tonight, Captain," he said. "That's a sight you really shouldn't miss, since you don't get to visit us too often. Sunset from Aces High is quite special, I'm sure you'll agree. Quite, ah . . . quite far out."

It worked. Cap'n Trips craned his head around, nodded, and started to take a step toward the balcony, but somehow those long pipestem legs managed to get tangled up in each other, and he started to trip. Before Hiram could step forward and catch him, Trips had thrown out a hand to steady himself, grabbed hold of the ice sculpture, snapped off the end of Peregrine's wing, and fallen flat on his face. His hat flew ten feet and landed at the feet of the Harlem Hammer, who picked it up with a look of disgust, carried it back to Trips, and pulled it down firmly onto the Captain's head. By then Cap'n Trips had gotten to his feet, an icy wingtip still in his hand. He looked very abashed. "I'm sorry, man," he managed. He tried to fit the missing piece back on the end of Peri's wing. "I'm real sorry, it was beautiful, man," he said, "maybe I can fix it."

Hiram took the ice away from him and gently turned him around. "Never mind," he said, "just go watch the sunset."

Jack leaned heavily against Bagabond as they came up out of the subway. Rosemary followed, scrutinizing the crowd. She took Jack's free arm tightly, lending support as the trio negotiated 23rd Street toward the Haiphong Lily.

No one paid any heed to them as the three moved slowly down the sidewalk. "In here." Bagabond steered them into a dark, narrow courtyard, ill-lit by two flickering streetlights on the block.

"I smell something good," Jack said miserably, raising his head.

"Rosemary, this is your scene." Bagabond helped Jack support himself against a bent steel railing leading up to a long-unrestored brownstone. She turned back toward the assistant district attorney. "How do you want to play it?"

Rosemary peered down the street toward the next dim pool of light. "What I want to do is use the notebooks to exert some control on the Gambiones. From there, maybe I can reach the rest of the Families." The regret was evident both in her look and in her voice. "Sorry to put you through this, Jack, but unless we de-escalate this war among the crime powers, the city will be in a state of siege." Her voice firmed. "By holding onto the books and releasing just enough information to maintain the balance, I want to influence the selection of the new don and his attitude toward the Families and the new gangs."

"Piece of cake," Jack said through gritted teeth.

"You really believe you can do that?" Bagabond was unconvinced that Rosemary could carry off the farfetched plan.

"Hell of a nice speech," said Jack.

"Rosa Maria Gambione can do that." Rosemary faced Bagabond.

"But what will they do when they find out who the assistant DA really is?" Bagabond frowned at the other woman. "You might as well step in front of an IRT."

"It's my choice. It's my heritage." She shrugged eloquently. "How else will I be able to make up for my father's acts?"

"A hundred Hail Marys," Jack said, weaving slightly. "Sorry about that."

"Your father chose to be what he was. You are not guilty of his sins." Bagabond grasped Rosemary's upper arm hard enough to hurt. "Your responsibility is to yourself."

"I don't see it that way." She pried Bagabond's hand from her arm and held it for a moment. "What I don't like is putting you and Jack into danger."

"Hey, we're used to it. We're aces, right?" Bagabond looked at Jack, who was swearing softly in French. Even in the poor light, they could see his skin starting to turn gray.

"How much longer?" Jack said.

"Just give it a little more time," Rosemary said reassuringly.

"Yeah, sure." Jack winced. "*Damn*, it hurts."

He froze when he saw the limos parked in front. Spector took a deep breath and a moment to calm himself. It wasn't the Astronomer, couldn't be, not yet. What did he expect Mafiosi to arrive in, Hondas and Yugos?

He saw the neon lily and knew he was in the right place. He stepped inside and walked up the creaky wooden stairs. A large man blocked his way at the top. The goon was over six feet high and built like a defensive lineman, obviously mob muscle. He would have been nothing more than a side of beef to Spector, except that he wore mirrored sunglasses.

"Reservations?" he asked, like it was the only word of English he knew.

"Yeah." Spector tried to slide past, but the man grabbed his bad wrist.

"Hold on."

Spector gritted his teeth. "You got some kind of problem?"

"We got a private party here tonight."

"Excuse me." An Oriental man put a hand on the hired muscle's shoulder. He looked at Spector, the corners of his mouth twitching slightly. "This gentleman is not with your party, but he does have a reservation."

"Will he stand for a frisk?" the big man addressed the question to the Oriental, then looked over at Spector.

"No problem." Spector unbuttoned his coat and raised his arms. The man frisked him in a quick, professional manner. "You Secret Service or something?" Spector asked.

"Okay. Do what you want with him." The big man took a step back toward the stairs.

The Oriental, Spector figured him for a manager, hustled him to a table near the entrance to the private room. He handed Spector a menu and smiled weakly. "No trouble," he whispered. "They told me there would be no trouble."

"Only if the food's bad."

"Food is excellent." The manager signaled a waiter and turned away, seeming relieved.

The menu was hand-printed in gold and silver on some kind of fancy card stock, not laminated like he was used to. Spector opened it and sighed. Bad to worse, not only was everything written in Vietnamese, but there were no numbers next to the entrées. It would be hard enough trying to find something edible without having to pronounce it, too.

"Excuse me, sir. Would you like some tea?"

Spector looked up at the waiter. "Sure." A little caffeine would be good for his reflexes when the time came.

The waiter turned over his cup with a white-gloved hand and filled it. "Would you like a few more minutes before you order?"

"Yeah. Come back in a while."

The waiter nodded, set the white china teapot on the table, and walked away.

Spector picked up the cup and blew the steam away from the surface of the tea. It looked a little greener than what he was used to. He took a tentative sip. The tea was almost too hot to be drinkable, but it was strong enough to do the job. He'd let it cool for a few minutes and then put away as much as he could. Spector smelled meat and vegetables cooking in hot oil. His stomach burned. He needed to get something solid into it soon.

Two people entered the restaurant. One was young; the other had to be pushing seventy. Both were wearing dark suits and hats. They talked briefly to the guard at the door, then disappeared into the private room.

Spector could hear their voices, but wasn't able to pick out enough words to follow the conversation. It didn't really matter. Most of them would be sleeping with the fishes before too much longer.

He turned back to the menu. If he ordered a beef dish, he could at least eat the meat.

Another group walked past the guard into the meeting room. Hello, he thought, I'm Demise. I'll be killing your asses stone-cold dead tonight.

His waiter wandered back over. "You ready now, sir?"

"Yes. I'd like something with beef in it. You understand. Plenty of hot stuff, too." The waiter nodded and left.

Spector checked his watch. 7:45. He picked up his cup and sipped at the tea. When he was sure everyone was there he'd make his move.

The cocktail hour was drawing to a close, and Curtis and his attentive staff were beginning to escort the guests to their tables when Jay Ackroyd finally showed up, with Chrysalis on his arm. Popinjay was in the same brown suit and loafers that he'd worn all day, tieless and a little rumpled. Chrysalis was wearing a glittering floor-length gown of metallic silver. It covered both breasts and one shoulder, but the slit up the side was high enough to make it perfectly apparent that she had decided to do without underwear. Her long legs flashed as she strode across the floor, muscles moving like smoke beneath transparent skin, the eyes in her skeletal face scanning the room as if she owned it.

Hiram met them by the bar. "Jay is as tardy as ever," he said. "I really ought to take him to task for delaying our meeting. I'm Hiram Worchester." He kissed her hand.

She seemed amused. "I'd guessed as much," she said in cultivated public-school tones.

"You're British!" Hiram said with a delighted smile. "My father was British. He fought at Dunkirk, you know. A male war bride, but not the kind who wore white."

Chrysalis smiled politely.

Ackroyd's smile was more cynical. "You two probably want to talk about Winston Churchill or Yorkshire pudding or something. I think I'll get a drink."

"Do that," Hiram said. Jay took the hint and wandered off to chat with Wallwalker. "I believe you have some information for me," Hiram said to Chrysalis.

"I might," she said. She glanced around. In a room full of celebrities and attractive women, she was drawing more than her share of glances. "Here? It seems rather public."

"In my office," Hiram said.

When the door was shut behind them, Hiram sank gratefully into a chair and gestured her to a seat. "May I?" she asked, producing a cigarette from a small handbag. He nodded. She lit up, and Hiram watched the smoke swirl inside her nasal cavities when she inhaled. "Let's dispense with the foreplay," Chrysalis suggested. "The sort of information you want is dangerous and expensive. How much are you prepared to spend?"

Hiram slid open his drawer, took out a ledger-sized checkbook, and began to fill out a check. She watched him carefully. He ripped it out and slid it across the desk.

Chrysalis leaned forward, picked up the check, looked at it. The ghostly musculature of her face worked as she raised an eyebrow. She folded the check in half and tucked it into her handbag. "Very good. That buys you a lot, Mr. Worchester. Not all, but a lot."

"Go on." He folded his hands on the desk. "You told Jay that Bludgeon was a part of something bigger. What?"

"Call them the Shadow Fist Society," Chrysalis said. "That's the name you hear on the street. It's as good as any other. It is a large and powerful criminal organization, Mr. Worchester, made up of many lesser gangs. The Immaculate Egrets in Chinatown, the Werewolves in Jokertown, Bludgeon's motley group along the waterfront, and a dozen others. They have allies in Harlem, Hell's Kitchen, Brooklyn, all over the city."

"The syndicate," Hiram said.

"Don't confuse them with the Mafia. The Shadow Fist Society is waging a very quiet war against the Mafia, in fact, and it is winning. It has fingers in a good number of pies, everything from drugs to prostitution to the numbers, as well as some legitimate businesses. Bludgeon and his protection racket are one of the smallest and least significant parts of this operation, but a part nonetheless. If I were you, I'd be very careful. Bludgeon himself is cheap muscle, but his sponsors are ruthless and efficient people who brook no interference. If you annoy them, they'll kill you as easily as you might swat a fly."

Hiram made a fist. "They might find that difficult."

"Because you're an ace?" She smiled. "On a day like today, that seems precious little to cling to, dear boy. Do you remember that rather sensational gangland murder on Staten Island last year? It was in all the papers."

Hiram frowned. "One of those ace-of-spades killings, wasn't it? I vaguely recall seeing the headlines. What was it the victim called himself?"

"Scar," said Chrysalis. "An instantaneous teleport, and a Shadow Fist hit man. Well, he's done, but they have other aces working for them, if rumors can be believed. With powers as potent as his. Maybe as many as a dozen. You hear names. Fadeout. The Whisperer. Wyrm. For all you know, one of your guests out there might be a Shadow Fist, sipping your champagne while he ponders the best way to dispose of you."

Hiram considered a moment. "Can you tell me the name of the man at the top of this organization?"

"I could," Chrysalis said coolly. "But passing along information like that could get me killed. Not that I wouldn't risk it for the right price, of course." She laughed. "I just don't think you have that much money, Mr. Worchester."

"Suppose I wanted to talk to them," he said.

She shrugged.

"Unless you can provide me with a name, you'll find I can easily stop payment on that check."

"We can't have that," she said. "Are you familiar with the name Latham, Strauss?"

"The law firm?" Hiram said.

"Attorneys from Latham, Strauss pried Bludgeon loose this afternoon, after Jay had teleported him into the Tombs. I had cause to ask a few questions about that firm today, and I discovered that the senior partner habitually takes a keen interest in men like Bludgeon. That seems strange, since his personal clients include a number of the city's richest and most powerful men, a few of whom have good reasons to be discreet. Do you understand what I'm telling you?"

Hiram nodded. "Do you have his address?"

She opened her handbag and produced it. Hiram's respect for her rose a notch. "I'll give you one more bit of advice for free," she added.

"And what is that?"

Chrysalis smiled. "Don't call him Loophole," she said.

CHAPTER 15

8:00 p.m.

It had become something of a ritual, the way these dinners began.

When the rest of them were all seated, when the waiters had brought the soup and the diners had chosen their entrées, then all eyes went to Hiram Worchester. He filled a tall, thin glass with champagne, made himself light, lighter than air, and floated gently up to the high ceiling, next to one of his chandeliers. "A toast," he said, raising his glass as he did every year. His deep voice was solemn, sad. "To Jetboy."

"To Jetboy," they repeated in unison, a hundred voices all together. But no one drank. There were more names to come.

"To Black Eagle," Hiram said, "to Brain Trust, and to the Envoy, wherever he might be. To the Turtle, whose voice led us back from the wilderness. Let us all hope that he is safe and sound, that, like Mark Twain, the reports of his demise have been grossly exaggerated. To all of our brother aces, great and small, living and dead and yet to come. To the jokers in their thousands, and to the memory of the tens of thousands who drew the Black Queen."

Hiram paused, looked down on the room silently for a moment, went on. "To the Howler," he said, "and a laugh that could shatter brick. To Kid Dinosaur, who was never as small as the one who killed him. To the Takisians, who cursed us and made us like gods, and to Dr. Tachyon, who helped us in our hour of need. And, always, to Jetboy."

"To Jetboy," they repeated once again. This time they drank, and perhaps one or two actually paused for a moment to remember the boy who couldn't die yet, before they lifted soup spoons and began to eat.

Hiram Worchester settled slowly back to the floor.

"You're not eating," Tachyon remarked gently, sneaking a glance at her almost untouched plate.

"Neither are you."

"I have an excuse."

"Which is?"

"My mouth hurts."

"That's not the real reason."

"Why should you care to hear the real reason?"

"I don't. I don't care." She looked away, but memory formed a transparent picture separating her from the room. *Josiah, nostrils tightening fastidiously, superimposed over Trips's kindly face. Her baby lying like some grotesque entrée on Mistral's plate.*

"What's your excuse?"

That I'm going to kill—have to kill—you, and I'm losing my nerve. Would that answer satisfy you?

Brain engaged with mouth, and she heard herself say, "I'm upset about what happened today."

"Which part?" the alien asked with a grim little smile.

"The Tomb, the killing."

His hand covered hers. "And you have hit on the reason for my lack of appetite. How can I eat when Kid . . . I think of his parents."

The French onion soup she had eaten earlier in the evening hit the back of her throat, and she swallowed convulsively. "Excuse me," she muttered breathlessly, and pushing back her chair fled from the dining room. The curious glances felt like blows.

In the bathroom she sluiced cold water across her face, heedless of her careful makeup job, and rinsed her mouth. It helped, but could not relieve the burning knot in the pit of her stomach. Her amber eyes stared bleakly out of the mirror, fawn wide and as frightened. She studied the perfect oval of her face, the high, chiseled cheekbones, the narrow nose (legacy from some white ancestor). It looked like a normal face. How could it hide such . . . Her mind rebelled at the word. Not evil. It hid memories.

Memories of evil.

Whose evil? The man whose kin had brought the hell-born virus to Earth, and broken her life?

Or her own?

She rested her hands on either side of the sink, bent forward, her breath coming in quick gulps.

"He lives, Roulette."

Fear drew a whimper, and she whirled to face him. Shrank back as he laid aside a nail file left for the convenience of the female customers of Aces High. Inspected knotted veins in the back of his hand, and swiveled slowly on the small dressing-table stool to face her. It was an incongruous sight. The Astronomer dressed as an Aces High waiter, framed by double rows of theatrical lights, the back of his balding head reflected in the mirror.

"Oh my God. What are you—"

"Doing here? Apparently finishing the business that you have failed to do. Dealing a little in death. I came expecting lamentations, fear, and loathing. What do I find?—a bunch of aces feeding their faces, and talking, talking, talking."

"You can't . . . not here."

"Oh yes, by all means *here*. Starting with Tachyon."

"No!"

"Concern?"

"He's . . . he's mine."

"Then, why haven't you killed him?" He had lost the jovial tone, his voice grating like rock across sandpaper. He came off the chair, the action made all the more menacing for its slowness.

"I—" Her voice didn't work, and she tried again. "I'm toying with him."

"What a dramatic—almost melodramatic—phrase. Toying with him," he repeated thoughtfully. His hand shot out, caught her by the throat. *"Well, don't toy with him! Kill him!"* Spittle wetted her cheek, and she twisted in his grasp.

The hand tightened, larynx aching under the pressure, blood rushing, beating in her ears. Roulette clawed at his hand, begging for mercy, but only mewling sounds emerged. He threw her contemptuously aside, and she came up hard against the edge of a toilet bowl.

"You can't make me. Fear of you won't be enough."

"True. I wish you would recognize the wisdom of what I've told you. Only your hate will free you. Only if you release the acid of your soul can you be at peace."

She dug her fingers into her temples. "I don't know what I hate worse. Your threats or your pop psychology."

He continued as if she hadn't spoken. "Only that ultimate catharsis can save you from a lifetime of memory."

He tore aside his carefully constructed mental shields, gripped and broke a part of her mind. The pictures fluttered past behind her eyes. *Nurse's hand hard on her chest, forcing her back. "Don't look." She looked. MONSTER! It lay in an incubator mewling out its life. Hidden away. Four days of watching it die. Disgust becoming love becoming hate. Nurse's hand hard on her chest, forcing–*

And so it went. A never-ending replay of a nightmare.

"Kill him, and it stops."

"Oh God! I don't believe you!" Her fingers writhed in her hair.

"That's unfortunate. For you really don't have any other option."

"Is it time yet?" Jack raised his head from the steel railing he was clutching.

Bagabond moved over to stand beside him. She put her arm around his waist. "Soon. It'll be soon." She reached up to push the sweat-soaked black hair away from his eyes. Obviously in pain, Jack stared back at her. Shadowed, his dark eyes blended invisibly with the night.

"You'll have to go in as yourself," she said. "I'll help you change when the time comes. I'll be there with you the whole time." Bagabond put her hand on top of his on the railing. He turned his hand over and clasped her fingers.

"I have a bad feeling about this," Jack said. He looked

down at their plaited fingers, but didn't take his hand away. "I wish the cats were here."

"Me too."

"Anything goes wrong," he said, "you get out. I mean it. I can take care of myself."

Bagabond said nothing, but squeezed a bit harder. She looked over at Rosemary. "Can we start in?"

The lawyer walked back to the corner and peered around the dingy brick. "It looks clear." She touched her digital watch, squinting at the dim glow. "It's twenty past eight. Everybody who's coming should have gone in by now. Let's go."

The entrance to the Haiphong Lily was marked by a huge water lily limned in red neon. Its buzzing flicker lit the quiet street. Half a dozen limousines were pulled up at the curb outside the restaurant. The uniformed drivers stood in a group at the head of the line, smoking and gossiping like ordinary cabbies. Each car was guarded by one or two unsmiling men. A couple of the guards impassively watched Bagabond and her companions pass, eyes tracking their progress like the sights on an M60 machine gun. All the guards wore black armbands.

The cilantro, fish, and hot pepper smells of the Vietnamese cooking engulfed them before they reached the door.

"Mon Dieu." Jack raised his eyes skyward and then looked toward Bagabond. "Can you believe it? Now I'm hungry."

"We'll eat as soon as we get this over with."

While the entrance was at street-level, the restaurant itself was up a flight of stairs. The stairwell was dimly lit and the red flocked wallpaper absorbed most of that light. In an alcove beside the inner doorway, a big man whose subdued suit matched those of the watchers outside stood gazing down the steps. He had stepped out at the sound of the outside door and now blocked the upstairs landing.

"Reservations?" he said.

"Of course." Rosemary didn't hesitate.

Bagabond felt the eyes behind the mirrored sunglasses checking them for the possibility of a threat. The big man shrugged. Apparently satisfied, he stepped back out of the way. He obviously did not recognize Rosemary.

Inside the restaurant was more of the dark wallpaper and a nervous, middle-aged Oriental man who greeted them with a sheaf of menus. "Good evening. Three? Yes?"

He had already started toward one of the many empty tables when Rosemary stopped him. "We're here for the meeting."

The small man halted abruptly. The dining room was nearly deserted. An elderly couple huddled in intimate conversation to one side. Nearer, a tall, gaunt man with a crooked mouth looked up from his meal. He and the Oriental manager exchanged looks. Bagabond thought for an instant that the lone diner looked *awfully* familiar, but her attention snapped back as Jack stumbled and nearly fell against a bubbling tank of carp. The maître d' looked distressed.

Smiling weakly, he said, "No meeting."

"Yes," said Rosemary. "There is. In the private room."

"No meeting here."

"What we have here," Jack said slowly through taut lips, is a failure to communicate."

Rosemary surveyed the room, stopping when she spotted two men in dark blue suits and expensive sunglasses sitting at separate tables in the back of the room. They too wore the armbands of mourning.

She addressed the nearer. "*Buon giorno* . . . Adrian, isn't it? Tony Callenza's son?"

"Lady, you got the wrong person." The soldier on the right glanced at his companion, who shrugged. Bagabond tightened her hold on Jack, prepared to pull him to cover if shooting started.

"Adrian," said Rosemary. "We used to play together. You'd kidnap my dolls and hold them for ransom. I'm hurt you don't remember." The assistant DA had left Bagabond and stood a few feet away from the table and the man she'd addressed. There was no tension in her stance, head high, arms loose at her sides. Bagabond had watched her once at a trial. Bagabond thought that she herself had never been so self-assured as Rosemary.

She was even less certain now that Rosemary really intended to use the books solely as a means to influence the family. There was too much of her father in her still. Bagabond remembered Rosemary's remark about wishing she had been a son, able to inherit control. Was she about to provide the means for Rosemary to get that control?

"I told you, my name isn't Adrian."

"Then I guess I'm not Rosa-Maria Gambione."

The man pulled off his mirrorshades. "Maria!" He smiled for the first time. "I remember once, I sent you the right hand from a kidnapped doll. You *still* wouldn't pay."

The other man spoke for the first time. "Be quiet, Adrian. Rosa Maria Gambione disappeared many years ago." He said her, "You look more like a district attorney to me, *Ms.* Muldoon."

"Very good. I don't know you, do I?"

"No."

"My father fought for the Family in the old ways. I chose few ones."

"Like hounding us?" said the second man. "Prosecuting us?"

"To be a useful district attorney, I have to be a good district attorney."

The thin, inexpressive mouth below the sunglasses twitched at one corner. "Adrian, get your father. I think he'll be interested in this." He leaned back in his chair and said, "Please sit down, you and your *friends*, Ms. Muldoon."

Rosemary pulled out a chair and sat, crossing her legs and smiling at the man on the other side of the table. She barely turned her head. "Suzanne, I think now would be an appropriate time."

Bagabond turned Jack toward her and extended a hand toward his head. The man pulled back sharply. "Not here!"

"You're right." She caught Rosemary's eye and pointed her chin toward the door of the men's rest room.

"Good idea," said Rosemary. To the man across the table, she said, "My friends will be rejoining me in just a moment. I can assure you they are not . . . armed." She looked directly into the opaque lenses. "*Do* you have a name?"

"Okay, make it quick." He waved idly at the rest room. "You always hang out with junkies?"

Rosemary reached across the table and poured herself a cup of tea. "No."

"Morelli," said the man.

"*Very* pleased to meet you."

Bagabond led Jack to the men's room door.

"Perhaps I'd best go first." Jack reached out to steady himself against the doorframe.

"You won't make it," Bagabond said matter-of-factly.

"Your faith is touching." Then he gasped in pain. "On the other hand . . ."

Bagabond pulled open the door and walked in. No one stood at the urinal, but a Vietnamese man dressed in a soiled kitchen apron was just coming out of the stall. He squawked in surprise, managed hurriedly to wash his hands, then left, muttering in a language Bagabond was glad she didn't understand. "Get in here," she said to Jack. The door swung shut after him.

"I don't know if I can do this," said Jack. "Sometimes I can't call him up. I hurt too much right now to concentrate. I–"

"Just take off your clothes."

"What?" He tried to smile. "Bagabond, this isn't the time." He shut up as she stared at him in exasperation.

"I don't have any spare clothing for you this time. If you don't take it off, you're going to destroy what you've got on. Okay?"

"Oh. Right." His back to her, Jack unbuttoned his shirt. Careless of her suit, Bagabond sat down on the dirty tile floor. After he had stripped, Jack looked dubiously at her. He held the bundle of clothes in front of him.

"Lie down."

Jack swallowed and prostrated himself in front of Bagabond. In the limited space, his feet extended under the green wooden partition dividing off the stall. She reached out and set his clothing safely aside. Holding his head in her hands, she began to send her consciousness inside his mind, searching for the key to his transformation.

"Let go of the pain. Stop trying to control it." Bagabond stopped using the rough voice she had adopted years before. Now she spoke in the rhythm she used when she calmed her animals. She synchronized her breathing with that rhythm and stroked Jack's head.

She knew the way. It was not the first time she had worked with Jack, although it was the first time she had sought to release the beast rather than contain it.

Jack relaxed under her hands. In his mind, he led her down through the levels of his consciousness. She dodged the barriers there and respected the private self which stood behind them. The cats had always urged her to pry. Out of friendship and because of her own near-pathological desire for privacy, Bagabond resisted that severe temptation.

Journeying through Jack's mind was a trip defined by smell. The city, its people, Bagabond herself, were all denoted by their individual scents, not by sight or words. Those came much later in the chain of consciousness.

Coming to a smell of swamp, rotting death and decay, and darkness, Jack stopped. Bagabond met his fear of never returning from the swamp with her reassuring consciousness. She was there. She would not abandon him. But it was the strength of her will that forced him back through the dark space and smell that lay at the core of his reptile self. As Jack's conscious mind was subsumed into the other, Bagabond fled back through his brain as it imploded into the reptile consciousness. The miasma of the swamp and the bellowing challenge of a bull alligator followed her like a riptide.

As she returned to her own body, the reaction flung Bagabond's head back against the side of the porcelain sink and jerked her hands away from the alligator whose head lay heavily in her lap. The reptile flipped over onto his feet again and roared the challenge Bagabond had just heard. Gasping quick, deep lungfuls of air, she entered the creature's mind and calmed him. Tail-tip twitching, he backed slightly away from her, cramped for space in the small rest room.

Bagabond looked up when she heard Rosemary's voice raised outside. The rest room door opened sufficiently to reveal the worried face of the Vietnamese maître d'. His eyes widened and his hand rose to his mouth before slamming the door on the impossible scene.

She looked back down at the alligator and began to search through his mind for the trigger to force him to vomit up the books. Bagabond directed the alligator toward the stall as she uncovered the memory of poisoned meat.

The psychic feedback almost did the trick for her too.

The alligator vomited the contents of his gullet onto the floor and into the stool. The stench of half-digested food shook even Bagabond, inured to most aspects of life and death. Calming the agitated reptile, she got up and gingerly fished for the plastic-wrapped books. Thankfully, it didn't take long. She rinsed off the package in the sink. The alligator whipped his tail, smashing the stall partition into kindling. He growled deep in his throat, a discontented, hungry rumbling.

Reaching out to the alligator brain, Bagabond began the process of separating Jack's humanity from the reptile mind. In little more than a minute, Jack lay shivering on the cold tile floor where the gator had been. She handed him his clothes as he curled up fetally against the smell and the memory.

"It had to be done." She moistened a paper towel and gently wiped his forehead.

"Each time, I think I will never be human again." Jack stared at the wall. "When that finally happens, perhaps it will be for the best."

"Not for Cordelia." Nor for herself, but that thought remained unspoken.

"Cordelia. Yeah. Okay." His voice was flat. "Let's get this thing done." Dressed now, he pushed open the door. Bagabond followed him. Across the room, Rosemary stood with two older men who had joined the group.

"Rosa Maria, we have only the greatest respect for your late father, but we cannot allow you to interfere with the business of the Family." The taller man spread his hands and regarded her paternally.

"The Family business is *my* business." Rosemary glanced over at the approaching Bagabond and Jack. "*I* am a Gambione." She took the slightly damp packet that Bagabond handed her. The two older Mafiosi exchanged exasperated looks. It was obvious to Bagabond that this conversation had been going on for some time while she'd been in the rest room.

"I have a proposition for the Family," said Rosemary. She held the books upright on the table, leaning on them slightly as she spoke. "All the capos should hear me."

The taller man said, "You are a woman."

"Roberto, let her speak. We must make decisions and this is delaying us." The smaller, heavyset capo touched his companion's arm. Resignedly, the other man nodded.

Morelli opened the door. Rosemary started in, followed by Bagabond and Jack. Morelli held out his hand to bar Rosemary's companions. She stared at the capos until they nodded. Morelli dropped his hand in a gesture for them to enter.

The private dining room was long and narrow, almost filled by the single table surrounded by the capos of the Family. They were angrily debating the proper method of exacting retribution for Don Frederico's death. The black crepe bands were ubiquitous.

Halfway down the white-linened table, one man stood listening to the discussion around him. He raised his eyes as Rosemary, Bagabond, and Jack entered. "These are the people with the notebooks?"

"Yes, Don Tomaso," said the tall capo who had questioned them outside. Rosemary moved to the near end of the table. Without releasing the books, she placed them on the tablecloth. Bagabond stood beside her. Jack wandered to the far end of the room and peered out the window at the dark alley.

"Thank you, Rosa-Maria." Don Tomaso's voice held an oily, unctuous tone. "Thank you for bringing these to us." Bagabond tensed and narrowed her eyes. This was one human she knew she especially did not like. Should it become necessary, his throat would be the one she'd spring at. She wrinkled her nose. The aroma of fish sauce made her realize she was hungry too.

"Signorina Gambione, if you please, Don Tomaso." Rosemary's fingers tightened on the books. She met his gaze across the table. Bagabond sensed the growing tension on both sides and felt her muscles echo the tautness. A garbage truck's hydraulic whine and the crash of an upturned dumpster came from outside. The moment of silence in the dining room stretched. It was Don Tomaso who finally inclined his head in acquiescence.

"The books are not a gift," said Rosemary. "They are mine. I decide who has access to their information."

"Then you speak as one outside the Family." Don Tomaso shifted his eyes toward a man to his right. Bagabond followed the slight motion. She again wished she had the claws and teeth of the cats.

"I *speak* as one who has seen the near destruction of the Gambione Family. We are threatened on all sides, yet you sit here debating revenge upon an enemy you cannot even name." Rosemary surveyed the room angrily and shook the books at Tomaso. "If you follow the ways of the Butcher, the Gambiones are *doomed!*"

Behind them, there was a cry of pain and the door crashed open.

"Uh oh," said Jack.

As Bagabond reached for Rosemary, she was shoved to the floor by the thin diner who'd burst into the room. He was fast. The gaunt man grabbed the books from Rosemary, tripping her as he sped past.

"Stop or die!" It was Don Tomaso.

As Bagabond struggled to catch Rosemary, she saw Don Tomaso draw a well-polished Beretta and aim at the fleeing thief. To her amazement, the man laughed hoarsely and halted. Mouth twisting, he turned and stared at the don, who convulsively fired once and then plunged heavily to the tabletop. It was a signal for the stunned capos to fire at the thief, who was now moving toward the window. The impact of the shots seemed barely to slow him down. Capos who tried to intercept him fell before his gaze as though their bullets were being deflected.

"Jack! Move! Now!" But even as Bagabond shouted her warning, she saw Jack face the killer. As the man caught Jack's eyes, the shapechanger's face grew scaly and the snout extended, teeth sharp and prominent. For an instant the thief hesitated, allowing the capos' bullets to slam into him. Then he attempted to bound over the giant alligator that now barred his path to the window.

As he leaped, the alligator's head swiveled up and clashed jagged-toothed jaws on the killer's foot. Screaming in shock and pain, the man pinwheeled in midair, blood spraying into the room from his truncated ankle. He crashed through the glass backward, still clutching the books to his chest as he curled up like a wounded snake.

Outside there was a thud and the groaning of transmission gears. The Mafiosi ran to the window and fired futile shots after the accelerating garbage truck.

"Bastard fell right into the truck!" The shooter at the window turned back to the room. "Don Tomaso, what do we do now?" he said off in the direction of the dead man.

The corpse said nothing.

The shooter did a little dance to avoid the alligator, which rumbled and swallowed contentedly.

Hiram had shifted a few guests around to make room for the refugees at his own table. With Water Lily on his left, Peregrine on his right, and beef Wellington, potatoes Hiram, white asparagus, and baby carrots in front of him, it was a delightful meal.

"Tuna?" Jane said in amazement. "This is tuna?"

"Not merely tuna," Hiram said. "White-meat albacore, flown in direct from the Pacific." No doubt she'd just eaten more than her share of chunk light meat out of cans. Tuna casserole, tuna surprise, tuna croquettes. He shuddered inwardly and covered another roll with butter. Food always made him feel better, even when the circumstances were dire. The thoughts of danger, death, and violence had receded into memory, smoothed away by fine wine, beautiful women, and an excellent hollandaise. Behind their table, the doors to the balcony were wide open, and a cool evening breeze moved through Aces High, perhaps gentled by Mistral's invisible hand.

"Well," Water Lily said, "this is *wonderful.*"

"Thank you," Hiram said. She was bright, no doubt of it, but her innocence was astonishing. She had a great deal to learn about the world, this Jane Lillian Dow, but he suspected she would be a quick and enthusiastic student. He found himself wondering if she were a virgin.

"You're no New Yorker," Peregrine said to Water Lily.

"Why do you say that?" She looked bewildered.

"A native would never say Hiram's food was wonderful. That's to be expected, after all. New Yorkers are more sophisticated than anyone on Earth, so they have to find something to dislike. That way they get to complain, and demonstrate their sophistication. Like this." Peregrine turned to Hiram and said, "I enjoyed the vichyssoise, really I did, but it just wasn't quite up to Parisian standards. But *you* know that, I'm sure."

Hiram glanced over at Jane, who looked as if she were afraid she'd committed some faux pas. "Don't let yourself be corrupted," he told her with a smile. "I remember when Peri first came to town. That was before the fashion shows and the perfume and *Peregrine's Perch*, before she had her name changed, even before the *Playboy* centerfold. She was a sixteen-year-old from—where was it, Peri? Old Dime Box, Texas?" Peregrine grinned at him, saying nothing, and Hiram went on. "The flying cheerleader, that was what the press called her. They were having a national cheerleading competition in Madison Square Garden, would you believe it? Peri was so sophisticated she missed the finals. She decided to save a little money by flying there herself instead of taking a cab, you see."

"What happened?" Water Lily asked.

"I had a street map," Peregrine said amiably, "but I was too shy to ask directions. "I didn't think I'd be able to miss a big place like Madison Square Garden. I must have flown over Madison Square a hundred times, searching for it." She turned and raised an eyebrow, and her gorgeous wings stirred the air behind her. “You win, Hiram,” she said. “The food *is* wonderful. As ever.”

“Flying must be wonderful too,” Jane said with a glance at Peregrine’s wings.

“It’s the second best feeling there is,” Peregrine said quickly, “and afterward you never have to change the sheets.” It was said glibly; a familiar answer to a question she’d been asked a thousand times before. The rest of the table laughed.

Jane looked slightly taken aback. Perhaps she’d expected something other than Peregrine’s offhand wit, Hiram thought. She looked so fresh and young and lovely in the gown he had bought for her—no, *loaned* her, he corrected himself, because that was so important to her. He leaned forward, put his hand lightly on her bare arm. “I can teach you to fly,” he said quietly. He could not give her true flight, of course, it was more a matter of floating, but no one had ever complained. How many men could make their lovers as light as a feather, or lighter than air itself?

Water Lily looked up at him, startled and beautiful, and drew back a little. Her eyes seemed to search him for something and he wondered what it was. What do you look for, Water Lily? he thought, as tiny droplets of moisture began to bead on her smooth, cool skin.

The raw nerve endings from his severed foot screamed white-hot into his mind. It was even worse than his death pain, which, after months of living with it, he could now manage to keep humming along in the back of his mind. Until he needed it. Luckily, Spector had stopped bleeding almost immediately. He hoped that damned fucking animal choked on it. Pain lanced through his leg every time the truck hit a bump or pothole. He shoved the notebooks into the front of his pants. They were his now. He could name his own price. He hurt too much to read them, even if the light was good, which it wasn't. Maybe it was just as well he couldn't though. He'd had more trouble than he could handle in a single day.

The truck slowed to a stop. Spector tried to crawl through the garbage toward the edge. No good. His stump hurt like hell every time he so much as twitched. He heard the hydraulic arms start, and looked up. The dumpster went up and over, dropping several hundred pounds of refuse on him. Spector took a deep breath before he was completely covered. Something heavy landed on his raw ankle. He tried to ignore the pain and claw his way up to the top, but suddenly felt himself moving backward. Bottles, cartons, paper, chicken bones, half-eaten TV dinners, all being compacted together and into him. He folded up with the garbage and tried to tuck his stump under his other leg. The pressure stopped. He heard the crash of the dumpster being set back down. The truck lurched and began moving again.

"Fuck," he said, and was rewarded with a mouthful of soggy coffee grounds. He dug frantically through the garbage toward the open air, trying to ignore the pain. He hoped the truck didn't have any more stops before heading to the dump.

CHAPTER 16

9:00 p.m.

He was too exhausted to try crawling out of the truck; regenerating was taking all his energy. Spector lay atop the garbage as the vehicle bounced down the street. He looked down at his bad foot. Flesh was sticking out several inches beyond the ragged edge of his pants leg. He was growing a new foot. Nothing like this had ever happened before and he'd been figuring he'd have to get some kind of prosthetic foot. His regenerating ability was even more powerful than he'd dreamed. His system was taking tissue from the rest of his body to build the new foot. No wonder he was so exhausted. It itched like hell. He shoved his hands in his pockets to keep from scratching it. He watched the buildings roll by and tried to figure out where he was. Dock area, maybe. There was some traffic, but the truck was still making pretty good time.

He pulled the plastic-wrapped notebooks out of his pants. He couldn't see much while the truck was moving;

the illumination from the streetlights was too irregular. Lucky he'd heard the girl talking about them. They'd better be the right ones after all the grief they'd cost him. No way he could have figured on a guy turning into an alligator. All the aces were supposed to be at Fatman's for the evening.

The truck slowed and he couldn't see buildings anymore. This was probably the end of the line. He tucked the books away and grabbed the rim of the steel wall with both hands. Spector pulled and kicked with his good leg. His muscles trembled for a moment, then failed him entirely. He settled back into the garbage, completely drained.

The truck stopped. Spector heard a metal chain being undone and the creak of a gate. He couldn't even manage to sit up. The truck moved slowly forward for a few moments, then stopped again. He knew what was coming next.

"Stop," he said. His voice was too weak for the driver to hear.

Hydraulic arms lifted the steel box of garbage off the truck and into the air. It began to tilt down. Spector covered his face and rolled into a ball. He caught his breath as he began to fall and pulled the notebooks to his chest. He landed on his head and shoulders and blacked out.

When the dessert carts started making their stately rounds, Hiram's table was, of course, served first.

He was feeling so relaxed and pleased with himself by then that his appetite had quite returned. He accepted a piece of the amaretto cheesecake from one of the new waiters, a wizened little man with a large head and thick glasses. He added a slice of chocolate mango pie for good measure.

The cheesecake was up to the lofty Aces High standards, and the pie was exquisite, its top covered with thin shavings of bittersweet chocolate.

Peregrine had chosen the pie as well. Chocolate, she had explained to Water Lily with that famous smile, was the *third* best thing there was.

Jane was staring at the waiter with a strange blank look on her face. "Is something wrong, dear?" the old man asked her.

She blinked slowly, and shook her head, like someone waking from a dream. "No. I mean . . . I don't remember." She shivered suddenly. "I feel funny."

"Chocolate cures all ills," Peregrine suggested.

But Jane selected the cherries jubilee. "Because," she told Hiram and Peregrine with a smile of her own, "I've heard that when choosing between two evils, you should pick the one you've never tried before." Hiram found himself laughing out loud at her unexpected Mae West intonations. The wizened little waiter laughed too, a shrill thin giggle that went on too long, as if he was amused by some private jest as he wheeled the dessert cart around the table.

All around them, attentive waiters were pouring fresh-brewed coffee from slender silver pots, and setting down little pitchers of heavy cream. Bottles of a delightful sweet wine were opened at tableside for who those who cared to imbibe.

After dessert, the seats would begin to empty, as the guests accepted brandy snifters and tiny glasses of liqueur and began the annual ritual of table-hopping. Modular Man had already gotten a head start; the android had bypassed dessert and was field-testing some Courvoisier.

Hiram dispatched his desserts in short order, washed them down with just the quickest taste of wine, and pushed back his chair. "Pardon my haste," he said to his dinner companions, who were eating more slowly, savoring every bite. "As the host, I have certain duties, though I hate to leave such delightful company even for an instant." He smiled. "Please don't rush off, the evening is just beginning."

Hiram drifted from table to table, smiling at the guests, inquiring about their dinners, accepting the compliments with a gracious smile.

Mistral, holding court at her table near the balcony doors, said her father would undoubtedly be pleased to know he'd been one of the ice sculptures. "We could hardly leave out Cyclone," Hiram told her, "even if he does miss far too many of these affairs. Living in San Francisco is really no excuse, and you can tell him I said so."

Hiram hardly recognized Croyd, who was looking around anxiously for the dessert cart, still two tables away. Next to him, Fortunato sat like a man in a dark shroud, and seemed to take no part in the dinner conversation that swirled about him. Hiram considered stopping by the table and giving him a reassuring word, but the look in those dark eyes beneath his massively swollen forehead seemed to forbid it.

Cap'n Trips had spilled a cup of herbal tea in the lap of Frank Beaumont's date, and was mopping at it ineffectually with a napkin, apologizing profusely, so Hiram was spared the necessity of learning about the dangers of processed sugar.

Wallwalker and the Harlem Hammer were talking together intently. When Hiram asked how their dinner had been, a curt nod from the Hammer was all the answer he got. Rahda O'Reilly, a petite red-haired lady who had been known to metamorphose into a full-grown Asiatic elephant with a startling capacity for flight, thanked him in a charming Indian accent. Fantasy had deserted the minor playwright who'd accompanied her, and was flirting with the Professor. Digger Downs had snuck in somehow, and was off in a corner by the window, interviewing Pulse. Hiram frowned, gave a signal, and two of Peter Chou's security men escorted Digger firmly toward the elevators. A man who could heat a pot of coffee with his bare hands tried to give Hiram a job application, and was directed to Chock Full O' Nuts. Ladybug reminisced fondly about the year they'd served a gigantic baked Alaska in the shape of Jetboy's plane.

Jay Ackroyd looked as though he was about to rupture and die. "I'll never eat again," he promised solemnly.

Hiram dropped down in a vacant chair next to Jay. "Things seem to have gone very well," he said, relieved.

A dessert cart made its way between the tables, but nobody seemed to be in charge of it. Not that it mattered, Fortunato didn't eat sugar, meat, or preservatives if he could help it.

It was one of the biggest disappointments the wild card virus had brought him. All his senses had gotten ridiculously sharp. The weird thing was that natural odors, even wet dogs or decaying vegetables, didn't bother him much. It was only the man-made smells—bus exhaust, insecticides, fresh paint—that irritated him. He'd even given up cocaine years ago. Now when he needed an altered state he used grass or mushrooms or fresh coca leaves.

He'd have preferred an altered state at the moment. Hiram had put him at the same table with Croyd Crenson, which was not itself the problem. Croyd had been a valued customer for years. The problem was Croyd's date. In a masterpiece of bad timing, Ichiko had set Croyd up with Veronica.

Veronica smiled and laughed and hardly touched her plate. Fortunato knew her good mood was nothing but bullshit and heroin buzz. He was glad he had both Cordelia and Croyd to separate him from her. She'd ignored him all the way through dinner, and her hand was in Croyd's lap enough that Croyd didn't pay attention to much of anything else. Except Cordelia, who'd gotten his attention right away.

Croyd was looking good—thin, tanned, high cheekbones, nice smile lines. Fortunato didn't ask how long Croyd had been awake, but he suspected it was already several days. There was an amphetamine brightness to his eyes. When it played out he'd sleep for days or weeks and wake up with a new look and a new power.

His power this time had something to do with metals. His knife and fork kept going limp in his hands. He would concentrate and they would stiffen up again. He and Veronica spent a lot of innuendo on the subject, and before long Cordelia had joined in.

Fortunato had eaten some of the salad and asparagus and let the rest of it go.

"Listen," Croyd said as a white-jacketed waiter switched his dinner plate for a clean one. "Do you think you could refigure my bill to include this one too?" He had one arm around Cordelia.

"There's a problem there," Fortunato said. "Cordelia isn't on the payroll. At least not yet."

"Oh," Croyd said. "I wouldn't want to cut in.

"It's not like that," Fortunato said. "You could say we're sort of auditioning one another."

Croyd looked embarrassed. "I didn't mean to mistake you for . . . uh, a professional," he said to Cordelia. "If you'd like to come to my place after, though, we could have a couple drinks and horse around. No strings, you understand. I wouldn't ask you to do anything you didn't feel up to. I've got a hell of a stereo in this pad down by the waterfront where they don't care how loud I play it . . ."

Suddenly there was a piece of cheesecake on Croyd's plate. Fortunato didn't know where it had come from. He glanced quickly around the room and when he looked back Croyd had added an apple cobbler and a slice of chocolate pie.

Something was badly wrong. Fortunato stood up. Various aces had moved to the balcony, and through the plate-glass window he could see Peregrine and Water Lily talking, their heads close together.

He couldn't seem to think. He leaned forward, palms on the table, and shook his head. The desserts. Where were the desserts coming from?

Think, goddammit. Pastries don't move themselves. That means somebody's moving them. Somebody you can't see. Is there anybody you know of that you can't see?

"Shit!" The huge round table was between him and the balcony. He grabbed the edges and hurled it out of the way, Croyd lunging futilely for his desserts. He was two steps away from the glass doors when Water Lily screamed.

There was about a half second of silence and then everything went to pieces. Modular Man charged the balcony, shouting, "Get away from her!" His body began to crackle with energy. Croyd lifted his hands like he was trying to channel his power. It didn't work. As Modular Man swept by them the radar dish inside his dome went limp and he veered off and crashed helplessly into a wall. He hit hard.

The impact must have scrambled something because he began firing off smoke and tear-gas grenades.

That was when the lights went out. In the first second of darkness Fortunato heard the unmistakable sound of a trumpeting elephant.

He blinked his eyes and let what light there was come to him. In another second he could see, dimly. The air was full of noxious gases so he stopped breathing.

Water Lily was on the balcony, her back to the rail. It started to rain all around her, and in the outline left by the falling water he could see the Astronomer reaching for her.

It was Kid Dinosaur and the park all over again. He fought to get to her and his muscles strained against an invisible force that made him seem powerless. "No!" he shouted, "goddammit, no!" as Water Lily rose into the air and spun around and hurtled off the edge of the balcony into darkness.

It was reminiscent of antiwar marches. The wet handkerchief across the mouth and nose to filter out the worst effects of the tear gas. The clouds of billowing smoke eructed harsh gags, coughs and screams.

Roulette shoved someone aside, making for Tachyon. She had seen him enter, focus on the balcony, move forward, but she had lost him when the lights failed. An ace let go with a burst of flame. Shading her eyes with a hand, she scanned the crowd. Modular Man struggling to his feet, a screaming woman, and Tachyon revealed against a backdrop of drifting smoke.

Tears streamed down his face, and his chest heaved as he struggled to hold back the coughs. His chin lifted as if he was steeling himself for some ultimate effort. Radiance flared about the Astronomer's wizened body as the blow from Tachyon's mind tested the limits of whatever power animated him.

Then Modular Man blew up.

Pieces of burnt steel and plastic shrapneled through the restaurant. One jagged chunk, still trailing a rag from the creature's uniform, struck Tachyon full in the forehead, and he went down, his face a mask of blood.

Screams tore from her throat, and she fought her way to the alien's side. *Don't be dead! Don't be dead!* But she was uncertain whether the mental cry arose from anguish over his loss, or anger at being cheated.

She dropped to her knees, and clutched his limp form to her breast, his blood staining the front of her white gown. Tearing the napkin from her face, she pressed it to the pumping, jagged cut. The tear gas raked at her throat and eyes, and she began to weep. Her tears rained down on Tachyon's face, leaving pale rivulets in the blood.

Water Lily's last scream still hung in the air. The restaurant was in complete chaos. Pieces of Modular Man spun harmlessly off Fortunato's force field. He watched random winds tear through the room as Mistral tried to clear the smoke. Some idiot with flame throwing powers tried to light the place up but only succeeded in setting the curtains on fire. Hiram ran toward the balcony, clenching his fist, shouting, "No! No!" Entire tables floated in the air and hung there, the aces who had lifted them not sure where to throw them. Someone ran upside-down across the ceiling. The noise of smashing china was almost continuous, almost loud enough to drown the sound of vomiting.

The Astronomer turned hazily visible on the balcony and bowed toward Fortunato. Jane, Fortunato thought, would still be falling. Peregrine had turned toward the rail to go after her. The Astronomer took her by the arm and tried to throw her to the floor.

She was clearly stronger than he realized. She gritted her teeth and went to one knee, and with her free arm she reached across and clawed for the Astronomer's eyes. His thick glasses fell to the concrete and blood ran down his cheeks.

The Astronomer smiled. His tongue flicked out and caught a drop of his own blood. The glasses rose by themselves and settled back on his face.

Fortunato took all the power Miranda had given him and centered it at the Manipura chakra at the center of his abdomen. A weird groaning noise came out of his throat and he pushed the prana, the pure energy, out of him and at the Astronomer.

It shot out of Fortunato as a glowing blue-green sphere the size of a softball. Fortunato pulled his arms back, fingers spread, his eyes stretched wide open. The prana bored through the lines of power surrounding the Astronomer and turned them inside out. From concentric circles they shrank to crescents, all on the far side of his body.

The little man's hold on Peregrine's arm began to slip. Peregrine whirled on him, slamming one knee into his crotch and breaking his nose with the palm of her right hand. Blood spurted from the Astronomer's face.

As soon as she was loose Peregrine dove over the side of the balcony, her wings beating furiously. The Astronomer spat at her and then turned back to Fortunato.

The little man's eyes were dead. The same eyes Demise had, the same eyes as the dead boy in the loft. The Astronomer had become Death itself, mindless, brutal, inevitable. You can run, the eyes said, but I will find you.

And then the Astronomer was gone.

The mass of aces wedged into the doors untangled like a slowly waking octopus. Mistral scrubbed at her tear-drenched face, raised her arms above her head, and summoned a breeze. The brisk wind whipping the choking fog into streaming white tatters seemed to free people from the horrified stasis that held them. There was an undignified rush for the door. More than a few remarks about "contacting my lawyer" hung ominously in the air, but Hiram seemed too distracted to notice. He continued to peer anxiously at the railing over which Water Lily and Peregrine had vanished. Somewhere a woman was crying, a horrible whimpering sound like an animal being tortured, then a man's voice called out desperately for a doctor. Unfortunately the only doctor available was out cold on the floor.

There came a thundering, rushing sound like a thousand swans taking to the air, and Peregrine, Water Lily cradled in her arms, landed lightly on the balcony, and glared about her. Hiram gave an inarticulate cry, and lunged forward. Gasps and murmurs of relief rippled through the remaining guests. Both women were drenched by the unending water that poured off Water Lily, but it did little to dampen the angry, darting hawklike glances that Peregrine cast about the room.

Her eyes met Fortunato's, and the fury faded from her face. The tension remained, her slender body vibrating like a plucked violin string, but it was not the tension of flight or fight, it was . . .

Roulette felt the blood rush to her cheeks as attraction flowed like waves off a powerful magnet between Peregrine and Fortunato. Perhaps it was a function of her power, or only an example of her disturbed mind, but the musky, heady odor of sex seemed to lay over the demolished room.

Hiram, treading with a light, fastidious gait through the carnage, stepped to Fortunato's side. "Well!" he gusted. "That was an uninspired mess. Virtually every ace in New York, and he makes a monkey of us all." His head poked accusingly at Fortunato, but the black was oblivious. "Thank God *I* was able to reach Lily. If she hadn't been light as air, Peregrine could never have reached her in time."

Fortunato grunted, but his eyes remained locked on Peregrine, who stood with an arm absently about Water Lily's shoulders and stared back.

"This was one time my power proved to be—"

Fortunato walked away, and Peregrine, abandoning Water Lily, met him halfway.

"Fortunato, for God's sake! I'm talking to you! Can you trace him?"

The pimp pulled his gaze away from Peregrine. "If I could trace him would I have let this happen?"

Hiram spread his hands helplessly. "Then we must try to locate his lieutenants. Someone must know of his plans."

Roulette pressed a hand to her throat, felt the pulse throbbing there. She stared resolutely down at Tachyon's pale face, fearful of Fortunato's piercing eyes. She lifted the blood-soaked napkin, and swabbed at his face, but it only made it worse. The bloody wad fell from her hand, and she stared, mesmerized by the blood staining the pale skin of her palm.

"Hiram, fuck off."

A stifled noise, rather like steam being vented from an engine, rose from Worchester. The burly ace seemed on the verge of apoplexy.

"*I* intend to do something."

"Please don't. I can do so much better without you."

Fortunato tucked Peregrine's arm beneath his, and walked swiftly away before Hiram could respond to this latest insult. The winged ace threw Hiram an embarrassed, apologetic look.

Water Lily was safe. Fortunato filed that away and went to look for Croyd and Veronica and Cordelia.

He found them behind one of the overturned tables. Croyd had rescued an entire Chocolate Death and they were eating it with their fingers. When he saw Fortunato his smile went away.

"I really fucked up with Modular Man," he said. "I'm sorry."

"It doesn't matter," Fortunato said. "As long as you're all okay."

"We're fine," Veronica said.

"I'm going back to his place," Cordelia said. "If you're sure you don't mind."

"It's fine," Fortunato said. "But I don't want you on the streets alone tonight. If anything should happen, Caroline will be home early. Call her and have her come get you in a cab."

"Yes, *o sensei*," Veronica giggled. They got up and headed for the elevators, Croyd with one arm around each, Cordelia with the cake in her free hand.

Fortunato turned back to find Peregrine staring at him. She'd been trying to calm Jane down, getting drenched in the process. He saw her break off in the middle of a sentence. He started toward her, broken glass and china crunching under his shoes.

Everything had faded into shadow except for her. She was tall and powerful and flushed with excitement and Fortunato wanted her. Drained as he was, weak as he was, he could feel her heat all the way across the room. Hiram tried to say something to him and Fortunato got rid of him, not even conscious of the words he used.

He stopped in front of Peregrine. She was breathing heavily, like she'd been running. "The party's over," Fortunato said.

"Yes."

"Can we go somewhere?"

"My Rolls is waiting downstairs."

Fortunato nodded. They walked to the door, side by side, her hand just resting on his arm.

"Wait!" Hiram said to Fortunato, coughing. His eyes were still watering from the tear gas. Fortunato glanced at him for a second, his mouth tight, and swept past, with Peregrine on his arm. Hiram stood helplessly, looking at their backs as they went through the wide double doors.

They were by no means alone. A steady stream of people were headed for the elevators, many still coughing, stumbling, holding onto each other, eyes red and sore. Chrysalis was among them. She stopped to thank him. "I've had a few lively evenings at the Crystal Palace," she said dryly, "but nothing quite like this." Fantasy staggered past with a cut on one cheek and her gown in ruins, and paused long enough to threaten him with a lawsuit.

Mistral had swept the last of the smoke and gas out into the night, then climbed onto the stone banister and leapt off into the darkness. Her cloak filled like a parachute as she climbed up toward the stars. As his friends and guests rushed for the door, Hiram Worchester surveyed what was left of Aces High. Tables were overturned, glasses and plates scattered and broken. The dessert cart the Astronomer had been pushing lay on its side, and panicked feet had ground slices of chocolate mango pie and amaretto cheesecake into the carpet. Several people had left their dinners behind in pools of vomit. In one spot the carpet was still smoldering, and there was a hole in the wall that looked as though someone had made their own exit into the night. At least four windows had been shattered; broken glass was everywhere. One of the chandeliers had come crashing down. Lying beneath it, unconscious, was a full-size Asiatic elephant. The ice sculpture of Peregrine was entirely wingless now, and the one of Dr. Tachyon had been knocked over and was melting slowly into a puddle.

Dr. Tachyon himself still lay on the carpet, groaning, a hand to his forehead. Roulette knelt beside him. Blood was seeping through his fingers, dripping onto the front of his tunic. Hiram moved toward him, and almost tripped over a jagged piece of Modular Man's torso, which looked as though it had been opened with a chain saw. "I'm sorry, Hiram," Tachyon said when he approached, averting guilty lilac eyes. Roulette helped the short man to his feet, but he looked none too steady. "I've got to go after Fortunato. He'll need my help."

"He's already left," Hiram said.

"Where?" Tach demanded in an agonized tone. He took

his hand away from the deep gash in his forehead and stared at the blood that covered his fingers.

"He didn't say. He left with Peregrine."

"I have to find him," Tachyon said.

"I don't think you're in any shape to be finding anyone," Hiram told him. "You ought to go to a hospital. Look at you!"

"Useless," Tach muttered. "I'm *useless*."

Hiram heard a trumpeting sound behind him, and turned to see Elephant Girl lurch to four unsteady feet. A moment later, there was a blinding flash of white light as she released her excess mass as energy. Tachyon cried aloud and Hiram covered his eyes. When they could see again, a shivering, naked Rahda O'Reilly stood where the elephant had been. Her companion, a handsome Egyptian knife-thrower from her circus, borrowed Mister Magnet's long chain-mail cloak and covered her with it.

He turned back to Tachyon and Roulette. The Takisian looked half dead. "Get him down to the Jokertown clinic," Hiram said to Roulette. "That gash needs to be looked after before it becomes infected. He ought to be X-rayed as well. He may have a concussion, or worse."

"But Fortunato . . ." Tach began.

Hiram tried to look stern. "You'd only be a liability to him, the shape you're in. Damn it, are you *that* anxious to add your name to the list of victims? You need treatment and you know it." He raised a hand. "If Fortunato calls, I'll tell him to contact you at the clinic. You have my word on it."

Dr. Tachyon nodded reluctantly and let Roulette guide him toward the door.

The restaurant was almost empty now. Hiram went back toward his office, and found Cap'n Trips on the floor outside the rest room. He was kneeling over a jumble of broken glass and colored powders, pinching the powder with the fingers of one hand and dropping it into a carefully cupped palm. "This is no time to be doing drugs, damn it," Hiram snapped at him.

Trips looked up at him through pale, watery eyes. "I just wanted to help, man," he burbled. "I was running to get one of my friends, but I tripped, and like, when I fell, everything must have gotten smashed."

"Just go home," Hiram said. Peter Chou appeared at his side. "Peter, help the Captain here find a cab before he cuts himself on that broken glass, will you?" Chou nodded.

Curtis intercepted him en route to his office. "There's a phone call for Fortunato. It's the police. What should I tell them?"

"He left with Peregrine," Hiram said. "I believe she's got a cellular phone in her car. Give them the number."

He pushed by Curtis and entered his office. Water Lily was sitting in his chair, still pale and shaken. Rivulets of water ran down her face as she looked up at him. Jay Ackroyd sat on the edge of Hiram's desk, holding Modular Man's head. "Alas, poor silicon chip, I knew him well," he was saying. Jane gave a small laugh that sounded to Hiram like incipient hysteria. Ackroyd tossed the head lightly from one hand to the other. The skullcap had fallen off, and Mod Man's radar dome was cracked.

"Put that down," Hiram said. He collapsed wearily into a chair, and looked at Water Lily. "I'm very glad you're all right. I don't think I could have endured another death today. Certainly not yours."

"What about him?" Jay said, placing the head on the desk. Mod Man's blind eyes stared out at Hiram.

"I'm sorry about Modular Man, but he wasn't precisely

alive and he isn't precisely dead. His creator will probably build another one."

"Ladykiller Mark Four? Another in the Silicon Valley's gift-to-women series?" Jane said. She gave another small ragged laugh. She put one hand over her mouth. He could hear her breathing unsteadily against it.

Hiram said, "Jane, if you have no objections, I'd take it as a favor if you'd stay here for a while. The Astronomer was gone by the time Peregrine returned with you, so with luck he thinks you're dead. Let's not disabuse him. He has a long list, after all." He ran a hand over his scalp. "I'm going to ask Peter and his staff to remain on duty. I know that's not much, but it's better than nothing."

Water Lily nodded and took her hand away from her face. "All right. I couldn't take much more tonight."

Hiram forced a smile he hoped was comforting. "I hadn't intended your first flying lesson to be quite so traumatic."

She straightened in the chair, seemingly trying to shake off the aftermath as much as she could, and looked at him in that searching way again. "What about you?" she asked.

Hiram Worchester folded his hands neatly atop his stomach. He looked a mess, he realized. He laughed, a short little humorless bark of a laugh. The shock was finally wearing off, but strangely, Hiram was not afraid. Instead he was conscious of a gnawing hunger, and a cold steady rage that was building within him. He thought of Eileen.

"Hiram?" Popinjay asked, breaking his reverie.

"I'd kill him if I could," Hiram said, more to himself than to them. "Perhaps I might have, but then Jane would have died. I'm not sorry I made *that* choice." He looked at her fondly, then turned to Ackroyd. "Jay, I believe I'll need to engage your services once more."

"Real good," said Ackroyd. "We going after the old guy?"

"Gladly," said Hiram, "if I only knew where to find him, or even how to begin the search." He made a short, impatient gesture with his right hand. "No, that's futile, and Fortunato made his feelings clear, so we'll leave those heroics for him. Still, there are other scores that require settling tonight. Call me quixotic, but after what happened here this evening, I cannot sit by passively and do nothing." He grimaced. "I feel strangely like righting a wrong."

"Take two aspirin and lie down," Jay said. "The feeling will pass."

"No," said Hiram. "I think not." He stood up, reached in the pocket of his tux. The slip of paper with Loophole's address was still there. "Start your meter. We're going to talk to a lawyer."

He felt rough hands chafing his wrists. Spector opened his eyes and put his hand over his mouth. The highly seasoned beef he'd eaten at the Haiphong Lily was threatening to come up. He could see the silhouette of someone kneeling beside him. Spector groaned.

"You're not dead. Knew it when I dragged you out. Lucky I was here. You'd have suffocated."

Spector could tell by the voice the person was old and male. He felt around with his hands. He was still lying in garbage.

"Where the fuck am I?"

"On a barge filled with garbage, friend. I might ask you how you got here, if you were of a mind to tell me." The old man flicked a lighter and lit a cigarette. He was completely bald with brown eyes and thin lips. His wrinkled skin had a slight orange tint. His lumpy body reminded Spector of the Michelin man. The lighter went off.

"Some crazy assholes beat me up and threw me in a dumpster. That's all I remember until you brought me to." It was as good a lie as any other he might tell. He reached into his coat for the notebooks. They were gone. "Any way we can get some light here? I want to see what those bastards left me with."

The lighter's small flame came on again. Spector checked his pockets and began looking through the garbage at his feet. He wanted those notebooks back. They'd give him the leverage to make the Shadow Fist boys help him take out the Astronomer. A few men with automatic weapons could make all the difference if the old man was as tired as Spector thought he might be. "What did you say your name was?" he asked, trying to divert attention from his search.

"I didn't. My name's Ralph. Ralph Norton." The old man held the lighter lower. He was wearing a blue long-sleeve shirt and matching navy vest and pants. The clothes were stained and rumpled. "You must have lost something, right?"

"Yep." He threw aside a plastic bag and dug into the garbage by his side. "Where did you get me out, anyway?"

"Down at the end of the barge, where they dumped you off." The old man pointed. "You tell me what you're lookin' for and I'll help. Got nothing better to do right now."

Spector looked at his injured foot. It was pink and pulpy, but still growing. He stood slowly, his knees wobbling as his feet sank into the refuse. His foot was like a bucket of coals at the end of his leg, but he'd have to live with it. "No thanks. But I'll buy that lighter from you." He reached into his pocket. The money was still there and he pulled out a bill.

"No need. You're welcome to it." Ralph handed the lighter over. "It's got plenty of fluid."

Spector took the lighter and flicked it, then began struggling to the other end of the barge. The lights of Manhattan were directly in front of him, but they didn't make him feel any better. He had to find those notebooks before the Astronomer came calling.

"Walk slow," Ralph said. "Otherwise you'll wind up on your face."

"Right." Spector was breathing heavily. "What the hell were you doing here anyway?"

"It's my taxi back home." Ralph laughed. "I live over in Fresh Kills on Staten Island."

"Fresh Kills?"

"The largest landfill in the country. Maybe in the world. They'll be taking these four barges over tomorrow morning. I only came over because some relatives of mine were in town for Wild Card Day. Wanted me to show them the town."

Spector plowed forward. "You live in a garbage dump?"

"Sure do. You'd be surprised the things people throw away. Perfectly good stuff. Sanitation workers tried to run me off a couple of times, but I always come back. The rent's too cheap to pass up." Ralph put his hand on Spector's shoulder. "Do you know any aces?"

Spector stiffened. "Not personally. Why?"

"Because I'm one. I've got power."

Spector was too tired to keep going, and sat down. "You're an ace and you live in a garbage dump. Do I look like an out-of-towner or something?"

Ralph smiled and picked up a milk carton, paused dramatically, then took a bite out of it. He chewed for a moment and swallowed. "I can metabolize anything. That's what that Dr. Tachyon said. What's garbage to most folks is food on my table."

Spector laughed. "You can eat garbage. That's your power? Bet everybody stays out of your way."

Ralph crossed his arms. "Go ahead. Laugh your head off. You know what I save in a year on food and rent alone? And I'm my own boss. Nobody tells me what to do. Nobody tells me when to come or go. That's more power than most people ever get to have."

"You got a point. Look, I'm pretty tired. Maybe you could help me. I'm looking for some notebooks wrapped in plastic. There's money in it for you."

"All right. But we've got to do better than a cigarette lighter or we'll never find them." He tapped his thumbs together thoughtfully. "Sparklers ought to work. Got plenty. I'll be back in a minute."

"Sparklers?"

"Yeah. I got a bunch of fireworks I was going to set off at midnight. Sort of my own little celebration. You wait here." He pushed through the garbage toward the other end of the boat.

Spector stuck his fingers through a couple of the bulletholes in his jacket and chewed his lip. If he managed to survive today, he wouldn't get out of bed for a week.

CHAPTER 17

10:00 p.m.

The Rolls was only a couple of blocks from Aces High when the phone started ringing. Fortunato looked at Peregrine, who shrugged and picked it up. "It's for you," she said.

"This is Altobelli," the voice on the phone said. "I made Hiram cough up your number, there. It's about Kafka."

"Fucking hell," Fortunato said, closing his eyes. "He's dead."

"No," Altobelli said. "Still alive. But it was close."

"Tell me."

"About fifteen minutes ago some weirdo in a white robe just appeared in the middle of the holding cell. But I believed you and I had a SWAT team there, and when he went for Kafka they opened up with everything they had."

"And?"

"They didn't hurt him. But the bullets kept knocking him down and each time he was a little slower getting up. Then he just disappeared again."

"You were lucky. He's weak right now, or nothing you threw at him would have stopped him." Fortunato didn't say anything about how weak he felt himself.

"This guy, whoever he was, had more than luck on his side."

"What do you mean?"

"Not over the phone. You remember that place we met last month? Don't say the name, just say yes or no."

"Yes."

"Can you meet me there? Like right away?"

"Altobelli . . ."

"I think we're talking life or death here. Mine."

"I'm on my way," Fortunato said.

When he hung up the phone Peregrine said, "The Astronomer."

Fortunato nodded. "I'll take a cab. You go back to Aces High, where you'll be safe."

"That's ridiculous. I'm safer with you. And there's no point in taking a cab when you can go in style in a chauffeured Rolls Royce." She raised one eyebrow. "Right?"

After shooing out the few remaining regular customers, the Gambiones had moved their meeting into the main dining room and scooted several tables together. Guns and wariness were much in evidence. Rosemary stood at one side, watching the men argue. Bagabond saw an undecipherable smile on her face. The bag lady sat with Jack at a banquette along a side wall.

"I want to start looking for Cordelia. It's been hours—much more time than I promised Rosemary." Jack glared across the room at the assistant district attorney.

"Until this is finished, she can't make the calls." Bagabond glanced sympathetically at Jack, who was tugging at the stained sleeve of his too-small white waiter's jacket. "Now eat."

Squeezing the lime over his soup, Jack shook his head and picked up the chopsticks. He pulled a mass of rice noodles and shrimp out of the bowl in front of him. "What's she going to do without the books?" He jabbed the chopsticks toward Rosemary.

"Don't know. She's made her choice now. She'll manage." Leaning her head back against the booth, Bagabond closed her eyes. "I'm going to find out if anyone has seen Cordelia. Quiet."

Jack eavesdropped on the Mafia maneuverings as he ate and refilled his bowl.

Two men were the faction leaders. The older man, black hair slicked back and dressed in a charcoal-gray double-breasted suit, stressed the sublime importance of continuing Don Frederico's plans in the interest of stability. A younger man, his dark brown hair expensively trimmed in what Jack would have described as a modified punk cut with a rat tail, pointed out that the Butcher had not been particularly effective in ending encroachments on their territory. The other men listened without comment.

"Not one of the other Families has ever challenged our authority." The older man leaned back in evident satisfaction.

"Christ, Ricardo. Of course, they haven't." The new-wave Mafioso rolled his eyes toward heaven. "They've all been busy with the *real* threats. The Vietnamese. The Colombians. The jokers. Jesus, can't you see that Jokertown's turning into a nickel-plated disaster area, man?"

"Respect, Christopher, please." Ricardo inclined his head sympathetically toward Rosemary.

"Thank you, Ricardo Domenici." Rosemary stepped toward the tables.

"She's heard worse, Ricardo. Even in the DA's office, I'm sure she's heard much worse." Christopher Mazzuchelli shook his head exasperatedly. "The *point* is that we must have as a leader someone who can face the new threats. You know, evolve."

"Mazzuchelli's right." The stares of all the Gambione capos pivoted toward Rosemary. "We *must* have new blood to lead us, or the Family will be destroyed. It's that plain."

The older man sounded placating. "Signorina Gambione, this is a serious issue. It is for us to decide. It would be better perhaps—"

"Yes, Ricardo, I am a Gambione. The last." Rosemary caught each man's eyes in turn. "This is *my* Family. I have a right to speak."

"Maybe she wants her father's job." Christopher Mazzuchelli grinned until her gaze returned to him.

"Maybe I do." Rosemary smiled a thin and enigmatic smile. "Donatello is dead, and likewise Michaelangelo, Raphael and Leonardo. Four dons. You understand what we face, but not what to do. Ricardo sees only the past."

"Wait a minute." Mazzuchelli's mouth hung slightly open in surprise.

"Who better?"

"You're a fucking district attorney!"

"Yes." Rosemary smiled as she appeared to consider the possibilities. "I couldn't protect us completely, but I could make a difference. And the information would be invaluable. My identity as a Gambione would have to be protected. No one outside this room must know. *Omerta.*"

"You can hardly command the Family in secrecy." Ricardo Domenici was obviously offended by the entire idea. "Even if we would consider such a thing."

"True enough. Someone else would have to be my . . . mouthpiece." She examined each of the capos in turn. "Mazzuchelli."

The capos began to babble as Christopher Mazzuchelli grinned insolently back at her.

"Gentlemen, have you any objections? Ricardo?"

"He is too young, too inexperienced. His very appearance . . ." Ricardo threw apart his arms at the obvious absurdity of it. "The other Families would laugh at us."

"This is insane. A woman, a boy . . ." A jowly man with a five o'clock shadow, wearing a traditional black coat, shoved back his chair and stood. "I will return when you are ready to choose a new don."

Mazzuchelli blocked his way but, at a gesture from Rosemary, moved aside. The dissenter walked across the room in the sudden silence and threw open the door.

Rosemary called out sharply, "Morelli!"

The man who had just exited backed into the room again, eyes fixed on the muzzle of the Uzi that Morelli pointed at his chest. "Yes, Signorina?" said Morelli. "A problem?"

"I think the problem has been solved. Do you agree, DiCenzi?" Rosemary watched the man across the room closely.

Under the gun, DiCenzi nodded. "*Sì*, Signorina. There is . . . no problem."

"Good." Rosemary scanned the seated, staring men. "Does anyone else have a problem?"

Ricardo glanced quickly at the men to either side of him.

They were ostentatiously ignoring him. "No, there is no problem, Dona Gambione."

"Signorina will do nicely, I think." She smiled a predatory smile at the capos. "Sit down, DiCenzi. Thank you, Morelli. Please have a seat."

Mazzuchelli was eyeing Morelli as he would a bad piece of steak.

"Christopher," Rosemary said, "you *are* too ambitious. I recognize it. Do not make any rash mistakes."

Mazzuchelli returned her look with a smile as lupine as her own. "You're the boss."

Rosemary nodded and gazed around the restaurant. "Has anyone seen the manager?"

"You want something to eat?" Ricardo was incredulous.

"I suspect Signorina would like to find out how that bastard who stole the books got in here." Mazzuchelli stared down at Ricardo. "Don't *you* think that would be an interesting question?"

Morelli stood and began walking toward the kitchen. "Signorina, he's yours."

While Morelli prepared the terrified Vietnamese for Rosemary's questions, the new head of the Gambiones called her contacts at the precincts and made inquiries about Cordelia. On the East Side, a patrolman remembered spotting someone looking a lot like the missing young woman walking downtown along one of the alphabet avenues. It hadn't been long before.

Bagabond wanted to enter the area on foot before she began an animal-by-animal search for the girl. Jack was ready to leave instantly, but Rosemary took the pair aside for a moment.

"Listen, thanks for your help, both of you. This wasn't

exactly what I'd planned, but it wouldn't have happened without you." Her smile looked political.

"Wasn't it?" Bagabond stared straight at Rosemary.

"Suzanne, I had no idea . . ."

"Yeah. I'll be in touch." Bagabond started to turn away. Jack was already moving toward the door.

"Suzanne, I'll call you later. Let me know what happens with Jack's niece."

Bagabond glanced at Morelli in the corner with the Vietnamese manager. In this light, the blood looked black. She shook her head slightly.

Rosemary colored and drew herself up. "I can do some good here, you know. Exert some controls."

Bagabond kept moving.

"Suzanne, I want to talk to you later about some ideas I had about the animals."

All the muscles of Bagabond's shoulders and upper back tensed as she followed Jack out through the door. She tried not to listen, but thought she heard whimpered cries from behind them.

Business was still hopping at the Donut Hole across the street from the Jokertown station. The sidewalks were filled right out to the gutters and every few minutes another black-and-white would drop off the latest load of drunk-and-disorderlies on the precinct steps.

The Rolls had let Fortunato off a block away and crawled away through the traffic in search of a place to double-park. Fortunato elbowed his way to a back table and found Altobelli wearing a Brooklyn Dodgers cap and a jogging suit. "I practically had to kill to save you that chair. Wanna doughnut?"

Fortunato shook his head. "Talk to me, Altobelli. I don't have much time."

"You do look a bit peaked. Okay, okay. It's Black, John F. X. Black, captain of the Jokertown precinct."

"I know the name."

"We leave Kafka here this afternoon. About an hour later I get a call from one of my guys. Black has ordered them off the Kafka watch. I drive over here to find out why and catch Black trying to take Kafka out in a squad car. He gives me a song and dance about a prisoner transfer. I say show me the paperwork. More songs, more dances. So I take Kafka away from him and bring him back uptown myself."

"You're telling me Black's dirty."

"You haven't heard dirty yet. Right after that guy in the robe and glasses tries for Kafka I get a call from my snitch at the Jokertown precinct. He wants to tell me he saw this weird guy in a robe and glasses in Captain Black's office not five minutes before."

Fortunato stood up. "Where is he?"

Altobelli hooked a thumb at the station. "Every cop in Manhattan is working double shifts tonight. I'm supposed to be back up on Riverside myself."

"Get on up there. And let yourself be seen."

Altobelli had to stop for a second and think about it. Finally he nodded. "Okay."

"Anybody else know about Black?"

"Just you and me. Fortunato?"

"Yeah?"

"Nothing, I guess. This ain't . . . it ain't the way I'm used to doin' things. I'm used to standing up for my own."

"He's not one of your own anymore. He's the Astronomer's. And now he's mine."

The address was on Central Park West. They took a cab; Hiram had no wish to involve Anthony or the Bentley in whatever unpleasantness might ensue.

Inside the heavy glass-and-iron doors of the apartment building, a doorman sat at an antique desk. Behind him was a bank of security monitors. He was built like a linebacker, and there was an obvious silent alarm built into the top of his desk, an inch or so from his hand. He could hardly have expected any trouble from a fat man in a tuxedo and a nondescript fellow in a cheap brown suit. "Yes?" he asked them through the intercom when they approached the door.

Jay Ackroyd made a gun out of his right hand, pointed at the doorman through the glass, and said, "Here's looking at you, kid." The man disappeared with a *pop* of in-rushing air.

Hiram rocked lightly on the balls of his feet, glanced around nervously. "Where did you—" he began.

"The main stacks of the New York Public Library," Jay said. "He looked like he needed to get caught up on his reading." He took out his wallet, removed a credit card, and opened the door in the blink of an eye. "Never leave home without it," he told Hiram as he slipped the card back into his wallet. They went into the lobby.

Latham lived in the penthouse, just as Hiram had expected. Jay pressed the button for the roof.

The embossed bronze plate above the doorbell said ST. JOHN LATHAM. Jay pressed it, and they waited in nervous silence by the elevator. He wasn't home, Hiram thought, of course he wasn't home, he was out somewhere, he was—then the door gave a soft buzz and swung open slowly.

They walked into a small foyer, empty but for a bentwood hat rack and an umbrella stand. The kitchen was to the right, a closet to the left. Ahead was a huge living room with a sunken conversation pit, a wet bar, and a solid wall of floor-to-ceiling glass that opened on a roof garden, a magnificent view of Central Park and the city and stars beyond. A lavish bedroom suite and den both opened off the living room, their doors standing wide. Voices were coming from the den. Hiram walked lightly, small quiet steps, but Jay's heels clicked loudly on the gleaming parquet floor as they crossed the room.

"That's fine. Yes. Yes, at all costs. Phone in when you have news." The man touched a button; the speakerphone disconnected. The only light in the room came from a brass banker's lamp with a green glass shade. Latham sat with a stack of maps under his left hand, his right hand working the keyboard of an IBM PC. He wore the vest and trousers of a gray chalk-stripe Armani suit, a perfect white shirt with the top button undone, and a dark foulard tie, the knot pulled down and to one side. He did not look up when they entered. "Do I know you?"

"My name is Worchester," Hiram said. "Hiram Worchester. My associate is Jay Ackroyd, a licensed private investigator—"

"Who earlier today illegally detained a client of Latham, Strauss, violating his constitutional rights and causing him untold psychological distress, not to mention disorientation, damage to his good name, and fear for his life and safety," Latham said. He still did not look up from the keypad. The screen displayed a grid of some sort. "An error in judgment that is going to cost Mr. Ackroyd a considerable sum of money, and probably his license." He finished his entry, stored it, and wiped the grid off the screen. Only then did he deign to swivel his high-backed chair to look at them. "If you're here to propose a settlement, I'm certainly willing to listen."

"A *settlement*?" Hiram was aghast. "You're suggesting we pay *money* to that unspeakable thug who—"

"I'd caution you aginst slander, Mr. Worchester. You're in sufficient trouble already." The phone rang. Latham didn't bother to pick it up. He reached out, touched the speaker-phone button, and announced, "Not now, I have company. Call back in ten minutes." The caller hung up without identifying himself. "Now, Mr. Worchester, what were you about to say?"

"Your client is scum," Hiram said clearly. "Frankly, I'm shocked that a distinguished man like yourself would even consider representing him."

"I'm a little curious about that myself," Jay Ackroyd said. He slouched against the doorway, hands in his pockets. "Usually you've got a little more class than that."

"I seldom involve myself in criminal matters," Latham said, "and I am not, in fact, the attorney of record in this case. But I make it a point to familiarize myself with all our pending litigation, even the most trivial, and Mr. Tulley briefed me on this matter only this afternoon."

"Who are you really working for?" Hiram demanded. Jay Ackroyd groaned. Hiram gave him a dirty look and then went on. "This is extortion, you know it and I know it. I want to know who's behind it, and I want to know now." He crossed the room, leaned over the desk, and stared in the lawyer's face. "I warn you, I'm an ace, and not an inconsiderable one, and I've had a *very* bad day."

"Are you threatening me, Mr. Worchester?" Latham asked in terms of polite interest.

"I don't feel so well," Ackroyd whined from the doorway. Hiram looked back in annoyance. Ackroyd was clutching his stomach, and his features did have a slight greenish tinge, but maybe that was just the light. "I wouldn't have eaten so much if I'd known I was going to get tear-gassed." He belched. "Where's the john?" he asked with some urgency.

"Through the master bedroom, to the right," Latham told him. Ackroyd bolted for sanctuary, and a moment later they heard the sound of retching. "Charming," Latham said.

Hiram turned back on him. "Never mind about him. Your client and his friends sent a decent, honest man to the hospital today. They broke his arm and two of his ribs, knocked out several of his teeth, and gave him a slight concussion. They also burned his delivery truck and vandalized his place of business. They poisoned my lobsters with *gasoline*, Mr. Latham."

"Did you see our client commit any of these alleged crimes? No? I thought not. Did Mr. Ackroyd?"

"Damn it, Latham. I was there this morning, I saw what they were trying to do—"

"Who?"

"Them," Hiram said. "His men. Three of them, they were called, ah, Eye and Cheech and, well, I don't recall the other one's name. Eye was the joker."

"I have no idea who you're referring to," Latham said. "In any case, Mr. Seivers is not a part of any gang."

"Mr. Seivers?" Hiram was momentarily confused.

"I believe he's sometimes known as the Bludgeon. If you're going to persecute the man on account of his appearance, you might at least trouble yourself to learn his real name, which as it happens is Robert Seivers."

Both of them heard the toilet flush. Latham leaned back in his chair. "Your friend is finished. Unless you care to propose a settlement, I believe our business is finished too. As you can see, I'm quite busy."

Jay Ackroyd reentered the room, looking a bit pale, dabbing at his lips with a handkerchief.

"Get out," Latham suggested coolly. "Both of you."

"You can't just–" Hiram began.

"Would you prefer I call the police?"

As they waited by the elevator, Hiram glared at Jay in indignation. "A fat lot of good you were," he said.

"You've got a great touch for interrogation, Hiram," Ackroyd said. "I didn't want to spoil your rhythm."

The doors opened and they got inside the elevator. "That got us exactly nowhere," Hiram said, pressing the button for the lobby with rather more gusto than required.

"Oh, I wouldn't say that," Ackroyd replied. He looked at his watch. "If Loophole's as smart as I think, he's searching his bathroom by now."

Hiram was lost. "Searching his bathroom?"

"Bedroom too. I didn't really expect him to *buy* my little tummyache," Jay said. "He's got to figure I ran to the john to plant some kind of bug."

"Ah," Hiram said, "so he wastes time searching . . ."

"I hope not. Hell, I didn't hide it very well. It's on the phone by his bed, how obvious could I get?"

Hiram gaped at him. "You planted a bug, but you want it to be discovered. Why?"

"Gives him something to find," Ackroyd said. "Once he has it, he ought to be satisfied. He thinks we're chumps anyway, and he's got other things on his mind tonight."

"Where did you get a bug?" They'd reached the lobby.

The doors opened, and they stepped out of the elevator.

Ackroyd shrugged. "Oh, I carry a few around. They're good for making people nervous. I get them real cheap at this place in Jokertown, this guy sells me all his broken ones, six for a dollar. Unless Loophole knows a lot more about micro-circuitry than I figure, he'll never know the difference." Ackroyd glanced at his watch again. "By now he should have found it, locked it up somewhere, and gone back to business, but let's give him a few more minutes just to play it safe. Did you notice the computer?"

"Eh? Yes, certainly, what of it?" Hiram opened the door and they walked outside.

"Manhattan streets," Jay said. "Times Square area. There were maps on his desk. Some kind of search is in progress, and our friend Loophole is coordinating it, I'd bet. Staying right by his phone, keeping everyone in touch with everybody else, charting the players on the computer. Real interesting."

"I don't know what you're talking about," Hiram said.

"Remember our little tête-à-tête at Tachyon's place? Tall-green-and-scaly was looking for some kind of book, and he didn't strike me as a real heavy reader. I think Loophole's looking for the same thing."

"I don't care a fig about stolen books," Hiram said. "I want something done about Bludgeon."

"Maybe the same guy owns them both," Jay said. He shrugged. "Or maybe not. Let's find out." He ambled back over by the building and began poking around in the shrubbery.

Hiram crossed his arms and scowled. "What are you doing?"

Popinjay looked back. "I'm going to hide in these

bushes. I'm real good at hiding in bushes. It's the first thing they teach you in detective school."

"How are you going to find out anything that way?"

"I'm not," Ackroyd said. He shaped his right hand into a gun and pointed a loaded finger. "You are," he finished. Hiram never heard the *pop.*

Fortunato's black tie and long coat were a little out of place in the Jokertown station house. It was like a human garbage dump. The dominant smell was a blend of cheap wine and vomit and stale sweat. The main hall was standing room only, with a special section for hookers. The sight of their streaked makeup and stained, gaudy clothes was more than Fortunato could stand.

It took him ten minutes to find Black's office. The door was open and Black was on the phone. Black was good looking in a five-o'clock-shadow, rolled-sleeve, cheap-haircut sort of way. Fortunato waited in the hall until Black hung up. Then he stepped in and closed the door.

"The name didn't mean much," Fortunato said. "But I recognize you now. It was seven years ago. I spent the night in a cell here while a woman I cared a lot about got her brain fried. You had a Sergeant Matthias and a guy named Roman interrogate me. They decided they weren't interested and turned me loose. You probably don't remember."

"Remember? I've never seen you before, *or* this bimbo you're talking about." Black was scared and not hiding it well. Fortunato liked that.

"You're going to tell me everything you know. I'm not going to fuck around, because I'm in a hurry. So you're just going to tell me, right now."

It was easy. Black wasn't an ace, just an ordinary guy. Fortunato was weak, but would never be ordinary again. Black leaned back in his swivel chair, tense but unresisting.

"What do you want to know?" Black said tonelessly.

"The Astronomer. He's escaping tonight. He's got a ship, some kind of spaceship. I need to know where it is."

"Spaceship? Like aliens from space? Like Dr. Tachyon and that kind of shit? You must be crazy."

Fortunato gave him another little jolt of power. He was starting to feel dizzy. "He must have been planning to take you with him. Otherwise he would have killed you."

Black looked puzzled. "Yeah, he was . . . but he decided to keep me here, keep me alive for 'contingencies.' "

"Like pulling the guards off Kafka?"

"Yeah. Like that."

"And where is it he's going?"

"It's funny. I really can't remember."

"Funny," Fortunato said. He let himself come loose from his physical body and went into Black's mind. The man wasn't lying. The memory of the ship, where the Astronomer got it, where it was hidden, where he was taking it, was gone. Neatly cut away. Just the way the Astronomer had cut up Eileen's brain.

Fortunato turned to go.

"You're just . . . going to leave me here?"

"You're no use to me."

"But . . . aren't you afraid I'd try to get back at you?"

"Yeah," Fortunato said. "I suppose you're right." With the last of his strength he reached into Black's chest and stopped his heart. Black made a noise like a cough and slumped sideways in his chair.

"Her name was Eileen," Fortunato said, and walked away.

Hiram's right foot was soaked up to the ankle; he'd appeared half-standing in the toilet, and it was sheer good fortune that an ongoing phone conversation had covered up the splash he made when extricating himself. As it was, he got nervous every time he took a step, fearful that the squishing sound would give him away. So he tried not to move much.

He crouched in the bedroom, near the door to the spacious living room. It was open, as was the door to the adjacent room. He couldn't see a thing but the empty living room, but he could *hear* everything, and that was what mattered. He'd been there twenty-odd minutes now, and he'd heard more than enough.

Ring. "Latham? This is Hobart. Subway's secure. The Egrets are down on the platforms, no way anybody gets on any trains without us knowing. I've got men hanging around every turnstile. You sure she's heading this way?"

"Our friend from Justice seem to think so. I spoke to Billy Ray a few minutes ago, he says that she's heading up Broadway and he's not far behind her. Wyrm has been informed, and he confirms. He's on his way."

St. John Latham of Latham, Strauss, obviously gave his clients a good deal more than legal representation.

Ring. "Cholly, man. We're at the Port Authority. I'm in a phone booth, we got guys at all the doors. Lots of pimps and ho's, man, but no sign of a white chick in a bikini."

"Keep watching."

The ringing of the phone was constant, as was the soft sound of Latham's practiced fingers on the IBM keypad. Hiram edged closer to the door.

He felt sorry for the prey, whoever it was. Latham and his people were closing a net around the whole Times Square area. Each phone call pulled the weave a little tighter, and the phone kept ringing.

Ring. "Sinjin? This is Fadeout."

"Where are you?"

"In front of Nathan's. No sign of her. It's not quite as bad as New Year's Eve, but it's not far off either."

"You visible?"

"For the moment. Otherwise I'd have nat assholes bumping into me every other second. Besides, I may need the energy if she shows."

"She'll show. Wyrm is certain of it."

"Where the hell is he?"

"In his limo, fighting traffic. Where are the rest of our people?"

"Egrets and Werewolves all over the place. Our jokers are all wearing Dr. Tachyon masks, so we know who they are. The Whisperer's up by the Cohan statue, Bludgeon is hanging around outside the Wet Pussycat, Chickenhawk's perched on top of the tower. He's supposed to be watching, but he's probably eating a goddamned pigeon. We've got a few guys in cabs too, in case she tries to hail a taxi, maybe she'll get one of ours."

Hiram tensed at the mention of Bludgeon's name. When the next call rang through, and he heard a familiar razor-cruel voice come out of the speakerphone, he edged forward until he was in the doorjamb. "Loophole, you fucker," the voice said. "It's me."

"Yes," Latham replied in polite, icy tones.

"I just spotted the gash. I'm watching her tight little butt right now. You ought to see her, nothing on but a fuckin' bikini, her titties just hangin' out there. Should I kill her?"

"No," Lathan said crisply. "Follow her."

"Shit, I could twist her fuckin' head off before she knew I was there." He laughed. "Fuckin' shame to waste the rest of her, though."

"She is not to be killed, not until we have the book. Obviously she's not carrying it. Keep her in sight, but don't touch her. Wyrm is on his way."

"Fuck," Bludgeon said. "Can I have a little fun with her, after we get the shit back?"

"Follow her, Seivers," Loophole said. He hung up.

The penthouse was strangely quiet for a moment.

Then Hiram heard the creak of Latham's swivel chair, followed by the soft sound of the lawyer's footsteps. *The bathroom*, he thought in sudden panic.

The footsteps moved closer.

Spector pushed another plastic garbage bag to one side. A rat the size of a dachshund launched itself toward him. The animal scrambled up his arm toward his throat. He grabbed it by the tail with one hand and banged its head into the edge of the metal barge. The rat squealed and twitched convulsively. He let it drop.

The sparkler was burning low, singeing his fingers. Tiny flakes of burning metal were irritating the back of Spector's hand. He tossed the sparkler over the side of the barge. There was a faint hiss when it hit the water.

"God, I wish it was daylight. We might have a shot at finding them," Spector said.

"If it was daylight, you'd have to fight the gulls. They swarm around these barges like bees to honey. Pick you to pieces if you're not careful. Don't give up yet," said Ralph.

He pulled another sparkler out of the box and lit it off the one he was holding, then handed it to Spector. "Those notebooks are on this barge somewhere, and we're going to find them."

Spector was feeling stronger as time passed. His foot didn't hurt nearly as much as before. The stump was getting longer and separating at the end, like toes were trying to reform. The smell on the barge was so strong that even Spector was bothered by it. He wished for a breeze and started digging through the garbage again.

"That's it. Don't give up." Ralph sorted through the trash quickly but carefully. But he'd had a lot of practice.

Spector liked Ralph, but he wasn't happy about it. He couldn't remember the last time somebody went out of their way to help him. He'd feel pretty rotten if he had to kill the guy, but it was probably the smart thing to do. He couldn't have somebody running around who could connect him with the stolen notebooks.

"Say, friend. You never told me your name."

"Allen," Spector said. "Tommy Allen." He didn't know why he'd bothered to lie; he was going to snuff Ralph anyway.

"Nice to meet you, Tommy." Ralph extended a garbage-smeared hand. Spector hesitated, then grasped it and shook once. "What's your line of work?"

"I'm, uh, an exterminator." Spector took a few steps away from Ralph and dug into some fresh garbage. He tossed a couple of paper sacks aside and unearthed a broken-down couch. The cushions were gone and the beige paisley fabric stained, but it looked okay otherwise.

"See what I mean?" Ralph was still right behind him. "Perfectly good stuff. I could clean it up with my Steamatic and it'd be almost as good as new."

Spector slumped onto the couch. The chance of finding the notebooks was getting worse and worse. Just his luck, to get hold of something like that and lose it right away. He could have nailed the Astronomer and set himself up for life.

Ralph sat down beside him and looked at Spector's clothes. The stains from the garbage helped to disguise the blood. "Boy, those guys worked you over good. That's one thing about living in a garbage dump, crime rate's mighty low."

Spector was silent. He stared directly at the sparkler, letting the magnesium brightness burn itself onto his retina. He wondered what the Astronomer was going to do to him. Things were probably going to get even worse than they were now, impossible as that seemed. Dying again was the simplest solution, but it wasn't what he had in mind.

Ralph stuck the handle of his sparkler into the edge of the couch, then leaned over and shoved his arms back into the trash up to his elbows. He turned to look at Spector and furrowed his brow, then pulled out a plastic-covered package. "Look familiar?"

Spector grabbed the package and wiped it off on his pants leg. He was seeing spots from looking at the sparkler, but knew it was the notebooks. He hurled his sparkler as far out into the river as he could. "Goddamn. Maybe my luck's changing."

Ralph nodded and smiled. "Told you we'd find them. Garbage can't hide anything from me for long."

"Well, you were right." Spector shoved the notebooks back into his pants. He wasn't taking them out again until he handed them over to Latham.

"Wait here." Ralph got up off the couch and began wad-ing away through the garbage. "This calls for a real celebration."

Spector looked at his watch. It was 10:55. He had to get moving soon. There was no telling when the Astronomer would come looking for him, and he wanted plenty of tough company around by then. The Astronomer was saving Fortunato for last, so Jumping Jack Flash and Peregrine were probably next on the list. Or maybe Tachyon. Taking them on was bound to push him to the limit, even with Imp and Insulin around to help out. Spector sighed. He might as well kill Ralph now and get it over with.

He saw Ralph light something at the other end of the barge, then move to another to touch it off. Two small flames slowly grew into cascades of colored light, fountaining twenty or thirty feet into the air. Ralph was standing well away from them, his back to Spector. He appeared to be keeping an eye on the fountains to make sure the barge didn't catch on fire. Couldn't have his ride home going up in flames.

Spector made his way to the shore end of the barge and stepped off. The fireworks would attract attention and that was the last thing he wanted. There was no time to kill Mr. Garbage right now. He'd do it later. If he survived the night.

He hobbled to the chain-link fence and climbed it slowly, trying to use his bad foot as little as possible. He hauled his body over the top and lowered himself down the other side. His foot still hurt if he tried to put his entire weight on it. He could see it now. It was pink and there were toes taking shape. He might be fully healed by this time tomorrow. If he was still alive by then.

Spector had to contact Latham first. He dug into his coat pocket for the card with the lawyer's phone number. Getting a taxi was going to be hell. He could always kill somebody and take their car, but he wanted to keep things as uncomplicated as possible.

He limped away down the street looking for a pay phone.

It took Jennifer nearly two nightmarish hours to make her way to the ground floor of the Empire State Building. She was afraid to use the elevators or the main staircases and had to continually ghost through ceilings, walls, and locked doors. Before long she had to rest between each phase of insubstantiality, balancing her weariness against the continual need to move on in case the federal agent was still tracking her. Kien, she realized, must have friends in very high places indeed. She wondered, not for the first time, what Yeoman's—Brennan's—connection with him was.

She finally made it, unobserved she thought, down to the street, where she merged with the pedestrian traffic and headed toward the corner of 43rd and Seventh, carefully keeping to the darkness and ignoring the occasional invitations to come party. The streets became more densely jammed with drinking, dope-smoking revelers as she approached Times Square, which was almost as crowded as it is on New Year's Eve. The people milling about the streets were determined, damned determined it seemed, not to let anything get in the way of a good time. Their desperate attitude tainted the atmosphere with a taste of depression, as well as something of menace.

Maybe, Jennifer thought, it was all in her head. Maybe the hulking man in dirty leathers and plastic Dr. Tachyon mask who seemed to be following her was just an innocent fellow out to have a little fun. Maybe, but she started walking faster when she realized he was following her, and her fear increased when she saw that he kept pace behind her.

She was never so happy to see someone as when she saw Brennan waiting for her on the designated corner. She broke into a ragged run toward him, dodging immovable knots of partiers. He turned as she approached, and Jennifer faltered. She could see his anger by the taut way he held his body, by his hard-clenched jaw and the thin line of his lips. Some of his tenseness drained away when he saw her, and was replaced by uncertainty. Some, but not all.

"I wasn't sure you'd show up," he said curtly.

"Why?" They spoke in low voices, even though none of the people milling around seemed to be paying them any attention.

"The Tachyon statue was smashed, scattered around the gallery. The books were gone," he said in clipped tones.

"Gone?" The astonishment in her voice and on her face softened his expression. He sighed, rubbed his chin wearily.

"Kien must have gotten to them . . . somehow . . . someway." He shook his head. "He's a tricky bastard. His reach extends farther and into more places than you'd ever dream of."

"It's not possible." Jennifer frowned and glanced sharply at Brennan, suddenly suspicious that he might have the books and was holding out on his promise to return the stamps to her. But his shoulders were slumped, and weariness and defeat was on his face. He can't be that good of an actor, Jennifer thought. But what possibly could have happened?

Brennan seemed to rouse himself. He straightened his shoulders, composed his features, and looked again at Jennifer. "Come on," he said gruffly. "It looks like I have to find you some more clothes." He frowned. "How'd you lose the ones you were wearing?"

"I'll tell you everything," she said, "but first let's get some food somewhere. I'm still starved. I only had half a cracker with some chopped liver at Aces High. Why don't we go for a late dinner somewhere? I'll buy. I'll tell you what went on at Aces High and you can tell me why you're after Kien's diary."

Jennifer told herself she made the offer out of simple curiosity, but part of her whispered that she was rationalizing. In reality, she didn't want Brennan to walk away from her.

He looked at her with a tight smile.

"I don't think that'd be wise," he began, then he lost his smile, grimaced, and swung his bowcase at Jennifer. "Duck!"

She ghosted.

A stocky man wearing a dark-blue satin jacket with a beautifully embroided white bird on the back—a crane? Jennifer wondered—passed through her. He stumbled forward, his arms windmilling as he tried to regain his balance. Brennan's case caught him flush in the face and he went down.

"Egret," Brennan snapped. "Let's get out of here."

He grabbed for Jennifer's hand, started to run, stopped, sighed half to himself, and waited for her to solidify.

"Sometimes you're difficult to cope with," he complained. Jennifer smiled and offered him her hand. It looked like this affair wasn't over yet. What, she wondered, is an Egret?

He took her hand and they ran.

It was impossible to make straight-line progress through the crowd. They left a trail of partiers in their wake cursing them or whistling catcalls at the sight of Jennifer's bikini-clad form, or both.

"We're never going to shake them at this rate," Brennan grumbled. He risked a glance over his shoulder and saw a pack of men wearing dark jackets—more Egrets, Jennifer realized—pushing through the crowd after them. They were less subtle than Brennan and Jennifer and simply shoved past anyone who blocked their way. Few cared to lecture them about their boorishness. "Eight of them," Brennan said, and his grip on Jennifer's hand was broken as she suddenly stopped in her tracks.

"Oh no," she said, staring.

"What is it?"

"Him."

A man wearing a skintight white suit was coming toward them.

"Who's that?" Brennan asked.

Jennifer shook her head. "He tried to arrest me at Aces High. Said he was a federal agent."

"Great." Brennan glanced around quickly. They were near a corner that was cluttered with a phone booth, mail repository, and several trash cans. "This way. Maybe he hasn't spotted you yet."

Jennifer and Brennan veered off to the side and the man in the battle suit called out, "Stop right there! You're under arrest!"

Jennifer groaned, jostled a man wearing a mask with an elephant's nose and ears—no, Jennifer realized, he wasn't wearing a mask after all—apologized, and stepped to the curb just as a limo pulled to a screeching halt. Its doors flew open and Wyrm and half a dozen thugs leapt out.

"Christ," Brennan swore. He let go of Jennifer's hand and everything happened at once.

A battered yellow taxi rear-ended the limo just as Wyrm screamed, "Get her! Get him!" The taxi bumped the limo forward and the open door on the passenger's side slammed into Wyrm. The reptilian joker went down as the Egrets burst through the onlookers surrounding the scene and tried to encircle Brennan and Jennifer. People trapped within the circle realized something heavy was about to come down and tried to get away. People outside the circle realized that something heavy was about to come down and pushed closer to watch. Billy Ray, now running toward them, screamed, "I'm a federal agent and you're under arrest!" and the huge man in dirty leathers and plastic Tachyon mask, who was also pushing through the crowd toward Jennifer and Brennan, whirled and clubbed him to the sidewalk with a single blow from his deformed, clublike right fist.

The Egrets looked at each other uncertainly and Brennan looked at Jennifer.

"What the hell?" he asked, and kicked the nearest Egret in the stomach. The Egret went down and two others leaped at Brennan and tried, unsuccessfully, to grapple him.

Billy Ray, to the astonishment of Jennifer, the onlookers, and most especially the huge joker who had struck him down, was already getting to his feet.

"Sucker," Ray said through clenched teeth. "I'm going to kick your ass."

The giant growled something inarticulate as Jennifer watched Brennan take out the two Egrets who had come at him. The hack leaped out of his taxi and screamed at the man who was driving the limo as one of the Egrets got by Brennan and grabbed at Jennifer. She smiled at him and ghosted and he tried over and over again to grapple her while she shimmered insubstantially on the sidewalk. Tiring of his attentions, Jennifer grabbed a lid from one of the garbage cans by the curb, solidified, and brought the lid down hard on his head. He stared at her with hurt indignation for a moment, then his legs went rubbery and he slipped, unconscious, to the sidewalk. Some of the onlookers applauded.

The giant spoke, his voice drawing Jennifer's attention back to him and Ray. "Fuck off, asshole." His voice was a monstrous rasping that sounded barely human. He was awesomely intimidating, but Ray smiled back at him. Jennifer thought he looked genuinely happy.

"You're under arrest for assaulting a federal agent."

The big joker growled and swung his deformed right fist, but Ray had already moved. He ducked under the punch and came up throwing one of his own that caught the giant in his hard, bulging gut. All the air whooshed out of his lungs and he stumbled and went down. But he wasn't out. He reached up as Ray tried to step by him, grabbed Ray's leg, and yanked. Ray went down again and the giant joker rolled over him like a tsunami, pinning him to the sidewalk. He struck before Ray could move, crushing Ray's jaw and mouth with his hammering right fist. Blood splattered everywhere. Jennifer, feeling faint, backed away, and felt herself bump into someone. Hands grabbed her waist and she whirled and found herself staring into a pair of pretty blue eyes. Eyes, and nothing else, except for tendrils that might have been nerve endings trailing off them. She suppressed an urge to scream and swung the garbage-can lid with all her strength. There was a satisfying loud *thunk* and the metal lid bent in her hands. The eyes disappeared, as if rolled up behind invisible eyelids; the invisible hands released her. After a moment a tall, lanky form blinked into sight, crumpled on the sidewalk. Jennifer dropped the bent garbage-can lid and backpedaled.

Three of the thugs who'd arrived in the limo with Wyrm started toward her while two others tried to help Wyrm to his feet and the other one rolled around on the street punching at and cursing out the driver of the cab that'd rear-ended them.

Out of the corner of her eye Jennifer saw the joker draw back to strike Ray again, but somehow, while spitting blood and fragments of teeth, Ray reached up and caught the joker's arm with one hand while raking across his masked face with the other. The mask came off, exposing a face that looked like a bombed-out battlefield. The man's scar-encumbered mouth was wide open and sucking for air.

"You're one ugly son of a bitch," Ray mumbled through mashed lips and broken teeth. A merry light danced strangely in his eyes. He twisted like an eel, jerked his leg upward, and caught the joker in the groin.

A stream of spittle ran down the joker's chin and he howled. Ray flipped him over, straddled his chest, and pummeled the joker's face until his fist was splashed with the joker's blood. The joker went limp, and Ray laughed lightly and stood up. His eyes, gleaming with an uncanny light, fastened on Jennifer. She glanced at Brennan, but he was busy with the Egrets. Ray started toward her, fastidiously wiping away the blood that dripped from his smashed jaw before it could fall on his uniform, as the three thugs from the limo approached from the other side.

"You're coming with me," Ray said. Jennifer could barely understand his mumbled words, but she let him take her arm.

"Hey, bug off, man. The chick's ours," one of the thugs said, and Jennifer let him take her other arm.

"I can only accompany one of you," Jennifer said, then ghosted and stepped aside. Ray grinned fixedly and advanced on the thugs as Brennan beat down another Egret with a crushing backhanded blow. The two Egrets still on their feet exchanged glances, decided it wasn't worth it, and beat cheeks down the sidewalk and through the crowd. Brennan turned back toward Jennifer. He wasn't even breathing hard, although he did look baffled as he watched Ray punch out Wyrm's thugs. Jennifer glanced at the limousine sitting in the street before them, motor running and door open.

"Come on," she called to Brennan, and dove through the open door. He followed her into the car, pulled the door shut, and a huge birdlike form hurtled out of the sky and slammed against the windshield. It was a skinny winged joker with a crown of dirty white feathers like the crest of a scraggly cockatoo, ugly purple and red wattles hanging from his jaw. He shook his head, stunned by the impact like a sparrow that'd flown into a plate-glass window, croaked something unintelligible, and slipped off the hood into the street, tripping Ray who had just disposed of his final adversary and was leaping toward the limo. Brennan watched them fall to the pavement in a tangle of limbs. Jennifer gunned the motor as Wyrm stood up groggily. The limo sped off as the reptilian joker looked around in bewilderment.

"What happened?" he asked, but no one could really tell him.

CHAPTER 18

11:00 p.m.

The toilet flushed. Latham paused to wash his hands, dried them on a monogrammed towel, and turned off the light as he emerged from the bathroom.

Hiram held his breath and tried to squirm closer to the ceiling. His fist was clenched very tight, and the slightest motion threatened to send him drifting across the room. He prayed Latham wouldn't look up. Thank god he hadn't turned on the ceiling light; a man of Hiram's girth floating up near the fixture would cast a noticeable shadow. He could thank Popinjay for getting him into this absurd situation.

He'd hoped Latham would head straight back to his computer, but he wasn't going to be that lucky. The attorney walked to his dresser and began to empty his pockets: money clips, keys, a handful of change. He undid his tie, removed his vest, hung them carefully in a walk-in closet, slipped into a smoking jacket. It was black silk, with a dragon motif worked in gold across the back, and it fit perfectly. Sitting on the edge of his bed, Latham untied his shoes, donned a pair of slippers. *No*, Hiram thought down at him, don't lie down, *please* don't lie down.

The phone rang.

Go away, Hiram thought wildly, go back to the other room. Loophole glanced at the door, as if he was considering it. Then he lifted the receiver off the bedside extension. "Latham."

There was a short pause. "You're not making any sense," the lawyer said curtly. "Yes, I understand that you're in pain." Silence. "He *ate* your foot?" The tone was incredulous. "No, I'm sorry, Mr. Spector, I don't believe you. If you've lost that much blood, perhaps you're . . ." A sigh. "All right, describe these books."

This time the silence was much longer. Hiram couldn't see Latham's expression from his vantage point against the ceiling, but when he spoke, his tone had changed. "No, James, don't read from it. It wouldn't be healthy. Where are you?" A frown. "Yes, but *what* dump, where, I don't . . . They're all in Times Square, she's been sighted . . . no, I don't know how long." He glanced at the bedside clock. "No. No, I want you here as soon as possible. Take a cab . . . I don't care how you get one, just do it, do you understand? You know the address."

Latham hung up the phone, rose thoughtfully from the bed, and then—to Hiram's immense relief—went directly back to the desk in the other room.

Hiram shuddered, unclenched his hand, and drifted slowly back to the floor. He touched down as lightly as a feather. *Spector*, he thought. Where had he heard that name before? What else had Latham called him? James, that was it, James Spector.

Suddenly it fell into place. Dr. Tachyon, that was where he'd heard the name, half a year ago, over a rack of lamb at Aces High. A man who'd escaped from the clinic and left a trail of death behind him, an accountant named James Spector, but he had a new profession now, and on the street they were calling him . . . Demise.

He heard Latham pick up the phone. Hiram glanced toward the front door, but to reach it he would have to cross the living room, in plain view. The window was a better bet. He tiptoed across the room, slid it open slowly and carefully, stuck his head out. It was a long fall, but not nearly as long as the fall from Aces High.

Grimacing with distaste, Hiram Worchester climbed up on the sill and pushed himself through the window. It was a tight fit, and for one horrible second he was afraid that he was stuck. Then he squirmed a little harder, the buttons gave on his jacket, and he popped free and began to fall. He only hoped that he wouldn't be blown *too* far off course.

And in fact there was enough power left for Fortunato to find the Rolls. He thought about Peregrine, about her mouth and her breasts and what she would taste like between her legs. Just the thought made him stronger.

He was going to have her. Even though it meant risking both of their lives. The Astronomer was not through with either one of them, and they'd be terribly vulnerable in bed.

But there was time. The Astronomer had to recharge, and so did he. He tried not to think about the Astronomer out there somewhere, maybe even now picking out his victim. Tried not to remember that the time he had was being bought at the cost of somebody else's life.

He turned a corner and saw the Rolls. Peregrine unlocked the door for him and he got inside.

"Your business?" she asked.

"Taken care of. For now."

"Good," she said. "I'd hate for you to be in a hurry."

Jennifer took a corner with enough speed to wring an angry whine from the limo's tires and a few angry curses from the pedestrians who had spilled off the crowded sidewalk onto the roadway itself. She glanced quickly to her right and saw Brennan leaning back against the luxurious upholstery, smiling.

"What are you so happy about?" she asked.

"Kien doesn't have the book."

"Hmmm?" Jennifer cut across two lanes of traffic and threw a fast left. She glanced into the rearview mirror. She didn't think they were being followed, but she wanted to make sure. "What makes you say that?"

"Simple," he said. "Wyrm is still following us. Or you, to be precise. Therefore Kien doesn't have the book." He suddenly lost his smile and frowned. "But if it isn't where you left it . . ." He left the sentence unfinished.

"Someone else must have it. Them." Jennifer realized that she was getting so caught up in Brennan's quest that she was forgetting the stockbooks full of stamps. The books that were, or at least should be, important to her. "Why do you want that damn book so much?" she asked suddenly, running through a red light. "What's your connection with Kien?"

Brennan stared out the window for a long moment.

"You handle this car very well."

"Come on," she said, frustrated beyond endurance by his reticence. "Cut the stall and answer my questions. You owe me that much."

"Maybe I do," Brennan said reflectively. "All right. Kien and I go a long way back. Back to Vietnam." Jennifer slowed to a reasonable speed so she could keep one eye on Brennan as he spoke. He was looking out the window distractedly, looking, seemingly, far beyond the street outside the window. "He's an evil man. Utterly self-absorbed, utterly ruthless. He was a general in the army of South Vietnam, but he worked for anyone who'd pay him. He caused the deaths of a lot of my men. He tried to kill me." Brennan's face became expressionless. "He killed my wife."

They drove on in silence, Jennifer wondering if she had probed too far, if she even wanted to know the rest of the story. After a while, Brennan spoke again.

"I had evidence implicating him in nearly every dirty scheme that was going on in 'Nam, but I . . . lost it. Kien stayed in power. I was almost court-martialed. When Saigon fell I left the army and Kien came to America. I spent a few years in the Orient, finally returning to the States a few years ago. An old comrade of mine spotted Kien a couple of months ago and sent me a letter that brought me to the city.

"I'm convinced that the diary would implicate Kien in countless criminal activities. Maybe it contains enough evidence to put him away for good . . . like he should have been put away by the evidence I'd gathered twelve years ago . . ."

"I don't know if this diary would be accepted as evidence in court."

"Perhaps not," Brennan conceded, "but it would contain innumerable clues to his activities, to his associates and underlings." He looked at Jennifer seriously. "Killing Kien would be simple, but, first, it wouldn't necessarily bring down the network of corruption that he's built up here in New York, and, second, it would be too easy on him." Brennan's eyes became shadowed with introspection. "I want him to lie awake at night and worry about the slightest noise, the fleetingest shadow that cuts across his dreams. I want him stripped of everything he has, all his wealth, all his power and riches. In the end I want him to have nothing but time, time weighing heavily on his head with nothing to change the endless succession of his dull and eternal days . . . And if he doesn't end up in a jail cell, I'll strip him of everything he has and make his life an inescapable hell of grinding poverty and fear. To do it I'll need the diary."

Brennan lapsed into silence again. Jennifer licked her lips. Maybe, she thought, it was time to tell him the truth. He should know. But something froze up inside of her at the thought of telling him. She licked her lips again, forced them open.

"Brennan–"

She was interrupted by the sound of a telephone ringing in the back of the limo. Brennan started and looked toward the back seat as she sighed, feeling like a condemned prisoner granted a reprieve.

The dashboard of the limo had more controls than a space shuttle.

"Which switch lowers the window between the seats?" Brennan asked.

Jennifer darted a glance at the dashboard and shrugged. Brennan slammed down a bunch of toggles, turning on the radio, locking the doors, putting up the television antenna and, finally, lowering the tinted glass barrier between the rear and front seats. He dove into the back. Jennifer heard a muffled curse as he banged his knee on the liquor cabinet and bar that faced the rear seat. He picked up the phone, switched on the speaker attachment so Jennifer could hear, and grunted into it.

"Wyrm? Wyrm, is that you? This is Latham."

Jennifer, glancing at him in the rear mirror, saw a strange expression fall upon his features. He smiled with pleasure, but no humor, as if he recognized the name, as if he were glad to hear the man's voice.

"Listen carefully. Demise is coming with the book. I repeat. Demise has the book. Call off your search and escort him in. Do you understand?"

Brennan's smile was savage.

"I do," he said quietly.

"You're not Wyrm."

"No," Brennan said.

"Who is this?"

"The past, spook. And I'm coming for you."

He hung up the phone.

The din, as they walked crosstown, was deafening. The crowds were virtually tidal in their power to ebb and flow, carrying most unanchored passersby with them.

"I'm *trying*," Bagabond said to Jack, eyes tightly closed as she leaned up against the brick pillar at an alley entrance off 9th Street. "The creatures of the city have never had to deal with this kind of human commotion before. They're terrified."

"I'm sorry," said Jack. The urgency in his voice belied the apology. "Just try. Please try."

"I am." She continued to concentrate. "Nothing. I'm

sorry." She opened her eyes and Jack found himself staring into their apparently infinite black depths. "There are eight million humans in this city. Probably there are ten times as many creatures, not even counting the roaches. Be patient."

Jack impulsively hugged her. "I'm sorry. Do what you can do. Let's keep heading downtown." His voice had turned weary now. Bagabond held the embrace a second more than necessary. Jack didn't object.

Bagabond suddenly cocked her head. "Listen."

"Are you picking up something?" Jack said.

"I'm *hearing* someone. Aren't you?" She started to walk rapidly down the block.

Jack heard it too. The music was familiar, the voice doubly so.

Blood and bones
Take me home

People there I owe
People there gonna go

Down with me to Hell
Down with me to Hell

"I'll be damned," said Jack. "It sounds like C. C."

"It *is* C. C. Ryder," Bagabond said. C. C. had been one of Rosemary's oldest and closest friends in the city. But triggered by acute trauma, her grotesque wild card talent had kept her under close care in Dr. Tachyon's clinic for more than a decade.

They stopped with several other onlookers, pressed up against the glass front of a Crazy Eddie's. There were several large video monitors set up in the display window. Overhead speakers piped the music out to the street. On the screens, sharp-edged geometric solids rolled and collided in black and white.

"Is she performing again?" Bagabond said. "Rosemary's said nothing."

"Not in person." Jack squinted through the glass. "Just in performance videos like this. I also heard she's been writing a lot of new stuff lately, songs for Nick Cave, Jim Carroll, people like that. I read in the *Voice* that Lou Reed's even considering one of her songs for a new album—and he *never* does covers."

"I wish she was doing concerts again," Bagabond said, voice almost wistful.

Jack shrugged. "Maybe. I guess she can't deal with more than maybe two people at one time. I think she's finally getting better."

"If she's recording now," said Bagabond, "then she's getting better."

"I bet Cordelia'd like to meet her," said Jack.

Bagabond smiled. "Cordelia's sixteen. Maybe C. C. knows Bryan Adams."

"Who?" said Jack.

"Come on." She took his arm and led him away from the display window. The lyrics followed them:

You can sing about pain
You can sing about sorrow
But nothing will bring a new tomorrow
Or take away yesterday

In the neighboring cubicle, screened only by a thin cloth curtain, someone was puking. Noisily, energetically, vigorously, a real tour de force of puking.

"So I sez to him, I sez, I'm gonna smear your ugly nat face all over–"

But where the beery-voiced joker had been going to smear the face was lost in the lonely cry of sirens and a loud aggrieved "Ow!" from Tachyon.

"Stop sniveling," ordered Dr. Victoria Queen, who looked as if thirty-six years of living with her improbable name had permanently soured her disposition. The frowning expression was at odds with her lovely face and lush body. She took another stitch in the alien's forehead.

"What are you using? A knitting needle?"

"Where's all this Takisian stoicism? To bear pain without flinching, to laugh in the face of vicissitude."

"You have a terrible bedside manner."

"I see you found him," the doctor said, ignoring Tachyon. Roulette felt a stab of anxiety. "Was he in a bar?"

Tachyon, rightly reading an insult, seized upon the remark without realizing its import. "I am not *always* in a bar. I wish you would stop telling people that."

There was the sound of growing confusion from beyond the cubicle. "Stay here!" ordered Queen, and twitched aside the curtain.

Tachyon tugged his bangs down over the half-opened gash, the needle still thrust through the white skin, and slid off the gurney. Roulette put out a hand.

"Where are you going?"

"To help."

"You're hurt, you're a patient."

"It's still my hospital."

She was too tired, and too obsessed with the images

passing behind her eyes to argue. She followed him into the emergency room of the Blythe van Renssaeler Memorial Clinic.

Every available chair and sofa was taken. Jokers of every description huddled, and hacked, and moaned, and mewed, and followed the overworked doctors with pleading eyes.

A three-legged joker was waddling after Dr. Queen. "I've been waitin' here for three fucking hours!"

"Tough!"

"Cunt!"

"You've got a broken wrist. There are others here with worse problems. We'll take you when we can. And I have no sympathy. Personally, I think Elmo should have broken your fucking neck."

Tachyon was examining a comatose old man on one of the gurneys, seemingly oblivious to the shouting match behind him. But when the joker took a swing at the woman doctor, the haymaker continued so he hit himself in the face, and then collapsed snoring on the floor.

"Nice work, Doc," called a huge scaly joker in a security guard's uniform. "Hey, you look like shit."

"Thank you, Troll."

"What do you want me to do with him?" He nudged the sleeping troublemaker with a toe.

"Have Delia set his wrist while he's sleeping." A quick smile. "Saves on anesthetic."

Another wailing ambulance disgorged its load. A gurney squeaked past, carrying a nightmare figure. Seven feet tall, head blunt like the head of a hammer. One ferocious red eye, and one bright blue eye glaring from beneath a heavy ridge of bone. Boils dotted his scalp in place of hair. Some had broken open and were oozing pus. The man looked as if someone had danced on his face with a jackhammer.

Roulette wrapped her arms about her stomach, trying to shut out the pain, the smells, the sounds. Queen discovered Tachyon administering a shot to a snuffling five-year-old, and chivied him back into the cubicle. When they reemerged, she was leading the tiny doctor by the wrist like an outraged school mistress with a recalcitrant student.

"Take him home." A sharp shove between the shoulder blades. "Give him these. Make him sleep."

"I'm all right. I'll stay."

"You're never here on Wild Card Day. Usually because you're face down in a puddle of cognac. Why break with tradition?"

Queen didn't seem to notice, or perhaps she didn't care, that Tachyon had been well and truly hurt by the remark. Roulette took his arm, and led him out the side door of the old brick building.

"I'm going after Fortunato," he abruptly announced.

"And do what?"

"Help him search for the Astronomer." His lips were pressed into a thin line.

"Tachyon, he must know after attacking the restaurant that every ace in Manhattan is after him. He'd be a fool to stay in New York."

"He's a madman. He won't care."

He shrugged off her hand, and closed his eyes. A great struggle seemed to be taking place, though it showed itself only through the increasingly haggard expression on his narrow face, the sweat that matted in the whorls of his sideburns, and the bright white points studding each knuckle. Suddenly he whirled, and slammed his fists against the wall of the hospital.

"He's blocking me!"

"Who?"

"Fortunato. *Damn him. Damn him. Damn him.*" Head thrown back, he screamed to the sky. "You've held me in contempt for years, you arrogant son of a bitch. Faggots from space. Well, fine! Handle it yourself, then, and be damned to you."

"Why worry? Maybe the Astronomer will come after you, and then you can handle it."

But he was already walking, head hunched forward, hands thrust deep into his pockets, and so missed the bitter irony in her words.

CHAPTER 19

12:00 Midnight

"Damn," Brennan muttered as he cradled the phone.

"Who were you trying to call?" Jennifer asked.

"Chrysalis."

"Still?"

"Yes. And she's still out."

"Who's Chrysalis, anyway?"

"She runs a bar called the Crystal Palace," Brennan said, looking out the window. "She's the information broker who put me on your trail. She knows just about everything worth knowing, so she'd probably know where Latham's apartment is. But she isn't available, and Elmo's getting annoyed by my constant calling. Damn," he repeated, hitting his left palm with his clenched right fist.

"There isn't much more we can do," Jennifer said, "than cruise around the better parts of town, like we've been doing, looking for some dude named Demise who's carrying a bag of books."

Brennan grinned sourly. "I know. It seems pretty hopeless, but let's stick to it for a while."

Jennifer shrugged. "Sure."

He was right, of course.

It was no wonder Demise had had trouble getting a cab.

He'd been shot a dozen times. The bullets had left holes in the front of his cheap gray suit, and his shirt was covered with powder burns and blood. He smelled of garbage, and his trousers had been soiled. As he opened the taxi door, a shudder ran all along the length of that scrawny body. Demise put one foot on the ground, supported himself on the rear door, pulled the other foot out after him. It was a twisted little thing, shoeless, sockless, pale under the streetlamp, soft and small like the foot of a child, growing from a ragged stump that was crusty with dried blood.

Hiram swallowed and looked away.

The cabbie was upset. "You motherfucker," he screamed. "I pick you up looking like that, and you stiff me!"

Demise grinned nastily. "You want to be stiffed, you come to the right place. You're lucky I'm in a hurry, you jerk." Gingerly, he lowered his raw new foot to the sidewalk, winced as it touched the pavement.

"Motherfucker!" the cabbie yelled. He peeled out so fast the force of his acceleration swung the rear door closed, and it caught Demise on the hip. He went sprawling in the gutter, and screamed. Something fell out of his pocket.

Books, Hiram saw.

They were in a plastic bag. Demise scrabbled for them, hugged them to his chest, got unsteadily to his feet. Then he hobbled toward the building, half-limping, half-hopping, trying to keep his weight off his new foot. His eyes were turned inward, on his own pain. The precious books were clutched tight, both hands wrapped around the bag. He didn't seem to wonder why the doorman was wearing a tuxedo. Hiram opened the door, almost feeling sorry for the wretch.

Jay stepped out of the bushes, finger pointed, thumb cocked. "Yo," he said loudly.

Demise looked back.

Hiram made a fist. Suddenly the books weighed something on the order of two hundred pounds. They slipped from Spector's fingers, crashed down on top of his foot. Hiram heard the tiny half-formed bones *crack*, saw the soft white skin split. Demise opened his mouth to scream.

And suddenly he was gone.

Hiram stooped, returned the book bag to its normal weight, gathered it up. He was drenched with sweat. "We could have died just then," he said to Popinjay.

"My mother could have been a nun," Ackroyd said. "Let's get out of here fast."

They caught a cab at the corner. It was the same one Demise had just gotten out of, and the cabbie was still complaining about his last fare. "Where to?" he finally asked.

Ackroyd's smile was faint and fast. "Times Square," he said.

"Well," Peregrine said. "This is it. Humble but mine own."

Fortunato closed the door and didn't say anything. The penthouse was a single wide room, the walls and carpets all different shades of gray. Each area was on its own level, each a step or two up or down from the ones around it. The furniture was steel or glass or upholstered in gray cotton, all of it long and low and expensive. One wall was nothing but windows, looking down on Central Park. The highest point in the apartment was an elevated king-size water bed in the far corner. There was no bedspread, just rumpled gray satin sheets.

"Can I get you a drink or something?"

He shook his head. Peregrine went to the bar and poured herself a snifter of Courvoisier. "Don't be so grim. We saved Water Lily, didn't we?"

"Yes, you did. You were very impressive."

"I can be when I have to be. I don't like being pushed around." She rested her hip on the edge of the bar and took a long pull at the cognac. Her wings fluttered a little as it burned its way down. Her sensuality was integral and unforced; her legs naturally turned to show off her long, rounded calves and lean thighs. "Which isn't to say I don't appreciate a certain amount of aggressiveness, in the right circumstances."

"A while ago you accused me of making a 'lame approach.' "

"I didn't hurt your feelings, did I?" Her eyes were glittering again. They didn't look away from him or hold anything back. "I mean, how was I to know you were telling the truth? Besides, all I complained about was the style. I didn't say I wasn't interested."

As Fortunato crossed the room she put down her glass and stood up. His left arm slid between her wings, his right around her waist. Her mouth was soft and tasted of cognac and opened immediately under his. Her tongue moved expertly across his teeth and then reached deep into his mouth. Her legs moved apart and her wings folded around him and he felt like they'd merged into a single organism. He could feel the heat of her pelvis through his pants leg and her wild card power roared through her body and into his like a nuclear explosion.

She broke the kiss, panting for air. "Jesus," she said. He picked her up and carried her toward the bed.

"You don't weigh anything at all."

"Hollow bones," she said in his ear, then ran her tongue around the edges of it. "Hollow, but strong as fiberglass." She tightened her arms around his chest, just for a second, to prove her point, then bit him on the neck.

He found the bed by instinct. The rest of his senses were out of control. He searched Peregrine's dress for a zipper and she said, "Forget it, I'll buy another one, I want you to fuck me, fuck me *now*." Fortunato grabbed the cups that covered her breasts and tore the dress down the middle. Her breasts spilled out, pale and perfectly rounded, the nipples broad and only a little darker than the skin around them. He took one in his teeth and she clawed at his tux shirt, popping the studs loose to bounce and clatter across the floor. She ripped off his cummerbund and pulled his trousers down to his knees. She gripped his penis in both her hands and it would have hurt if it hadn't already been so swollen and aching that he'd thought it was going to split lengthwise like an overripe fruit.

Underneath the velvet dress she had on nothing but a garter belt and black silk stockings. Her wings pulsed in time with her breathing. Her pubic hair was thick and soft as lambswool. She lifted her feet, still in their black pumps, onto Fortunato's shoulders and reached up to grab him around the neck. "Now," she said. "Now."

When he went into her it was like plugging into an electric socket. Hot, bright purple lines of energy pulsed around their bodies. He'd never felt anything like it in his life. "Jesus, what are you doing to me?" she whispered. "Don't answer. I don't care. Just don't ever stop."

After the initial moment of vertigo Spector had almost fallen, but managed to grab hold of the catwalk railing before he went over. His foot felt like it had been stuck into molten lava. He sat down and tried to figure out where they'd sent him. He was up high and could see a street packed with cars in front of him. He stood and hobbled to the end of the catwalk, using the cold railing for support. He stared out into the deserted darkness of Yankee Stadium. The little shit who did this to him was going to pay. He should have recognized Fatman at the door. Should have been more careful all around. Now the books were gone and he'd have to deal with the Astronomer on his own.

"Fucking assholes. Sent me to the goddamn Bronx." He wiped his nose and looked for a way down. After a few minutes he found a ladder. It was a good fifty feet to the concrete walkway below. He lowered himself carefully, holding his leg away so that his injured foot didn't touch anything. A gust of wind whipped his dirty hair into his eyes and sent pain humming through the tissue that was trying to become toes. It took him ten minutes to reach bottom.

Spector looked around for something to use as a crutch, but came up empty. There was nothing on the other side of the chain link fence but a nasty drop. He struggled around the edge of the walkway toward the stands. It was the only way he was sure would get him out.

He hauled himself over another fence. Spector figured

he was under the right field bleachers. He tripped over a box filled with bags of peanuts, and went to the ground screaming.

The light hit him almost immediately. "Hold it right there, buddy." A voice came from behind the flashlight.

Spector heard a snap being undone. Safety strap on a revolver, probably. "Help. I need a doctor. Point your light at my foot." He had to get the guard close enough to see his eyes.

The watchman shifted his light to Spector's feet. His bad foot was black and purple where the books had landed on it. "Jesus. What the hell happened to you?"

He was close, but his eyes still weren't visible. Spector pulled the lighter out of his pocket and flicked it. The watchman's eyes were ice blue, pretty in the light of the flame. Spector locked eyes. The man whimpered softly. Spector's death assaulted him with swift and sure results. He fell and was still.

Spector searched the guard's body, taking his flashlight and keys. If he could get into one of the dressing rooms, he might find something to wrap his foot in. He could certainly find some kind of crutch, and maybe even a change of clothing.

He limped up the ramp into the bleachers and down the steps toward the field.

"The best bets," said Bagabond, "are the rats. I'm pulling in impressions from as many of them as possible—and there are a lot."

"A rat's-eye view of the Big Apple," Jack said. "That's

something the tourist commission hasn't done much with." He tried to keep the words light.

Down the block there was a snake dance—jokers or normals dressed as jokers, Jack couldn't tell. The dancers had set fire to several derelict cars parked in loading zones. Or maybe they hadn't been derelict when the torches were set to them. It was hard to tell. At any rate, now they blazed merrily, smoke curling greasily.

Jack and Bagabond had stopped at a Terrific Pizza for takeout drinks. Both of them were parched. "Your syrup's low," said Jack to the counterman. He grimaced at the taste of his drink.

"Tough titty," said the counterman. "You don't like it, try the immigrant soda jerk down the block."

"Let's go," said Bagabond, mentally urging six hundred rats from the alley in back to slip into the back of the Terrific Pizza and check out the dough and cheese storage.

Out on the sidewalk, Jack said, "Oh my God!"

"What's wrong?"

"Come on." Jack led her toward the snake dancers. The line had started to break up. Apparently misshapen dancers, some of whom wore even more grotesque costumes, straggled toward them.

Jack confronted one of the dancers. The man was tall and dark, skin virtually blue-black in the mercury-vapor glare and the flickering fire-scatter. He wore a parody of tribal gear, beads and feathers in profusion. His skin was covered with a sheen of sweat. The droplets running down his face, however, were beads of blood from slashes runnelled into his cheeks. The slashes were cut in regular chevrons, slanting down along the planes of his cheekbones. His eyes were infinitely deep caverns ringed by white makeup.

He wore a red Bozo the Clown nose.

"*Dieu!*" Jack said. "Jean-Jacques? Is it you?"

The dancer stopped and stared at Jack. Bagabond came up to them and watched.

"You recognized me," said Jean-Jacques sadly. "I am sorry, my friend. Now that I am not human, I thought no one would know who I am."

"I recognize you." Jack reached out tentatively, checked the motion. "Your face—what have you done?"

"Do I not look more like a joker?"

"You're not a joker," said Jack. "You are my friend. You are ill, but you are my friend."

"I am a joker," said Jean-Jacques firmly. "I have a sentence of death laid across me."

Jack stared at him mutely.

The black man looked back at him, then brushed the tips of his fingers across Jack's face. The motion was fleeting and tender. Others of the dance line had gathered around them. Jack saw they were all normals dressed in outlandish garb, some bright and desperately garish, others muted and more subtly grotesque.

"Good-bye, friend Jack. I shall miss you." Jean-Jacques turned away and started to chant the letters, "H, T, L, V!" The others took it up: "H, T, L, V!" roared along the street.

"HTLV?" Bagabond said to Jack as the pair stood there while Jean-Jacques and the other dancers whirled frenetically away.

"The AIDS virus," said Jack flatly.

"Oh." Bagabond looked at him strangely. "Jean-Jacques—that's his name?"

Jack nodded.

"You and he? . . ."

"Friends," said Jack. "Very good friends."

"*More* than just friends?"

He nodded.

"We need to talk," said Bagabond. "We'll talk when this is over."

"I'm sorry," said Jack, starting to turn away.

"For what?" She took his arm again. "Come on. I mean it. We'll talk." She reached up and touched him as Jean-Jacques had. His face was rough with stubble. "Come on," she said again. "We've still got to find Cordelia."

Their eyes met. Each thought, *things are going to be different now*. But neither knew just how.

The shower was hot, but that was the way Spector liked it. The water spattered off him and ran down his thin body. He opened his mouth and let it fill up, then swished the water around and spat it out. His foot still hurt, but he was used to pain. At least it was clean now.

He turned off the shower and walked across the cold tile floor to the locker area, still favoring his foot. He whistled the beginning of "Take Me Out to the Ballgame," then stopped. The sound echoed off the walls. The locker room was less impressive than he'd expected. Plain showers and lockers; wooden benches to sit on. Not that different from high school.

He walked over to a basket filled with dirty baseball uniforms and started sorting through them, looking for something close to his size. Most of it was much too big and he hated pinstripes. Better than his shot-up suit, though. If anybody asked, he could just say he was in costume. He managed to find a uniform that didn't fit him like a tent and got dressed.

He wandered into the equipment room, past the caged-off space that held bats and gloves and beat-up practice balls, into the trainer's area. He picked an elastic bandage off the floor. Spector took a breath, then started wrapping his broken half-foot. He had to stop twice, it hurt so much, but after a few minutes he had it fairly well covered. He put his foot down and shifted a little weight onto it. A sharp pain ran up his leg, but he could stand that. He walked back toward the dressing area, trying to limp as little as possible.

Spector dug out a pair of tennis shoes and shoved a sock in the end of the one, then painfully slipped his mangled half-foot in. He tied the laces loosely and slipped on the other shoe.

"Outside, Demise. Right now. I'm waiting."

Spector looked up. The Astronomer's image was floating a few feet in front of him. The projection didn't have the normal knife-edge clarity Spector was used to. It was faint, colorless, and ghosted around the edges. The old fuck must be low on power.

"Where are you, uh, exactly?" Spector asked.

"In the parking lot. Look for the limo. I want you *now.*"

"On my way."

The Astronomer's image vanished.

Spector picked up his suit and headed for the exit. He rubbed his forehead. The old man's energy was down; if he was going to do anything now was the time. He flipped off the lights in the locker room and started whistling "The Party's Over."

CHAPTER 20

1:00 a.m.

The limo was running low on gas and Jennifer could see that Brennan was running low on patience. An hour had passed and they had seen no sign of anyone who might be Demise carrying the books. They had seen plenty of suspicious and strange and downright weird sights, but nothing that was of any use to them.

"We might as well forget it," Brennan said. He checked his watch. "I want to get some equipment that's at my apartment. Then we can plan our next move."

As they headed toward Jokertown the streets became even more crowded with late-night revelers.

"It'll be quicker if we abandon the limo," Brennan decided. "Besides, it's just too conspicuous. We'll have Egrets all over us in a minute if we try to take it through Jokertown."

They pulled over and Jennifer reached for the keys to

turn off the engine, but stopped with her hand resting on the keys, listening to the radio.

"What's wrong?" Brennan asked.

"Shhhh."

"... beat the Stars 4–2 today at Ebbets Field, Seaver winning his fourteenth. But the events of the game took a back seat to the bizarre story that nearly the entire Dodger team had seen a ghost in the locker room before the game. According to the normally stolid, one might even say unimaginative, Thurman Munson, the ghost wished them good luck before vanishing through the clubhouse wall. Descriptions of this specter state it was a female in her twenties, tall, with long blond hair, and very good looking. It—or she—wore a black string bikini. Well, if you're going to be haunted—"

Jennifer turned off the engine, killing the radio, and got out of the car. Brennan looked at Jennifer critically, then frowned.

"What's the matter?"

"We've really got to get you out of that bikini now. Talk about conspicuous." He looked at her closely and she would have blushed had she thought he wasn't being analytical. "Well, I'll get something. I wish you wouldn't lose your clothes so often. Although . . ."

He seemed to think better of finishing the sentence, and turned and walked off, shaking his head.

They'd been tailing her for several minutes, since she left Fortunato's place in a cab. Spector was sitting in the back seat with the Astronomer. The old man's eyes were closed and he was completely silent. Imp and Insulin were sitting in the middle seat. Imp had his arm around her. They were probably sleeping together. Imp had made a joke about the baseball uniform, but the Astronomer had stepped in before Spector could kill him.

The girl wasn't what he'd been expecting. She was pretty enough and carried herself well, but wasn't dressed like a high-priced whore. She had on faded blue jeans and a red-and-white. University of Houston sweatshirt. Her hair was short, dark blond, and tightly curled. She'd bounced down the stairs with a smile on her face when the cab showed up. Saved them the trouble of going inside. It would be simple enough to grab her wherever she got dropped off.

Spector looked at the Astronomer. The old man was breathing noisily and his hands trembled. When he opened his eyes again, Spector would try his power. There wouldn't be a better opportunity. Spector stared at the Astronomer's eyelids and waited.

The Astronomer opened his eyes. There was still power there, too much for him to challenge. Spector turned away. "I wonder where the hell she's going?" he asked.

"The Jokertown clinic." The Astronomer laughed wheezily. "That's right, Demise. The place you were born, so to speak."

"I'm not going in there," Spector said, shaking his head.

"Yes, you are, Demise. You really have no choice." The Astronomer closed his eyes again. "No choice at all."

Spector clenched his teeth. The old bastard was right. "You're sure she's going to the clinic."

"That's what she told the cab driver, Demise. There will be two other women. I want them all. Imp and Insulin will go inside with you." The Astronomer paused. "Just to back you up."

They rode in silence until the cab pulled up in front of

the Jokertown clinic. The limo pulled past the cab and parked in front of a fire hydrant. The girl got out of the cab.

"Go get them." The Astronomer jerked his thumb in the direction of the clinic entrance.

Spector opened the door and stepped out of the limo. He walked slowly toward the brightly lit entrance. His guts were ice. He'd spent the worst days of his life in the clinic, most of them screaming. He'd had to kill an orderly to escape, and someone might recognize him and remember. Two women were coming down the stairs to meet the girl from the cab. One had dark hair and was wearing a black sequined dress. The other, also a brunette, had on a low-cut electric-blue lamé dress slit up to mid-thigh.

"What happened?" asked the girl in the sweatshirt.

"It's Croyd," said the brunette. "We think he went into a coma or something. One minute he was fine, the next he's passed out and we can't wake him up."

"Bet you tried everything you could think of, though." The girl in the sweatshirt smiled. Spector wondered what her expression would be if she knew what was in store.

He heard car doors close behind him. Imp and Insulin were moving in. Spector couldn't make a break for it with Insulin around.

Spector heard muffled screams from inside. Glass from the entranceway shattered outward. A security guard bounced bleeding down the steps. Spector ran forward.

"Get the fuck out of my way, jerk-offs. Get away, or I'll feed you your own assholes." The speaker was one of the biggest, ugliest jokers Spector had ever seen. The thing's face was badly bruised. He raised a clublike hand, tearing the white hospital gown that only partially covered his oversized body.

The joker saw the girls and smiled. They backed away from him toward the cab which was pulling away, tires screaming.

"Come to Poppa, little pussies."

Spector moved in as the joker grabbed the woman in the lamé dress. She tried to knee him in the balls, but couldn't hit high enough. Spector looked at the dark-haired woman and squinted. It was the same girl who'd been in the subway station with the pimp. She looked even better dressed up. Spector took a step toward her.

"Who the fuck are you?" The joker had slung the other woman over his shoulder and leapt down the stairs at him. "One of the boys of September?"

Spector saw the punch coming and ducked; the blow grazed his left cheek and spun him to the ground. He rolled out of the charging joker's path. There was no way to lock eyes while he was moving so quickly. He turned at a scream behind him. Imp was dragging the dark blonde toward the limo.

Insulin faced the giant and smiled.

The joker went to one knee. "Goddamn, what the fuck are you doing to me?" He dropped the woman and slumped over. The brunette pulled herself out from under him, tearing her dress. Insulin grabbed her by the elbow and pointed her down the street.

Spector sat up, thought about running, and looked at the limo. The Astronomer was staring at him. No chance to get away. There wouldn't be, ever. He went for the dark-haired girl, putting his arm around her. She didn't look scared, but there was something in her eyes that made him feel she wasn't all there.

"Me again," Spector said. "Looks like your visit is going

to be kind of short." She didn't react. "Tonight nobody's getting out alive." Still no reply.

He kicked the fallen joker in the face with his good foot as he walked past.

CHAPTER 21

2:00 a.m.

She glanced back, arched until her shoulder blades etched bony wings beneath her skin, but Tachyon failed to take the hint. He was agitatedly pulling the brush through his tumbled curls and staring sightlessly into the mirror. Frowning with irritation, Roulette reached back and unzipped the white silk gown. It whispered to the floor, brushing softly at her ankles.

The brush crashed onto the antique marble-topped dressing table scattering crystal bottles. "This day! What is it about this day that it always engenders so much grief? And they celebrate." He swept out an arm toward the closed window which could not completely block the sound of continued revelry. "Would you celebrate?" His violet eyes seemed to blaze in his pale face as he swung around to face her.

"No, but mine's a bleak nature." She took several steps toward him, but stopped short of touching him. "And I don't think you fully understand why they celebrate. It's not heedlessness, it's an attempt to survive. We have very few options when life plays its little jokes on us. We can laugh, hiding the hurt. We can die. Or we can be revenged. You hear the laughter, but I hear cries of pain."

"Pain. You talk to me of pain, I who have lived with it every day for forty years. You humans are fortunate. Your present time memory is mercifully short. The tragedies you endure fade quickly. Your minds draw a veil. It's not so with us."

He lifted the picture in its silver frame, staring at the delicate face captured there. His lips hardened, deepening the lines about eyes and mouth.

She felt again that tearing as the Astronomer stripped from her those buffering veils and released her demons. They lovingly presented each moment of loss and abandonment, and each repetition was as exquisitely painful as the one before. Her hand lashed out, and swept away the picture. It landed face down on the cold marble, and the glass shattered with a sound like frozen music. Tachyon lifted the photo, and held it protectively against his chest while Roulette stared in fascination at the crystal pattern left by the broken glass.

Reflecting waterfalls as the mirror broke, window glass like a scintillating snowfall across the streets . . .

His eyes were on her, seeming to burn her cheek. Slowly she faced him. Long lashes lowered as he studied the picture. Then the full force of his gaze was once more on her.

"You are absolutely right," he murmured cryptically, and opening a drawer in the dressing table he slid in the photo. Before it closed she saw the gleaming black metal of a .357 Magnum.

In the midst of the public chaos, it seemed to Jack and Bagabond that they were starting to walk in circles. In the middle of the very core of the Big Apple, the pair started getting the feeling that they might as well have been in trackless woods with no sign of the sun for navigation. The faces in the crowds started to look the same. The costumes all began to look alike. The only thing missing was a sixteen-year-old girl, tall and slim, with straight, black hair and dark eyes.

They passed an alley and heard what sounded like cries.

Bagabond shook her head and started to walk past.

"Hold it," said Jack. He walked a few steps into the narrow passage. He saw several people he'd already encountered today on separate occasions. One was Jean-Jacques. He crouched protectively over one of the other dancers. This one, in tattered and dirty formal ballet getup, was lying sprawled on the alley floor. There was blood around his mouth.

Standing over the pair was the punkish young man with whom Jack had had the run-in the morning past, outside the Young Man's Fancy. The young man's rainwater eyes were masked by the alley shadows.

"Try sucking this," he said. Jack and Bagabond heard the *snickt* of spring steel. The blade snapped out of the young man's stiletto and locked into place.

The young man crouched with the knife and feinted toward Jean-Jacques. The Senegalese didn't move. "Fuckin' faggots! I'm gonna cut off everything that moves."

Jack started forward. Bagabond tripped him. Jack sprawled forward into the alley, partially catching himself with his outthrust palms, feeling skin grate across the ragged brick.

"Wait." Bagabond frowned, concentrating.

Alley cats erupted from the stinking pyramids of garbage bags stacked further back in the darkness. Howling, they bounded toward the young man with the knife. He snarled in turn and swung around to face them.

"Come on," said Bagabond, helping Jack up. "It's taken care of. Everything's cool." She tugged at his arm.

Jack hesitated, but saw that Jean-Jacques was helping his friend up. He followed Bagabond.

The alley cats screeched and yowled triumphantly behind them, as all humans exited the alley, save for the young man.

"Couldn't happen to a nicer homophobe," muttered Jack.

Spector had never been inside the Astronomer's penthouse apartment before. It was in the Seventies off Central Park. The decor was surprising subdued, dark wood floors and furnishings complemented by off-white walls and ceilings.

The Astronomer unlocked the door to a room off the library and motioned them to enter. The old man leaned heavily against the doorframe. Spector pulled the dark-haired girl inside. The captive women had been quiet, probably Insulin's doing. The room was dim, the only illumination coming through a large skylight. Underneath it was a mahogany altar. There were steel manacles at each corner, and a large V-shaped notch at one end. Spector didn't have to wonder what that was for.

"That one." The Astronomer pointed to the girl in the University of Houston sweatshirt and closed the door.

Imp pulled off the woman's sweatshirt and dragged her to the altar. He quickly manacled her hands and then unzipped her jeans and began working them down her legs. He tossed them on the floor and tore off her red cotton panties, then fastened her feet down.

Spector felt the dark-haired woman tense and he gripped her arms tighter.

"Get her ready." The Astronomer opened a drawer in the altar's side and pulled out a syringe. He made a fist and tied his arm off, then sank the needle in and slowly injected what Spector knew had to be heroin. The old man took a deep breath and pulled out the needle, leaving a tiny red dot. His arm was lined with them. The Astronomer unsashed his robe and let it drop. Imp kneeled between her legs and began moistening her with his tongue.

The Astronomer walked unsteadily over to the altar, stroking his erect penis. "What's your name, my dear?"

"Caroline." She struggled ineffectually against the chains. "You have any idea whose girls we are? You're going to be in deep shit if anything happens to us."

The old man laughed and pinched her nipple between his thumb and forefinger. "Fortunato the pimp. He's been a nuisance to me for years, but not much more than that. What could be more appropriate than using his own women to insure his destruction." He turned to Imp, who still had his head buried between her legs. "That's enough."

Imp stood and walked silently over to where Spector and Insulin held the other two women. He tugged at the end of his tongue trying to pull away a stray pubic hair. "We taking him with us?" Imp indicated Spector.

"I think so." The old man ran his finger down the naked

woman's body as he walked around the altar.

"You leave her the fuck alone." The woman in the electric-blue dress strained to get away from Insulin, then went limp in her arms.

"No more interruptions." The Astronomer stood in the altar's notch, between Caroline's legs. He pushed into her and closed his eyes. The only sounds in the room were the Astronomer's labored breathing and the soft rattle of the manacles.

The Astronomer put his hands under her armpits and drew his fingers slowly down her rib cage, leaving deep red furrows in her flesh. Caroline screamed. The old man brought his hands to his mouth and nibbled at the skin he'd torn from her. Blood began to pool on the polished wood. The Astronomer carved a symbol into the skin around her navel.

The dark-haired girl looked away and began to shake. Spector pulled her close. "What's your name?"

"Cordelia."

"He's going to do this to all of you, unless somebody stops him. Only an idiot would try, though." Spector wondered about Imp's comment. Where the hell were they going? The Astronomer had said something about other worlds that morning, but it hadn't sunk in until now.

The Astronomer straightened his back. His body was covered in a sweaty sheen; he was gaining vitality with every stroke. Caroline rotated her pelvis down as far as she could, trying to push the old man out of her. She clenched her teeth in pain, but was no longer screaming.

"Stupid bitch." The Astronomer pulled out and climbed on top of her. "Imp, take care of her." He pointed to Cordelia. "Demise, get over here."

Spector waited until he was sure Imp had a good grip

on the girl, then walked to the head of the altar.

"You don't mind if I fuck you in the mouth, do you, my little bitch?" The Astronomer slid up her body.

"You just try it, asshole." She opened her mouth wide, baring her teeth.

"That won't be necessary. I've got my own special way of doing it." He reached for her throat and sliced it open with a finger.

"Look at me, sweetheart," Spector said, bracing himself. He grabbed her head and twisted hard. There was a *pop* as her neck gave way. Caroline convulsed and was still.

"Idiot." The Astronomer grabbed Spector and threw him across the room. "You killed her, wasted her energy." He grabbed Caroline's head and bounced it hard against the altar. "I'll kill you for this. As soon as I'm done with them. Pain like you've never imagined, Demise. Imp, bring me the next one." He undid the manacles and dumped the corpse on the floor.

Spector stood up and looked for something he could use as a weapon. There were knives in the altar's open drawer if he could get that far. He felt his knees getting weak. Insulin again.

Imp tore at Cordelia's dress and dragged her forward. Her face was white. "No." She screamed and pulled away from Imp. The little ace gritted his teeth and clutched at his chest.

"What the fuck?" Spector righted himself. Whatever was happening had distracted Insulin enough to make her forget about him. He ran toward the Astronomer, ignoring the pain from his crippled foot.

Imp dropped to the floor, gasping and tearing at his shirt. "She's doing it." The Astronomer pointed at Cordelia, who took a step backward. "Stop the little bitch. Insulin, look out."

The warning came too late. Veronica was awake and clawing at Insulin's face, dragging her to the floor. Spector slammed into the old man, knocking him over the altar, then turned to Insulin. Veronica was out again. Insulin didn't notice Spector moving in from behind. He spun her around and hit her hard on the chin, twice. Her eyes rolled up into her head.

A final gasp came from Imp's now bluish lips, then he was still. "Very impressive, my dear. You somehow stopped his cardiac and respiratory functions simultaneously. A painful death." The Astronomer wiped his bloody hands on the altar as he pulled himself into a standing position. "Yours will be even more painful."

Spector knew the Astronomer could negate Cordelia's power with his own. It was what happened every time he tried to kill the old man. He decided to try something. They were dead anyway if he just stood around. He moved in closer.

"Whatever you did to Imp, lady, try to do it to him." Spector pointed to the Astronomer, who turned to look at him. Spector locked eyes and tried to force his death into the old man's mind. He felt the Astronomer block him off. "Do it now," he yelled at Cordelia. Pain flickered in the old man's eyes and he reached for his heart. It was like Spector figured. The Astronomer couldn't block two ace powers at once, and Cordelia's was getting through.

Spector kept pushing hard mentally. The Astronomer couldn't look away now that their eyes were locked.

The Astronomer dropped to his knees. "Kill you all," he said, just loud enough for them to hear.

"Not this time, you old fuck." Spector's breathing was getting ragged from the strain.

"What are you doing?" Veronica was awake and looking at Cordelia.

"I don't know. I've never done it before."

The Astronomer slid his right hand underneath the skin and into his own chest. He screamed.

"Jesus, let's get the hell out of here." Veronica grabbed Cordelia by the wrist and dragged her toward the door.

Spector broke contact and stared for a moment at the muscles in the Astronomer's forearm. The old man was massaging his heart to keep it going. The Astronomer stared hatefully at Spector. "Dead. All of you."

Spector ran after the women. "Hey, come back. We have to finish him now." He heard a hiss as the Astronomer started breathing again. "Fuck it. Somebody else will have to do it."

Spector ran through the apartment toward the elevator. Veronica had her dress caught on the elevator door and was tearing at it to get free. Spector dived inside the elevator, knocking Veronica down and putting another tear in her already-ruined dress. Cordelia punched the button for the groundfloor. The cables creaked and the car began to go down.

"I don't get it," Jay said. "I just don't get it. Not milk. Not lemon juice. Heat doesn't do a thing. The impressions are too faint to be worth a bucket of warm spit. I just don't get it." He slammed the notebook shut with a sound of disgust, and stared down morosely at the bamboo pattern on the blue cloth cover.

Hiram stood by the window, peering out around the corner of a torn shade. Jay's tiny two-room office was on the fourth floor of a dilapidated brick building on 42nd Street, half a block off Broadway. From the window he could see the marquee of the Wet Pussycat Theater. Alternating messages flashed in blue and red on the neon sign to his left. GIRLS GIRLS NAKED GIRLS was blue, while ALL-DAY ALL-NIGHT ALL-TOPLESS was red. Popinjay said he met a nice class of people in the building.

Hiram dropped the shade and turned away from the lights. Jay's desk was covered with the remains of the pizza—sausage, mushrooms, extra cheese, anchovies on Ackroyd's half—that they'd finished an hour ago. Hiram had been giving his power a workout, and it had left him drained and famished. The pie had helped. He wished they had another. Instead, they had three rather troublesome books.

"We can't stay here," Hiram said, lowering himself to sit on the radiator. He'd let his real weight return for the last few hours, to give himself a rest, and the ladderback chair Jay kept for clients hadn't been equal to the task. Hiram wasn't sure he was either; he felt exhausted. "They have to be looking for us," he continued. "Sooner or later they'll find your office."

"I don't know why," Ackroyd said. "The clients never do."

"Droll," said Hiram. "I hope you retain your sense of your humor when people begin shooting at us."

"No one's shown yet," Popinjay pointed out. "Hey, Yankee Stadium's a long walk, especially on one foot."

"A foot and a half," Hiram said.

"For all we know, Demise is still up on top of the scoreboard, and Loophole is still sitting by the phone, wondering whatever became of him."

Hiram stood, frowning. He was very tired. Lack of sleep was beginning to catch up to him, now that he was no longer in any immediate danger. He needed coffee. Better yet, he needed eight or ten hours in bed, preferably without having to worry about someone breaking into his house to kill him. "Enough is enough," he declared. "I seem to recall vaguely that we had a good reason for getting involved in this, but I can't recall just what it was." He crossed the room, picked up the two notebooks with the black leather covers. "My interests run to numismatics rather than philately, but I know these stamps are worth hundreds of thousands of dollars, at the very least. As for that other book, I don't know what to make of it, and neither do you. It's of no value to us."

"Makes us the odd men out," Ackroyd said. "Everybody else sure as hell wants it."

"Precisely," Hiram told him. "I'm going to call Latham. I want you on the other line."

The detective lifted an eyebrow. Hiram fished the paper Chrysalis had given him out of his jacket pocket and went out to Ackroyd's waiting room, a tiny cubicle filled to the point of claustrophobia with a dead orange sofa, a gray steel desk, and the receptionist, an extremely buxom blonde whose mouth was pursed in a perpetual O of surprise. Her name was Oral Amy; Jay had found her at a place called Boytoys somewhere in the East Village. Hiram lifted her by her hair, seated himself in her chair, picked up the phone, and dialed.

It rang twice. "Latham."

"I won't mince words with you," Hiram said crisply. "This is Hiram Worchester. We have your books." He heard Jay pick up the extension.

"I don't know which books you're referring to."

"Of course you do," Hiram said in aggrieved tones.

"Hiram," Jay said, "he's just covering his ass, in case we're recording this. Isn't that right, Latham?"

There was a moment of thoughtful silence. Finally Latham said, "It's quite late. Let's speed this along. What's the purpose of this call?"

Hiram pulled at his beard and considered his words. "A legal matter," he said. "Let us suppose a hypothetical case, purely for purposes of discussion. Say I had, very innocently, acquired some books. Two black leather books filled with valuable stamps, let's say, and one blue cloth notebook whose contents are, ah, interesting. Are you with me?"

"Assuming these books had indeed been acquired innocently, I'm sure that you would want to see them returned to their rightful owner," Latham said.

"Certainly," Hiram said. "In fact, in our hypothetical case, I'm sure that very thought might have been on my mind when I liberated the books from the custody of a notorious wanted felon. I can't help but speculate on how the felon acquired them. Theft, perhaps?"

"If so, the owner might be quite grateful for their safe return. A reward might even be in order."

"The act is its own reward," Hiram said.

"Hey!" Jay protested.

"Quiet," Hiram said, "Now, Mr. Latham, since we're discussing stolen property here, the correct procedure would be to turn over the books to the police."

"Technically, yes, but if there was a question of charges, the property might be impounded as evidence. The rightful owner might conceivably find that inconvenient."

"I see," Hiram said. "Now I think we understand each other. Let's be blunt. I don't know who the owner is, and I'm not likely to, am I?"

"Perhaps not."

"I do know that you represent him, however. No, don't deny it. I'm too tired for more of these games. Your client wants his notebooks back? Fine. I'm a businessman, Mr. Latham, not a stamp thief or a racketbuster. Let us do some business, and you can have the books back. Here are the terms. First, no charges or retaliation against me, my restaurant, or any of my friends, including Mr. Ackroyd. The lawsuit against him will be dropped." Hiram cleared his throat and leaned forward. Oral Amy was staring up at him from the floor, mouth open wide as if even she were a little surprised at what he was doing. "Second," he said firmly, "the protection racket at the Fulton Street Fish Market will be terminated immediately. Gills and the other fishmongers will be free to conduct their business without any further harassment or fear. Third, I want Bludgeon to go to prison."

"I'm not a judge," Latham said. "I can't guarantee who will and won't go to prison."

"If your client promises that Gills will not be harmed, then his testimony will do the job. If it doesn't, fine. I'll take that chance." He took a deep breath. "That's it."

"I'll need to consult my client. Offhand, I think these terms might be the basis for an agreement. I'll get back to you. What's your number?"

"No way," Popinjay put in. "How dumb do you think we are? No, we'll do a meeting. The four of us, me and Hiram, you and your client."

"Where and when?" the attorney asked.

"The Crystal Palace," Ackroyd said. "After closing. Chrysalis will act as broker, for a fee. She's got a telepathic bartender who'll make sure no one is stacking the deck."

"Agreed," said Latham.

His hands played across her, caressing, almost worshiping. She was dimly aware that something had changed. Something had been added. His attention was almost obsessively focused upon her. It would have been disturbing had she been more aware. But he was competing with a Dantesque vision—*it's hidden away. Wish it would die. She keeps going to see it. It tries to nurse.* And his murmured endearments could not be heard over the other voices. *"You are obviously both latents. Unfortunately the virus chose to express in your child."*

"That Thing *has nothing to do with me! It is apparent that my wife has been less than faithful." Reproachful brown eyes, the face set in lines of heroic betrayal. "I could forgive almost anything else, Rou, but family is everything."*

"Josiah, why are you doing this to me? When I need you so?"

No pity.

Tachyon entered her, and she tensed, closing her moist softness close around him. Cobweb fingers brushing at the shields. Her body seemed to be shrinking in on itself as she gathered her will, summoning death from every cell. For an instant she hesitated, and the indecision was a physical pain.

This man, so . . . good. They had shared music, love, and fear. No other path to freedom from . . . monsters.

A conscious, willful choice, the release of death, it flowed softly, a gentle implacable love.

And her shields fell. They were an artificial construct. And as she released, her mind broke under the stress, and, with it, the shields.

Roulette felt his ecstasy as for one brief flicker of time

they were one. Then horror replaced joy. She felt him touch it all. The child, Howler, Josiah, the Astronomer, *Baby*, DEATH!

He recoiled, falling from the bed in a tangle of bedding, and crawled to the far wall. He huddled, retching for several minutes, then the spasms gave way to sobs, and he rocked back and forth hugging himself as tears ran down his bruised face.

Get out of here. For god's sake, *run*! But she couldn't force strength into her legs, so she curled against the pillows, and watched him cry. It was pointless anyway. They would run her down soon enough. And she wanted it to end. She couldn't go on living with the memories. Perhaps it was because she had failed to kill Tachyon that the nightmare kept replaying. She considered for a moment then rejected the notion. No, it was because the Astronomer had *lied*. And she realized she wasn't quite ready to die. First, there would have to be a reckoning.

CHAPTER 22

3:00 a.m.

Spector looked around before darting across the street. Cordelia and Veronica trotted after him.

"Slow down for god's sake," said Veronica. She was holding her lamé dress bunched up above her knees. "That old man isn't going to bother us anymore. He looked pretty bad when we left. Might even be dead by now."

Spector shook his head and guided Cordelia toward the darkness between streetlights. "You don't know what the fuck you're talking about, lady. He's got power enough to waste all of us. All he has to do is pull someone off the street and finish what he started with your dead friend. What was her name? Caroline?"

Veronica stopped and grabbed Cordelia's shoulder. "That's right. And you killed her." Veronica sniffed. Spector couldn't tell if Caroline's death had finally sunk in or if it was just the cold. "Let's dump this guy. He won't give us any trouble." Veronica pulled Cordelia close. "If he does, you let him have it. Same as that Imp guy."

"Fine," he said. "Get the fuck out of here. You're only slowing me down. Go help your pimp. He's going to need it."

Cordelia turned slowly and let Veronica escort her away. He thought for a moment about following the women and killing them. It would be easy to blindside Cordelia before she could use her power. The other one was just a skirt. But he really didn't feel like it. All he wanted was to kill the Astronomer, or at least have him dead. What smarts Spector had told him Cordelia and Veronica alive could be trouble for him. They could finger him for Caroline's death. As Button-Man Tony had told him once, "It's not the people you kill you regret; it's the people you don't kill."

"Fuck it. I can't ice everybody." He walked down the street toward the subway stop at Seventy-Seventh. He could take the Number 5 train to Jokertown. From there, he just didn't know.

Fortunato lay with his head on Peregrine's naked stomach. She was spread-eagled in the chaos of sheets and shredded clothes and pinfeathers that had come loose in the heat of the last couple of hours. Just a few minutes before, Fortunato had used three of them to bring her to something like her fourteenth or fifteenth orgasm. He'd lost count long before, forgotten the minutes ticking away, even forgotten where he was.

"What in God's name did you do to me?" she moaned. "I feel like I just ran a marathon."

"Sorry," Fortunato said. "It kind of goes with the territory." He'd never had sex with another ace before. The fusion of their powers was beyond anything he'd ever experienced. His energy body was too large to be contained in his flesh; it overflowed all around him in a bright white aura.

He'd come three times himself, each time blocking the flow and turning it back inside him. He'd lost a couple of drops in the process, enough to give Peregrine her own faint luminescence, though it didn't do much for her energy level.

She stroked his chest. "I've heard of afterglow, but this is ridiculous."

He rolled over and kissed her on the thigh. "I have to go, you know."

"The Astronomer."

"Something's supposed to happen in an hour. He's got some kind of escape set up, something that'll get him away from me for good and all. I can't let that happen."

"Why not? Just let him go. What good is killing him going to do?"

"I'm not out for justice, if that's what you're thinking. Making him pay for his crimes, or any of that shit. It's just that I'm not going to spend the rest of my life looking over my shoulder, worrying about him showing up again."

"Bullshit. You want him dead, and you want to be the one to kill him."

"Yeah. Okay. I want the little ratfuck dead. I admit it. I want it enough I can taste it." He got up and into his pants. He rolled up the sleeves on his tux shirt and let it hang open rather than search the apartment for the missing studs.

She came to him and put her arms around his neck. "I'd offer to help, but I'm getting dizzy just standing."

"All I want you to do is come back to Aces High with

me, and stay there till this is over. One way or another."

"Wait . . ."

"I can't wait. Time is running out."

"No, I mean, listen. Do you hear something?"

His senses were overloaded from the glut of power. There seemed to be a low, electrical hum coming from all over his body. But beyond that he could hear something else, a sound like wet plates squeaking in dishwater. He glanced at the digital clock next to the bed. It was vibrating on its pedestal.

"Oh shit," Fortunato said, just as the water bed exploded.

The force of it knocked them across the room. The water was boiling at first, but cooled as it expanded. Fortunato landed against a gray earthenware pot full of bamboo. It shattered under him. Before the air even came back into his lungs a dead, broken body hurtled through the wall of windows and he was surrounded by flying glass.

Fortunato reached out to slow time, but time itself resisted him. He strained against it and saw the lines of power in the room in topographic relief. He saw that the body was a woman's, but he didn't let himself see any more, not yet.

He pushed at the lines of power with his mind. Tight cones of force rose up where he and Peregrine lay. The broken glass followed the new contours of the room's spacetime and curved away around them, smashing itself to dust against the walls.

Peregrine crawled across the floor. Fortunato saw where she was heading and shaped his power around her to protect her. She got to where her gloved talons hung on the wall and put them on. There was a costume there too but she didn't bother with it.

The roof groaned and then split all down its length like a broken saltine. Chunks of concrete and rebar rained down on them, but the shields around them were solid. It took hardly any of Fortunato's new power to hold them. Peregrine gave herself a running start and flew out into the darkness.

The floor buckled under Fortunato. Jets of water shot up from broken pipes and the air stank of natural gas. He crawled toward the dead woman and turned her over.

Caroline.

It was Caroline.

Her neck was broken. Her skin was clawed and bitten and torn.

She'd been his favorite for seven years. He could never predict her violent moods and sarcastic humor, could never get enough of the sheer physical intensity of her lovemaking. Between the new girls he'd always come back to her.

For a long time he couldn't feel anything. A huge piece of concrete, studded with broken rebar, missed him by inches while he knelt beside her body.

The anger, when it finally came, transformed him.

It was life and death, that simple. The Astronomer took his power from killing. The Astronomer was Death. Fortunato took his strength from sex, from life. And Life was hiding in its burrow, too shit-scared to come out and look Death in the face. Shouting out empty threats and hoping it would just go away.

He opened his eyes wide. All it took was a blink of the eye and everything he'd missed jumped out at him. The shimmering heat lines he'd seen in the dead boy's apartment seventeen years before funneled out into the night.

Fortunato stood up, the power of his anger levitating him a foot off the floor. He reached out to the conical net of power, ready to fly into it, to shoot out into its vortex and tear the source of it to pieces.

He reached out and the lines were gone.

He walked through the shattered glass wall and hovered there, glowing, thirty stories above the streets of Manhattan. High overhead he could see Peregrine, gloriously naked, banking steeply over the park. The lights of the city turned the sky flat and gray behind her, and she seemed two-dimensional herself, like a sexually explicit kite. She circled him once, then settled on the broken edge of her apartment.

"Jesus," she said. "So tired . . ."

"Did you see him?" he asked her.

"No. Nothing. You?"

"For a second. I saw the traces he left behind. For the first time. For the first time I'm stronger than he is. If I could find him, find that goddamned ship, I could . . ."

"What is it?"

Ship, he thought. Spaceship. Like aliens from space, Black had said. Like Tachyon.

Tachyon. Christ, Tachyon had a ship!

The longer he thought about it, the more convinced he was. The Astronomer was going for Tachyon's ship.

He walked back over to Peregrine and kissed her. The smell of their sexual juices hung around them like perfume and it was hard for Fortunato to stop. She staggered a little when he let her go.

That was when she saw Caroline's body.

"Oh my God," she said.

Fortunato took the broken thing in his arms. "This isn't about you," he said. "This is about me. You should forget about it." He made it an order without meaning to. She nodded.

He walked out into space again.

"Fortunato . . . ?"

He wanted to look back but there was nothing else to say. He let the power take him on into the darkness.

The streets were still crowded despite the lateness of the hour, and everyone who was still out seemed to be drunk, stoned, belligerent, crazy, or all of the above. Jennifer attracted an unwanted amount of attention, and if it hadn't been for Brennan's glowering presence she couldn't have walked half a block without having to use her power to foil someone's unwelcomed advances.

The long day was taking its toll on her. Her feet hurt, she was dead tired, and her hunger had grown until it felt like a small animal gnawing away at her insides. She'd have to get some food. She couldn't ghost until she did. Turning insubstantial burned a lot of energy, and there weren't many calories stored in her lean frame.

Jennifer noticed a street vendor who looked as tipsy as the revelers around them and told Brennan that she needed something to eat. They stopped and he brought her a couple of the soft pretzels the man was selling.

"Sorry this is the best I can do," Brennan said, munching on one of the doughy pretzels himself. "Tonight most restaurants are closed, reservation only, or already so crowded that we couldn't even get in the door."

"These'll be fine," Jennifer said through a mouthful of dough. She grimaced and took a big swallow of her drink. "This mustard is *hot!*" she said, trying to speak and roll ice on her tongue at the same time.

"Hmmm?" Brennan stopped, then turned back to the vendor and bought a whole bottle of the condiment.

"What's that for?" Jennifer asked as he stashed it away.

"For later." He didn't elaborate and Jennifer was too busy tearing into her food to worry about it.

They went on through the streets until Brennan led them down a narrow alley that was, amazingly enough, totally devoid of partiers.

"You'll be safe here until I get back," he said.

"Where're you going?"

"To my apartment. I'll be right back."

Jennifer watched him go down the alley, stung that he obviously didn't trust her enough to take her to where he lived. He returned as he had promised, bringing a cloak for Jennifer to wrap herself in and a pair of thonged sandals for her feet.

"They're a little large," Brennan said, "but it'll be better than running around barefoot."

She was still stung by his distrust, but couldn't resist asking about the pack on his back.

"What's in there?"

"Some things we might need before the evening is over."

"Informative as always," she said. "Can you tell me something straight out? Where are we headed now?"

"The place we might be able to get some answers. The Crystal Palace."

For seventeen years Fortunato had kept to the shadows. Not from modesty, but to avoid distractions. He didn't fly to the rescue of trapped miners or break up muggings on the subway. Except for a few months of covert politics back in the sixties he'd stayed in his apartment and read. Studied Aleister Crowley and P. D. Ouspensky, learned Egyptian hieroglyphics and Sanskrit and ancient Greek. Nothing had seemed more important than knowledge for its own sake.

He couldn't say when that had started to change. Sometime after a woman named Eileen had died in a Jokertown alley, her brain wiped clean by the Astronomer. Sometime after everything he read, from particle physics to Masonic ritual to the *Bhagavad Gita*, told him the same thing, over and over: all is one. Nothing mattered. Everything mattered.

Tonight he flew over Manhattan Island in the remains of his evening clothes, glowing like a neon tube, a dead woman in his arms. Drunken tourists and cranked-up jokers and the last of the theater crowd looked up and saw him there and it didn't matter.

He looked at the idea that he might not live through the night and that didn't seem to matter much either. What was one pimp more or less?

He saw Jokertown spread out below him. The barricaded streets were crammed with people in costumes and people who *were* costumes, all of them carrying candles and flashlights and torches. Every streetlight and every light in every window up and down the Bowery was at full power.

He left Caroline on the steps of the Jokertown clinic. The crowds opened up to let him through and then closed again after him. There wasn't a lot of time for sentimental gestures. Caroline was dead now and beyond caring.

He levitated straight up into the sky. He floated there and cleared his mind and pictured Tachyon, in his effeminate clown suits and Day-Glo hair. *You dead yet, Tachyon?* he thought. *Yo, Tachyon, do you read me?*

Tachyon's thoughts filled his head. *Finally! Where have you been? I've been trying to get through to you! There was some kind of wall of power around you!*

I'm a little charged up tonight, Fortunato told him.

I have to see you. The image of a warehouse on the East River formed in his mind. *Can you meet me here? It's desperately important. It's about the Astronomer.*

Fortunato turned the picture of the warehouse inside out. The ship was inside. Shaped like a jewel-studded conch shell and bigger than most houses.

I know, Fortunato thought. *I already know.*

Tachyon was still weeping. *An inexhaustible flow,* Roulette thought wearily, followed by an irritated flash: *What does he want from me?*

"Stop it," she said, and her voice seemed to be coming from a long way off.

The alien caught his breath on a sob, lifted his blotchy, tear-stained face from his hands.

"Nobody cares. You can cry your soul out, but nobody will care."

"I loved you." His voice was a husky rasp in the shadows of the room.

"Always in the past tense." And the remark struck her as being unbearably humorous. She never noticed when the laughter became tears.

His hands gripped her shoulders, shaking her until the teeth chattered in her head and the crystal beads in her hair set a cold ringing. "Why? Why?" he shouted.

"He promised me revenge, and peace."

"The peace of the grave. The Astronomer destroys everything he touches. How many bodies must it take to convince you?" He was screaming into her face. "And now *Baby, Baby,*" he groaned, thrusting her aside.

"And what about *you,* Doctor?" she cried. "What about

a lifetime of bodies?" The demons began their play, and she clutched at her head whimpering. "My baby."

His mind met hers, but this time there was no blending of thoughts. The chaos of her mind rejected the meld.

"It's happening again," Tachyon cried in an anguished whisper. "I can't bear it. Not again. What should I do? Who can help me?"

He pulled her off the bed, and shoved her toward her clothes. "Get dressed. We must hurry, hurry. If I can reach *Baby* before the Astronomer does. Then, later . . . later I'll do what I can for you, my poor, poor darling."

Roulette, mechanically pulling on her dress and shoes and gathering up her purse, tried to concentrate, but Tachyon's nervous babblings raked across her nerves, destroying thought. She tried to shut him out.

"Personality deterioration," he mumbled from within the large walk-in closet. "It will be necessary to find the core, rebuild memory compartments." The litany continued like a schoolboy trying to cram for an exam. A hanger screeched across the rod.

Roulette moved swiftly, slid open the dresser drawer, removed the Magnum, secreted it in her purse. An instant later Tachyon, dragging a coat over his unbuttoned shirt, raced into the room, and caught her by the wrist.

She didn't resist. He was taking her to her master. And then she would deal with them both.

Before he could even see the place, Fortunato heard the screaming in his head. It was the noise of a squalling infant, but refined, purified, maddening. He put up a mental block against it just to keep his mind clear.

He flew in over a rundown block and saw the warehouse. It was surrounded by kids in black leather jackets, the last of the gangs that had run wild in the Cloisters. They had M16s and holstered .357 Magnums, like twenty-first-century cowboys. As Fortunato came down at them from the sky they all leaned their heads back to look.

"Run!" Fortunato ordered them. "Run away!" They dropped their rifles and ran.

Fortunato hit the street by the entrance to the warehouse. Something inside hummed like a monstrous carrier wave. There was a single floodlight over the door, but Fortunato himself glowed like a small sun. In that light he saw Tachyon and Roulette running toward him from the direction of Tachyon's apartment.

The Astronomer was already inside. His energy spoor covered the walls and leaked out into the street. Fortunato was reaching for the door when a thin cylinder of pink light punched through the wall next to him, then winked out. There was a sharp cracking noise as air imploded into the vacuum the laser left behind. Somebody inside the warehouse screamed. A second later the laser cut another hole a few yards away, and another. The noise was like cannon fire. Then the humming and the laser stopped together. At the same time the squalling in his head got even louder.

"I'm going in," Tachyon said. "He's hurting *Baby.*"

"*Baby,*" Fortunato said. "Christ."

"It's the name of his ship," Roulette said.

"I know," Fortunato said. "What's your part in this?"

"She's working for the Astronomer," Tachyon said. "She tried to kill me tonight."

Fortunato nearly laughed. So she wasn't freelance after all. Too bad she hadn't pulled it off. Fortunato jerked open the door and saw the Astronomer crawling into the side of the ship.

There was a body on the floor, a kid with a smoking black hole instead of a chest. In the corner were four others: a woman with a nurse's uniform and an M16, another woman in white, a man with a cat's face and long claws, and a plain Oriental woman who looked somehow familiar. The Cloisters, Fortunato thought. He'd seen her there and in the old Masonic temple in Jokertown, just minutes before he'd blown it up. As he watched she became beautiful. Fascinating. He couldn't look away. He could feel the neurons in his brain misfiring.

"Stop it," he ordered. His brain cleared and she became plain and frightened again. The nurse raised the M16 and Fortunato melted it, the plastic stock turning to hot liquid in her hands.

"It's over," the Oriental said, "isn't it? We're not getting out of here."

"Not in that ship," Fortunato said.

"All the way from San Francisco for nothing," she said.

"The door is still an option."

She looked hard to make sure he meant it, then ran for it. The others followed more slowly, not willing to turn their backs on Fortunato.

"Gresham?" Tachyon said. His voice warbled with anger and hurt. "Nurse Gresham?"

"What?" the nurse said.

"How could you? How could you betray my trust?"

"Oh, fuck off," Gresham said. "What do I care about your fucking trust?"

Tachyon put both hands to his head. His fingers pulled the flesh into a monster face. Fortunato wondered if he was going to combust. Instead Gresham's eyes rolled up in her head. She spun around once and slammed into the decaying wall next to the door.

"Jesus," Fortunato said. "Did you kill her?"

Tachyon shook his head. "No. She's not dead. Though she deserved it."

"Then you need to get her out of here," Fortunato said. "Both of you. While you still can. I'm going to split that ship like an oyster."

"No!" It was practically a scream. "You can't! I forbid it!"

"Don't get in my way, little man. The Astronomer is one of yours. It's your virus did this to him. I'm going to finish this. If you get in my way I'll kill you."

"Not the ship," Tachyon said. The little bastard really didn't know when to be scared. Fortunato had to give him that much. "She's alive. It's not her fault this is happening to her. You can't punish her for it."

"There's more at stake here than a goddamn piece of machinery."

Tachyon shook his head. "Not for me there isn't. And she's not a machine. If you try to harm her, you'll have to stop to fight me first. You can't afford that. The Astronomer will kill us all."

The little fuck was not going to back down. "All right. Okay. We play it your way. But you get the Astronomer out of that ship. Or I'll get him out any way I have to."

Tachyon paused for a second and then said, "Agreed."

"What about me?" Roulette said.

"You're coming with me," Tachyon said. He took her hand and pulled her into the ship after him.

The Astronomer leaned nonchalantly against a post of the bed. The sleeves of his robe were encrusted with blood, and there was the sour odor of death about his bony form. But for the first time since meeting him Roulette sensed confusion and hesitation.

He turned his maddened, red-rimmed eyes upon them. "You didn't kill him."

The Takisian stepped forward, boot heels ticking on the polished floor. "I proved tougher than you anticipated." The awful gaze switched to Tachyon. "And only a coward sends a woman to do his killing."

"Is that the best you can do? Toss a few insults in my direction? You're pitiful, little man."

Suddenly the master Mason staggered, groaned, and clutched at his head. Tachyon, hair like a fiery cloud on his shoulders, eyes bright in a pale face, began to tremble with strain, and beads of sweat lined his forehead. Then, with menacing slowness, the Astronomer straightened, shook off the alien's mind control. Tachyon's eyes widened in fear.

"Die, you irritating gnat." The talonlike fingers curled, and Tachyon flung himself to one side as a ball of flame exploded on the spot he had been standing.

The floor tilted wildly as *Baby* flinched.

"It's no good. This ship can't be your escape." Tachyon scrabbled across the polished floor as another ball of flame exploded a delicate chair behind which he'd been hiding. "She doesn't navigate herself. How's your astrogation?"

Roulette squeezed herself into an alcove praying to be overlooked, praying to avoid being incinerated by one of her master's errant energy bolts.

"And you better not sleep if you do get off the planet. She's a sentient being, but of course you've figured that out." Tachyon yelped, and the shoulder of his coat blackened. "You drop your coercion, and she'll blow the locks, or fly into a star. One of the drawbacks to a living ship, as other enemies before you have discovered."

The pyrotechnic display died. The Astronomer eyed Tachyon with something approaching pleasure. "You've made some interesting points, Doctor. So I'll take you with me."

"No . . . I think . . . not." Gasping breaths punctuated the words. "I've set a deathlock. All that I am, body, soul, and mind, oppose you now. To possess me you will have to destroy me."

"A pleasing image."

"Which still leaves you with your original problem." They were circling the room, Tachyon edging warily away from the Astronomer, the Astronomer pacing him with the patience of a predator. "And there's another small matter, but I thought I ought mention it. Fortunato's outside. Waiting. He'll crack this ship to get at you. I'd prefer that he not. Which is why I'm here—though I can think of nothing I'd rather do less than face you."

But the Astronomer had stopped listening. At the mention of Fortunato his face had suffused with blood, and an explosive expletive left his lips flecked with spittle.

"You've plagued me long enough, you useless piece of shit. *This* time I will finish it."

He plunged out of the ship, and Tachyon, seizing Roulette by the wrist, raced after him. And into hell. Balls of flame screamed through the air, searing the concrete floor and igniting the warehouse walls. There was a backblast of air that sent them tumbling, and Tachyon's hand slipped from her wrist. Masonry and girders rained down as *Baby*, terrified beyond reasoning, burst through the roof and fled into the night. Choking from the plaster dust, Roulette crawled for the door, ignoring Tachyon's frantic calls, first for *Baby*, then for her.

Cradling the Magnum she huddled in an alley, and watched the sky.

CHAPTER 23

4:00 a.m.

Fortunato felt his legs come off the ground and fold into a lotus. His thumbs touched his forefingers and settled on his knees. He felt as if his final orgasm with Peregrine was still going on. When she held him and drove the power back into him it was like being blown to atoms and coming back together with the entire universe inside him. He felt like the core of a sun, with flares of energy shooting off him uncontrollably. He felt like it would never end.

It was five minutes later when the Astronomer came out of the ship. Fortunato had lived through his entire life again in every detail, the feel of silk against his skin, the sound of every note of music he'd ever heard, the taste of the breath of every woman he'd ever kissed. It had taken forever and no time at all.

"Motherfucker!" the Astronomer screamed. "You're a worm, a maggot, a fucking amoeba! Why do you keep buzzing around my head, you fly, you mosquito, you locust?

Why do you not fucking die and depart?" He raised his thin hands and the sleeves of his blood-caked robe slid back past his elbows. The insides of his arms were dotted with bruises and sores. Fortunato remembered the heroin he'd seen at the Cloisters.

The Astronomer's hands swelled like canteloupes and then exploded with balls of flame, hundreds of them, screaming through the air at Fortunato. Each one peeled off a layer of his power as he deflected it and he couldn't rebuild his shields fast enough. The last fireball singed the hair off his left arm.

The roof of the warehouse exploded. The Astronomer shot through it into the sky, still screaming. "A dog that chases me down the street, trying to chew my shoes. Magick? Your kissing and hugging and fucking and sucking? You're a child, a larva, a little, helpless, wriggling sperm. You've never seen power." He pulled Fortunato up in his wake, and the warehouses, and then the island, fell away under them.

Now the Astronomer was glowing. Hotter, brighter than Fortunato. "Death is the power. Pus and rot and corruption. Hatred and pain and war."

Fortunato saw that the Astronomer was more powerful than he'd ever imagined. It left him strangely calm. The city was far below and behind him, nothing more than a grid of lights. They were over the East River between Manhattan and Queens. The Williamsburg Bridge was just to Fortunato's right, the cables clanking hollowly in the wind.

They were high enough up that Fortunato's skin felt cold where his tux shirt hung open. The air was clean and a salt smell blew in from Long Island Sound. His legs had unfolded and he stood in midair, his arms curled at his sides. He knew he was going to die.

He saw himself as the hexagram Ken, the Mountain, keeping still. His opponent was Sung, Conflict, boiling with chaos and destruction. There was no point in rebuilding his shields. He drew all the power inside him into the middle of his body, formed it into a sphere and compressed it. Harder, tighter, until all his strength and knowledge and energy was compacted into a grain the size of a pinhead, just behind his navel.

There would be no second chance. He launched it at the Astronomer. It shot through the air, leaving Fortunato limp and frail and empty. It was so bright he had to put his hands in front of his eyes, and even so he could see the bones through his flesh.

He felt rather than saw it penetrate the Astronomer, going through his shields like a bullet through jelly. When he could see again the Astronomer was doubled up in shock and pain.

The Astronomer burst into flame. He burned hot and red, and dense black smoke boiled off him. His arms stuck out of the fireball at odd angles and Fortunato watched them turn black and crusty.

And then the flames died.

The Astronomer's body was blackened, mummified. The wind blew charcoal-scented flakes of burnt skin off him as he floated.

Fortunato took a breath. He had a little power left after all, enough to keep them afloat, but that was all. And it would soon be gone.

He couldn't seem to move. A sense of nothingness surrounded him.

The Astronomer opened his eyes.

"Is that all?" he said. He screamed with laughter, and slowly straightened his body. Burned skin showered off him and Fortunato could see the scalded pink flesh underneath. "Is that your best shot? Is that really all you can do? I would pity you. I would pity you except you hurt me, and now you have to die."

Fortunato saw the hideous, blistered little man gathering himself, and the nothingness around him told him what to do.

He chanted silently, banishing his fear. He cleared his mind, found the last thoughts that still snagged there—Caroline, Veronica, Peregrine—pulled them loose and let them flutter down toward the lights below.

He slowed his heart and it started thrashing again and he calmed it, finally.

It was, after all, only death.

He touched the Astronomer's mind and saw the power beginning to uncoil, and reached in to help. He loosened the bonds and pulled the damping rods and opened all the switches. He turned the dials up to ten.

We go together, Fortunato thought. You and me. Nothing mattered; he became nothing, less than nothing, a vacuum. Come to me, he thought. Bring everything you have.

The night filled with cold white light.

Most of the crowd couldn't even see the battle over the East River because of their angle of sight being limited by the Manhattan skyline. It was mainly the observers standing in the intersections who could look along the numbered streets east to the spectacle.

Even those onlookers weren't completely impressed as the fireballs coruscated and exploded. One joker, staring at the sparks cascading down toward the river, said in range of Jack's hearing, "Hey, I saw a lot more spectacular stuff during the Bicentennial. This ain't nothing. Why don't they go do something over the Statue of Liberty?"

"Yeah!" said someone else. "That'd be *neat.*"

No one peering goggle-eyed from the intersection of 14th Street and Avenue A had any idea just what was going on above the river.

"I've got a date in three hours," said Bagabond. "It's my first date in twenty years, and now the world's ending."

The fireworks dimmed and died.

"I think it's over," said Jack. "The world's not ending. You've still got your date. Who's the lucky guy?"

She recoiled and stepped away from him.

He realized what she was thinking and hastily said, "I'm not being sarcastic. I mean it. Who is he?"

"Paul Goldberg."

"The lawyer? Rosemary's office?"

"That's right."

"What're you going to wear?" said Jack.

Bagabond hesitated. "The usual."

Jack laughed. "Bag lady outfit?"

She shook her head angrily. "Business suit."

"Come on."

This time it was Jack who grabbed Bagabond's arm and tugged her along the street. "It's maybe three blocks to All Nite Mari Ann's," he said. "It's the in place this season."

"What do you mean?" said Bagabond.

"You need an all-night boutique," said Jack. "This is going to be fun."

"I'm not looking for fun," said Bagabond.

"You want to look really great at your breakfast date?"

She resolutely stared straight ahead.

"Then, let's go, kiddo."

She tried to lag as he led the way down the street. Jack waited for her, took her elbow, merrily steered her along. He was whistling an off-key version of "We're Off to See the Wizard."

"You're no Judy Garland," Bagabond said.

Jack just smiled.

The crowds were starting to thin out, almost as though the epic battle over the East River had been equivalent to the nightly fireworks at Disneyland, signaling families it was time to take the kids home. More than that, the crowds seemed simply to be exhausted. It had been a long, long day.

All Nite Mari Ann's was sufficiently successful; it could afford to spread out more than the average boutique. It sprawled through the ground floor of what had once been a parking garage.

Jack led Bagabond along a window-shopping tour of the front of the store. "Yes," he said. "Oh yes. A silk dress, see?" He pointed. He looked into her face and then back into the interior of the shop. "Teal, I think. Perfect." He moved ahead of her. "Come on, Suzanne. It's Cinderella time."

Bagabond made one final attempt to stall. "I don't have much money with me."

Holding the door for her, Jack said, "I have an account."

When the burst of power went through him, there was nothing left of Fortunato to resist it. Nothing resisted it, and so it passed through him. And as it passed it left particles behind, particles of knowledge and memory and understanding.

Fortunato saw a little man in thick glasses crawling out of the East River, twenty years ago. There were no memories before that. Where there should have been memories there was only a seared place, self-inflicted. The Astronomer was self-made; there was no human identity, no human history left to him.

The little man had crawled into the grass of East River Park and he had looked up into the night sky. And the wild card virus uncoiled in him for the first time and his mind shot out into that sky and moved between the stars. It saw clouds of gas that burned in reds and purples and blues. It saw planets striped and whorled and ringed and haloed. It saw moons and comets and shapeless lumps of asteroid.

And it saw something moving. Something dark and nearly mindless, something vast and rubbery and foul, something hungry. And his mind began to scream.

The little man found himself outside a brick building in Jokertown, naked except for his glasses, still screaming. A door opened and a man named Balsam took him in. Took him in and taught him the secrets, taught him the name of the thing he'd seen, the name that was the ultimate Masonic word: TIAMAT.

Taught him about the machine, the Shakti device that the brother from the stars had brought to Cagliostro. Cagliostro who had founded the Order, to protect the knowledge of TIAMAT—the Dark Sister—and the Shakti device.

Until Balsam had nothing left to teach the little man, and it was time for the little man to become the Astronomer, and remove Balsam, with the unwitting help of a bumbling magician named Fortunato. To take control of the Order. To realize their destiny. To found a religious tyranny of Egyptian Masons that would rule the world. A world that would come begging to be ruled out of awe and gratitude. For the

Astronomer would use the Shakti device as it had always been meant to be used . . .

"No," Fortunato said. "No."

But the knowledge would not go away. The knowledge that the Shakti device had been given to the Masons to *save* the Earth from TIAMAT, not to lure her there. To call the Network to destroy her.

The Shakti device could have saved them and Fortunato had destroyed it. Because of him, thousands had died. For all his claims of wisdom he was still only a creature of impulse, nothing but a temperamental child.

The Astronomer still lived. The filmed glasses were still hooked around his ears, the tatters of his robe snapped in the wind, his chest moved up and down. His eyes had rolled back in his head, and his power was gone. Completely.

It would take nothing at all for Fortunato to drift across the thirty feet that separated them, put his hands around the little man's throat, and finish him.

Instead he left him fall.

Long seconds later Fortunato heard the splash as the little man came full circle, back into the East River again.

Henry Street was still and deserted, its revelry closed with the Crystal Palace. Sawhorses still closed off both ends of the block, though the street fair was long over. Hiram and Jay walked down the middle of the street, past the darkened rowhouses. The gutters were choked with litter: napkins, paper cups, plastic forks, newspapers.

Halfway up the block, a dark shape stepped out from the shadows to accost them. Popinjay's hand came out of his pocket fast, but Hiram grabbed his arm. "Don't," he said.

The shape moved under the light of a streetlamp. It was a heavy gray-haired woman in a shapeless green army jacket. The bottom half of her body was a single huge white leg, moist and boneless. She pushed herself forward like a snail. "Spare change?" she asked. "Spare change for a poor joker?"

Hiram found he could not look at her. He took out a wallet, gave her a five-dollar bill. As she took it from his hand, his fist clenched, and he cut her weight in half. It wouldn't last, but for a little while it would be easier for her.

A fire was burning in the vacant, debris-strewn lot beside the Crystal Palace. A dozen small twisted forms were huddled around it, and an animal of some sort was turning on a spit above the flames. At the sounds of footsteps, some of the creatures got up and vanished into the ruins. Others turned to stare, eyes hot as embers in the darkness. Hiram paused. He didn't often come down to Jokertown, and now he remembered why.

"They won't bother us," Ackroyd said. "This is their time, when the streets are empty and the world's asleep."

"I think that's a dog they're cooking," Hiram said.

Jay took him by the arm. "If you're that interested, I'll have Chrysalis get you the recipe. Come on."

They climbed the steps, knocked.

The sign on the door said CLOSED, but after a moment they heard the dead bolt slide back and a man stood before them. He had a pencil-thin mustache, oily dark hair, and an expanse of taut skin where his eyes should have been.

"Sascha, Hiram," Jay Ackroyd said. "They here?"

Sascha nodded. "In the taproom. Only two. They're clean."

Hiram heaved a sigh of relief. "Let's get this over with,

then." Sascha nodded, and led them through a small antechamber to the main taproom of the Crystal Palace.

The only lights were those behind the long bar. The room smelled of beer and cigarette smoke, and the chairs had been upended on the tables. They sat in a booth, three of them. In the dimness, Chrysalis looked like a skeleton in an evening gown. The end of her cigarette glowed like the eyes of the lost souls outside. Loophole Latham was impeccably dressed in a charcoal gray three-piece, and his briefcase was on the table in front of him. Between them, wrapped in shadow, was the third man.

"Thank you, Sascha," Chrysalis said. "You can leave us now." When the echoes of his footsteps had died away, it was deathly quiet in the taproom.

Hiram wondered once again what the damnation he was doing here. Then he thought of Gills, swallowed hard, stepped forward. "We're here," he announced, his deep voice full of confidence he did not really feel.

Latham stood up. "Mr. Worchester, Mr. Ackroyd," he said, as easily if this were just a business lunch.

The third person hissed. Something long and thin flickered out of his mouth and tasted the air. "We weren't assure you would come." He leaned forward, thrusting his gaunt reptilian face into the light. He had no nose, just nostrils set flat into his face. His forked tongue moved constantly. "Ssso we meet again."

"Sorry you had to rush off like that this afternoon," Jay said. "I didn't quite catch the name."

"Wyrm," the reptile man said.

"Is that a first name or a last name?" Jay asked.

Chrysalis laughed dryly. Latham cleared his throat. "Let's get on with this," he said. He sat down, spun the combination locks on his briefcase, clicked it open. "I've consulted with my client, and your terms are acceptable. No legal action will be taken against either of you, and the false-imprisonment charges will be dropped. I have the papers here, already signed by Mr. Seivers, who waives all his claims against you for the amount of one dollar."

"I'm not going to—" Hiram began.

"I'll pay the dollar," Latham said quickly. He handed a sheaf of legal papers to Ackroyd. The detective looked through them quickly, signed them in triplicate, returned two sets. "Very good," the attorney said. "As for the fish market, without admitting any prior guilt or involvement, my client and his organization will henceforth take no interest in that area of the city. This is not something that can be committed to a legal instrument, of course, but Chrysalis is a witness to these proceedings and the organization's reputation is your surety."

"Their business is built on trust," Chrysalis confirmed. "If they're known liars, no one will deal with them."

Hiram nodded. "And Bludgeon?"

"I reviewed his case after our last conversation, and frankly, he is not the sort of man Latham, Strauss, cares to represent. We're dropping him."

Wyrm's smile showed a mouth full of yellowed incisors. "Would you like his head ssserved up on a platter?"

"That won't be necessary," Hiram said. "I just want him to go to prison for what he did to Gills."

"Prissson it isss, then." His eyes were fixed on Hiram, and his tongue flickered out greedily. "And now, Fatman, you have all you wanted. Give usss the booksss! Now!"

There was a moment of tense silence. Hiram looked at Jay. The detective nodded. "Looks like all the bases are covered."

"Good," Hiram said. Now all that remained was to get

it done, and get out of here alive, back to the sanity of his own life. He was about to speak when, out of the corner of his eye, he saw something move behind the bar. He turned.

Wyrm said, "I want the booksss. Quit wasssting my time."

"I thought I saw a reflection in the mirror," Hiram said. But there was nothing there now. The polished silver surface gleamed softly in the dim light, but no one moved.

"Where are the booksss?" Wyrm demanded.

"I'd like to know the answer to that question myself," another voice added.

He was standing in the door, a black hood pulled over his face, a complex bow in his hands. An arrow was nocked and ready.

Wyrm's hiss was pure poison.

Hiram gaped. "Who in damnation are you?"

As he spoke, a young woman wearing a black string bikini and nothing else stepped out of the mirror behind the bar.

"Oh, shit," Popinjay offered.

Wyrm grabbed Chrysalis by the arm. "You ssset usss up, cunt. You'll pay for thisss."

"I had nothing to do with this," she said. She wrenched her arm free of his grasp, and looked at the masked man in the door. "Yeoman, I don't care for this," she told him.

"My regrets." He raised the bow, drew back on the arrow. "Unless the book is handed over, I'm going to put an arrow in the right eye of the gentleman in the three-piece suit."

Latham regarded him emotionlessly.

"And you're always telling me to dress better," Jay Ackroyd said to Hiram. "See what it gets you?" He turned to the bowman. "The book isn't here. You don't think we'd be dumb enough to bring it with us?"

"Wraith, pat them down."

The woman in the bikini walked right through the bar and approached the table. Suddenly Hiram recognized her. She'd been wearing rather more clothes at Aces High, but he was sure she was the same young woman who'd vanished through his floor when Billy Ray had tried to apprehend her. It made him sad. She was young and attractive, far too lovely to be a criminal. Undoubtedly she'd been corrupted by evil companions.

She frisked Jay first, then Hiram. When she touched him, her hands seem to go insubstantial, sliding through the fabric of his clothes and even his skin as they moved up and down, searching. It gave him a shiver. "Nothing," she said. The archer lowered his bow.

"You know, I'm a little slow," Popinjay put in. "You're the bow-and-arrow vigilante, right? The ace-of-spades man. How many guys have you killed? Gotta be in double figures, right?"

Wraith's eyes went to her partner, and she looked a little startled. An innocent in over her head, Hiram thought. His heart went out to her. He had read the accounts of the ace-of-spades killer in the *Jokertown Cry* and the *Daily News*, and he couldn't imagine how a sweet young lady like her had gotten involved with such a homicidal lunatic.

"Where's the book?" the archer said.

Hiram stared at the arrow. He ought to have been cold with dread, but curiously, he felt nothing but annoyance. It had been a very long day. "In a safe place," he said. He took a step forward, his fist clenching his side. He had had entirely enough. "Where it's going to stay." He began to walk toward the door, his bulk shielding the others behind him.

"I've gone to a great deal of trouble to set this up, and I'm not having Gills hurt or Bludgeon freed because you want these books for your own undoubtedly criminal purposes."

The eyes behind the mask looked absolutely astonished as Hiram strode forward. The archer hesitated, but only for a second. Then the bow came up again, Hiram tensed as the string was pulled back smoothly, pulleys turning, and Hiram clenched his fist as the gravity waves shimmered around the arrow, invisible to all but him, the moment of truth almost at hand, and–

–there was a *pop*, and the archer was gone.

Hiram heard Wraith gasp, and then Wyrm screamed in sibilant triumph. The lizard-man shoved at the table that trapped him inside the booth, and it came out of the floor with a metallic ripping sound. Wyrm hurtled over it toward the woman, who back-stepped away from him. "Leave her alone!" Hiram yelled.

Wyrm ignored him. He lunged, hissing, clawed hands grasping to embrace her, and passed right through her body, smashing hard up against a barstool. Popinjay laughed.

Wraith spun around wildly, wide eyes searching for her ally for a moment before she gave up and ran. She dashed through the bar again and vanished back into the mirror, its silvered surface closing over her like a pool of mercury.

"Nice of you to drop in," Popinjay called after her. He turned back to the others. "I don't suppose anyone got her phone number?" He sighed. "Oh, well . . ."

Wyrm climbed back to his feet, screeching in dismay. "I'll kill her! I'll kill them both!"

"Later," Loophole suggested. The lawyer folded his hands as if the little interruption had never happened. "Do we still have an understanding?"

"I don't want the damnable books," Hiram said. "If you'll honor my terms, they're yours."

"Fine. Where are they?"

"We hid them," Hiram told him, "in Jetboy's Tomb. In the cockpit of the JB–1 replica."

"If they're there, our agreement will be honored."

"If not," Wyrm added, "you'll all be very sssorry."

Chrysalis crossed to the bar and took down a bottle. "Perhaps we should have a little toast, to the successful conclusion of a difficult transaction."

"I'm afraid we don't have the time," Latham said, closing his briefcase. Hiram wasn't listening. He was staring past Chrysalis, staring at the silvered surface of the long mirror where—for just an instant—he thought he had seen something move.

She watched him struggle against the current, his stick-thin arms flailing wearily at the dark water. A dying water spider skimming hopelessly toward shore. Roulette had waited for him to die in the sky over Manhattan. Instead he had fallen like a tiny fleshy meteor, and her imperative continued. Now, watching his battle against the water, she again waited for him to die. The small dark knob of his head vanished, but she forced herself to wait. The Astronomer had cheated death before.

His head broke the water, and the violence of his thrashings shattered an oil slick into a hundred rainbow drops. *Die*, Roulette prayed, but the black, oily waters of the East River were carrying him to the refuse-strewn shore.

The Astronomer came crawling out, the vomit of the river. His naked body, pink flesh showing between the cracking flame-seared skin, lay like a rotting animal among the rusted cans and soggy hamburger wrappings like tiny disintegrating paper hillocks on the muddy shore. His left hand gripped his glasses, and slowly, skin flaking and cascading from him with every move, he tried to replace them.

Roulette, the heels of her dainty strap sandals sucking at the ooze, ran to him. Her kick caught him in the back of the hand. Fingers jerked open like scattered twigs, the glasses flying free to lie glinting on the mud. Roulette fell on them as if they contained the essence of the Astronomer, the soul of Tachyon. Drove down with a heel only to have it slide harmlessly off the thick lens and bury itself in the mud. The muck released her with a sad, repellent sound. Sobbing, she scooped up the glasses.

"Cunt! Filthy whoring pussy! My glasses, give me my glasses!" His voice spiraled to a frenzied shriek.

A splintered plank offered support. Pulling off her shoe she knelt in the mud, and hammered at the glasses with the sharp heel. The rhinestone studs cut into her hand, drawing blood. She tightened her grip on the blood-slick leather.

"Kill you! Kill you!" howled the Astronomer, groping about on his belly, hands outstretched, touching and recoiling from the various bits of detritus.

One lens broke with a sharp crystal sound.

"No!"

The second.

"Kill me? You can't even see me. Where will you run to this time? They're hunting you. Who will you kill to find the power? Tachyon's coming. Then only one of you will be left. For me. Better crawl."

His face, nose burned away, mouth a pale slit, eyes red from rupturing capillaries, was turned to her. "Over, all over," he quavered. His hands dug deep into the mud, fingers squeezing shut on the noisome ooze as if remembering other, more glorious, moments.

Finally he began to crawl, and Roulette followed. Bare feet slapping on the slick mud, hem trailing, chain of her evening bag cutting deep into her shoulder from the weight of the Magnum.

CHAPTER 24

5:00 a.m.

The streets were finally emptying. Only the hardiest revelers were left to cry up the dawn, or the least hardiest who had passed out—or worse—and were lying like abandoned rag dolls in the street.

The Crystal Palace was about a mile from Jetboy's Tomb. Jennifer knew that there was no way she was going to beat them to the mausoleum. It was difficult to run in the thonged sandals Brennan had lent her, but it was better than going barefoot down the refuse-littered streets.

Brennan. What in the world had happened to him? The little guy had pointed a finger at him and, whoosh, he was gone. Just like that. Well, she thought, her breath coming a little faster as she ate up the blocks between the Palace and the Tomb with an easy, long-legged stride, she had started this caper by herself, and she would finish it.

Big talk, she thought. Already she was missing Brennan's gruff presence. She hoped he was all right.

The great edifice that was Jetboy's Tomb was a looming black silhouette before the quiet waters of the Hudson River. It looked deserted, but there was a long limousine, brother to the one Jennifer and Brennan had borrowed, parked next to the twenty-foot-tall statue of Jetboy that stood in front of the Tomb's main entrance.

There was no one in or around the limo. Wyrm and the others, Jennifer realized, must already be inside the vast building.

She went quietly up the marble steps, as silent as the namesake she had chosen for herself, stripped off the cloak Brennan had lent her, and kicked away the sandals. A surge of adrenaline pushed back the weariness that threatened to overwhelm her.

It's been a long day, she told herself. But soon it's going to be over. One way or another.

The tomb was vast. A full-sized replica of Jetboy's plane, the JB-1, hung from the ceiling, bathed in muted light shining from hidden lamps also hanging from the inside of the dome.

The light filtered to the floor of the tomb where it vaguely illuminated three men staring up at the plane hanging from the ceiling. She recognized Wyrm, of course, and the man called Loophole. The third was a stranger, of average size and build, his features unrecognizable in the gloom.

Jennifer smiled to herself. Unless one of them could fly, there was no way they could reach the cockpit of the mock plane. It was a different matter, of course, for her.

She worked her way around to the far side of the tomb, keeping to the dark shadows along the walls. The acoustics inside the place were excellent and she could hear the men discussing what to do.

"That fat ssson of a bitch mussst have fffloated up to the ceiling and put the bookssss there."

"It doesn't matter how they got there," the unidentified man said in a hard, angry voice. "I want them down. Immediately."

They argued the problem as Jennifer reached the rear of the building. Still in shadows, she ghosted, fighting off a brief wave of vertigo, and pulled herself up through the wall to the ceiling. That was the easy part. Now it got a little tricky. She kept the body of the plane between her and the men below as she slipped into the cockpit and saw a small plastic bag, the bag she'd put the books in—was it only this morning? It seemed like a year ago.

She couldn't risk solidifying herself and checking them. She touched them, ghosted them, then, instead of feeling the triumph she anticipated, an uneasy tremor passed through her insubstantial form.

She was reaching the end of her endurance. She had pushed herself hard, ghosting more in the last twenty-two hours than she'd ever done in her life, and she hadn't had much food or rest between her periods of insubstantiality. She had only a little time left to get solid, or else she'd be in trouble.

She slipped out of the cockpit, but was careless in her haste. Loophole had walked around the plane to get another viewing angle, and he saw Jennifer's insubstantial form, shimmering like a Halloween specter as she was silhouetted against the wing.

"It's her again! She's got the books!"

She looked down and was assaulted by a sudden wave of dizziness. She had to get solid fast. Instinct took over and she stepped off the wing of the plane.

She floated as gently as a feather to earth, barely conscious, and when she touched ground her body took over and became solid. The transformation ate up all her energy reserves, and she blacked out.

"But what about Cordelia?" Bagabond said, as they carried the packages down through the City Hall station toward the passageways leading to Jack's home. The cats had joined them, the calico and the black rubbing contentedly against Bagabond's legs.

"The Cajuns have a saying," said Jack, opening the metal access door.

"What saying?"

The calico and black purred like Rip Van Winkle's snoring.

"I don't remember any more," said Jack. His voice seemed to Bagabond to possess a manic edge. "Something to the effect that if you do the best you can, then the breaks'll come. Or they won't."

"Right," said Bagabond.

"I'll find Cordelia. She'll be okay."

"You're tired," said the woman. "You're exhausted."

"So are you."

"I'm fine."

Racing ahead, the cats beat them to Jack's door. As he unlocked it and they all started in, Bagabond suddenly stiffened. "Jack," she said, staggering a little. "I've got–something."

Jack halted in midmotion, keys halfway into his pocket.

"It's a rat," she continued. "It's in the shadows, on top of a cabinet. It sees . . ." Bagabond hesitated. "Damn it, Jack, it's *her!*"

He hustled the cats and her inside the Victorian living room and shut the door. "Where?"

"That's what I'm trying to find out. There are other rats in the building. I'm switching from one to the other... There!" She grinned. "I've got one outside, peeking out of the alley. It's a bar, a club of some sort. There's a big neon sign that moves." She shook her head. "It's in the form of a woman, a stripper with six breasts. You, uh . . ." Bagabond hesitated. "You have to walk between the legs to get in."

"I've heard of it," said Jack. "Freakers. Never been there." He picked up an *East Village Other*, scanned the ads. "Nothing." He grabbed the *Fetish Times*. "When all else fails . . ." Leafing through the pages, he said, "Okay! Here it is. Chatham Square."

"Not too far," said Bagabond. She was already up and heading for the door, the cats on her heels.

"No," said Jack.

She turned to look at him. "No?" Tails switching, the cats stared at him too.

"You've got things to do. I can handle this."

"Jack—"

"I mean it." Jack set down the parcels he was still holding. "You get ready." He unwrapped a smaller package and took out some cosmetics. "I took the liberty of buying these."

"What are you *doing*?" she said as he set her down in front of the antique silvered mirror.

"It won't take long," he promised. "Then I'll drop in at Freakers."

"You're crazy," she said.

"Absolutely."

Jack juggled the lip gloss and the blush. He tilted her head so that she was staring at herself in the mirror.

"It's showtime," he said.

"Jack . . ." Bagabond shook her head stubbornly. "This talk we're supposed to have . . ."

"Tomorrow." He glanced up at the railway clock. "Later today. When there's time."

Bagabond uncharacteristically persisted. "*Why*, Jack?"

He bent down and looked levelly into her eyes. "You might as well ask why the wild card virus, Suzanne. It happens. You deal with it."

She was silent for a bit. "It'll take getting used to."

"It did for me too."

"I . . . still . . ." Her words dwindled to silence.

"Me too, love." Jack kissed her. "Me too."

Spector knew Fortunato had won. If it had been the other way around, the Astronomer would have cut Fortunato into fishbait before dropping him into the drink. Spector had watched the fight, same as everybody else. The difference was he knew what was going on. He couldn't believe that stupid simp Fortunato had let the old man go. Now the Astronomer could hide out, lick his wounds, and wait until he could build his power up again. Spector figured the old man would try to make shore on the Manhattan side of the river. If Spector could find him, he'd take care of the Astronomer once and for all.

"It's Judgment Day," he said, rubbing his bad arm.

He walked down the deserted alleyway. It was cold enough to frost his breath. He was tired and numb. The alley dead-ended in a wall.

"Fuck." He turned to leave, then stopped. There were voices on the other side. Familiar voices. He walked to the base of the wall and jumped, his aching muscles slowly pulling him up.

The Astronomer paused, breath wheezing and rattling in his chest. A cracked litany of hate dribbled from his mouth, the words hanging like beads on the long threads of saliva that were expectorated with each gasping breath. Roulette too stopped, waiting for him to find the strength to continue. Wondering with irritation why Tachyon was so slow. He should have been here by now. All of them joined in a final deadly union.

The Astronomer vanished into the dark mouth of an alley, and Roulette waited again for Tachyon. Who didn't appear. She fled after the Astronomer. And almost blundered into the Takisian who stepped from a connecting alley. Shrank back among a jumble of packing crates. Watched as the alien covered his eyes, cast about like a fox on a trail, froze, followed unerringly the path taken only moments before by the Astronomer. Roulette fell in behind, Magnum clutched in both hands, barrel leading like a dousing wand.

A sharp right into another alleyway, which dead-ended a hundred feet further on in a brick wall. Tachyon, hands clenched at his sides, stared down at the Astronomer, fury etched in his delicate face.

"God damn you, Fortunato!" He threw back his head, and howled into the overcast sky. "You gutless wonder, you honorless piece of shit, you motherless procurer! I thought you were going to finish this. Instead you leave it to me! And I don't want it," he ended in a soft, sad voice.

The Astronomer continued his dogged crawl, not seeming to realize that he had entered a trap. Tachyon inspected his hands, drew a fighting knife from his boot, dithered. And Roulette cursed.

The scrape of a shoe on brick as a figure hauled itself onto the top of the wall. Squatted there like a man-sized gargoyle. Dropped into the alley, a curse exploding from him as his mangled, half-grown foot struck the pavement. *Demise.*

Roulette wept with vexation, licking away the salty tears as they streamed down the corners of her mouth. Lifted the gun. Demise would not be allowed to cheat her.

"James!"

He strolled forward, the half-formed foot throwing him into a lurching, rolling gait. "So you remember me, Doc."

"Yes," Tachyon replied, edging cautiously away from the menace in Demise's acne-scarred face. "We've been worried about you." They revolved about the prone body of the Astronomer, until Demise's skinny back came up square in front of Roulette, blocking her aim.

"I'll just bet, you fucker." He turned his awful gaze from the Takisian to the pitiful figure at his feet. "Well, well, look what you've found." He nudged the Astronomer with his partly regenerated foot. "Hey, *Master,* I'm still here. And you're dead."

Tachyon started forward, and Roulette danced from side to side, trying to get a clear shot past Demise. "What are you going to do?"

"Kill him. You gonna try to stop me, you little puke?"

"No."

Demise stared hard at the alien's knife, threw back his head, and laughed, the sound echoing wildly off the walls. "Gonna deal a little death yourself tonight, eh, Tachy?

Gonna play God again? Give a little life today, take it away tomorrow."

"Stop, please." A broken whisper.

The words crashed through Roulette touching—something. Violent shudderings ripped through her body, the gun fell from nerveless fingers, hit, detonated, the chambered round ricocheting off the brick wall over Demise's head.

"Shit!"

Tachyon and Demise whirled to face her, and the Astronomer, with a burst of hoarded strength, came to his feet.

The Astronomer's voice was a dry rasp. "Help me, James. Kill them. I'll reward you. Help me. Anything you want. Just help me now. So weak. No power left."

Spector grabbed the Astronomer, blackened bits of flesh coming off in his hands. "I don't think so, old man."

The Astronomer lunged for the wall. Spector spun him around, but the Astronomer became insubstantial in his hands, stepped back, began to melt into the brick wall. Well, *one* power left.

Pale, almost-blind mole eyes locked with Spector's. The perfect sharing of the perfect moment. This time there was nothing to block him. The death flowed quick and hard into the Astronomer. The old man gasped and began to solidify.

The bricks around him split and glowed red with heat. Blood poured hissing into the cracks and down the wall. Bricks closed lovingly on flesh.

Spector let out a sigh of relief. He'd done it. Nobody in the world would have given him a chance in hell of killing the old bastard, but he was dead. The Astronomer, Lord Amun, the Master, Setekh the destroyer.

And he was still around to talk about it.

The sound of pursuing footsteps echoing loudly in the empty street. Closing in! Hands seizing her. Roulette, sobbing, choking with fear, whirled, attacking her captor with teeth and nails. A steel-like grasp closed about her wrists, pulling her into a tight embrace. The fresh and now familiar scent that was Tachyon washed across her. She slumped in his arms, and a slim, small hand stroked her cheeks, wiping away the tears.

Tachyon's mind flowed through hers like a clean, icy-cold stream, soothing the wounds left by the collapse of the shields. Washing away the memories, drowning deep the Astronomer's touch. What remained was a vast, aching emptiness.

She could feel the Magnum forming a cold wedge between them. He stepped back, hands dropping limply to his sides, and the pistol dropped from her hand. They regarded each other across a space of air that seemed impossibly wide. The gun lay on the ground between them.

"You're not healed. It's not my gift. But I have done what I can."

"I wanted to kill you."

"You should avoid undue emotional and mental stress."

"I did kill Howler."

"You should perhaps enter therapy."

"And there've been others."

He stooped, swept up the gun, and extended it to her butt first. "Then finish it. If that is what you must have in order to find peace."

"Oh, God damn you!" A garbage can rang like a sour bell as the heavy pistol slammed into it. "I killed Howler!"

"I know. There is very little about you that I don't know." His thin lips twisted in a sad, sick, little smile. "I have an amazingly elastic and creative conscience. Part of my upbringing. I can raise three excellent reasons to justify your vendetta. To be avenged is—"

Her hand lashed out and took him across the face. "That is *crap*! Stop worming out of it, and give me a decision. What are you going to do?"

The tip of his tongue touched the newly opened cut on his lip. "Are you planning to turn yourself in to the authorities?"

"No."

"Then I am going to do nothing. A telepathic reading is not admissible evidence in a court of law." Again that sad smile. "I also would not relish describing the situation in which I made that reading. It would do little for my dignity." A hand slid in an unconscious protective gesture to his crotch.

Turned, walked away. Aware now of the filth beneath her bare feet, the mud caking the silk gown. A fitting envelope for her soul.

"Roulette." She paused, but did not look back. "Earlier I said I loved you. I think I still do."

"Don't burden me this way."

"Call it my punishment for you."

"I've lived on hate. Now there's nothing. Let me see if I'm capable of anything beyond those two states."

"I'll be waiting."

She smiled despite herself. "Damn you, I think you will."

Spector sat in the alley, his back to the cold brick wall. The others were gone; he was alone with the old man.

"Didn't quite turn out the way you planned, eh, Astro?" He patted the Astronomer's cheek. "Or maybe it did. Might be just what you had in mind all along."

Spector felt empty and tired. He'd thought with the Astronomer dead there would be some kind of relief. Ever since the fight at the Cloisters earlier in the year he'd had a look-behind-you fear of the old man. There was no focus for him now.

He looked into the Astronomer's dead eyes. "Now you know what I went through. Not that you'd care, even if you could say anything. Probably just scream at me for fucking up."

Spector heard someone throwing up at the mouth of the alley. He backed up the wall into a standing position, took a last look at the Astronomer, and headed toward the street.

The man was on his knees, wiping his mouth. He stood and stepped back from the pool of vomit. He was about the same height as Spector, young, and not smart enough to stay out of alleyways in Jokertown. The suit he wore was gray, Spector's color.

Spector could use some new clothes, again. His baseball uniform was almost no help against the early morning chill. He tapped the man on the shoulder. "I'll give you this authentic Yankee uniform for that suit of yours."

The man jumped, then recovered and gave Spector a tough look. "Don't give me no static, man. I'll cave your head in."

Spector was dead tired. He didn't want to use up his remaining energy undressing another corpse. "If you don't do what I say, you're going to die. That suit worth dying for? I don't think so."

The man raised his fists.

"Stupid," Spector said wearily. "You've got something in your eye."

"What?"

"Me." He locked eyes and put the man down. "Dumbass." Spector pulled off the man's coat and threw it over his shoulders. The pants would be more trouble than they were worth to him.

It was time to attend to a little unfinished business. Time to head back to the garbage barge and visit Ralph.

"So long, suckers," he said to dead men in the alley. No sound. He thought about some poor city worker trying to chip the old man's body out of the wall, and smiled.

Jennifer regained consciousness with pain stinging her cheek. Her eyes fluttered open to see the palm of an open hand approaching her face, and she felt rough, strong hands holding her up. The palm connected with her cheek again, bringing her consciousness to full resolution.

They were outside the Tomb, clustered by the limo parked before the statue of Jetboy. Wyrm was holding her upright and Loophole was slapping her silly while the third man—middle-aged, Oriental, running a little to fat—was watching. He idly swung the bag containing the books as Loophole slapped her. He was, she realized, Kien.

They finally saw she was conscious again. Wyrm released her and stepped aside. She slumped against the side of the limo, unable to stand by herself, and glared at them. Another figure, vague in the darkness, stood beyond Kien and Loophole. Hope flared, then died, when Jennifer realized that it was just another of Kien's omnipresent goons.

"You've been quite an inconvenience," Kien said in a mild voice. "A great inconvenience indeed. I wanted you to be awake for this." He nodded at Wyrm and the joker drew a small, ugly-looking snub-nosed pistol from a holster clipped at his waist. "It shall be a pleasure to watch you die."

Wyrm raised the pistol and Jennifer closed her eyes. She tried to ghost, but couldn't. The energy she needed to power the transformation just wasn't there. She'd never pictured herself dying this way, never really pictured herself dying at all.

"Not there, you fool," Kien said with a trace of exasperation, "you'll ruin the finish on the limousine." He turned to the man standing in the background. "Take her away from the car."

The collar of his jacket was turned up against the chill of the early morning, his hat was pulled down low over his face. Jennifer glanced at him dully, and her eyes stayed on his face and stared.

Her lips formed the name, Brennan, and in a single motion he grabbed her by the arm, whirled her out of the way, and ripped the gun from Wyrm's hand with a sidekick that sent it clattering into the night.

Wyrm hissed in surprise, his tongue twisting like a blind snake. Jennifer glanced at Kien and saw shock and anger and finally fear chase themselves across his face.

"It's him!" Kien said in a low voice, half to himself. Then he screamed. "Kill him! Kill him!"

Brennan faced Wyrm empty-handed, one hand open, the other clenched into a fist. He stood and smiled at the joker, seeming, to Jennifer, to invite an attack. Wyrm leaped at him and they grappled. Brennan was borne back against the side of the limo by the superior strength of the joker, and Wyrm, triumphant, drew back to strike.

But Brennan moved faster than the joker. He opened his clenched fist for the first time and reached out and grabbed the joker's tongue with it, close to the root. He slid his hand down Wyrm's tongue, smearing it with a sticky brownish substance, then released it.

Wyrm's eyes tried to jump from their sockets and he screamed, fell to the ground, and thrashed about like a man on fire while pawing at his tongue.

Loophole grabbed Jennifer as Wyrm howled in agony, and she heard the approaching footsteps of running men. Kien dropped the bag with the precious books in it, drew the pistol holstered at his waist, and pointed it at Brennan.

Brennan looked at him calmly.

"My joy is doubled," Kien said between clenched teeth. "After all these years you've come back to devil me. And now you'll die by my hand."

Jennifer saw Brennan tense to leap and she knew that he'd never make it across the impossible distance that separated him from Kien. She lunged away from Loophole, unable to break free of him, but pulling within reach of Kien's pistol. She grabbed it.

He snarled, tried to yank away, but Jennifer held on, frowned in fierce concentration, and ghosted most of the gun and most of Kien's hand. Loophole yanked on her arm hard, hard enough to pull her away from Kien, and he screamed.

He fell to his knees, what was left of his hand dropping what was left of the gun. The ghosted molecules of both, since they were no longer in direct contact with Jennifer, drifted away on the breeze. A stunned Loophole released

Jennifer and bent down to help Kien staunch the river of blood fountaining from his mangled hand.

Jennifer snatched up the bag, turned, and grabbed Brennan by the arm.

"Come on," she shouted. He resisted for a moment, staring remorselessly at his longtime foe, then he followed her into the dark, running.

Fortunato rang the bell of the brownstone for a long time before Veronica's voice came through the intercom. When he told her who it was, she ran downstairs to open the door.

She threw herself into his arms and started to cry. "It was so horrible. So horrible. This . . . man . . . took me and Caroline and Cordelia. He killed Caroline. He—"

"Shhh," Fortunato said. "It's over. He's finished. His power is gone."

"I thought we were all going to die."

"Where's Cordelia now?" he asked gently. "Is she okay?"

"She went out. She's okay. She said she'd be back. Maybe. But Caroline . . ."

She started to cry again. Gradually she got herself under control and Fortunato took her inside. He had to put his suitcase down to shut the door, and Veronica saw it.

"What's that?"

"I'm leaving town for a while."

"Fortunato? Look, I can quit the smack. It's not a big deal. We can work this out."

"It's not about you."

She reached up and touched his forehead. It was smooth

and flat. The bulge, where his reserve power built up, was gone. "Are you all right?" she asked.

He nodded. He'd been back to the apartment to pack and clean up. He put some food out for the cat and sat for a couple of minutes with her on his lap. There didn't seem to be anything physically wrong with him, just this overwhelming detachment.

"I have to see Ichiko," he said. "I'll need some paper and a pen. And get your mother to bring her notary seal."

He had it all worded in his head, and it took less than five minutes for him to get it on paper, witnessed and notarized. He handed it to Ichiko. "It's yours now," he said. "Everything. You can keep it going if you want, or stop it. It's up to you."

"What happened?" Ichiko said.

Fortunato shook his head. "I don't want to change anybody any more. I don't want to make them into geishas or hookers or heroin addicts. If someone else does it that's fine, but it's not going to be me anymore. I don't want to change anybody but myself. I can't . . . I can't take the responsibility."

"And the suitcase?"

"I'm going home. Back to Japan. To the Shoin-ji temple at Hara."

Miranda said, "What about your power?"

"It'll come back," Fortunato said, "I think. As to what I'm going to do with it, I don't know. I just don't know."

Miranda looked at Ichiko. "Well," she said. "I don't want to give up the business. But I don't know if we can make a go of it without help. The Gambiones are always lurking like vultures, waiting for a sign of weakness."

"We've always protected ourselves with influence and

money," Fortunato said. "You can do that as well as I ever could."

"Ah," Ichiko said. "But there was always the fist inside the glove."

Fortunato picked up a deck of cards from the end table. He took out the ace of spades and threw the rest of the cards away. He took the pen again and wrote. *Help if you can. Fortunato.*

"There's a man called Yeoman. You can trust him. If you need him, leave word at the Crystal Palace, and show him this card."

Veronica walked with him to the door. "What are you going to do?" he asked her.

"Fuck men for money," she said. "It's all I've got. What are you going to do?"

"I don't know."

"You're lucky," she said. She kissed him good-bye. Her mouth was soft and sweet and almost enough to change his mind.

CHAPTER 25

6:00 a.m.

After Jack left, Bagabond was left to stare at her transformation. The mirror revealed an attractive woman in her mid-thirties who tried to smile, but gingerly, as though her face might crack. She turned away. The suits had been barely tolerable, and only because she saw them as protective color. This dress revealed too much of someone she didn't know. For a moment, she considered changing into the dirty, torn clothing she had worn for so long. This new persona frightened her.

The black and the calico cats came up to her in response to her broadcast of pain. The calico leaped into her lap and licked her under the chin while the black rubbed his back against her calf. They questioned her about the sending. Bagabond tried to explain. She sent a picture of Paul to them both. Neither cat was impressed by the human they saw. Even Bagabond's emotional shadings of the face she remembered were not enough. The black looked up at her and imagined Paul's throat torn out. It was the simplest solution to him. If something annoys you, kill it. Bagabond shook her head and rebuilt Paul's image.

The calico sent a scene of Bagabond, back in her normal dress, sitting on the floor of Jack's home and playing with the kittens. Bagabond stroked the calico, but blocked out the sight of the familiar group. The black snarled and placed his huge paws on Bagabond's knees. He stared into her eyes and she knew his anger and frustration.

Bagabond looked back at the mirror and saw a girl in a beaded leather headband and a tie-dyed T-shirt. The younger woman seemed to smile at her in encouragement. Bagabond reached out to touch the girl's hand, wondering if she could ever have been so young and happy. As she touched the glass, the image changed to herself, teal dress, mascara, and blush. Examining herself again, Bagabond thought she saw something of the girl's eyes still in hers.

The shrill ring of the phone broke her reverie. Dumping the calico onto the floor, she wondered if this was more bad news for Jack. But the voice at the other end was Rosemary's.

"Suzanne, did I wake you?"

"No." Bagabond sat down on the floor beside the phone.

"Can you meet me at home? I mean, the penthouse?"

"Why?"

"I just feel as if . . ." Rosemary's voice grew thin for a moment. "I guess I want to tell my father what I'm doing. Maybe it's why I held on to the place. But I don't want to go there alone. Please, Suzanne."

"Why me?"

Rosemary hesitated. "Suzanne . . . I trust you. I can't trust anyone else. I need you."

"That's not new." Bagabond clenched her jaw and her hand tightened on the phone.

"Suzanne, I know you don't agree with what I've done, but I promise I'm going to change things."

"All right. But I have an appointment at seven." Bagabond closed her eyes in disgust at her need for Rosemary's approval.

"Thanks. I'll meet you there." Rosemary hung up.

Bagabond looked down at the cats.

"I don't think this night is ever going to end."

She pulled on the long, open, ankle-length black sweater Jack had insisted she get. The black and calico accompanied her to the door. Bagabond mentally told them both to stay. The cats responded with yowls of anger, but backed away from the door. Closing the door, Bagabond knew the black was using another exit to follow her.

At the subway station, she held the door of the car so the cat could enter. The black was not happy he had been spotted, but was glad he would not have to chase the train or find another route. He panted as he lay at her feet. For him, now, it had been a long run.

She got off at 96th Street, abruptly aware of how few people had been on the subway. The crowds really *had* given up. She went upstairs to the street. Two blocks down Central Park West, Rosemary waited on a bus bench. Her eyes widened as she saw Bagabond's dress, but she did not comment.

"Let's go in." Bagabond was impatient to get this done. She suddenly felt the gray cat watching her from the park across the street. She looked up, but saw nothing in the trees.

"I suppose I'm ready." Rosemary hesitated before pulling open one of the heavy glass doors.

"Signorina, you'd better be." Trailed by the black, Bagabond followed her in.

The doorman was no longer a Gambione man. He was young, and Bagabond noticed he was studying a book on contract law. Rosemary showed him her key and signed in, as Rosa Maria Gambione, on the guest register.

In the elevator, she used another key to send the car to the penthouse.

"I haven't been here in five years." Rosemary looked up at the ceiling of the car.

"Are you sure you want Rosa-Maria to return?" Bagabond reached out to touch the other woman's shoulder. "You were desperate to leave all this behind. Your father, the Family, all of it. You wanted to atone for what he did. Now you want to be like him?"

"No!" Rosemary glared at Bagabond for an instant before she lowered her head. "Suzanne, I could do a lot of good, turn the Family around."

"Why?" Bagabond barely kept her balance in the high heels as the elevator jerked to a halt. "Let them be destroyed. They deserve it. They're criminals."

Rosemary stepped out into the hallway. "It looks wrong without the men. There were always guards here for my father."

"You want to live that way?"

Rosemary unlocked the double oak doors, then turned and was framed against the darkness behind. "Suzanne, don't you understand that I can make a difference? I can stop the violence and the killing."

Bagabond was skeptical. "You could destroy yourself instead."

"It's worth the risk." Rosemary pushed the doors open wide and walked in. "I believe that."

Behind her, Bagabond watched the new head of the Gambione Family walk down the dark entry. She murmured to herself and the black, "I know you do, God help you."

Rosemary showed Bagabond the apartment, telling her of the happy things that had happened there. There were some: the holidays, family gatherings, birthdays. The last room they entered was the library. Books lined the black walnut walls and heavy draperies seemed to absorb most of the light. Despite the oppressive atmosphere, Rosemary laughed.

At Bagabond's look, she explained. "It's awful. All these books? My father bought them by the yard. He didn't care what they were, so long as they had leather bindings and looked impressive. I used to sneak in and read some of them. There was Hawthorne and Poe and Emerson. It was fun." She looked at Bagabond defensively. "It wasn't always bad to live here."

Running her hand over the backs of the chairs that lined the central table, she walked to the chair at its head. For a moment she put her arms around the back as though she embraced a person. Then Rosemary pulled the chair out and sat down, contemplating Bagabond down the length of the table.

"Can you find the door?" Rosemary leaned back and was dwarfed by the massive, carved back of the chair. "I just want to think for a while."

Bagabond walked out of the room feeling as though she had seen a ghost. Back in the elevator, she knelt and stroked the black until he purred at her. Then she stood and pulled the sweater more tightly around her.

Outside, the sun was up and traffic had increased on the streets until the horns and diesel fumes made it clear the day had begun. The gray still watched from the park. She was unable to pick up the animal's emotions without effort. She left him his privacy. Bagabond patted the black's head and sent him across to the park to see his son.

She stepped to the curb to hail a cab to take her downtown to the restaurant.

As the taxi wove through the thickening morning traffic, Bagabond started attempting to think of good conversational gambits. Nothing she remembered from the sixties somehow seemed appropriate.

Bagabond wondered if Paul liked cats. He had better.

"Okay, how did you track me to Jetboy's Tomb?"

Brennan shrugged. Jennifer was carrying the book sack and he had two bags full of Chinese food that Jennifer had insisted on buying at a take-out place near her apartment.

"It was easy. I'd put a bug on the cloak I'd given you. That little fellow with Fatman teleported me to the middle of the Holland Tunnel, which, luckily enough, isn't far from Jetboy's Tomb. Though I must say I was worried that you'd do something foolish before I managed to reach you. And I was right."

"Humph. And then?"

"And then? Wyrm had planted lookouts to make sure they wouldn't be bothered while they were recovering the books. You must have come through while they were either still securing the perimeter or rousting someone else. At any rate, I took the place of one of them just as Wyrm and the others were dragging your unconscious body out of the tomb. Then it was simply a matter of waiting for my chance. I saw it, and jumped Wyrm."

"What did you do to him, anyway?"

Brennan held up his hand. The palm was still stained brown.

"Remember the mustard I brought from the street vendor?" She did. "Wyrm's tongue is an extremely sensitive sensory organ that doesn't take too well to spices. Besides discomforting him, I'm sure the mustard also wiped away all traces of your scent. So you should be safe from him."

"Thanks. And thanks for saving my life."

"You did the same for me. I'd have never gotten that gun away from Kien."

Jennifer nodded. She'd never used her power that way before, and, even though it had been unintentional and Kien had, after all, tried to kill her, now that she had time to think about it, she felt nauseated. All that blood . . .

They walked on in silence for a while. She felt Brennan's eyes on her, but said nothing until they'd gone up the four flights of stairs to her apartment.

"Well, here we are."

Books were everywhere about the living room, giving it a comfortable, lived-in look. At least that's how Jennifer thought of it. Brennan put the bags containing the food on the counter that divided the kitchen nook from the rest of the room.

"Make yourself at home," she said as she turned to put the coffeepot on the stove and got two plates and utensils from the cupboard. She turned back to see Brennan standing in the middle of the apartment, an impatient expression on his face. "You want to see the book?"

He nodded. She took the bag off her shoulder and put it on the counter next to the food. She selected a box, ladled a portion of shrimp fried rice onto her plate, and reached for the box with the sweet-and-sour chicken.

"Well, go ahead."

If Brennan noticed the resignation in her voice he gave no sign. He strode forward eagerly, took the pouch, and looked inside. Jennifer kept her eyes on the food. She took a forkful of the chicken and somehow it didn't taste as good as she had thought it would.

"Is this a joke?" Brennan asked after a moment, his voice flat and emotionless.

He was holding up Kien's diary.

Jennifer swallowed. "No, no, I don't think so," she said in a small voice.

He thumbed through it, disbelief on his face.

"It's blank," he said, fanning the pages for Jennifer to see.

"I know." She put her fork down and looked at Brennan for the first time.

"What the hell happened?" Brennan demanded, anger growing in his voice. She could see his jaw muscles jump as he clenched his jaw tighter and tighter.

"Well, the nearest I can figure is that the ink didn't translate when I ghosted the book. You see, it takes special effort to make dense material like lead, or gold, insubstantial, and he must have used something like that to write . . . with . . . you see . . ."

Her voice ran down as the storm gathered on Brennan's face.

"I. Went. Through. All that shit. For. A. Blank. Book." He said each word as if it were a sentence.

"I couldn't tell you," Jennifer said. "At first I didn't totally trust you. Then, when I saw how important it was to you, I just couldn't find a way."

Brennan stared at her silently, and she flinched, expecting him to scream, to throw the book, to strike at her, to do just about anything but what he did.

"A blank book," he repeated. The storm on his face broke and vanished as quickly as it had gathered. He sank down unseeingly into the large stuffed chair near the bookcase, rose up slightly and picked up the hardcover copy of *Scaramouche* that was open, face down on the chair. He looked at it as if he'd never seen a book before and muttered, "Ishida, my roshi, if you could only have experienced the events of this day. What lessons could be learned. Tell me." He looked at Jennifer with serious, questioning eyes. "What lessons can one learn from a blank book?"

"I—I don't know," she faltered.

He shrugged. "I don't know either, yet. A new koan to meditate upon." Brennan thumbed through the diary again, a bemused expression on his face. "Of course," he said after a moment, "Kien doesn't know the book is blank. Doesn't know that at all."

He smiled, the first real smile that Jennifer had ever seen on his face. He looked at Jennifer and his smile broadened, turned into laughter. It was joyful, cleansing laughter. Jennifer sensed he hadn't laughed out loud in a long time. She felt herself smiling as well out of relief and because of the recognizable, binding companionship that already lay between them.

Brennan stood, still laughing and shaking his head. He walked over to the counter. His eyes and Jennifer's were on the same level. If anything, he had to look up to see into hers. She'd never seen him before with a true smile on his face, and she liked it. He told her, without saying anything, that he liked what he saw when he looked into hers.

He took his hood off and dropped it on the counter. Some of the tension had gone out of his face and he looked years younger than when Jennifer had first seen him.

"Did you get any egg rolls?" he asked.

She looked down at the little boxes filled with Chinese food, and felt a strange, unexpected, unanalyzable stab of joy.

When Jack finally managed to find Freakers, he understood why it wasn't the kind of all-night dive that advertised itself strenuously. Those who needed to know where it was, found out. Looking at the moving neon woman astraddle the door, Jack thought that maybe some people arrived here simply by following their darkest instincts.

The neon seared his retinas like a branding iron. This hour of the early morning, there was no one guarding the door. Presumably this was the time of day when only the most dedicated clientele showed up.

Ignoring the swooping, glowing lines above him, Jack pushed open the door and entered. Smoke, muted conversational noise, geometric patterns in neon primaries—these were what he noticed first.

Across the main room, an obviously tired stripper desultorily went through the motions on a cylindrical revolving stage. Bathed in a rose spotlight, she undulated to a slow beat Jack couldn't even hear. He squinted, trying to focus in the smoke. He realized the stripper's abdomen was covered with what looked like pairs of vertical lips. She was down to her last G-string.

Jack turned away, scanned the tables. He headed toward the cheap, plank-hewn bar. Then he saw the row of booths at the back. There was a girl in one of them—a young woman with black hair falling straight along the sides of her thin face. She was dressed in a startling, clingy blue dress. She stared directly at him.

There was a nondescript man in a brown suit standing over the booth, talking to the young woman. He straightened as Jack approached. Jack faltered, then walked up to them. Ignoring the man in brown, Jack looked down at the woman. She started to smile.

"Uncle Jack?" The malachite eye in the silver alligator hanging from her left earlobe flashed as it caught light from the follow-spot clicking off on the stage.

"Cordelia!"

She was instantly out of the booth and holding onto him as though she were traveling steerage and he had the only life preserver on the *Titanic*. They stayed that way for long seconds.

The man who had been talking to Cordelia said, "Hey, you want that, maybe you should rent a room." It seemed to be spoken without real malice. Jack looked up across Cordelia's shoulder at him. The man's suit jacket was rumpled. He wore no tie. To Jack, he looked as one might imagine a cashiered, down-at-the heels FBI agent on the skids. The man offered a wry grin. "Hey, I figured it wouldn't hurt to try. No offense."

"Do I know you?" said Jack.

"The name's Ackroyd," said the man. "Jay Ackroyd, PI." He put out his hand.

Jack ignored it. The two men looked each other in the eye for a few seconds. Then Ackroyd smiled. "It's over, man. For now, at least. Everybody's dead-butt tired. Truce." He gestured around the bar. "Besides, nobody'd do anything while Billy Ray's nursing his beer." Jack followed the line of Ackroyd's finger. He saw a guy wearing a white stretch fighting suit sitting alone at a table. The man's features were mismatched, asymmetrical. His jaw looked inflamed and he was sipping his beer through a straw. "Pride of the Justice

Department. Baddest of bad-asses," said Ackroyd. "Listen, cool out, have something to drink, visit with your niece." He stepped away from the booth. "I gotta get some fresh air anyway." Ackroyd headed for the door, weaving just a little in his scuffed brown loafers.

"Sit down, Uncle Jack." Cordelia tucked him onto the seat beside her in the booth.

"What are you drinking?" He touched the glass.

"7-Up." She giggled. "I wanted RC, but they don't have any up here."

"We've got it," said Jack. "You can get anything in Manhattan. You're just in the wrong neighborhood."

A barmaid in satin top and shorts, her visible skin showing a stitchwork of granular tumors, came over to the booth. "Something to drink?" Jack ordered a beer. Iron City. That was the sort of imported brew you could order in a place like this.

"What the hell are you doing here?" he said. "Bagabond—my friend—and I have been looking all day for you. I saw you at the Port Authority—you got away before I could get through the crowd. You were with someone who looked like a pimp."

"He was, I guess," said Cordelia. "There was a man named Demise . . . He saved me." She hesitated. " 'Course then he helped try to kill me. This is a confusing town, Uncle Jack."

"I owe him," said Jack. "One way or the other." For a split second, his face started to alter and his jaw to deform. He took a deep breath, settled back, felt his teeth resume their human size. "Why are you here? Your folks are going crazy."

"Why are *you* here, Uncle Jack? I always heard things

from Mama and the relatives about how you ran away and why you came to this place."

"Fair enough," said Jack. "But I could take care of myself."

"So can I," Cordelia said. "You'd be surprised." She hesitated. "You know what all's happened today?" The young woman didn't wait for Jack to shake his head. "I can't even tell you what all. But some of it is this: A slaver tried to kidnap me, I was rescued, I've met some really strange and some really fabulous people, I found the most fantastic man—Fortunato—I almost got killed, and then . . ." She paused.

Jack shook his head. "And then *what*, for God's sake?"

She leaned close to his face, looked him straight in the eyes, and said seriously, "Something incredible happened."

Jack wanted to laugh, but didn't. He accepted her seriousness and said, "What's that, Cordelia?"

Even in the neon-lit dimness, he could see that she was blushing. "It was like when I started my periods," she finally said. "You know? You probably don't. Anyhow, it was when I was up there in this penthouse and this old guy was about to kill me? Something just *changed*. It's hard to describe."

"I think I know," said Jack.

She nodded soberly. "I think you do. It's why you left the parish all those years ago, isn't it?"

"I expect so. You—" It was his turn almost to stammer. "You changed, didn't you? Now you're not the same person you were."

Cordelia nodded vehemently. "I still don't know what it is I'm becoming. All I know is that when that Imp guy tried to grab me—he was going to help the old guy rip out my heart or something like that—there was this feeling inside like things were really tight and then . . ." She shrugged expressively. "I killed him. I *killed* him, Uncle Jack. What really happened was it felt like I could use something down deep in my brain I didn't know how to use before. I could *do* things to the men who were trying to hurt me. I could make them stop breathing, keep their hearts from beating—I don't know what all. Anyhow, it was enough. So I'm here." She put her arms around his neck again. "I'm really glad."

"You've got a way of understating things," Jack said, grinning. "Listen, are you ready to come home?"

"Home?" She sounded puzzled.

"My place. You can stay with me. We'll get things settled. Your folks are sweating toad spit."

She drew back. "I'm not going back, Uncle Jack. Not never."

"You've got to talk to your folks."

She shook her head. "And the next thing, you'll be putting me on a bus. I'll get off at the next stop. I'll run away. I swear it." She turned away from him.

"What's the matter, Cordelia?" He felt confused.

"If I go back, there's Uncle Jake. *Grand*uncle Jake."

"Snake Jake?" Jack started to understand. "Did he—?"

"I can't go back," she said.

"Okay. You don't go back. But you've still got to talk with Robert and Elouette." To his amazement, she was crying.

"No."

"Cordelia . . ."

She wiped away the tears. There was something hard now in the fragile features of her face, a toughness in her voice. "Uncle Jack, you've got to understand. Things have *happened* today. Maybe I'm going to be one of Fortunato's geishas, or serve drinks in a place like this, or go to Columbia University and be a nuclear scientist, or something.

Anything. I don't know. I'm not who I was. I don't know what I am—who I am now. I'm going to find out."

"I can help you," he said quietly.

"Can you?" She was staring at him hard. "Do you know who *you* are, really?"

Jack didn't say anything.

"Yeah." She moved her head slowly. "I love you very much, Uncle Jack. I think we're very much alike. But I'm willing to find out who I am. I've got to." She hesitated. "I don't think you admit much to yourself or to the folks around you." It was as if she were looking inside him, shining a searchlight around inside his head and his mind. He was uncomfortable with both the uncompromising glare and the shadows.

"Hey!" The shout came from Ackroyd, ducking his head past the front door. "You gotta see this! All of you." He retreated back outside.

Cordelia and Jack looked at each other. The young woman joined the others heading for the door. Jack hesitated, then followed.

Outside, the night retreated. Dawn was breaking over the East River. Ackroyd stood out in the street and pointed toward the sky. "Will you look at that?"

They all looked. Jack squinted and at first didn't realize what he was staring at. Then the details coalesced.

It was Jetboy's plane. After forty years, the JB-1 soared again above the Manhattan skyline. High-winged and trout-tailed, it was indisputably Jetboy's pioneering craft. The red fuselage seemed to glow in the first rays of morning.

There was something wrong with the image. Then Jack realized what it was. Jetboy's plane had speed lines trailing back from the wings and tail. *What the hell?* he thought. But for the moment, he was as transfixed by the vision as everyone else around him. It was as though they were all collectively holding one breath.

Then things came apart.

One wing of the JB-1 started to fold back and tear away from the fuselage. The plane was breaking up.

"Jesus-fucking-jumping-joker-Christ," someone said. It was almost a prayer.

Jack suddenly realized what he was seeing. It wasn't the JB-1, not really. He watched bits of aircraft rip loose that were not aluminum or steel. They were fashioned of bright flowers and twisted paper napkins, two-by-fours and sheets of chicken wire. It was the plane from the Jetboy float in yesterday's parade.

Debris began to fall slowly down toward the streets of Manhattan, just as it had four decades before.

Jack saw what had been masked within the replica of Jetboy's plane. He could make out the steel shell, the unmistakable outline of a modified Volkswagen Beetle.

"God bless!" Someone said it for all of them. "It's the Turtle!"

Jack could hear cheering from the next block, and the block beyond that. As the last bits of the JB-1 replica sifted down toward the city, the Turtle snapped into a victory roll. Then he swept around in a graceful arc and seemed to vanish in the east, occulted by the sun now edging above the tops of the office towers.

"Can you beat that?" said one of the refugees from Freakers. "The Turtle's alive. Fuckin' terrific." The grin on his face echoed in his voice.

Jack realized Cordelia was no longer standing beside him. He looked around in confusion. From just behind his shoulder, Ackroyd said, "She said to tell you she had things to do. She'll let you know how things work out."

Jack spread his hands helplessly. "How will I find her?"

Ackroyd shrugged. "You found her this morning, didn't you?" The man hesitated. "Oh yeah, she also said to tell you she loves you." He put his hand on Jack's shoulder. "Come on, I'll buy you a brew." He turned toward the neon woman. She had paled now in the breaking daylight. Back over his shoulder, the detective said, "I'll give you my card. Worst comes to worst, you can hire me."

Jack hesitated.

Ackroyd said, "Also I'll introduce you around. I heard you started to *change* in there. I don't know you, but I've got a feeling there are quite a few of our colleagues you don't know either. It's about time you made their acquaintance."

Billy Ray had overheard. "Fuck you, Ackroyd," he said.

Ackroyd grinned. "Those Justice boys have a thing about us gumshoes."

Before Jack followed him into Freakers, he looked one more time into the east. In the sun-glare, he couldn't see the Turtle.

It was a new morning. But then they were *all* new mornings.

It had taken Spector the better part of an hour to track down a cab in Jokertown. He sat in the back seat, thumbing through the early edition of the *Times*. Except for the Astronomer, all the dead aces had their pictures on the front page, surrounded by a black border. There was a question mark next to the Turtle, but he was obviously still alive and kicking. Spector was almost glad. But he couldn't figure out why he wasn't dead too. He'd always managed to survive. Most losers did.

"Yesterday was a hell of a day, I'll tell you," the cabbie said.

"Yesterday?" Spector shook his head. Too much had happened in the last twenty-four hours. It was like a long, bad dream.

"Yeah. It would suit me fine if all those aces killed each other off. I got no use for them."

Spector ignored him and pulled out the sports section. He wondered if the Nets would be any better this year.

"What about you?"

"Huh?"

"What do you think about aces?"

"I don't. Why don't you just shut your mouth and drive."

It was several minutes before the cabbie spoke again. "Here we are. What the hell do you want down here?"

Spector opened the door and got out, then handed the cabbie a hundred-dollar bill. "Wait here."

"Fine. But I can't sit around all morning."

Spector walked down to the chain-link fence. It was time to visit Ralph again. Maybe he'd be too tired to kill. The king of the garbage dump really didn't deserve it.

A young black man wearing a green windbreaker and red cap met him at the fence. "You need something?"

"Yeah, there was a bunch of barges full of garbage here last night, and a guy named Ralph. Where are they?"

The man turned around and pointed out to the river. "They're halfway to Fresh Kills by now. Just garbage, though."

"Right. Thanks." Spector watched the man walk away,

then looked out across the water. "You get to live, Ralphie. Unless you say something stupid."

The cabbie honked his horn. One thing Ralph had been right about. There's no substitute for being your own boss. Doing work for the Astronomer and Latham had gotten him shot, broken, bitten, and zapped to the top of the scoreboard in Yankee Stadium. He was sick of it. No more being a loaded gun who some big wheel pointed at someone else. From now on he'd decide who he killed and when.

Another honk. "One more time, shithead," Spector muttered. "Just one more time."

The sky was beginning to brighten, but the light brought no warmth. The docks were already alive. Most people were waking up or downing their first cup of coffee. Spector was going to go to bed and sleep for a week. The talk about this Wild Card Day probably wouldn't die down for a week or even a month.

"Yessir, Ralph, you showed me the way. From now on, I look out for number one. No more cleaning up after other people's shit."

There was a third long honk. Spector turned slowly. "You asked for it moron." The endless pain hummed through him like a fresh papercut.

It was going to be hell finding another cab.

Even in that darkest hour that comes before the dawn, Manhattan never truly sleeps, but Riverside Drive was motionless and empty as Hiram Worchester climbed from his cab. It was almost eerie. He tipped the driver, found his keys, and climbed the stoop to his own front door. Nothing had ever looked as welcoming.

Inside, Hiram climbed the stairs wearily, without bothering to turn on the lights. He undressed while he trudged upward, hanging his jacket on the wooden acorn at the foot of the polished banister, dropping his tie and shirt on the steps, abandoning his shoes on the first landing and his trousers on the second. The maid could pick them up tomorrow, he thought. Except that it was already tomorrow, wasn't it? No, he decided. No, no matter what the calendar might say, this was still Wild Card Day, and it would be until he got to sleep.

His third-floor bedroom looked out over the Hudson. Hiram went to the window and opened it wide, taking a deep breath of the chill night air. The western sky was black satin, and over in Jersey the lights were beginning to come back on. But the most beautiful sight in the room was his king-size water bed, its pillows plumped and ready, its covers turned back on clean flannel sheets. It looked so warm and comfortable. Hiram lay down with a sigh of gratitude, feeling the water slosh gently beneath him. He slid under the blankets and closed his eyes.

Somewhere the Howler laughed, and Hiram's dreams shattered into crystal shards. Kid Dinosaur swooped through Aces High, dropping pieces of his body onto the dinner plates. A maniac with a bow aimed an arrow at his eye, but Popinjay sent it away with an off-color quip. Faces turned toward him, bruised and bleeding, eyes full of pain: Tachyon, Gills, an old joker woman who walked like a snail. Water Lily smiled, the moisture running off her naked skin as if she had stepped fresh from a shower, her hair gleaming in the soft light of the chandelier, and she walked outside to look at the stars, climbing up on the edge of the parapet, straining toward them, reaching, reaching. Hiram tried to warn her, shouted that she needed to be careful, but her foot slipped, and as she began to fall he saw that it was not Jane after all, it was Eileen, Eileen who reached out her hand for help, but Hiram was not there, and she fell away from him screaming. In dreams you fall forever.

Then he was in his kitchen, cooking, stirring a great pot, and in the pot was a thick liquid that bubbled slowly and looked like blood, and he stirred frantically, because they would be here soon, the diners would be here soon, but the food wasn't ready, it wasn't any good, they wouldn't like it, they wouldn't like *him*, he had to get it ready, had to make sure everything was perfect. He stirred faster, and now he heard footsteps, growing louder and louder, heavy pounding footsteps on the stairs, someone coming closer and closer . . .

Hiram jerked upright, scattering pillows and bedclothes, just as a fist the size and color of a smoked Virginia ham crashed through the closed bedroom door. The door was kicked, once, twice, and on the third kick it few apart, and Bludgeon stepped through. Hiram gasped.

He was seven feet tall, dressed in tight-fitting leather. His head was square and brutal, seamed with callous and twisted horn, eyes set beneath a heavy ridge of bone, one a clear bright blue, the other a vivid red. The right side of his mouth was closed by the slick, shiny scar tissue that had grown over it, and his flesh was mottled by a huge greenish bruise. His ears were veined leathery things like the wings of bats, his scalp covered by boils instead of hair. "*Fucker,*" he screamed in a voice that whistled out of half his mouth like scalding steam. "*Fucking cuntface ace,*" he shrieked. The fingers of his right hand were closed permanently in a fist, rough calloused skin grown over fingers and knuckles in great ridges. When he made a fist of his left hand, his muscles bulged, and the seams of his leather jacket split open.

"I'm gonna kill you, you fucking cuntface asshole fatboy."

"You're only a nightmare," Hiram said. "I'm still asleep."

Bludgeon screamed and kicked the bed. The wooden frame shattered, the plastic burst, and water began spraying out from underneath the blankets. It looked like a sprinkler. Hiram sat there numbly, the water soaking through his underwear, blinking in shock. This wasn't a dream, he told himself as he got wetter and wetter. Bludgeon reached through the spray and grabbed the front of his undershirt with his left hand, lifting him bodily in the air. "You fucker," the giant was screaming over and over. "I'm out, you cuntface bastard, you stinkin' piece of lard, they cut me fuckin' *out* and it's all because of you, I'm going to fuckin' kill you, you shitface cunt-lapping fatboy, you're fuckin' *dead*, you hear that, you fuckin' *hear* that?"

His right hand waved under Hiram's nose, a misshapen ball of bone and scar tissue and horny callus cocked into an eternal fist. "I can dent fuckin' *tanks* with this, you cuntface fucker, so just imagine what it's going to do to your pussy-eating face. You see it? *Do you see it, fucker!*"

Dangling at the end of Bludgeon's arm, Hiram Worchester managed to nod. "Yes," he said. He raised his own hand. "Do you see this one?" he asked, and made a fist.

As Bludgeon bobbed off the floor, his clubfist came around and caught Hiram on the cheek. It smarted quite a bit and left a red welt. By then Bludgeon was floating, hanging onto Hiram for dear life, his feet scraping against the ceiling. He began to scream threats. "Oh, keep quiet," Hiram told him. He tried to disentangle Bludgeon's fingers from his undershirt, but the joker was too strong.

Frowning, Hiram restored himself to full weight.

Then he doubled it.

Then he doubled *that*.

Instead of trying to push Bludgeon away, he pulled him nearer, hugged him tightly to his ample stomach, and did a bellyflop onto the hardwood floor. It was the second time that day he heard bones crack.

Hiram climbed to his feet, panting, his heart triphammering away in his chest. He lightened himself and stood frowning down at Bludgeon, who was hugging his ribs and screaming. As he drifted up off the floor again, Hiram caught him by wrist and ankle and heaved him right out the open window.

He fell up. Hiram went to the window and watched him rise. The wind was from the west. It ought to blow him over the city, toward the East River, Long Island, and eventually the Atlantic. He wondered if Bludgeon could swim.

The bed was ruined. Hiram went to the linen closet. He paused with the sheets in his hand, shook his head, stacked them neatly back in the closet. What was the use? The night was almost gone, and he had so much to do—Aces High was supposed to be open for lunch, someone would have to supervise the repairs, and in a few minutes the dawn would be coming up, the start of a whole new day. He was too tired to sleep anyway.

Sighing deeply, Hiram Worchester went downstairs and began to cook. He made himself a cheese omelet and a triple rasher of bacon, fried up some small red potatoes with onions and peppers, and washed it all down with a large orange juice and a fresh-brewed pot of Jamaican Blue Mountain.

Afterward, he was almost certain that he would live.

Around her the city was coming alive. Several million people performing the routine little actions that give form to a life. A litany of the ordinary, the mundane, the comfortable. And Roulette felt a stir of interest, a flare of anticipation. So humdrum when compared to the obsession that had ruled her life. But so restful in its simplicity. She thought she would start by brewing a cup of coffee. And after that? The possibilities were limitless.

There were still merchant ships headed for the Far East. It was still possible to get a cabin on one, though with this short a notice it had been expensive.

But it was done. Fortunato stood at the rail as they steamed out past Governor's Island and into Upper New York Bay.

The sun was coming up over Brooklyn. Underneath him the sea moved at its own pace, vast, balanced, fluid yet unchanging. It was the first of Fortunato's new teachers.

CLOSING CREDITS

starring	*created & written by*
Bagabond	Leanne C. Harper
Fortunato	Lewis Shiner
Jennifer (Wraith) Maloy	John J. Miller
Jack (Sewer Jack) Robicheaux	Edward Bryant
Roulette	Melinda M. Snodgrass
James (Demise) Spector	Walton Simons
Hiram Worchester	George R. R. Martin

co-starring	*created by*
Daniel (Yeoman) Brennan	John J. Miller
Dr. Tachyon	Melinda M. Snodgrass
The Astronomer	Lewis Shiner
Jay (Popinjay) Ackroyd	George R. R. Martin
Rosemary (Gambione) Muldoon	Leanne C. Harper

featuring	*created by*
Peregrine	Gail Gerstner-Miller

St. John (Loophole) Latham .... Lewis Shiner
Jane (Water Lily) Dow .... Pat Cadigan
Chrysalis .... John J. Miller
Kid Dinosaur .... Lewis Shiner
Modular Man .... Walter Jon Williams
The Howler .... Stephen Leigh
Wyrm .... John J. Miller
Cordelia Chaisson .... Edward Bryant and Leanne C. Harper
The Great &-Powerful Turtle .... George R. R. Martin

with — *created by*

Billy Ray .... John J. Miller
The Bludgeon.......................... George R. R. Martin
Cap'n Trips .... Victor Milán
Imp and Insulin .... Lewis Shiner and Walton Simons
Ralph Norton .... Walton Simons
Digger Downs .... Steve Perrin
Senator Gregg Hartmann (D., NY) ... Stephen Leigh

WILD CARDS

THE TOM PALMER GALLERY

Frontispiece: Peregrine flies to the aid of a plummeting Water Lily during an attack by the Astronomer.

Gallery title page: Hiram Worchester welcomes one and all to the annual Wild Card dinner.

Page 503: Jennifer Maloy—the underdressed thief known as Wraith—helps herself to the riches contained in Kien Phuc's wall safe.

Page 504: Bagabond feeds the other strays who call the streets of New York their home.

Page 505: At the Freakers club, the beauteous Roulette Brown-Roxbury comes face-to-chest with the always flamboyant Dr. Tachyon.

Page 506: Yeoman is about to put paid on Lizard Man's unwanted advances on Wraith.

Page 507: A street punk is about to learn why it's not such a good idea to make Sewer Jack mad.

Page 508: Having bared most of her flesh to Father Squid of the Church of Jesus Christ, Joker, Wraith decides baring her soul is the next logical step.

Page 509: Astronomer gets hot under the collar, and everywhere else courtesy of the super-powered pimp, Fortunato.

Page 510: The Astronomer meets his well-deserved end at the . . . hands of James Spector, one of the deadliest Aces around.

AFTERWORD

BY GEORGE R.R. MARTIN

The great boom in shared world anthologies began in 1979, when Ace Books published Robert Asprin's *Thieves World,* the first volume in a long-running fantasy series about the imaginary city of Sanctuary and the motley cast of swordsmen, sorcerors, princes, rogues, and thieves who roamed its streets, with occasional guest appearances by an equally motley assortment of gods.

Thieves World had its precursors, to be sure. In comic books, both and the Marvel and DC universes were shared worlds, wherein the heroes and villains lived in the same world, constantly crossed paths with one another, and had their friendships, feuds, and love affairs. In prose there was H.P. Lovecraft's Cthulhu Mythos. Lovecraft encouraged his writer friends to borrow elements from his stories, and to add their own, and Robert E. Howard, Clark Ashton Smith, Robert Bloch, August Derleth, and others gleefully took up the game. HPL himself would then make mention of the gods, cults, and accursed books the others had contributed, and the mythos became ever richer and more detailed.

Much later came *Medea: Harlan's World,* wherein Harlan Ellison assembled a group of top-rank science fiction writers to create an imaginary planet and work out all the details of its flora, fauna, geography, history, and orbital mechanics, whereupon each writer penned a story set on the world they had created together.

But *Thieves World* was the breakthrough book that defined the modern shared world, and it proved so successful that it soon spawned a whole host of imitators. *Ithkar* and *Liavek* and *Merovingan Nights* had fantasy settings and the flavor of sword and sorcery, as did *Thieves World* itself. *Borderlands* was more urban fantasy, with its punk elves and contemporary setting. *The Fleet* and *War World* brought the shared world format to space opera, *Greystone Bay* extended it to horror, and *Heroes in Hell* took it to hell.

Some of these series came before ours; others followed us. Some had long runs; others only lasted for a book or two. In the end, *Wild Cards* would outlast all of them to become the longest-running shared world series of them all, with twelve volumes from Bantam and three from Baen . . . and now two more in the works from ibooks. Which means that I now have more experience with shared worlds than any other editor, I suppose.

When *Wild Cards* was starting out, however, my editorial experience was limited to *New Voices,* the annual (in theory) collection of stories by the finalists for the John W. Campbell Award. I knew going in that a shared world was a very different sort of animal, and not one easily tamed, so I set out to learn as much about the beast as I could. Bob Asprin and Lynn Abbey were gracious enough to sit down with me and share all the trials and tribulations they had undergone editing *Thieves World,* and the lessons they had learned from them. Will Shetterly and Emma Bull were equally forthcoming about their own experiences editing *Liavek.* From the Master Agreements that governed those two series, I was able to devise a Master Agreement for *Wild Cards* that provided a firm but fair legal foundation upon which to build the series.

A shared world also poses some difficult artistic questions, the most crucial one being the amount of sharing involved and the rules that govern it. All of the shared worlds of the '80s answered these questions in their own ways, I found, but some of the answers were more satisfactory than others. Some books shared only their settings; the characters never crossed paths, nor did the events of one story have any impact on those that followed. Each story existed in isolation, aside from a common geography and history. In other series, the characters did make "guest star" appearances in one another's tales, while the stories themselves continued to stand alone. But the *best* shared world anthologies, the ones that were the most entertaining and the most successful, were those that shared characters and plots as well as settings. In those books, and those alone, the whole was more than the sum of its parts. The "shared worlds" that minimized the sharing were missing the point of the exercise, it seemed to me.

Wild Cards would not make that mistake, I decided. We would maximize the sharing. More, we would strive to go well beyond what anyone else had ever done in the shared world game. So much so that when I drew up my "immodest proposal" for the first three *Wild Cards* books, I eschewed the old term "shared world" and promised the publishers a series of "mosaic novels."

That initial proposal was for three books, for no particular reason but that we wanted to do more than one, and no publisher was likely to buy twelve at a shot. That set a precedent, and later on we continued to plot, sell, and write the books in groups of three–"triads," as we called them, since they were not quite trilogies (the second triad turned into four books and the third one into five, but those are stories for another afterword). The first two volumes of that first triad (which would eventually become *Wild Cards* and *Aces High,* though they had other titles in the proposal) would feature individual stories, each with its own plot and protagonist, a beginning, a middle, and an end. But all the stories would also advance what we called the "overplot." And between the stories we would add an interstitial narrative that would tie them all together and create the "mosaic novel" feel we wanted.

But the *true* mosaic novel would be the third book, wherein we brought our overplot to a smashing conclusion. No other shared world had ever attempted anything quite like what we proposed to do with *Jokers Wild:* a single braided narrative, wherein all the characters, stories, and events were interwoven from start to finish in a sort of seven-handed collaboration. The end result, we hoped, would be a book that read like a novel with multiple viewpoints rather than simply a collection of related stories.

In my proposal I spoke of *Jokers Wild* as "a Robert Altman film in prose." Like *Nashville* and *A Wedding* and several other of Altman's trademark films, *Jokers Wild* would feature a large and varied cast of characters whose paths would cross and recross during the course of the book. The setting would be New York City on September 15, 1986–Wild Card Day, forty years after Jetboy's death and the release of the Takisian xenovirus over Manhattan. All the action would take place within twenty-four hours, giving us a strong chronological framework on which to hang our story threads. The first two *Wild Cards* books had featured the work of eleven writers and nine writers, respectively, but because of complexity of what we were about to attempt, I decided to limit *Jokers Wild* to six stories (there are seven names on the title page, to be sure, but Edward Bryant and Leanne C. Harper were collaborating, as they had in Volume One). Each of the seven viewpoint characters had his dreams, his own demons, and his own goals, the pursuit of which would take him back and forth across the city, up skyscrapers and down into the sewers, bumping into other characters and other stories as he went.

It was seven stories and it was one story, but mostly it was an enormous headache. I did a lot of cutting and pasting and shuffling of sections as the manuscripts came in, striving for the perfect placement of all our cliffhangers, climaxes, and foreshadowing while simultaneously trying to keep chronology and geography firmly in mind. Half a hundred times I thought I had it, until noticing that Yeoman had taken six hours to get to Brooklyn, that Fortunato was in two places at once, that it been three hundred pages since we'd last seen Demise. Then it was time to sigh and shuffle again. But I finally got it right. (I think).

In truth, we were creating a new literary form of sorts, though none of us quite realized that at the time. We did realize that what we were doing was an experiment, and there were days when none of us were at all certain that that the beast was going to fly. It was the hardest, most challenging editing that I ever did, and the writing was no day at the beach either.

In the end, though, all the effort was worth it. Readers and reviewers both seemed to love the mosaic novel form (although one reviewer amused me vastly by making a point of how seamlessly I had blended the styles of such dissimilar writers, when of course I'd made no attempt to "blend" any styles whatsoever, preferring that each character retain his own distinctive individual voice).

And my writers and I agreed: *Jokers Wild* was the strongest volume in the series to date. The experiment had been a success, and the template was set. The full mosaic was too difficult and time-consuming a form to be used in every volume, but every third volume was just about right. So the template was set: all the *Wild Cards* triads to come would also conclude with a climactic mosaic, fully interwoven in the same manner as *Jokers Wild.*

Before I close, let me add one last aside. This being an afterword, I presume that all of you reading these words (yes, I'm talking to you, don't look over your shoulder, there's no one here but you and me) have already finished *Jokers Wild*

If you haven't, STOP. What follows is in the nature of a spoiler, and not meant for your eyes. Why do you think we call them *After*words, damn it! Go read the book.

Is he gone?

Good. Now I can tell you about Kid Dinosaur and the Howler.

Over the course of *Wild Cards,* probably the single thing that upset our fans the most was the Astonomer's hideous murder of Kid Dinosaur in *Jokers Wild.* For years thereafter, whenever we did a *Wild Cards* panel at a convention, one of the questions would inevitably be, "Why did you kill Kid Dinosaur? He was my favorite character." The Howler was less prominent and far less popular, yet he had fans as well, some of whom wrote us in dismay when Roulette did the nasty with him.

The truth is, both characters had been marked for death from the day they were created. Remember, we plotted the *Wild Cards* book in *triads.* We knew, even before we started writing our stories for Volume One, that come Volume Three the Astronomer and the surviving Masons would be trying to hunt down and kill all the aces who had smashed them at the Cloisters at the end of Book Two. A number of our major ongoing characters would be on that hit list, of course, and we wanted the readers to feel as though their lives were in desperate peril, the better to keep them on the edge of their seats.

But superheroes don't die. Not in comic books, not really, not for good.

We needed to establish that *Wild Cards* was something different, that this danger was *real,* that we were playing for keeps here, that even our good guys could indeed die, and die horribly.

With that in mind, early on in the going I sent out a call for "red-shirt aces" (anyone who's ever watched the original *Star Trek* will get the reference), secondary characters that we could introduce in Book One and include in the Cloisters raid in Book Two, thereby setting them up to be Astronomer fodder in Book Three.

A number of my writers obliged by creating throwaway aces. One such was Steve Leigh's Howler. Another was Kid Dinosaur, introduced by Lew Shiner in the epilogue to Volume One. The poor Howler had, I seem to recall, exactly one line of dialogue in the first two volumes, before Roulette got him into her bed in Book Three, so to this day I don't understand how our readers could get attached to him. Kid Dinosaur was pushier, though. The little snotnose managed to force his way into several juicy scenes in *Aces High*—including one wherein the Turtle *warned* him what was going to happen if he kept trying to play with the big boys.

Is it my fault that the kid wouldn't listen?

—George R.R. Martin
September 16, 2001

ALSO AVAILABLE

WILD CARDS™

Edited by George R.R. Martin
Illustrations by Mike Zeck
Cover art by Brian Bolland

ISBN: 0-7434-2380-1

When a group of SF's most imaginative writers discovered they shared a secret love of the larger-than-life heroes of the four-color comics and Saturday matinee serials, they gave each other a challenge: What would our world be like if these superhuman heroes and villains had been real flesh-and-blood men and women who lived through this century's most turbulent history?

The alien virus arrived on Earth just after World War II—and the world was never the same. For those who become infected, there are two results: death, or transformation. And depending on the recipient, death is sometimes the preferable outcome. Only a few lucky ones become superhuman "aces" as a side effect of the virus; the rest are turned into horrible, grotesque "jokers." It's a strange and wonderful, terrible and terrifying world where anything can go. A world that, in a twist of fate, could lie just outside your door.

A world of Wild Cards.

Featuring stories by
ROGER ZELAZNY • STEPHEN LEIGH
MELINDA M. SNODGRASS • GEORGE R.R. MARTIN
EDWARD BRYANT • LEANNE C. HARPER
VICTOR MILAN • JOHN J. MILLER • LEWIS SHINER
HOWARD WALDROP • WALTER JON WILLIAMS

WILD CARDS™ II: ACES HIGH

Edited by George R.R. Martin
Illustrations by Floyd Hughes
Cover art by Brian Bolland
ISBN: 0-7434-2391-7

It all began in 1946, when the bizarre, gene-altering "Wild Cards" virus was unleashed in the skies over New York City. A virus that created super-powered Aces and bizarre, disfigured Jokers.

Now, thirty years later, the victims face a *new* nightmare. From the far reaches of space comes The Swarm, a deadly menace that could very well destroy the planet. Putting aside their hatred and mistrust, Aces and Jokers must form an uneasy alliance and prepare for a battle they must not lose. . . .

Featuring stories by
ROGER ZELAZNY • GEORGE R.R. MARTIN
MELINDA A. SNODGRASS
WALTER JON WILLIAMS • PAT CADIGAN
VICTOR MILAN • JOHN J. MILLER
LEWIS SHINER • WALTON SIMONS

X-MEN™/DR. DOOM™: THE CHAOS ENGINE, Book 1

by Steven A. Roman
Illustrations by Mark Buckingham
Cover art by Bob Larkin

ISBN: 0-7434-3483-8

Returning from another dimension, the X-Men discover that Earth is now ruled by one of the most notorious tyrants the world has ever known—Doctor Doom. Far more disturbing than the police state in which they find themselves, however, is the fact that some of the world's greatest Super Heroes—including the X-Men's closest friends—have allied themselves with the legendary villain.

Searching for answers, hunted by old enemies and former allies, the mutant adventurers face their greatest challenge: deposing an armor-clad madman with an entire world against them. Standing between them and victory, though, is their deadliest enemy—the malevolent Magneto, who has his own plans for dominating the world. . . .

SPIDER-MAN: REVENGE OF THE SINISTER SIX

by Adam-Troy Castro
Illustrations by Mike Zeck
Cover art by Mike Zeck and Phil Zimelman

ISBN: 0-7434-3466-8

Peter Parker, the amazing Spider-Man, has made an astonishing discovery—he has a sister! But that's not the only surprise, for not only is his sister a deadly super-villainess known as Pity, but she's working alongside the manipulative Gentleman—a man who masterminded the deaths of Peter's parents! Together with Doctor Octopus, Electro, the Vulture, and Mysterio, the Gentleman and Pity have formed the newest incarnation of The Sinister Six—a group dedicated to destroying Spider-Man!

Faced with the challenge of trying to save Pity from her predicament while, at the same time, stopping The Sinister Six from carrying out the Gentleman's world-threatening plans, Spider-Man must turn to the super-spy organization S.A.F.E. and its volatile director, Col. Sean Morgan, for help. But can the wall-crawler trust an agency that regards him as a public menace and wanted man—or is he just stepping into an even worse situation . . . ?